Resilience and Development

Positive Life Adaptations

LONGITUDINAL RESEARCH IN THE SOCIAL AND BEHAVIORAL SCIENCES
An Interdisciplinary Series

Series Editors:

Howard B. Kaplan, *Texas A&M University, College Station, Texas*
Adele Eskeles Gottfried, *California State University, Northridge, California*
Allen W. Gottfried, *California State University, Fullerton, California*

DRUGS, CRIME, AND OTHER DEVIANT ADAPTATIONS
Longitudinal Studies
Edited by Howard B. Kaplan

DRUG USE AND ETHNICITY IN EARLY ADOLESCENCE
William A. Vega, Andres G. Gil, and Associates

RESILIENCE AND DEVELOPMENT
Positive Life Adaptations
Edited by Meyer D. Glantz and Jeannette L. Johnson

A Continuation Order Plan is available for this series. A continuation order will bring delivery of each new volume immediately upon publication. Volumes are billed only upon actual shipment. For further information please contact the publisher.

Resilience and Development

Positive Life Adaptations

Edited by

Meyer D. Glantz

National Institute on Drug Abuse
Bethesda, Maryland

and

Jeannette L. Johnson

University of Maryland
Baltimore, Maryland

Kluwer Academic/Plenum Publishers
New York, Boston, Dordrecht, London, Moscow

Library of Congress Cataloging-in-Publication Data

Resilience and development : positive life adaptations / Meyer D.
Glantz and Jeannette L. Johnson, eds.
        p.   cm. -- (Longitudinal research in the social and behavioral
sciences)
    ISBN 0-306-46123-4
    1. Substance abuse--Psychological aspects. 2. Resilience
(Personality trait) 3. Substance abuse--Prevention. 4. Mental
illness--Prevention. 5. Developmental psychology.   I. Glantz,
Meyer D. II. Johnson, Jeannette L.   III. Series.
HV4998.R47 1999
362.29--dc21   99-38203
                                                                CIP

ISBN 0-306-46123-4

© 1999 by Kluwer Academic/Plenum Publishers, New York
233 Spring Street, New York, N.Y. 10013

10 9 8 7 6 5 4 3

A C.I.P. record for this book is available from the Library of Congress

Printed in the United States of America

To Benjamin and Amy Elizabeth,
two very wonderful and resilient children.

Contributors

Fred Beauvais, Tri-Ethnic Center for Prevention Research, Colorado State University, Fort Collins, Colorado 80523.

Bonnie Benard, Resiliency Associates, Berkeley, California 94703.

Gretta Cushing, University of Utah, Salt Lake City, Utah 84102.

Norman Garmezy, Department of Psychology, University of Minnesota, Minneapolis, Minnesota 55455.

Meyer D. Glantz, Division of Epidemiology and Prevention Research, National Institute on Drug Abuse, National Institutes of Health, Bethesda, Maryland 20892.

Jeannette L. Johnson, Department of Psychiatry, Division of Alcohol and Drug Abuse, University of Maryland, Baltimore, Maryland 21201.

Howard B. Kaplan, Department of Sociology, Texas A & M University, College Station, Texas 77843.

Karol L. Kumpfer, Center for Substance Abuse Prevention, Substance Abuse and Mental Health Services Administration, Rockville, Maryland 20857.

Alan I. Leshner, National Institute on Drug Abuse, National Institutes of Health, Bethesda, Maryland 20892.

Suniya S. Luthar, Department of Human Development, Teachers College, Columbia University, New York, New York 10027.

Ann S. Masten, Institute of Child Development, University of Minnesota, Minneapolis, Minnesota 55455.

Eugene R. Oetting, Tri-Ethnic Center for Prevention Research, Colorado State University, Fort Collins, Colorado 80523.

Jon E. Rolf, Center for Substance Abuse Prevention, Substance Abuse and Mental Health Services Administration, Rockville, Maryland 20857.

Zili Sloboda, Division of Epidemiology and Prevention Research, National Institute on Drug Abuse, National Institutes of Health, Bethesda, Maryland 20892.

Ralph E. Tarter, Center for Education and Drug Abuse Research, Western

Psychiatric Institute and Clinic, University of Pittsburgh Medical School, Pittsburgh, Pennsylvania 15213.

Michael Vanyukov, Center for Education and Drug Abuse Research, Western Psychiatric Institute and Clinic, University of Pittsburgh Medical School, Pittsburgh, Pennsylvania 15213.

Emmy E. Werner, Department of Human Development, University of California, Davis, California 95616.

Michael Windle, Department of Psychology, University of Alabama at Birmingham, Birmingham, Alabama 35294.

Preface

Attempts to understand, predict, prevent, and treat substance abuse and mental health disorders usually start with the question, "Why?" Questions such as, "Why do people abuse drugs?", "Why do they become depressed?", "Why do they drink even after they have seen the consequences of their alcoholism?", and a thousand other *why* questions are raised. As important as these questions are, in the last few decades scientists and practitioners have come to see the importance of also asking "Why not?", "Why don't most people lose control of their use of alcohol including those who seem to have risk factors associated with alcoholism?", "Why is it that even though many people have some experience with illegal drugs, most do not become dependent on them?", "How is it that some people who appear to be subject to influences that lead many people to affective or other mental health problems overcome or avoid these presumably likely consequences?" Questions such as these and a wide range of clinical and research observations supported by common everyday experiences have led to a great interest in the topic of *resilience*.

With this attention, the field has been broadened beyond the questions about what goes wrong and why to include questions about what makes it possible for at least some people to resist or resolve those detrimental influences that lead to substance abuse and mental health problems. This broader view is not just an academic matter. An understanding of resilience offers the possibility of more effective interventions. Currently, mental health and substance abuse prevention and treatment are based primarily on attempts to avoid or overcome negative behaviors and circumstances. If characteristics of resilience could be taught or somehow made available to others, then prevention and treatment would have a second major dimension—that of building on the positive and strengthening the individual.

With this recognition, six major national institutions jointly sponsored a conference on resilience. On December 5 and 6, 1994, the National Institute on Drug Abuse (of the National Institutes of Health, NIH), the

National Institute on Alcohol Abuse and Alcoholism (NIH), the National Institute of Mental Health, (NIH), the Center for Substance Abuse Prevention (of the Substance Abuse and Mental Health Services Administration, SAMHSA), the Center for Mental Health Services (SAMHSA), and the National Association for Children of Alcoholics collaborated to organize a national conference entitled "The Role of Resilience in Drug Abuse, Alcohol Abuse, and Mental Illness." This widely attended meeting brought together the foremost researchers and practitioners who have focused on resilience. While the conference did not produce a consensus on the nature of resilience, there was a strong consensus that resilience is a critical phenomenon in need of more study. The conference also laid the groundwork for this book.

The papers and discussions in this volume collectively review the research on resilience and represent the diverse perspectives and opinions common among the community of scientists and practitioners who have been concerned with resilience. A number of these papers and discussions were presented in some earlier form at the conference. All of the pieces in this volume, those that are later versions of these presentations, as well as those pieces written specifically for this book, have been newly revised or prepared to be rigorous considerations and to enable the book as a whole to be a generally comprehensive presentation of the current state of research and thought on resilience.

The book includes in-depth reviews by expert researchers examining critical aspects of resilience, as well as discussions and alternative perspectives prepared by noted researchers and practitioners. Also included are an overview of the field by Ann Masten, a leading resilience researcher, and an interview with Norman Garmezy, generally considered to be the founder of research on resilience, who discusses the history and the future of the field.

It is our hope that this volume will reinforce and serve as a resource for the growing interest in resilience both in research and in interventions. We also would like this book to be a tribute to all of the resilient people who resisted and overcame adversity through their hard efforts, persistence, and resolution and who inspired our interest in resilience.

Acknowledgments

A great many people contributed ideas and support for this book and the conference that inspired it. We particularly want to thank Judith Funkhouser, Sis Wenger, Zili Sloboda, and Eliot Werner, without whom there would have been neither a conference nor a book. We also want to thank Elaine Johnson, Jan Howard, Diane Sondheimer, Lynn Huffman, William Bukoski, Donald Ian Macdonald, Mary Jansen, Steven Wolin, and Steve Gardner who played a critical role in developing the resilience meeting.

We are very grateful to the agencies that sponsored the conference, bringing to national attention the relevance of resilience research to substance abuse and mental health issues. The conference was a pioneering collaboration of the National Institute on Drug Abuse (of the National Institutes of Health, NIH), the National Institute on Alcohol Abuse and Alcoholism (NIH), the National Institute of Mental Health (NIH), the Center for Substance Abuse Prevention (of the Substance Abuse and Mental Health Services Administration, SAMHSA), the Center for Mental Health Services (SAMHSA), and the National Association for Children of Alcoholics.

Our greatest appreciation is for the authors who contributed not only their considerable expertise, time, and effort, but also their unflagging support, patience, encouragement, and good counsel.

Contents

1

Introduction

Alan I. Leshner

Historically, the major focus in both prevention research and in the development of interventions targeting problem behaviors has been on identifying both so-called "risk factors" and "high risk" people. This is a familiar and logical approach that assumes that the best way to prevent a problem is to focus on what "causes" it and on the group of people who seem to have most of those causal or risk characteristics.

However, a variety of intersecting observations suggest that focusing on risk alone is not the best approach. First of all, it is generally the case that in terms of problem behaviors, the majority of "high risk" children and adolescents do not develop the anticipated problem behavior. For example, most "high risk" adolescents do not use illicit drugs or become drug abusers. Even most high risk adolescents who have some exposure to illicit drugs do not become established drug abusers. Clearly there is more to the picture than the influence of risk factors.

Further complicating the picture, risk factors do not seem to be specific to particular outcomes, they seem to relate to broad developmental outcomes. In fact, the risk factors that have been identified for any given adolescent and young adult problem behavior are typically very similar to those that have been identified for other problem behaviors. This is especially true for deviant/delinquent problem behaviors. This strongly suggests a complex multi-dimensionality to the development of problem behaviors. Theories and research which assume that there is a simple, direct correspondence

Alan I. Leshner • National Institute on Drug Abuse, National Institutes of Health, Bethesda, Maryland 20892.

Resilience and Development: Positive Life Adaptations, edited by Glantz and Johnson. Kluwer Academic/Plenum Publishers, New York, 1999.

between given risk factors and single problem behavior outcomes have rarely considered the broad spectrum nature of risk influences. This has sometimes led to the generation of myopic and less powerful models and interventions. Of even greater concern, the purported risk factors are generally not amenable to change.

Attempts to ameliorate many behavior problem risk factors face significant pragmatic difficulties. Some, such as poverty, are major recalcitrant societal issues. Some are difficult to identify factors (e.g., familial dysfunctions), unrecognized circumstances (such as child abuse) or sub-clinical/pre-morbid conditions (e.g., impairments in regulatory functioning). Some predispositions seem to be biologically based and currently not readily susceptible to intervention. Still others, such as anti-social personality disorder, are not only very difficult to treat but tend to insulate individuals from intervention, for example by leading them to be classified as delinquents or criminals rather than as individuals who need help.

For some time, a small group of researchers and program providers have been focusing on, basically, what keeps some of the most at high risk individuals from engaging in the problem behavior, what are called "protective factors". Several researchers have studied resilient individuals who have defied others' expectations and survived or surmounted daunting and seemingly overwhelming dangers, obstacles and problems. This research has provided some very important insights and is part of the founding body of information which has launched the relatively new field of developmental psychopathology. One of the cardinal tenets of this field is a systems approach that incorporates a focus on the interaction of risk and resilience factors. This more holistic perspective is not only heuristically useful but also encourages interventions that both attempt to minimize risk factors *and* maximize protective or resilience factors. The approach also recognizes the interaction between risk and protective factors, since what constitutes an effective protective factor can vary significantly with both the level and form of risk.

Recently, researchers, program developers and service providers have increasingly begun to build on these insights about what keeps most of even children and adolescents at high risk protected from bad behavioral outcomes. Researchers are starting to ask these more sophisticated questions and the answers they are finding are being built into prevention and treatment programs. For example, in my own field of drug abuse research, the standard for investigations into the origin and development of drug involvement is to explore not only why some people become drug abusers but also to explore why most people do not, even those who have been exposed to substance abuse. The standard for developing new prevention and treatment programs is to strengthen resilience factors as well as to minimize the harmful ones. This is particularly critical because in many cases it is more practical to increase resilience than to eliminate risk. Problems and risk factors are ubiquitous and inevitable. Helping people to develop the strengths and resources to resist and overcome them is the most rational and effective approach.

Just as risk factors do not seem to be specific to particular outcomes, it is likely that protective factors are not specific either. This gives everyone who is concerned about any problem behavior a stake in the whole complex of risk and resilience factors. It is not surprising that the writing of this book on resilience and the conference which inspired it were a collaborative effort from people in the diverse fields and organizations concerned with mental health and problem behaviors. While targeted intervention programs may be more effective in some cases, we are all concerned about overall life and functioning and ultimately we are all concerned with the same problems and the same goals. And we must all be concerned with understanding the nature of resilience and building on that knowledge. This book is a state of the art guide in that effort.

2

Resilience
An Interview with Norman Garmezy

Jon E. Rolf, edited by Meyer D. Glantz

Introduction

Norman Garmezy is Professor of Psychology, Emeritus, at the University of Minnesota. He is generally credited as being the founder of the contemporary research study of resilience. Following is an interview (in edited form) conducted by Dr. Jon Rolf in which Dr. Garmezy discusses the origins of his interest in resilience and some of his current thinking.

Jon Rolf: How did you become interested in resilience?

Norman Garmezy: My interest in resilience started with the work on schizophrenia that I began with Eliot Rodnick, my collaborator and my mentor at the Worcester State Hospital in Massachusetts. We were interested in the study of schizophrenia, but the study of schizophrenia at the time that I am talking about, which was in the 40s, had a considerable range of outcomes for people so diagnosed. In the mid 40's and 50's when the work was being done in schizophrenia, there were two "types" of schizophrenic patients. There were "process" patients and there were "reactive" patients. The dif-

Jon E. Rolf • Center for Substance Abuse Prevention, Substance Abuse and Mental Health Services Administration, Rockville, Maryland 20857. **Meyer D. Glantz** • Division of Epidemiology and Prevention Research, National Institute on Drug Abuse, National Institutes of Health, Bethesda, Maryland 20892.

Resilience and Development: Positive Life Adaptations, edited by Glantz and Johnson. Kluwer Academic/Plenum Publishers, New York, 1999.

ferences between the two were striking. For example, if you looked at length of stay in a mental hospital, the process cases, which were the chronic schizophrenia cases, stayed an average of 13 years and even longer whereas reactive schizophrenics were marked by very different kinds of histories. The reactive cases were much more functional. They were more competent, they held jobs, they were often married, and when they had a "schizophrenic breakdown", it was a very active kind of manifestation of the disorder usually accompanied by recovery and return to the community. At that time, when schizophrenics came to the hospital, there wasn't much that could be done medicinally. But, if one allowed the reactive schizophrenics to rest in the hospital and to have an opportunity to talk and so on, their stays were rather brief. So here you had two groups given the same classification, but manifestly different in their work history, marital status, and participation in family activities. This observation seemed very important to us and trying to understand this phenomenon led to the study of resilience.

In the current diagnostic view, "process schizophrenia" is called "schizophrenia" and "reactive schizophrenia" is called "schizophreniform". We were very interested in the differences of the two groups and Eliot Rodnick and I looked into the history of these patients and found that their backgrounds were very different. There was a long pattern of incompetence in many areas for the chronic schizophrenics but more competence in general for the reactive schizophrenics. And so we set out to try to learn as much as we could about these two different types; that was the beginning.

It was very difficult to decide what to study in order to learn what differentiated these groups. We decided to study a group of children and try to understand the attributes of competence and its development in children; and this was the leap that we took at Minnesota. The good, confident work histories, family patterns and the like of the reactive schizophrenic raised the critical question of a different pattern of adaptation in the presence of uncommon stress.

I think that was really the route we started on in our preliminary investigation. We initiated a search for school children who came out of highly stressed environments and yet seemed to be very adaptive. We made some visits to the school system. In early conversations with the superintendent of schools he was captured by the fact that we wanted to take a look at children under stress who have competent histories and, we hoped, competent outcomes. We were given a great deal of support from the schools. We began in a very simple way. We called school administrators and made appointments with the school principals; then we asked the principal if he could bring his school social worker or nurse to a meeting with us. I remember what I would say upon entering the principal's office. I asked whether there were any children in his school who when he first heard of their backgrounds he had a great deal of concern about them and now when he sees them in the hall he has a sense of pride that they are part of his school. What I was saying was "can you identify stressed children who are making it here in your school?" There was a long pause after my inquiry before the answer came. If I had said, "do you have kids in this school who seem to be troubled?" there wouldn't have been a moment's delay. But to be asked about children who were adaptive and good citizens in the school and making it even though they came out of very disturbed backgrounds, that was a new sort of inquiry. But that's the way we began. It was always interesting. The principal would turn to the social worker and say "what about what's-his-name?" and they would tell the child's story.

The story that I found most moving was the description of a boy, a young boy about 9 years old whose mother was an alcoholic. There was no father in the family and the boy was basically on his own. He would bring a sandwich to school but there wasn't much food available to him and so he took two pieces of bread with nothing in between and he became known to us as the boy with the bread sandwich. The reason that he took a "bread sandwich" to school was so no one would feel pity for him and no one would know of the ineptitude of his mother. You know if you get hit with a case like that and you begin to think, "Let's look beyond this case. Let's take a look at other children who are resilient in other kinds of stresses and circumstances." There was literature that dealt with kids in accidents, children who suffered burns and became functional children. There were certainly "wartime" stories of children under the gun who were adaptive in contrast to others who were not adaptive. We decided to focus on children who despite impoverished backgrounds were manifestly competent. What were the roots of their adaptation? The term "resilient" came in not as a simile for competence but as an extension of their competencies despite their early background of very high stress experiences. That focus was the essence of resilience and that is the way we launched our research efforts.

J.R. Define resilience for us and is it different than competence?

N.G. I think that the original concerns of the principals and teachers were based on their knowledge of the child's background. Their subsequent delight was the evidence that the child in class was manifestly competent in the school despite the stressors in the life of the child and this reflected what we are interested in. I think "competence" is really the term for a variety of adaptive behaviors and I think that resilience is manifest competence despite exposure to significant stressors. It seems to me that you can't talk about resilience in the absence of stress. The point that I would make about stress is the critical significance of cumulative stressors. I think this is the most important element. We in the study of resilience have had a tendency to go with great stressors, such as bombings and what the consequences might be. What in effect we were asking was whether there were identifiable children who were exposed to very acute stresses under which many people would flag and that resilience in some cases was reflected in manifest recovery over time. But there are also many cases in which if you were to summate the stressful experiences it would seem to point very much to maladaptation. So you can go two ways in your approach, you can go with a markedly acute stress. Bombings in London in World War II, that would be a great stressor. Combined with deaths in the family, with the bombs coming down, that is the beginning of the summation of stresses. And I think that you can either focus on great stressors and study its consequences or you can look into the environment of ordinary families and so forth and really begin to make a tabulation of the cumulating impact of stressors.

I think such a cumulation is very critical. Recently, the direction of my thinking now has turned toward children in poverty. When you study children who are caught up in the midst of impoverishment, you find numerous stressors in that child's environment and background; that is the nature of cumulation. It is extremely important. And so I have to think two ways about this. I have to think of a single great stressor and its consequences and I think also of the cumulation of stressors in which the environment, the family, and the background all add up to generate negative events and circumstances that ordinarily would bring a child down, but in many instances do not.

J.R. You have talked about children in poverty as providing a good opportunity to observe resilience and it's development. You have also expressed concerns about poverty that go beyond scientific issues. Why do you focus so strongly on poverty?

N.G. Well, if you think of the cumulation notion of stressors, poverty bares it. I might just say, not speaking scientifically now, that poverty is one of the great issues for the country to cope with. And the amelioration of poverty ought to be a goal of government and so part of me is political and part of me is a researcher. One part is aware of what it means when you live in dire physical circumstances, when you are presented with a marked threat of violence, when you attend over-crowded schools, when you have only a partial family, if at all, when you have the absence of a husband, when you have multiple children, or when you have out-of-wedlock children who are also caught up in economic disadvantage. That piling up of negative events is probably as strong a summation of stressors as one can imagine.

At the same time the other part is almost a philosophy of government. The escape from poverty is part of the American heritage. As successive generations have come to this country, whey have survived under the multiple stresses of being in a new country, living in ghettos and so on. But these negative factors have also provided us with some of our great figures. And so one part of me looks to the political side with the view that if we can come to understand and help people escape from poverty this country will benefit to an extraordinary degree. So I'm political on one side and a researcher on the other side. On the second side I know that one finds cumulation, and the study of cumulation of stressors and the way of measuring children's adaptations and competencies begins to give us the leverage for change. For me, resilience is a compound and I find myself caught between the political and the scientific in reflecting on escape from poverty.

All of those things I think present for me a major picture of American distress. And when we use the word "distress" we are really talking about the cumulation of stressful events. My focus on poverty comes out of the American experience. It comes out of the fact that successive generations of children reared in poverty in this country over successive centuries have seen positive outcome more frequently than negative outcomes.

However, now we have a new stressor that's been introduced—rampant violence in our cities and in our communities. And the threat posed to children who succumb as well as to those who don't want to join gangs but who are forced to do so, threatens their survival. So all of these things I believe are critical in the choice of poverty and its consequences as a focus. I might just add one thing and that is the study of children encompasses multiple disciplines . . . medicine, social work, psychology, political science, sociology, economics, physiology and so on. All of those disciplines are contributors to our understanding of poverty—the guiding forces, the early forces and their outcomes. I believe that since it's one of the great problems in our country at the moment and since scientists can find in political issues important areas to research, I would hope that poverty becomes a target for people who are interested in stress, its antecedents, and its consequences.

J.R. Studies of resilient children have revealed processes, which seem to protect them and propel them toward growth and adaptation.

N.G. Well, we've begun to get tabulations of positive factors in the world of children even under deprived circumstances—a caring parent, even a single parent, the effort of the parent to insure that the child doesn't miss out on education, and the like; trying to protect the child from becoming a part of a gang in some big urban centers because there the cumulation is toward even more stressors. Yet there remain protective factors.

J.R. May I interject one thing . . . another stressor frequently found in impoverished neighborhoods is substance abuse?

N.G. I would certainly include that. There are so many crises that intervene for children and substance abuse is one of them. It locks a child as it does as adult into a situation of great danger. It anticipates failure experiences in the broad areas of work, family and government.

J.R. As well as a kid getting involved with substances and troubles using drugs or alcohol are kids who have a family member, even an alcoholic parent, or who are in a family headed by somebody who is a seller or an abuser of alcohol or other drugs. Maybe you could discuss the factors within the child that seem to enable him or her to rise above, to escape from decline in others.

N.G. Well let me add that this is another factor that is quite pervasive in our society. And now we're moving out of the slum environment and into the middle class environment as well. Substance abuse, alcoholism, drugs, and so on. It seems to me that this is one of the most incapacitating stress factors and it really overcomes whatever might be the more positive aspects of a person's personality and environment. So we must confront one very great problem here in the United States most certainly as well as in other nations, but particularly here I think. And its contributions to the sense of hopelessness in the poor neighborhoods are very profound.

J.R. Let's turn if we can to protective processes. These are the mechanisms whereby children escape, move or grow towards more protective things. I was wondering what are some of the protective processes within the individual?

N.G. That is one of our major needs for good research. Answering the research question, it seems to me, begins with a determination of the manifest stressors present in the lives of children marked by adaptive behaviors. From this you develop inferences about protective processes both in the child's environment and the attributes of the child—what factors lead to a positive outcome or which lead to a negative outcome? There lies the central issue of "protective processes." What protective processes really speak to is the unanticipated avoidance of failure and deficits by a child subjected to multiple stressors. It's when you say, "well how can that be?. . . . that child should have gone under a long time ago, but he or she hasn't." So let's look into the world of the child and lets look into the child himself or herself in order to try to make a tabulation of what we call "protective processes." Those protective elements which seem to, in some way, compete against the stressors children are exposed to with a certain degree of victory in overcoming the stressful elements. What accounts for the negative influences that are being overcome? I would say here we could make all kinds of lists. But the important thing is the research to that needs to be done. That is the task for the researcher, to begin with the stressors and then to look to the adaptive versus the non-adaptive groups of children. Then to move back into the world of the child, particularly in the context of the family, in order to see all the things that separate these two groups.

Now the thing we haven't talked about is biology, genetics and the environments of children. I say that knowing that there are some people who become inflamed when you talk about biology and genetics. But we recognize temperament differences in the infant and the child—where do they come from? They can't come from environmental factors unless you begin to consider, for example, the environment of the womb such as the mother who is taking drugs or using alcohol during pregnancy. I would not retreat from the critical importance of bio-genetics to try to understand this phenomenon. The good part of bringing in genetics in this way is there is no such thing as "good genetics" for the middle class and "bad genetics" for the lower class because there are too many kids that escape from their lower class environments. So if you're going to accept genetics you're going to have to turn, and I think you should, to where the powerful biological factors are playing a role here—interaction with the environment. And if for example one said, "well, good mothering is critically important," I would say, "absolutely true; now we go to the mother and we try to find the positive protective attributes of the mother". And in many ways we might indeed find that there is the powerful thrust of the mother protecting her child, knowing the dangers of the environment the child is in and protecting the child. And someone could say, "it's good mothering." And then the researcher could say "Yes, but what are the antecedents of good mothering?" and they might well be what the mother grew up with in her own childhood interacting with temperament factors and some of the other qualities which she herself was born with.

You know there's a story worth telling here and if I have time I'd like to tell it. I was invited to speak by one of our departments on the Saint Paul campus of the University, which is our agricultural campus. I was asked to talk about resilience and I asked, "Instead of talking about resilience, do you think that you might be able to locate a person who you see as powerfully resilient who has children so that we could know some of the story behind it?" And they did find a young mother of two children, and this is her story. She lived in Harlem on the fifth floor of an apartment building with her husband and two children. The family income level was very low. The husband earned a spare living but he worked, he was employed. One day they went to the beach and within sight of both mother and children, the husband drowned. They brought him to shore but he couldn't be resuscitated. Now this mother never allowed her children to walk up the five stories alone in the apartment building. Because there was a crack house on the forth floor, there were all kinds of degradations within that building and she feared for the well being of her eight year old daughter and the younger boy and so she kept them in their apartment all the time. She would stand out on the stoop of the tenement looking down two streets to see when her daughter was coming home and then she would take her right up the stairs. But as debt accumulated and the stress of trying to protect the children grew more and more difficult, at one point she simply felt she was breaking down and could not survive any longer. She called her sister who lived in Saint Paul and she said to the sister "I'm going under and I can't do anything about it". The sister said to her, "pack what ever you have, ship it out here and come out here immediately". Talk about a protective factor. This mother came to Saint Paul and went to the social agency and the social agency set her up in a lovely apartment in one of the outside suburbs with furniture provided for the family and so on. And the children were placed into school. Now the mother needed a car and so a car was provided for her and she then found that she couldn't pass the driver's test. She took the exam seven times before she finally passed the test. In the meantime, her daughter was going to school and loved it. Now comes a tragic moment. The daughter went home with one of the children in her classroom and they made sandwiches and they were sitting on the couch and the dog in the house leaped for the sandwich of the little girl and gashed her terribly. There was a rush to call 911, the ambulance came, and the child was in surgery for three hours with three hundred small stitches put into her mouth. She recovered; she came home quite bandaged up. And the mother said to her "you're not going to school tomorrow". And this little girl said, "yes I am". And the mother said, "no, you can't". And the little girl said, "I'm going to school". And the mother said to her, "they'll laugh at you". And the little girl said, "I don't care I'm going to school". She went to school the next day and what happened? The teacher told all the students what had happened and all of them grouped around this little girl and welcomed her in the classroom. Now where are the protective factors in that story?

If you begin to cumulate your cases, which is the way science operates, you can lay out the resilience of this mother. The stressors on her were overwhelming. She was going under, she would have been lost in New York. What if she didn't have a sister in Saint Paul, what if the Saint Paul welfare agency wasn't welcoming and helpful? what if she simple no longer had the strength and determination and other safety factors? And what about this little girl talking back to her mother, insisting on going to school. "Yes I will." "No you won't." "Yes, I will." "No, you won't." This mother met her difficulties and this little girl had earlier picked it up but perhaps also carried some of the biological aspects of her mother. That's a long story. But for me it summarizes the resilience of the family and their good fortune. The whole thing, the resilience, is a combination of psychosocial elements and biological predispositions, an aggregation of protective factors. And this story also shows how resilience can be the resilience of a family as well as the resilience of an individual. And perhaps larger social units as well. I think that organizational supports are critically important for people.

J.R. If I can make a comment on the side, you are advocating a change in societal intervention. Some strengthening of inherent resiliency processes through external support.

N.G. Well, you know you could ask anyone the question, "how would you explain people who are under great stress and yet behave very adaptively?" and everybody would give different reasons and examples. For me, there is no such thing as a single set of protective factors. Although you can set out certain things, like intelligence. This little girl, our Saint Paul girl, was very bright and her intelligence played a role. Her mother was bright and that's a very helpful thing. So you can begin there in terms of genetics. Now, we are inclined to talk about high intelligence in terms of genetics. In terms of low I.Q. We get upset with genetics but these are elements that are extremely important. And there are other protective elements as well. How much does society seek to protect its underprivileged and help them to develop their potential including their genetic potential? That I think is a very crucial problem in the United States. The image of the poor, and I'm sorry to politicize this, but the image of the poor in the eyes of middle and upper class people is really one of all too often of saying "If you want to make it, you can make it." But that isn't quite so. One needs to have a great deal of assistance in reaching a position of safety in this country. Middle class people never think of that. But the offspring of middle class people have a tremendous protective factor in their parents. They go off to high school, they go off to college, and they move in a different environment of safety and support and so on. But we are very spare in what we try to provide for people who are in poverty. And I think that that's a most unfortunate thing. And quite unfair. Especially since so much of resilience is a function of the interaction of multiple, complex factors.

J.R. *Before we end, are there directions or projects or ideas about the future for resiliency, resilience research that excite you because of their promise?*

N.G. I think ... you know we're so often talking about resilience in terms of it's antecedent factors because we first spot the child who is making it or the child who isn't making it and now we try to double back to look at the past to understand this. I have not been active in the therapeutic scene. But one can begin to think of these things that might be very helpful. My own feeling about this is to ask, "How might you approach getting a handle on adaptive behavior in dire circumstances?" This is something that I've said when speaking to clinicians who work in various agencies and clinics, therapists who see adults and children who come in for treatment. When a person comes in for a first interview, for a second interview, the clinician should begin to formulate in his mind what is the nature of the risk elements there and from a therapeutic stand point what are the protective elements that he might be able to count on. Rather than launching into the therapy right at the beginning, search out what really are the risk factors and the protective factors. Make a tabulation and take that tabulation and then build on it then follow through on the therapy and other positive factors provided by agencies and other support groups. In addition, I have urged clinicians to help advance the study of resilience by participating in it. If clinicians examined risk and protective elements and correlated them with outcomes in therapy, we might begin to get a handle from clinicians about what some of these multiple factors might be that engender positive outcomes as opposed to negative outcomes.

J.R. *Thank you for sharing your thoughts about the study of resilience.*

N.G. Thank you for the opportunity.

I

THE CONCEPT OF RESILIENCE

3

Toward an Understanding of Resilience
A Critical Review of Definitions and Models

Howard B. Kaplan

Introduction

Over the last four decades increasingly a new vocabulary was adopted by behavioral scientists interested in explaining more or less benign/malignant outcomes of the developmental process. The evolution of this vocabulary is illustrated with reference to a longitudinal study that traced the developmental paths of a cohort of children who had been exposed to conditions that were widely believed to be predictive of poor developmental outcomes (Werner, 1993):

> "We began our study by examining the children's vulnerability, that is, their susceptibility to negative developmental outcomes after exposure to serious risk factors, such as perinatal stress, poverty, parental psychopathology, and disruptions of their family unit . . . As our longitudinal investigation progressed, we also looked at the roots of resiliency in those children who successfully coped with such biological and psychosocial risk factors and had protective factors that aided in the recovery of troubled children and youths as they made the transition into adulthood" (pp. 503–504).

Howard B. Kaplan • Department of Sociology, Texas A & M University, College Station, Texas 77843.

Resilience and Development: Positive Life Adaptations, edited by Glantz and Johnson. Kluwer Academic/Plenum Publishers, New York, 1999.

Arguably, the most provocative among these constructs is resilience. When a concept such as resilience captures the imagination of a large group of scholars we should perhaps be grateful. Science can only win when scholars focus upon an idea and bring their unique perspectives to the elucidation of this idea. Yet at the same time we should be wary. For whenever we concentrate on something, we exclude something else from consideration. We must continually reexamine exciting ideas to make sure that they are serving a positive rather than inhibitory purpose and that they are worthy of the intellectual resources focused upon them. As Liddle (1994) observes:

> "Concepts have a life all their own. Sometimes they appear and then suddenly depart like fashion trends. These early exits are not necessarily premature, at least when the ideas were insubstantial to begin with. With this in mind, consider our current fascination with the notion of resilience. Does resilience qualify as an organizing concept with sufficient logical and emotional resonance to yield systematic theoretical and research inquiry that will make it a lasting contribution" (p. 167).

Liddle (1994) concludes that it is too early to answer this question. However he notes that the potential resiliency of resilience should be examined with an eye to consideration of continued revision or extension of the construct. It is in this spirit that I offer the present chapter.

In the following pages I review issues concerning the definition of resilience and note areas of commonality and variation in the conceptualization of resilience and related constructs. I then review models that incorporate resilience by focusing on component constructs and the dimensions along which these models vary. Finally, I offer an assessment of the functions that the construct of resilience has served and of its future usefulness in the study of human behavior.

Defining Resilience

As part of the literature on the concept of resilience, I include commentaries and research dealing with functionally equivalent terms such as invulnerability and stress-resistance (Garmezy, 1985). The functional equivalence of these terms has been recognized by numerous researchers, each selecting one of the terms and indicating the functional equivalence of the other terms. For example, Losel, Bliesener, and Koferl (1989, p. 187) observe: "There is a multitude of constructs that are related to invulnerability, such as resilience, hardiness, adaptation, adjustment, mastery, plasticity, person-environment fit, or social buffering."

I also encompass constructs such as vulnerability when they are defined relative to resilience. Thus, resilience and vulnerability are often viewed as opposite poles of a continuum reflecting susceptibility to adverse consequences or benign consequences upon exposure to high risk circumstances (Anthony, 1987a,b). Rutter (1990, p. 181) defines resilience as a positive pole of ubiquitous phenomenon of individual differences in people's response to stress and adversity. Occasionally the negative pole is defined in terms of nonresilience rather than vulnerability. As Radke-Yarrow and Brown (1993) use these terms:

> *"Resilience was defined as having no diagnoses and not being on the borderline of reaching criteria for a diagnosis. Nonresilience was defined as the presence of one or more diagnoses of a serious nature, with problems persisting over time"* (p. 583).

The definitions of resilience, their functionally equivalent terms, and their polar opposites are highly variable. The variability in definition may be traced to four main sources. The first source is in the distinction between the relationship between resiliency and outcome. According to some definitions resiliency is coextensive with the outcome of having survived in the face of adversity; according to other definitions, resilience is analytically distinguished from and is causally related to more or less desirable outcomes. Frequently, the defining language is so imprecise that it is easy to misinterpret the intent of the investigator regarding which meaning is applicable.

The second source of variability is the variation in outcomes among those definitions that equate resilience with outcomes. The third source is in variation in the defining characteristics of resilience that influence outcome, where the analytic distinction between resilience and outcome is drawn. Finally, the definitions of resilience are highly variable because the outcomes and their putative causes are defined in terms of risk factors that are themselves highly variable. Each of these sources of definitional variability is considered in turn.

Resilience as Outcome Versus Cause of Outcome

Definitions of resilience vary according to the answer to the following questions: Should resilience be defined in terms of the nature of the outcomes in response to stress or in terms of the factors which interact with stress to produce the outcomes? Is resilience the variation in good outcomes among individuals who are at-risk for bad outcomes, or is resilience the qualities possessed by individuals that enable them to have good outcomes? Is resilience a phenomenon that moderates the influence of risk factors on more or less benign outcomes? Or is resilience the fact of having achieved benign outcomes in the face of adversity? In the latter case, resilience would be defined in terms of the presence of desirable outcomes and the absence of undesirable outcomes. In the former case, resilience would be defined in terms of the characteristics that moderate the effect of risk factors on benign outcomes and, less directly, the influences upon these factors.

Resilience as Outcome

Resilience is frequently defined in terms of the fact or process of approximating valued outcomes in the face of risk or adversity. Resilience refers to the fact of "maintaining adaptive functioning in spite of serious risk hazards" (Rutter, 1990, p. 209). Consistent with this definition, Losel, Bliesener, and Koferl (1989) states, *"Our main interest is in resilient adolescents who are (still) psychologically healthy despite high multiple exposure to stressful life events and circumstances . . ."* (p. 194).

Individuals are considered as vulnerable to particular negative outcomes or to the absence of positive outcomes by virtue of being at-risk. Vulnerable individuals are those who turn out poorly while invulnerable individuals turn out well (Seifer & Sameroff, 1987). As one team operationalized the concepts, children who are being reared in chaotic and threatening conditions by emotionally ill parents are labeled "invulnerable" or "resilient" if they have no psychiatric diagnoses, relate well to peers and to adult authorities in school and at home, have a positive self-concept, and are performing at grade level in school (Radke-Yarrow & Sherman, 1990). For Masten (1994), resilience relates to *"how effectiveness in the environment is achieved, sustained or recovered despite adversity"* (p. 4).

Resilience as Cause or Influence

Resilience, in addition to or instead of being defined in terms of the fact of having benign or less malignant outcomes in the face of life stress, may be thought of as a general construct that reflects specific characteristics and the mechanisms through which they operate that moderate the relationships between risk factors and outcome variables. One construct that is the functional equivalent of resilience used in this sense is hardiness.

Individuals who are said to be characterized by hardiness have high levels of three adaptive characteristics: commitment (belief in the importance and value of oneself and one's experiences or activities), control (the belief that life events and experiences are predictable and consequences of one's actions), and challenge (the belief that change is normal and represents a positive rather than threatening circumstance) (Kobasa, 1979). The hardiness components moderate adverse effects of stressful life circumstances by permitting individuals to reinterpret stressful experiences in such a way that stress is reduced, and through the use of adaptive coping patterns following the experience of stress (Gentry & Kobasa, 1984).

Hardy individuals are more likely to engage in adaptive coping strategies and are less likely to employ maladaptive responses such as behavioral avoidance or denial. Wiebe (1991) reported results that are interpreted as consistent with conceptualizing hardiness as a moderator of stress. High hardy men when compared with low hardy men appraised an aversive task less threatening and more controllable. Further, they responded to this task with less negative affect, more positive affect, and lower physiological arousal. The conceptualization of resilience and vulnerability in terms of personal characteristics that enable approximation of desirable outcomes is nicely represented in the following statement by Rauh (1989):

> *"A continuum of adverse events may produce in the child a specific or generalized vulnerability, a proneness or preparedness to disintegrate in the face of specific or general stress. Vulnerability can be described as reduced flexibility or adaptational potential . . . Also, the child in its specific characteristics may attract reactions from its environment that exacerbate its adverse situation as, for example, in the case of a physically deformed, a sick, or an extremely irritable infant that may provoke rejection or even neglect . . . These characteristics may be dependent on genetic endowment, on the intactness of the central nervous system, and on physical appearance and health. In addition, vulnerability may be defined by the individual's abilities and skills under development or by emotional and motivational reaction styles that become stabilized with significant others.*
>
> *The positive counterpart to vulnerability is 'resilience' . . . Resilience is characterized as the ability to draw on personal or social resources, the ability to detect contingencies and predictability in complex situations, and the ability to react flexibly. Resilience is enhanced, for example, by self-efficacy beliefs, a positive self-concept and self-esteem . . . Vulnerability, and its positive counterpart, resilience, is usually conceived as relatively stable personal characteristics of the child . . ." (p. 165).*

The implication that resilience reflects characteristics of the person or environment that influences (other) desirable outcomes is apparent in Cohler's (1987) comments about the nature of resilience:

> *"In sum, the children of psychiatrically ill parents who are better able to cope with the adversity of unreliable and often emotionally inaccessible caretakers have innate ego strength, creative abilities, and increased per-*

*sonal and physical attractiveness; these traits enable these children to con-
tinue to reach out to others for support. To the extent that their parents
are able to provide care and assistance, these more resilient children
appear to be successful in engaging the parents. When a disturbed parent
is not accessible, these children do not give up in their efforts to obtain
adult care, turning instead to such other available adults as relatives,
teachers, and family friends. Finally, these children often have greater
intelligence and come from families higher in social status; in turn, these
qualities foster increased instrumental mastery and greater social skills"*
(p. 395).

The definition of resiliency in terms of one or several stable and
general characteristics that are responsible for desirable outcomes (or the
forestalling of undesirable outcomes) has caused great concern among a
number of observers. For example, Bartelt (1994) dealing with the subject
of educational resilience observes:

> *"Frankly, I feel that we are imbuing resilience with the same overarching
> powers that early chemists attributed to phlogiston, the mystical sub-
> stance that was ostensibly released during combustion and, being con-
> tained within the object being consumed enabled it to successfully burn.
> Resilience, as a psychological trait, that is seen as a component of the self
> that enables success in the face of adversity, and may either be consumed
> or, paradoxically, reinforced by adversity.*
>
> *In short, I make the case that resilience, as a concept is difficult, if
> not impossible to empirically specify, and is too easily conflated with
> measures of situational success or failure. It suffers from its roots in
> subjective interpretations of biographical events, and it is too closely
> dependent on observer-imputed stresses and resources for dealing with
> stressors"* (pp. 98–99).

In many instances it is difficult to determine which of the two
definitions, resilience as outcome versus resilience as influential quality,
is intended by the researcher. As Staudinger and her associates (1993)
observe, *"the distinction between the protective factors and mechanisms
underlying resilience, as an outcome can be quite arbitrary"* (p. 544). Indeed,
outcomes in one context may be treated plausibly as influences upon outcomes in another context:

> *"'Outcome' is a complex set of variables that reflect the interaction,
> across a number of areas, of multiple processes of coping with and adap-
> tation to internal and external demands . . . The existence of 'false posi-
> tives' underscores the necessity of studying the factors that negate, buffer,
> or interact with risk in the majority of studied individuals who do not
> succumb to mental disorder. These factors overlap with measures of pos-
> itive outcomes; when adjustment is viewed as a process or long-term tra-
> jectory rather than as level of functioning at one point in time, it become*

mediate and outcome variables. The same current indices can be viewed *either as signs of positive adjustment* or as protective or compensatory f*actors; in both cases the variables will* predict future good outcomes" (Sc*h*uldberg, 1993, pp. 139–140).

Variability in Outcome Definitions

Resilience often is defined in general terms of the forestalling of adverse developmental outcomes in the face of characteristics of the individual or the individual s environment that would have led to the prediction of the adverse developmental outcome. However, except for this similarity, variation in the nature of the desirable or undesirable developmental outcomes has led to widely different definitions of resilience.

> *"At present, various researchers employ different definitions of resilience that can range from the absence of psychopathology in the child of a mentally ill parent to the recovery of function in a brain-injured patient. Definitional diversity results in sometimes disparate profiles of competent adaptation as well as in different estimates of rates of resilience among similar risk groups"* (Cicchetti & Garmezy, 1993, p. 499).

The subject may be manifesting resiliency according to one criterion, but not according to another. For example, Spencer and her associates (1993), conceptualizing resilience as adaptive coping, tested a model of risk and resilience to examine coping methods and competence outcomes as measured by academic performance and academic self-esteem. It is possible, those individuals may be judged to be resilient by these criteria but not according to criteria representing competence in other spheres (peer relations, family). The fact that individuals may vary in adjustment depending upon the domain under consideration has implications for the conceptualization of resilience. Luthar (1993) concludes:

> *"The current evidence indicates, then, that notions of overall resilience are of questionable utility. In future research, it would be more useful if discussions were presented in terms of the specific domains of successful coping (e.g. academic resilience, social resilience or emotional resilience), along with those areas in which apparent survivors show high vulnerability"* (p. 442).

Even within the same sphere of operation, judgments of resiliency may vary as outcome measures vary.

> *"While a child may appear to be adapting positively within the school arena if outcome measures focus solely on cognitive abilities, the same*

child may manifest impaired social relationships. Unless multiple domains of development are assessed, only a partial picture of adaptation can be formulated" (Cicchetti & Garmezy, 1993, pp. 499–500).

The outcomes that define resilience will vary according to developmental stage and sociocultural milieu. As Masten (1994) observes:

"Resilience implies a qualitative evaluation of functioning based substantially on normative expectations for adaptations that vary according to age and environmental context. The markers of good psychosocial development, developmental tasks, change as a function of age and vary across culture" (p. 19).

Finally, the outcomes that define resilience vary according to the level of organization to which the individual (or other unit of observation) contributes.

"In this discussion we are viewing coping at three levels. At a biological level, children are said to be coping successfully if their behavior contributes to their chances of physical survival and health, and the continuation of the species. At a societal level, successful coping behaviors are those that contribute to the survival and well being of others. At a psychological level, we regard positive coping as the exercise of behaviors that contribute to the well being of the self. A child who becomes a survivor is one who is happy about one's self, who is physically healthy, whose behavior is masterful, and who is learning to be a positive contributor to one's immediate society" (Radke-Yarrow & Sherman, 1990, p. 100).

Variability in Protective Factor Definitions

Where vulnerability is defined in terms of the protective factors or related phenomena that permit the approximation of desirable outcomes or the forestalling of undesirable outcomes, a good deal of definitional variability may still be observed. Variability in definition is observed because the forces of resiliency vary according to the causes of diverse outcomes, the view of vulnerability as process rather than static trait, and the variable definition of the unit of observation.

Since the same factors may not cause one outcome as cause another outcome, factors which mitigate the effects of stressors on one outcome may be expected to be different from those that mitigate the effects of stressors on another outcome. The implication of this is that,

"... differences across spheres of adjustment must be carefully appraised, and discussions on resilience should be presented in terms of

the specific spheres of successful (and less successful) adaptation. While it is more important to demonstrate which children survive relatively well and why, it is equally critical that researchers address the costs that at-risk children may pay even as they maintain positive profiles across some adjustment domains" (Luthar, 1993, p. 442).

In contradistinction to definitions of resiliency in terms of state-trait or individual characteristic, some conceptions deal with resiliency as a process. For example, resiliency is the

". . . process of coping with disruptive, stressful, or challenging life events in a way that provides the individual with additional protective and coping skills than prior to the disruption that results from the event" (Richardson, Neiger, Jensen, & Kumpfer, 1990, p. 34).

One implication of processual definitions of resilience for definitional variability in the construct relates to the upper bound of resilience. In some definitions resilience seems to imply reaching an acceptable level of developmental outcome in the face of adversity. Presumably resilience resulting in individuals who do not experience stress will reach a plateau that is the equivalent of that which is reached by individuals who do not experience the stress. However, according to other definitions, resilience permits achieving levels of development that go beyond that which would have been reached in the absence of stress. Resilience is fostered by stress rather than representing evidence of having overcome stress. According to such definitions,

"Life crises are viewed as constructive confrontations that spur develop- ment. *Personal growth can be fostered by the disruption that crises generate and the subsequent reorganization that occurs in their wake. Stressors are a natural and potentially positive part of life; resilience develops from confronting stressful experiences and coping with them effectively . . . people in crisis often experience disruptions in significant relationships, challenges to their basic values and beliefs, role changes, and new demands. The process of confronting these experiences can promote a cognitive differentiation, self-confidence, and a more mature approach to life. A person who experiences pain and loss may develop a deeper understanding and empathy for others with similar problems. Exposure to novel crisis situations may broaden a person's perspective, promote new coping skills, and lead to new personal and social resources"* (Schaefer & Moos, 1992, p. 150).

Finally, variability among definitions of resilience in terms of causal influence is accounted for in part by attribution of resilience to various agents including the individual, the organization, and the community. At each level are definitions in terms of what it takes for that unit to survive in its respective environment. At the level of the individual, the requirements for successful adaptation are summarized in the construct, akin to resiliency/vulnerability, ego-resiliency and its opposite extreme ego-brittleness:

> *"Ego-resiliency, when dimensionalized, is defined at one extreme by resourceful adaptation to changing circumstances and environmental contingencies, analysis of the 'goodness of fit' between situational demands and environmental contingencies, and flexible invocation of the available repertoire of problem-solving strategies ('problem solving' being defined to include the social and personal domains as well as the cognitive). The opposite end of the ego-resilience continuum (ego-brittleness) implies little adaptive flexibility, an inability to respond to the dynamic requirements of the situation, a tendency to perseverate or to become disorganized when encountering changed circumstances or when under stress, and a difficulty in recouping after traumatic experiences"* (Block & Block, 1980, p. 48).

The definitions of the requirements for organizational adaptation may differ somewhat from the requirements of individual adaptation, although certain similarities may be noted at higher levels of abstraction. Anderson (1994) concludes with reference to school organizations,

> *"What emerges clearly from much of the recent literature is that successful organizations are those that (a) recognize and actively structure and restructure themselves to support proper and consistent articulations of a mission, (b) support the optimal development of shared decision making, (c) build trust, (d) encourage openness, and (e) are tireless in their efforts to support the growth of individual and collective competence ... Organizations exhibiting these characteristics are considered healthy, and are the ones most likely to survive typical external intrusions and to avoid persistent incompetence"* (p. 143).

Variability in Risk Factors

Definitional variability with regard to the concept of resilience is linked to variation in the conceptualization of stress or risk factors in a number of senses. First, definitions of resilience assume that the individual who has achieved a desirable developmental outcome or who has forestalled an undesirable outcome has nevertheless been exposed to some risk. However, the nature of the risks that are assumed are highly variable. Consequently, the definitions of resilience, which are tied to the nature of the risks, will also be highly variable. The nature of the at-risk person's response will be such that the risk factor is obviated if the person is in fact resilient or invulnerable. This is illustrated with reference to certain of the invulnerable types described by Anthony (1987a):

> *"First, there is the 'invulnerable' who has a 'sociopathic' uninvolved approach to the world and is strategically estranged from it . . . The individual may be alienated or emotionally responsive, but the crucial element of intimacy is missing. They do not, cannot, or will not get close to the object because of early experiences of suffering at the hands of primary objects . . . A special subgroup of 'invulnerables' comprise those who have bounced back and continue to rebound from high risks and vulnerabilities. They frequently begin life as frail, weak and ailing infants and children; despite this fragility, they gradually develop a seemingly implacable resolve 'not to be broken' and demonstrate an extraordinary degree of persistence in their continuous struggles with adversity. In the service of survival, they can display a high degree of creativity, which tends to be inner-directed and agonizingly expressed. Their capacity to transform intolerable reality through fantasies is of a high order, and at its best, gains the lasting attention of the world. Their creative activity relieves their overwhelming sense of vulnerability, but as it abates, they become susceptible to breakdown. It is life long struggle by often very miserable people, but society benefits from it"* (pp. 43–46).

The definitions of resilience are tied to risk factors in a second sense as well. In addition to the nature of risk factors, the number and intensity of risk factors inform the definition of resilience. The nature of resilience is only meaningful relative to the enormity of the stresses under which the individual operates. As the adversity experienced by the individual increases, the characteristics of the individual that are required to overcome the adversity must necessarily increase. As Werner (1989a) observes,

> *"The number of ameliorative factors that discriminated between positive and negative developmental outcomes in this cohort increased with stress (in both middle and lower class children) and deprivation (among lower class children). As disadvantage and the cumulative number of stressful life events increased, more protective factors in the children and their caregiving environment were needed to counterbalance the negative aspects in their lives and to ensure a positive developmental outcome"* (p. 162).

Definitions of resilience are restricted as well as proliferated by recourse to risk variables. Since resilience is imputed only when individuals avoid a negative outcome or achieve a positive outcome under conditions when the reverse would be expected, it would appear that resilience has little relevance where risks associated with particular outcomes have not yet arisen. In the absence of those conditions it could not be determined whether or not the achievement of the positive outcome or the avoidance of the negative outcome was the result of the absence of the risks. The notion of resilience does not encompass the potential of individuals to survive risks should they arise. At the very least, the concept of resilience should include the capability as well as the actuality of surviving in the face of stress. In fact, Anthony (1987a) refers to this situation when he identifies,

> "... pseudovulnerables who are vulnerable or extremely vulnerable individuals who have been 'blessed' with an overprotective environment (particularly the maternal portion of it), and are relatively unchallenged and thriving until the environment fails, and they fail along with it" (pp. 27–28).

The conceptualization of risk factors has yet another consequence for definitions of resilience. Whether stress or other risk factors are thought of as constants or as variables has implications for the conceptualization of resiliency. Where stress is a constant, resiliency/vulnerability is defined as having direct or indirect effects on outcome measures. Where stress or the occurrence of risk factors is variable then resiliency/vulnerability is defined as moderating the relationship between stress (risk factors) and outcome variables.

The definitions of resilience that have reference to risk factors have been widely and justifiably criticized. Two statements illustrate and summarize the range of concerns. Each makes reference to the fact that there are no definite criteria by which a particular variable may be defined as a risk factor. Therefore, no clear criterion exists by which particular behaviors or outcomes may be defined as resilient. Judgment is always made after the fact and is based on the assignment of risk to particular conditions. Seifer and Sameroff (1987) also note:

> "There is currently no criterion by which a particular variable is determined to be a risk factor, a protective factor, or merely a measure that is related to the outcome in question. The current situation is that individual researchers make informed, but arbitrary, choices in this matter. However, when investigators with different points of view examine the same populations, conflicts are bound to arise...
>
> This issue of defining 'risk' might be a trivial matter, except for the fact that what determines vulnerability or invulnerability is dependent upon the initial determination of risk. To some extent, this is a logical dilemma. One could assume that any factor shown to affect child outcome adversely should be considered a risk factor. But then there would be no possibility of finding a set of measures that consistently differentiate vulnerables from invulnerables, since anything that differentiates children with good outcomes from those with poor outcomes would be considered a risk factor. At the other extreme, one might rigidly restrict the conception of risk factors to a small set of measures. But in this case

a different type of problem arises. If . . . we had considered only parental mental illness to be a risk factor, then we could have concluded with certainty that SES and race are the essential factors that differentiate vulnerables from invulnerables. However, we consider this form of analysis relatively uninformative, since it fails to account for variables at different levels of individual, family, or societal organization as potential risk factors. In sum, to accomplish the goal of identifying factors that protect at-risk children from poor outcome, it is necessary to define the meaning of 'risk' somewhere between two extremes. At one pole is a rigid set of single factors, and at the other is an operational definition that includes any factor related to poor outcomes in children" (pp. 64–65).

Finally, Cicchetti and Garmezy (1993) observe the difficulty of distinguishing between the factors that indeed place the individual at risk, and factors that happen to distinguish between good and poor outcomes but have no causal significance. Frequently risk factors are stated in terms of marker variables rather than in terms of underlying constructs. Therefore, the assumption of being exposed to risk may be faulty. The individual may have been exposed to the marker variable but not to the underlying construct that is said to be represented by the marker variable.

"Investigators must be cautious that children who are labeled resilient are not simply children who have not been exposed to the stressor under investigation . . . For example, a child with a mother who has been depressed will not necessarily experience poor-quality caregiving. Moreover, the maternal depression may have been situationally based, and the child may not have inherited a genetic predisposition for depression. In a situation such as this, the child might be better classified as low risk than as resilient. The issue of magnitude of risk cannot be minimized, and risk should not be assumed merely in response to the presumed presence of a stressor. Rather, more comprehensive information on risk must be attained in all samples" (Cicchetti & Garmezy, 1993, p. 500).

In the last analysis, the meaning of any concept of resilience is dependent upon a specific causal model. If the causal model specifying antecedents of a desirable outcome is not valid, then the imputation of resilience as the characteristic which permits attainment of the desirable outcome in the face of the causal risk factors is itself invalid. If no theoretical model is presented, then the putative risk factor and the related definition of resilience are a function of accidental empirical associations between the variables said to represent risk factors and the variables said to reflect resilience. Since the conceptualization of resilience depends upon the contextual theoretical model I turn now to a consideration of the range and viability of theoretically informed models that encompass resilience as an explanatory construct or as the object of explanation.

Models of Resilience

The meaning of resilience may be properly understood only in the context of causal models that attempt to explain some outcome that has socially evaluative significance. Resilience is defined in terms of the nature of the relationship between putative causes of the outcome and the outcome itself. I consider in turn the components of such models, and the range and viability of the types of models that have incorporated resilience as a component whether as an independent, dependent, mediating, or moderating variable.

Components of Models

Since resilience is generally defined either in terms of more or less desirable outcomes or in terms of the linear or interactive influences exerted on such outcomes, the components should include, as a minimum, constructs representing outcomes and those reflecting the "causes" of such outcomes. These variables as they have appeared in the literature may be considered parsimoniously under three rubrics: outcomes, risk factors (and their complements), and protective factors (and their complements).

Outcomes

Resilience has no meaning except in relationship to more or less desirable outcomes. It is defined either in terms of the fact of having approximated desirable outcomes or having distanced oneself from undesirable outcomes, or in terms of characteristics that enable the approximation of desirable outcomes.

The Normative Basis of Outcomes.   The very notion of resilience connotes evaluative significance.

> *"Resilience is a quintessentially U.S. concept. It has roots in the U.S. hero myth commemorated in books and stories by Horatio Alger in the latter half of the 19th century"* (Rigsby, 1994, p. 85).

The outcomes to which definitions of resilience have references similarly have normative significance. The evaluative connotations of certain of the outcomes is apparent in terms such as "Problem-Behavior Theory" (Jessor, Donovan, & Costa, 1991). Outcomes are ordinarily defined in terms of normative judgments regarding appropriate intrapsychic and behavioral responses taking into account culture, environmental circumstances and stage of development. As Masten (1994) observes,

"In developmental psychopathology, adaptation is judged according to psychosocial milestones called developmental tasks for example, in the United States and other industrialized societies, lists of developmental tasks in middle childhood usually include school adjustment (attendance, appropriate behavior), academic achievement, peer acceptance, having at least one friend, and moral conduct (following the rules of social organizations such as family, school, and community, for example by not stealing). In adolescence, new tasks become salient, including adjustment to pubertal change, romantic relationships, and a coherent identity. In adulthood, achievements related to earning a living, establishing a family, and performing community service become important" (p. 4).

When these expectations are not met, the individual will be judged in psychopathological or other terms signifying deviance. However, when these expectations are met in circumstances where it would be understandable (if not forgivable) that the expectations were not met, the individual would be evaluated in terms of being resilient, heroic or otherwise extraordinary.

As a consequence of the phenomenon of normative relativity we are cautioned not to generalize too easily on the basis of studies conducted in our own culture (Werner, 1993).

"Most studies of risk and resiliency undertaken during the past decade have focused on the development of children who live in urban, industrialized societies where parents have options to pursue different child-rearing philosophies and techniques, where children are expected to spend some 10–12 years in compulsory schooling, and where much of their socialization is undertaken by a succession of strangers who prepare them for entry into a competitive economy that prizes acquisitiveness, assertiveness, and mobility and values a person's control over his or her social and physical environment. Future research on risk and resilience in children and youth needs to look more systematically at other 'developmental niches' that characterize the interface of child and culture . . . The physical and social settings in which children live, the customs of childcare and sex role socialization, and caregivers' beliefs concerning the nature and needs of children vary greatly in those parts of the world where five out of every six children are born today: in Asia, the Middle East, Africa, and Latin America. So do the risk factors that increase the vulnerability and challenge the resiliency of children" (pp. 513–514).

A major limitation of the concept of resilience is that it is tied to the normative judgments relating to particular outcomes. If the outcomes were not desirable, then the ability to reach the outcomes in the face of putative risk factors would not be considered resilience. Yet it is possible that the socially defined desirable outcome may be subjectively defined as undesirable, while the socially defined undesirable outcome may be subjectively defined as desirable. From the subjective point of view, the individual may be manifesting resilience, while from the social point of view the individual may be manifesting vulnerability. Bartelt offers the following example (1994):

> "*Several representatives of Hispanic community organizations have put the following question to me: If family income is lower for Puerto Rican communities, if the day-to-day needs of the household for additional economic resources are strongly present; and if there is a strong pro-family ideology within the community that is threatened by continued poverty; why should we not expect that our teenagers will seek to leave school and obtain full-time employment as soon as possible? In turn I must ask myself, isn't this a form of resilience as we have come to define it? How then do we distinguish academic success as resilience from dropping out as resilience*" (p. 103).

Positive and Negative Outcomes. Outcomes may be stated in positive or negative terms. In the latter case the reference is some undesirable state (illness, maladaptive behavior, substance abuse, psychopathology). Individuals are described as approximating or distancing from the state. In the former case, the reference is a desirable state (health, competence, self-actualization, optimization of gratification, reality-oriented self-acceptance). The individual is evaluated as approximating or distancing from the desirable standard. As Luthar and Zigler (1991) remind us,

> "*Frequently, researchers have used the absence of psychopathology, or of maladaptive behavior, as an indicator of resilience against high-risk conditions . . . Over the last two decades, developmental psychopathologists have increasingly explored the concepts of 'invulnerability', rather than focusing predominantly on vulnerability and maladjustment. Recent investigations on risk and vulnerability have tended more frequently to use aspects of health and competence as outcome measures, correcting empirical psychologists' traditional neglect of successful adaptation under adverse conditions . . . With regard to definitions of social competence, two major criteria have been delineated . . . : the success of the person in meeting societal expectations, and aspects of the individual's personal development or self-actualization . . .*" (pp. 11–12).

Among those who focus on positive outcomes, Aaron Antonovsky (1984) suggests as an antidote to the pathogenic paradigm that proposes we focus on the causes of sickness a salutogenic orientation and seeks to understand how individuals are able to overcome adverse circumstances and achieve a state of wellness. Rather than asking what keeps one from getting sicker, one asks how one becomes healthier. Among the outcomes that are specified in more benign terms is positive mental health (Jahoda,

1959; Offer & Sabshin, 1966) and self-actualization (Maslow, 1970). Schaefer & Moos (1992) identify three broad categories of positive outcomes: enhanced social resources such as development of a confidante relation-ship or formation of new support networks; enhanced personal resources such as cognitive and intellectual differentiation or self-reliance and self-understanding; and, the development of new coping skills including cognitive skills, problem solving and help-seeking skills, and the ability to regulate and control affect.

Whether or not positive and negative outcomes should represent polar opposites or the nature of the range between polar opposites remains problematic in the literature. Each desirable state does not necessarily have an undesirable state as a polar opposite. The presence of an undesirable state (illness) implies that absence of a desirable state (health). However, the absence of an undesirable state does not necessarily imply the presence of a desirable one. One may not be characterized by self-hate and yet may not be fully self-accepting. A person may be asymptomatic without having fulfilled his potential for health.

> *"In studies of adaptation to life crises, investigators typically equate good outcome with the absence of physical symptoms and psychopathology. They usually fail to consider the possibility of a new and better level of adaptation that reflects personal growth rather than a return to the status quo"* (Schaefer & Moos, 1992, p. 149).

The way these issues are resolved has important implications for the definition of resilience and the other components of paradigms of resilience,

> *"Should positive factors associated with the reduction of risk and vulnerability be considered as leading to optimal development and thus be considered as benefits to the growing child, or should one assume that they contribute primarily to adequate development, and should thus be seen as protective? One view would hold that the possible influence of positive and negative factors could affect development on a full continuum running from poor to optimal functioning. The other possibility is that positive and negative factors affect the organism on a continuum ranging from poor to adequate functioning only but do not affect optimal functioning"* (Greenbaum & Auerbach, 1992, p. 12).

Range of Outcomes. A wide variety of outcomes of varying degrees of specificity have been examined in models of resilience. The range of outcomes encompasses emotional disorders, conduct problems, and physical dysfunction. Among the particular patterns of psychopathology that have been investigated are anti-social disorder, schizophrenia, and the major affective disorders (Garmezy, 1985; Rutter, 1985). Park and her associates

(1990) investigated the protective function of religious coping in moderating the relationship between life stress and depression and trait anxiety. Topf (1989) considered correlates of occupational burnout. Carro and her associates (1993) examined maternal and paternal characteristics at one month postpartum as risk and protective factors for children s internalizing and externalizing problems at two to three years of age.

For Rubenstein and her associates (1989) suicidal behavior was predicted by life stress and depression as an independent risk factor that was offset to a degree by family cohesion. Gest and his associates (1993) tested process-oriented models of resilience for conduct problems in adolescence. Stevenson and Rhodes (1991) examined risk and resilience in teenagers who avoid pregnancy. Mulholland and her associates (1991) considered psychological resilience and vulnerability in relationship to academic performance in children of divorce, and Masten and her associates (1990) identified a number of variables that moderated the relationship between stressful life events and competence in the school setting.

Among those who considered outcomes that had important implications for physical health, Chandy and his associates (1994) investigated disordered eating behaviors of adolescents with substance misusing parents, and Rodin, Striegel-Moore, and Silberstein (1990) examined risk and protective factors for bulimia nervosa with particular reference to the influence of biological variables, genetic disposition, development of body image, and personality and behavioral characteristics that may contribute to differential risk for bulimia. Other studies examined resilience with reference to the immune system. Wiedenfeld and her associates (1990) reported that the development of a strong perceived self-efficacy to control phobic stressors had an enhancing effect on the immune system, and Baron and his associates (1990) investigated the relationship between social support and immune function among spouses of cancer patients. Finally, Brown (1991) investigated the moderating role of physical fitness on the adverse effects of life stress on health status.

The range of outcomes, of course, has implications for the definition of resilience. For each outcome the definition of resilience varies. Thus, Wang, Haertel, and Walberg (1994) speak of educational resilience, defined as *"the heightened likelihood of success in school, and in other life accomplishments, despite environmental adversities, brought about by early traits, conditions, and experiences"* (p. 46).

Multiple Outcomes/Variable Resilience. In the real world, events never have only one outcome. They have several outcomes, each of which is evaluated in a more or less favorable light. Each outcome has its own set of causes. Those outcomes that have the same set of causes may in fact represent separate indicators of the same underlying construct. However, to the extent that the separate outcomes have different causes, then resilience would be defined differently, depending upon the causal model that accounts for the particular outcome. If, on the basis of the causal model an individual were expected to reach a particular undesirable outcome but in fact did not reach that outcome, the person would be judged to be resilient. The same person who, on the basis of the appropriate causal model, was predicted to have a particular outcome and in fact achieved that undesirable outcome would be judged to be not resilient. In short, resilience is relative to the putative causal model and the nature of the outcomes, as well as the desirability of the outcomes. Where multiple outcomes are considered in the same model, multiple evaluations of resilience would be in order. As Fisher and his associates (1987) observe,

> "When multiple criteria are used to define competent and incompetent functioning so that environmental or parental factors can be identified, inconsistencies and discrepancies develop. The children identified as competent or incompetent using one criterion may be different from those identified when another criterion is used. There is little doubt that single indices of competence are insufficient to reflect the complexity of adequate adjustment; yet it becomes clear that the use of multiple criteria produce discrepant results when used singly or reduce sample size considerably if used in combination" (p. 222).

The frequent lack of congruence between outcome variables is reflected in a number of studies. Luthar, Doernberger, and Zigler (1993) report that children under stress who showed behavioral competence were at the same time vulnerable to emotional distress over time.

The implications of the multiple and uneven evaluations of resilience for models that attempt to explain behavioral adaptation are clear. As Luthar (1993) summarizes,

> "... differences across spheres of adjustment must be carefully appraised, and discussions on resilience should be presented in terms of the specific spheres of successful (and less successful) adaptation. While it is important to demonstrate which children survive relatively well and why, it is equally critical that researchers address the costs that at-risk children may pay even as they maintain positive profiles across some adjustment domains" (p. 442).

Relationships among Outcomes. Frequently, diverse outcomes are related to each other in at least two ways. First, they may represent separate indicators of a latent construct. It is quite possible, for example, that several indicators of behavioral adaptation represent a common construct.

Certainly, diverse indicators have often been classified as if they represent a smaller number of basic constructs. As Masten (1994) states,

"Psychological adaptation historically has had two major components: mental functioning and external behavior. Internal health has been described in terms of psychological well being, internal equilibrium, and ego strength. Internal problems have been described in terms of psychological distress, decompensation, and anxiety. Externally, 'good' psychological adaptation has been referred to as competence and social adjustment, whereas 'poor' adaptation has been called externalizing symptoms, antisocial behavior, and social maladjustment" (p. 4).

Second, the outcomes may bear causal relationships to each other. Outcome variables may be treated as precursors of other outcome variables that in different models are represented as risk factors or protective factors. Situations where outcome variables are themselves risk factors for other outcomes are illustrated by a prospective study of life stress, social support, and adaptation during early adolescence (DuBois, Felner, Brand, Adan, & Evans, 1992). Time 1 stress and support variables predicted subsequent psychological distress, and earlier psychological distress was associated with subsequent stresses and supports. In short, the nature of the outcome variable, and, hence, the nature of resilience may be determined only in the context of particular causal models.

Risk/Ameliorative Factors

Definition of Risk Factors

Evaluating the contemporary field of developmental risk research, Greenbaum and Auerbach (1992) state:

"... the basic concepts of risk research, including the concept of risk itself, are not well-formulated and have been used in various ways by different researchers working in different areas of risk. The result has been a lack of clarity regarding the meaning of outcomes or risk research and their implications for theory and practice" (p. 10).

The term "risk" has been used in many different senses. It refers to probable negative outcomes, a predictor variable, and as a descriptor of negative life conditions (Rauh, 1989). Probable negative outcomes include sudden death syndrome, mental deficiency, psychopathology, criminal behavior, drug abuse, or school dropout. Most often, however, the term is applied to specific early predictors of such later unfavorable outcomes. Risk factors might include complications of pregnancy and delivery, perinatal health problems, irritability, developmental retardation, and familial socioeconomic adversity. The predictive value of these factors *may* signify factors that are causally related to the development of the later problem behavior, or they may signify early manifestations of the later behavior. Risk also has been used to signify unfavorable life conditions and events including family conflict, adverse urban environment, and poverty. While these meanings have generally been employed in infancy research, they are applicable also in research in any stage in the life course.

The most prevalent definition of risk factors involves some variation of the following (Clayton, 1992), *"A risk factor is an individual attribute, individual characteristic, situational condition, or environmental context that increases the probability of drug use or abuse or a transition in level of involvement with drugs."* (p. 15). However, some investigators draw distinctions between characteristics of the individual and characteristics of the environment, reserving the term for external influences.

The ambiguity regarding definitions of risk factor, particularly with reference to whether the actors include environmental as well as individual factors is clearly reflected in the use of alternative definitions by the same observers. Thus, reviewing the literature on drug abuse, Gerstein and Green (1993) define a risk factor as,

> *"... any observable (measurable) characteristic of the individual (including duration of exposure to specified environmental conditions) that has been shown to correlate significantly (in population or case-control studies) with a criterion behavior or outcome—in this case, with the onset of illicit drug use, some threshold level of consumption, or the clinical occurrence of drug abuse or dependence. This specification makes the risk factor model more empirical than theoretical. The risk factor must precede or at least occur simultaneously with the drug behavior; that is, a risk factor must be a potential cause or precursor, not a direct or indirect effect or symptom, of the criterion behavior"* (p. 47).

Elsewhere in the same chapter the authors state, *"Risk and protective factors may be characteristics of the individual or of the environment"* (Gerstein & Green, 1993, pp. 50–51).

Risk and Vulnerability

Closely related to the concept of risk is the construct of vulnerability or psychosocial proneness. Risk factors render the person vulnerable to adverse outcomes. For example, in one well-known study (Werner, 1993) risk status was frequently defined by such factors as being born into poverty, perinatal stress, chronic discord in the family environment, and parental alcoholism or mental illness. In fact, such groups of risk factors predicted the development of disvalued outcomes. Of the *vulnerable* children (those who encountered four or more risk factors by age two) two out of every three develop serious learning or behavioral problems by age ten and had experienced by the age of eighteen mental health problems, delinquency, or teenage pregnancy.

Generally then, vulnerability is taken to denote *"a characteristic that predisposes an individual to a negative outcome"* (Tarter, 1988, p. 78). Vulnerability, as opposed to vulnerability factors, often refers to the observation that individuals are differentially at risk for some evaluatively significant outcome such as engaging in drug use or in making the transition from drug use to drug abuse (Glantz & Pickens, 1992). For some researchers, risk and vulnerability are conceptually the same. For others, risk is used to refer to environmentally based influences while vulnerability is used to describe child characteristics.

The following statements are representative. Tarter (1988) observes:

> *". . . that there may be numerous vulnerability characteristics that exist across multiple levels of biological organization which portend future alcohol or drug abuse. These vulnerability features may be manifest either dispositionally (i.e., in the drug-free state) or specifically during drug or alcoholic intoxication. From a methodological and sampling standpoint, the identification of vulnerable individuals can be made according to empirical criteria, such as the frequently documented association of substance abuse within families, or according to some theoretical supposition regarding the physiological or psychological propensities for substance abuse. The heterogeneity of the population of alcohol and drug abusers and the fact that the vulnerability characteristics may be evident only during specific stages of an individual s life illustrates some of the difficulties involved in elucidating the predisposition to substance abuse"* (pp. 78–79).

Jessor, Donovan, and Costa (1991) offer a statement that more explicitly relates the dispositional notion to risk factors:

> *"As a dispositional concept, psychosocial proneness represents the strength of the tendency to engage in a particular problem behavior and, therefore, its likelihood or probability of occurrence. It is a resultant or outcome of the balance of instigations toward and controls against engaging in problem behavior. Such instigations and controls have parallels or analogs in the epidemiological notions of risk and protective factors. The interaction or balance of the latter is often summarized simply as psychosocial risk. The concept of psychosocial proneness is essentially synonymous with that latter concept of psychosocial risk and the theoretical variables in the three systems of Problem Behavior Theory can just as well be characterized as psychosocial risk (and protective) factors for problem behavior"* (pp. 18–19).

Nature of Risk Factors

Two kinds of risk factors appear to be considered in the resilience-related literature. The first kind of risk defines the at-risk status of a population (having a parent who received a psychiatric diagnosis, having an alcoholic parent). The second kind of risk factor includes those that distinguish between more or less positive outcomes among the group at primary risk or among groups that have no specified risk as a defining characteristic. Over the years, a relatively standard field of risk factors has been identified for various outcomes. For example, Losel, Bliesener, and Koferl (1989) observe:

> *"In the field of juvenile delinquency as an example, numerous cross-sectional and longitudinal studies since Glueck and Glueck (1950) have repeatedly shown that the characteristics of a multi-problem milieu, such as parental criminality, poor parental supervision, cruel, passive, or neglectful attitudes, erratic or harsh discipline, mutual conflict, large family size, and socioeconomic disadvantages, correlate with the development of persistent delinquent careers . . . Even long-term longitudinal studies report a substantial predictive power of risk variables . . ."*
> (p. 190).

Hawkins, Catalano, and Miller (1992) review a number of risk factors that increase the probability of alcohol and other drug problems. The risk factors include factors related to laws and norms, availability of drugs, economic deprivation, neighborhood disorganization, physiological factors (including biochemical and genetic influences), family drug behavior, family management practices, family conflict, low bonding to family, early and persistent problem behaviors, academic failure, low commitment to school, peer rejection in elementary grades, association with drug using peers, alienation and rebelliousness, attitudes favorable to drug use, and early onset of drug use. Risk status has often been defined in terms of the experience of adverse life events such as parental divorce or separation, living in single-parent families, being a stepchild, being raised in a foster family, loss of a sibling, teenage pregnancy, attention deficit/hyperactivity disorder, developmental retardation and adjudication as a delinquent (Rhodes & Brown, 1991).

Risk factors vary according to the outcome under consideration. For example, Chandy and his associates (1994) defined the primary risk factor for disordered eating as having substance misusing parents. Factors that distinguish between those who did and did not develop disordered eating symptoms were satisfaction with present weight and pride in body, less worry of being sexually abused, and the perception that school was relatively alcohol-free. Williams and her associates (1990) reported that sex, maternal depression, marital status of the parents, and reading problems, as

well as a number of other risk factors, distinguished between children with
and without behavioral and emotional disorders in preadolescent children.
Risk factors are identified with varying degrees of specificity. Thus,
Rutter (1979) identified six family variables, which were strongly associated
with child psychiatric disorder. These included severe marital discord, low
social status, overcrowding or large family size, criminality of the father,
psychiatric disorder of the mother, and admission into the care of a local
authority. Using more general categories, Garmezy (1985,), notes that antisocial behavior in adolescence and adulthood is predicted by such risk
factors as *"family background, parental maladaptation, individual personality dispositions, potential hereditary influences, deprived ecological settings,
and societal/institutional indices"* (p. 214).

Complementary Constructs

As a complement to risk factors a number of other constructs were
introduced to signify factors that increased the likelihood of desirable outcomes or decreased the probability of negative outcomes. Such factors were
viewed as counteracting risk factors and/or as the opposite poles of the risk
factors on continua. These factors were known as compensatory, resource,
ameliorative, or (to some) protective factors. Preferred contemporary usage
is to reserve this last term for factors that moderate, rather than counteract the relationship between risk factors and outcomes. Nevertheless, the
term has been used to denote the opposite end of the continuum from risk
as in the statement by Gerstein and Green (1993):

> *"Much research attention has been focused on risk factors—variables
> that exist before or during the typical age of onset of drug use (the second
> decade of life) and predict an elevated probability of developing abuse
> or dependence—and on their mirror image, protective factors—those that
> seem to confer a degree of immunity against drug involvement. By and
> large, risk and protective factors are opposed ends of a set of continua,
> for example, impulsivity versus planning, strong versus weak family
> bonding . . . Risk and protective factors thus refer to relative degrees of
> vulnerability on a set of continua"* (pp. 50–51).

Similarly, Glantz and Pickens (1992) in connection with their consideration
of vulnerability to drug abuse observe:

> *"Protective factors also play a role, and their involvement is as complex
> as that of the risk factors. Protective factors appear to work in opposi-
> tion to risk factors and, if sufficient in magnitude, may nullify the pre-
> dispositional influence of even potent risk factors. At least in some cases,
> the bipolar contrast of the risk factors may serve as protective factors; for
> example, poor academic achievement is a risk factor, whereas strong
> school achievement seems to have protective influences"* (p. 7–8).

Conrad and Hammen (1993) prefer to use the term resource factor "as a variable that contributes to good outcomes for a person regardless of risk status . . ." (p. 594). A resource factor is the opposite of a risk factor. It does not interact with risk level or stress. It could be studied by having a high-risk group alone or in addition to a low-risk control group. Others have called resource factors compensatory factors (Gest, Neemann, Hubbard, Masten, & Tellegen, 1993). Stress or risk factors and resource or compensatory factors combine in an additive manner to predict outcomes. Such a model examines main effects whether in an analysis of variance or regression design. I suggest the use of the term ameliorative to refer to factors that have direct or indirect effects on the increase of benign or the decrease of maleficent outcomes. Alternative terms such as counteracting or compensatory factors presume the presence of risk factors that are counterbalanced by these more benign variables.

Some investigators found support for the conception of protective and risk factors as opposite poles of the same variable (Stouthamer-Loeber, Loeber, Farrington, Zhang, van Kammen, & Maguin, 1993). Empirical analyses by these investigators, focusing on extremes of distribution, showed that risk and protective effects often co-occurred in the same variables, and that few variables had risk effects only. No variables were observed to have protective effects only.

Individual ameliorative factors include physical health status, life events, intellectual resources, group membership, and genetic assets. Environmental ameliorative factors include climatic conditions, systems of social expectancies, and the resources possessed by the groups in which subjects hold membership. Although general variables such as hardiness tend to be viewed as protective (moderating) variables, empirical studies more frequently than not model hardiness as a variable that is linearly related to adverse outcomes whether as an independent or mediating variable. For example, Williams and her associates (1992) reported that hardiness was positively related to adaptive coping variables and inversely related to maladaptive coping. Coping patterns mediated the hardiness-illness relationship. Banks and Gannon (1988) reported that hardiness tended to have additive and opposite effects to that of stressors in impact on symptomatology. Further, those higher in hardiness experienced less frequent stressors and perceived the events they did experience as less stressful.

Risk Factors–Outcome Relationship

As indices of adjustment vary so do the risks and ameliorative factors that are associated with them vary. Thus, Cauce, Hannan, and Sargeant (1992) report that family support was positively related to adjustment in several domains, while school support was only related to school competence. Further, peer support was positively related to peer competence and anxiety, but negatively related to school competence. In another study, the patterns of risk and protective factors that predicted to outcome varied according to the outcome variable (mood, deviance, self-esteem, grades) as well (Grossman et al., 1992).

Interrelationships Among Risk Factors

Risk factors exert direct or indirect influences upon each other, and interact with each other to have synergistic influences upon outcome variables, in addition to the additive effects that they exercise. The causal relationships among risk factors is reflected in the statement by Baldwin, Baldwin, and Cole (1990) who recognize that risk factors are highly variable in the degree to which they directly affect the child. Social class is a risk factor but its effect on the child is mediated by the requirement that both parents work, the fatigue experienced by the work, and consequent irritability which influences the relationships between the parent and the child. The effect of poverty on developmental outcomes may be mediated by the absence of the working mother from the home and her associated inability to exercise supervision over the child.

> *"We distinguish between distal risk variables that do not directly impinge on the child but act through mediators, and the proximal risk variables that do impinge directly on the child. The terms 'distal' and 'proximal' should be thought of as ends of a continuum. Some distal variables are more distal than others. Poverty, for example, is a distal variable. Maternal anxiety is closer to the proximal end of the scale, but its effect on the child is still mediated through maternal behaviors such as irritability, restriction of the child's freedom, or excessive nurturance. We picture a causal chain beginning with the distal variable, proceeding through its consequences (the mediating variables), and finally impinging on the child through one or more proximal variables"* (Baldwin, Baldwin, & Cole, 1990, p. 258).

Consistent with these observations, Gest and his associates (1993) noted that, in addition to being risk or compensatory factors,

> *"There are at least two other ways in which a characteristic might be implicated in the transactions between adversity and adaptation. First, several recent reviewers have suggested that a characteristic may either decrease or increase the chances of experiencing adversity: These processes could be called adversity preventive or adversity producing, respectively. Second, a characteristic may mediate the relation between adversity exposure and adjustment, with adversity affecting adjustment*

through its effect on the characteristic. This process could be referred to as adversity mediating" (p. 664).

The interrelationships among risk factors has been noted particularly with regard to the influence of some undesirable outcomes as risk factors on other outcomes (Kaplan, 1995). Thus, with regard to vulnerability to substance abuse,

> *"At least some psychopathologies seem to have an etiological influence. Antisocial personality, conduct disorder, and criminal behavior are clear vulnerability factors. Childhood conduct/behavior problems aggressivity, acting out, and a high childhood activity level are also risk factors for abuse. There is a risk-factor cluster associated with emotional/ behavioral arousal, self-regulation difficulties (possibly including sensation seeking), impulsivity, and hyperactivity/attention deficit disorder. Other factors include generally poor function, difficulties in coping, social isolation, interpersonal difficulties, traumatic experiences, including childhood physical and sexual abuse, and not having good school achievement"* (Glantz & Pickens, 1992, p. 10).

The interrelationships among predictors of outcomes are illustrated by the report of Roosa and his associates (1990) who reported that children of alcoholic status was related to higher levels of negative and lower levels of positive events which, in turn, had a contemporaneous effect on adolescent symptomatology. Further, Baldwin and his associates (1993,) noted the *"contribution of proximal variables such as parenting behavior, intermediate variables such as other family factors, and the more distal variables such as social class and minority status"* (p. 71) to the mental health of a sample of 18-year-olds (see also, Taylor, 1994).

In addition to linear effects by one risk factor on others, the experience of one stress may moderate the effect of another stress. In the presence of one stress, another stress may have a strong effect on a developmental outcome, but in the absence of the stress the other stress may have no effect at all on the developmental outcome. For example, the interaction of risk factors on adverse outcomes is suggested by findings reported by Landerman, George, and Blazer (1991) that parental mental health increases the likelihood that stressful life events will result in depression, and that parental separation/divorce interacts with stressful life events to increase vulnerability to alcohol problems and psychiatric disorders.

The effects of risk factors or ameliorative factors may be additive. The more that are applicable the greater is the effect on the outcome. The observations of Gordon and Song (1994) suggest both the additive and interactive effects of risk or resource factors. They cite a number of personal characteristics, environmental characteristics, and situational constraints that are associated with positive outcomes despite the presence of factors that are associated with negative outcomes. These factors include the presence of significant others, support for development and learning, a sense of community, models and heroes, opportunity, challenge, manifestations of developed ability, networking, specific responses tendencies (that is, personality), and specific environmental influences. They note that these factors are mutually influential and should be viewed collectively with regard to their impact on outcomes.

> "*It appears that these factors and others interact dialectically and reciprocally to accommodate and influence each other. Furthermore, they appear to be expressed in clusters, in which several factors are associated collectively to produce the dependent variable. To understand the relationship from which causation is often inferred requires that one not focus on the presence or absence of specific unitary factors, but examine the nature of the interactions within the collectivity of factors. Success may be conceptualized as the product of the interactions between the person s various characteristics, the characteristics of the environment, and the characteristics of the situation in which both development and achievement can occur*" (Gordon & Song, 1994, pp. 32–33).

Finally, risk/ameliorative factors are related to each other insofar as they often reflect common antecedents and are, perhaps, indicators of common constructs. This is in addition to any mutual causal effect they may have.

> "*From the perspective of temporal order . . . the first involvement in delinquent activity usually predates illicit drug use. But findings from a number of longitudinal studies . . . suggest that drug use and antisocial behavior in adolescents have similar precursors: aggressive behavior, school conduct problems, poor grades, and, less certainly, shyness, anxiety, depression, and problems in peer relationships. Early alcohol and drug use along with violent or predatory behavior and early and aggressive sexual behavior seem to be part of a general pattern of rebellion and nonconformity variously called a 'deviance syndrome', 'antisocial personality', 'conduct disorder', or 'adolescent adjustment disorder'*" (Gerstein & Green, 1993, pp. 56–57).

Theoretical Issues

Gerstein and Green (1993), reviewing the literature on drug abuse, note that approaches which focus upon risk factors are the *"least theoretically structured and the least empirically focused"* (p. 47) among the several approaches that might be used. The requirement for a theoretically informed definition of vulnerability has been noted by several observers. Tarter (1988), for example, observes:

"A major, if not central, issue concerns delineating both the general as well as the specific aspects of childhood vulnerability that predisposed to an adverse outcome. In carrying out such research, a multidisciplinary theory-driven strategy is essential that not only distinguishes children at high risk for alcohol and substance abuse from normals, but also from groups of other children at risk for other psychopathological disorders" (p. 83).

Variables that are categorized as risk factors frequently are done so solely on empirical grounds. Hence, the inference of resiliency on the basis of individual s having good outcomes when they are characterized by the "risk" factors may be unwarranted, as Masten (1994) observes, *"If a person in a risk group develops well despite risk status, it is always possible that the key causal influences were not present. Hence, it is 'risky' to infer resilience just because an individual from a high-risk group does well"* (p. 6). Implicit in the notion of resilience is the expectation of a known nomological network.

"The very definition of resilience suggests that we must know something of the causes of success and failure. In the first place, the definition by implication, distinguishes successful and unsuccessful adaptation and presumes to identify risk and asset factors that affect adaptations. This means we have made judgments about desirable and undesirable outcomes from some normative frame of reference. Further, employing some predictive framework we have been able to assess the likelihood of successful and unsuccessful outcomes given some predictive contingencies" (Rigsby, 1994, p. 88).

The implication of this is that the prediction model which we use to explain outcomes must be adequate, taking into account the many levels of causal structures involved in human behavior. In the absence of a relatively complete explanation, we might be led to call behaviors resilient that would be otherwise explainable in the context of a more complete theory.

Protective Factors

As noted previously, the two main definitions of resilience refer to the fact of having achieved desirable outcomes in the face of adversity or to the qualities that facilitates achievement of the desirable qualities under adverse conditions. In the case of the former definitions the relationship between adversity and evaluatively significant outcomes is said to be moderated by protective factors. In the case of the latter definitions, resiliency is equated with these same variables. In either case the issues we raise (with the exception of those related to definitions) will be equally applicable.

Defining Protective Factors and Resiliency

Although the term "protective factors" has at least two meanings in the literature—as individual or environmental characteristics that reflect the absence of risk factors or the presence of ameliorative factors, and, as variables that mitigate the effects of risk factors or strengthen ameliorative effects, it is the latter meaning that is more often accepted to define protective factors, and its complement, "vulnerability factors." Gest and his associates (1993), for example, employ a set of definitions used by others that is, or is likely to become, common usage in the field. Thus,

> "... a characteristic was called a compensatory factor when it predicted better outcomes at both high and low levels of adversity exposure (i.e., a statistical main effect). A characteristic was called a protective factor when it was associated with sustained adequate functioning in the face of adversity by persons with high levels of the characteristic or a vulnerability factor when it was associated with a decrease in functioning under adversity only for people with high levels of the characteristic. Protective and vulnerability factors moderated the relationship between adversity and outcomes; they were suggested by a significant statistical interaction effect between the characteristic and adversity exposure..."
> (p. 664).

Similarly, the distinction has been drawn between protective and resource factors.

> "A protective factor is one that moderates against the effects of a stressful or risk situation so that the individual is able to adapt more successfully than they would have had the protective factor not been present ... A study of protective factors thus requires a research design with a high-risk group and low-risk control group and the protective factor model proposes that certain factors interact with risk (or stress) in such a way that the protective factor modulates the impact of the risk factors. This relationship is tested by looking for interaction effects in an analysis of variance or by including an interaction term in a multiple regression analysis ... A protective factor is the opposite of a vulnerability factor..." (Conrad & Hammen, 1993, p. 594).

The distinction is drawn, also between resilience and protective or vulnerability factors. Whereas resilience is concerned with individual variability in response to risk factors, vulnerability and protective mechanisms refer to changes in the person s response to the risk.

> "Thus, it requires some form of intensification (vulnerability) or amelioration (protection) of the reaction to a factor that in ordinary circumstances leads to a maladaptive outcome. The effect is indirect and dependent on some type of interaction. It must be in some sense catalytic

in that it changes the effect of another variable, instead of (or in addition to) having a direct effect of its own" (Rutter, 1990, p. 185).

As Rutter (1990) suggests, vulnerability factor is often thought to be the negative pole of a continuum, the positive pole of which is protective factors. However, he also suggests that although protective factors frequently reflect the absence of vulnerability, it may be wise to maintain the two terms since circumstances exist in which the process in question involves a change in life trajectory from risk to adaptation rather than from adaptation to risk, and in which the mechanisms for the positive end of a scale differ from those of the negative end. With reference to the latter, Rutter (1990) points out that at the bottom end of the scale, variation in IQ score may suggest organic brain dysfunction, while this is not implied by the variation within the scores at the more positive end of the scale.

It might be pointed out, further, that new experiences may exacerbate the ill effects of a risk factor but the absence of the experience might not ameliorate the effect (but, rather, might have no effect at all). Thus, vulnerability factors may be defined by the absence of protective factors *or* the presence of other factors that exacerbate the effects of risk factors. For example, the absence of self-confidence or the presence of an experience whereby the individual was unable to meet a new set of expectations that the subject regarded as legitimate exacerbate the influence of an earlier risk factor. In any case, putting aside the question of how interactive processes are confirmed, it is clear that the essential nature of vulnerability and protective mechanisms *"is that the vulnerability or protective effect is evident only in combination with the risk variable"* (Rutter, 1990, p. 185). Either the vulnerability/protective factor has no effect in low-risk populations, or its effect is magnified in the presence of the risk variable.

The Nature of Protective/Vulnerability Factors

The nature of resilience or of the protective/vulnerability factors that influence resilience by moderating the effects of risk or ameliorative factors has been summarized by numerous commentators in more or less specific and general terms, based on their own work and that of others. The protective factors offered in the literature are so numerous that they invite categorization as in Garmezy's tripartite classification:

"A review of the literature on resilience suggests the presence of three core factors for individuals in stressful life situations. One set implicates temperament and personality attributes such as activity level, reflectiveness when confronted with new situations, cognitive skills, and positive responsiveness to others. Another core of variables is to be found in families, including those in poverty: warmth, cohesion, and the presence of

some caring adult such as a grandparent who assumes a parental role in the absence of responsive parents or if there is marital discord or dissolution between the parents.
    A third factor is the availability of social support. This can come in the form of a strong mother substitute, a concerned teacher, a caring agency, institution, or a church that fosters a child's tie to the larger nondelinquent community" (Garmezy, 1993a, pp. 391–392).

Rutter (1985) also offers a parsimonious set of resilience-related qualities. According to this view, resilience *". . . seems to involve several related elements. Firstly, a sense of self-esteem and self-confidence; secondly, a belief in one s own self-efficacy and ability to deal with change and adaptation; and thirdly, a repertoire of social problem solving approaches"* (p. 607).

Kumpfer (Kumpfer & Hopkins, 1993) concluded following a review of research studies that seven major self-factors compose increased resiliency in youth. The seven factors are optimism, empathy, insight, intellectual competence, self-esteem, direction or mission, and determination and perseverance. These characteristics are associated with specific coping skills acquired by resilient children through interaction or transaction with their environment. The skills are emotional and management skills, interpersonal and social skills, intrapersonal reflective skills, academic and job skills, ability to restore self-esteem, planning skills, and life skills and problem-solving ability. The challenge to researchers now is to translate these personal characteristics into programs or protective mechanisms to increase resilience to drug use. Radke-Yarrow and Sherman (1990) identify a number of protective factors:

"In addition to the generally established protective factors of intelligence, curiosity, pleasing physical appearance, and socially winnings ways, each survivor-child has been found to fulfill a need of one or both ill parents that also serves the child positively, at least for the present. By meeting parents' needs, the child receives as much of the family's scant social and emotional resources as the family can muster—more than do other children from similar backgrounds of risk who are not faring as well. It is in the context of the match between child characteristics and parent need that we have observed the development of the child's positive self-regard and effective style of responding to stress and relating to others" (p. 118).

In another study, Losel, Bliesener, and Koferl (1989) reported that resilient adolescents relative to those who have become more deviant tended to be more intelligent, to report more active problem solving and less passive and fatalistic coping behavior, to perceive themselves as being less helpless and more strongly self-effective, and generally to have a more positive self-evaluation. The resilient adolescents tended to be more approach-oriented and more flexible in style. The resilients also consistently report a larger network of social support and a higher satisfaction with their support. The resilients report a more autonomy-oriented and open climate in their institutional homes. These findings are consistent with the literature on the resiliency construct.

Among the general factors that have been conceptualized as buffers that mitigate effects of stressors on positive outcomes is the sense of coherence postulated by Aaron Antonovsky (1984). The sense of coherence has three components: comprehensibility, manageability, and meaningfulness.

> *"The comprehensibility component . . . refers to the extent to which individuals perceive the stimuli that confront them as making cognitive sense, as information that is ordered, consistent, structured, and clear—and, hence, regarding the future, as predictable—rather than as noisy, chaotic, disordered, random, accidental, and unpredictable. It does not mean that they are unwilling to enter open-ended situations, but that when they do so, they have confidence that sense and order can be made of the situations. The manageability component refers to the extent to which people perceive that resources are at their disposal that are adequate to meet the demands posed by stimuli . . . 'At one's disposal' may refer to resources under one's own control but it may also refer to resources controlled by legitimate others—friends, colleagues, God, history—upon whom one can count. No implication exists that untoward things do not happen in life. They do; but when people are high on manageability, they have the sense that, aided by their own resources or by those of legitimate others, they will be able to cope and not grieve endlessly. The meaningfulness component . . . is, in a sense, the emotional counterpart to comprehensibility . . . People who are high on meaningfulness feel that life makes sense emotionally, that at least some of the problems and demands posed by living are worth investing energy in, are worthy of commitment and engagement, and are challenges that are welcome rather than burdens that they would much rather do without"* (Antonovsky, 1984, pp. 118–119).

A follow-up of a high-risk cohort into adulthood (Werner, and Smith, 1992) revealed several clusters of protective factors in the records and interviews of the high-risk children who made a successful adaptation in adult life.

> *"Cluster 1 included temperamental characteristics of the individual that helped him or her to elicit positive responses from a variety of caring persons. Cluster 2 included skills and values that led to an efficient use of whatever abilities they had: realistic, educational and vocational plans, and regular household chores and domestic responsibilities. Cluster 3 included characteristics and caregiving styles of the parents that reflected competence and fostered self-esteem in the child. Cluster 4 consisted of supportive adults who fostered trust and acted as gatekeepers for the future. Finally, there was the opening of opportunities at major life tran-*

sitions, from high school to the work place, from civilian to military life, from single state to marriage and parenthood that turned the trajectory of a significant proportion of the high-risk children on the path to normal adulthood. Among the most potent forces providing a second chance for such youths were adult education programs and community colleges, voluntary national service, and/or an intrinsic religious orientation" (Werner, 1993, p. 508).

Less attention has been paid to the grouping of factors in terms of vulnerability although these may be inferred from the prior statements. Vulnerability factors include the absence of resources which are required to meet emotionally significant expectations, and the absence of prior experiences regarding how expectations may be met. The experience of new demands in the absence (but not the presence of) adequate resources and prior experiences may be expected to have adverse outcomes. That is, the absence of resources and of prior experience exacerbates the adverse effects of new demands for performance or mitigates the benign effects of such demands.

Operationalizing Moderating Effects

The protective and vulnerability factors that have been noted in literature reviews of theoretical statements and large-scale studies have informed a plethora of empirical tests. The nature of the protective factors that have served moderating effects varied, of course, with variable risk/ameliorative factors, and outcomes. With regard to protective factors, Wyman and his associates (1993) reported that early positive future expectations predicted enhanced socioemotional adjustment in school and more internal locus of controls and acted as a protective factor in reducing the negative effects of high stress on self-rated competence; Moran and Eckenrode (1992) reported that high self-esteem and internal locus of control orientation serve a protective function in reducing the effects of maltreatment status on depression scores among female adolescents; Kernis, Grannemann, and Mathis (1991) reported that stability of self-esteem moderated the relationship between level of self-esteem and depression; Cauce, Hannan, and Sargeant (1992) reported that family and school support moderated the relationship beween negative life events and school competence; and, Bradley and his associates (1994) identified general quality of care as a protective factor from the consequences of poverty and prematurity for cognitive, social/adaptive, health, and growth parameters. Shepperd and Kashani (1991) reported interaction of stress, gender and hardiness for several health measures. While males under low stress conditions experience few physical and psychological symptoms regardless of levels of hardiness components, high stress males experience more problems when they were low rather than high in either commitment or control. No interaction between the hardiness components and stress in the prediction of health outcomes was noted for females.

> *"In addition to varying with the nature of stress and outcome, protective factors vary in their influence along the life course. In discriminant function analyses, in which we contrasted resilient and problem children and youths, we found that constitutional factors within the child (health, temperament), had their greatest impact in infancy and early childhood; problem-solving and communication skills, and alternative caretakers played a major role in middle childhood; and intrapersonal factors (internal locus of control; self-esteem) in adolescence..."* (Werner, 1989a, p. 171).

With regard to the moderating effects of vulnerability, MacEwen and Barling (1988) reported that marital adjustment was influenced by the interaction of inter-role conflict/family support interaction such that high family support exerted a negative impact on marital adjustment when inter-role conflict was high; and, Bonner and Rich (1991) found empirical support for the hypothesis that the factors of emotional alienation, cognitive distortions, and deficient reasons for living anticipate vulnerability to the development of hopelessness under conditions of negative life stress. Having reported a number of instances in which significant effects of predictors of depressive episodes were confined to a subsample of respondents with a history of depression, Kessler and Magee (1994) conclude:

> *"The reason for these stress-buffering effects disappearing in sub-sample analyses is that history of depression (which was strongly related to all of the stress buffers) was the vulnerability factor. That is, it was people with a history of depression who were vulnerable to the effects of life stress on [major depression]; the other risk factors only appear to be stress buffers because they were associated with history. When history was, in effect, controlled in the subsample analyses, the evidence of stress-buffering effects of the risk factors disappeared"* (p. 250).

The same variable may be protective in certain contexts but exacerbate developmental disability in another context:

> *"Family policies that will shield a child from noxious elements in a high-risk environment, may unnecessarily limit a child's opportunities in a low-risk environment. Similarly, encouraging what would be reasonable self-reliance for a child in a low risk environment might overwhelm the coping abilities of a child living in a high-risk environment"* (Baldwin, Baldwin, & Cole, 1990, p. 259).

To illustrate further how the same variable may assuage the effects of distress on outcome in some circumstances and exacerbate the effects of stress on outcomes in other circumstances, Myers and his associates (1992) reported that active health-seeking strategies (family mobilization, acquiring social support) moderated the effects of maternal psychological distress and family risk attributes for boys but exacerbated the effects of dysfunctional maternal social and psychiatric histories for girls. Similarly, intellectual ability has variously been observed to operate as a protective factor, a vulnerability factor, or to not have significant interactions between intelligence and risk in predicting adjustment (Luthar & Zigler, 1991).

Multiple Functions of Variables

The same variables might reflect risk factors, vulnerability/resilience, and outcomes. The inability to attend to the environment (that is, poor concentration, inattention to novel stimuli) might increase stress by virtue of evoking punitive responses from parents and teachers. At the same time, the inattention might exacerbate the adverse effects of other stress factors by forestalling problem-solving attempts; or inattention might mitigate the adverse effects of stress by permitting the person to ignore the distress-inducing expressions of disapproval by others. Finally, inattention may be regarded as a socially undesirable outcome. Further, if having the good opinion of one's fellows is highly desirable, then any indication to the subject that such good opinion is withheld constitutes a risk factor for a particular outcome (subjective distress). At the same time, the absence of social support (reflected in the good opinions of others) exacerbates the adverse effects of assault upon one's self-esteem (e.g., being fired). That is, in the presence of perceiving that one is held in high esteem by one's peers, the effect of being fired on subjective distress is mitigated.

The notion of adversity as a protective factor is implicit in observations by Gordon and Song (1994):

> *"Constraining and negative factors do not necessarily depress development. They sometimes operate as catalytic agents of resistance, or of more constructive responses. For reasons that have not as yet been definitively explained, disadvantagement is not consistently associated with negative effort or outcomes. In many instances, misfortune, rejection, discrimination, deprivation, and racism are responded to as challenges to defy the implicit negative prediction. Subjects spoke of 'showing them they are wrong', or 'proving that I am as good as they are', or having to demonstrate to one's self the fallacy of inferior status designation"* (p. 38).

It may be reasonable to assume that so-called risk factors operate both as independent variables more or less directly affecting outcomes, and as moderating variables which interact with certain stress factors (perhaps, the need for self-enhancement, that is, self-rejecting feelings) to influence redoubled effort and the search for resources that in turn lead to positive outcomes. Thus, protective conditions have been observed to operate as both direct (main effects) and interactive (moderators of risk) influences on drug use (Felix-Ortiz & Newcomb, 1992). Or, a particular variable may serve as a vulnerability factor for one outcome, and as a direct risk variable for another outcome. For example, lack of parental care may serve as a vulnerability factor for depression, while the same variable may function as a direct risk for conduct disorder and personality disturbance (Rutter, 1990).

One should be careful, however, not to confuse two different variables as the same factor. Rutter (1990), for example, observes that the *"loss of a love relationship because of death or divorce serves as a direct precipitant of depression, but chronic lack of such a relationship constitutes a vulnerability factor in conjunction with other life stressors..."* (p. 186) (referring to the work of other investigators). However, these are not in fact the same variable. One variable refers to a discrete life event, while the other refers to a more stable and undesirable situation. Nevertheless, the point may be made that the chronic absence of loving relationships may serve both as a risk factor and as a vulnerability factor in the presence of other life stressors.

In like manner, variables may be in fact different if they refer to different periods in the life cycle. For example, the absence of a caring adult in the environment during infancy may reflect a risk factor, while the presence of a caring adult during adolescence may represent a protective factor that assuages the adverse effect of the deprivation of a caring adult or of other risk factors during infancy or later.

Interrelationships among Protective Factors

The factors that have been identified as protective or vulnerability factors have their own causes (other protective factors), have their own consequences (act through mechanisms), and moderate the influence (interact with) each other to affect the relationship between risk/ameliorative factors and more or less desirable outcomes.

First, I consider the sources of protective/vulnerability factors that must then be considered protective/vulnerability factors once, twice, or further removed. Where do the general factors that moderate the relationships between stress derive from? Antonovsky's (1984) sense of coherence is said to derive from life experiences that have the characteristics of consistency, and underload-overload balance, and participation in decision making. Experiences of consistency allow us to make accurate predictions about what is likely to take place. The underload-overload balance involves the congruence between demands made upon us and our capacities to fulfill those demands, a circumstance that is reflected in variable degrees of success. Participation in decision-making implies that people approve of the tasks that they must perform, that the people have responsibility to perform and their own behaviors influence the outcome.

The constructs of resiliency and vulnerability that moderate the effects of ameliorative and risk factors have their own causes. Thus, Block and Block (1980) reported that,

> ". . . individuals we would call ego-resilient tended to come from families earlier and independently characterized as having loving, patient, competent, and integrated mothers, free interchange of problems and feelings, sexual compatibility of parents, agreement on values and concern with philosophical and moral issues, among other qualities" (p. 51).

Interrelationships among protective factors is apparent in the work of Werner and her associates (Werner, 1993) who examined the links between protective factors within the individual and outside sources of support or of stress. Werner (1993) reports,

> ". . . a certain continuity that appeared in the life courses of the high-risk men and women who successfully overcame a variety of childhood adversities. Their individual dispositions led them to select or construct environments that, in turn, reinforced and sustained their active, outgoing dispositions and rewarded their competencies" (p. 508).

Scholastic competence at age ten was associated with a number of sources of help that the teenager attracted from teachers and peers as well as family members. Scholastic competence at an earlier age was associated with a sense of self-efficacy at age eighteen. Self-efficacy at age eighteen, in turn, was inversely related to distress and emotionality for the high-risk men at age 32 and generated a greater number of sources of emotional support for the high-risk women in early adulthood, including support from a spouse or mate. Educational level of opposite sex parent was a protective factor. Better-educated parents had more positive interactions with their children in the first and second years of life and provided more social support during early and middle childhood. Parental education was also linked to the infant's health and physical status. More educated parents tended to have more scholastically competent children.

Spencer, Josephs, and Steele (1993) wonder *"why some people are more resilient to the vicissitudes of life than others, that is, why their sense of worth and the psychological states that vary with it (e.g., defensiveness, efficacy, positive affect) are less affected by particular threats to their self-image"* (p. 21). These authors argue that resiliency is related to self-esteem. High self-esteem people have more resources (that is, positive aspects of their self-concept) which may be used to affirm their sense of self-integrity. Therefore, they are less disturbed by threats to self-worth. Self-esteem, in turn, is affected by (among other factors) the effectiveness of ego-defenses that permit justification of one's behavior in social relations that are perceived as threatened by the subject's thoughts or behaviors (Kaplan, 1986; Swanson, 1988).

Risk factors that anticipate more or less desirable outcomes also may influence factors that moderate the relationship between the risk factors and the outcome. Thus, adolescent females who first experienced maltreatment during childhood were significantly less likely than those who first experienced maltreatment during adolescence to have higher levels of self-esteem and internal locus of control orientation, two personality characteristics that moderated the effect of maltreatment on depression (Moran & Eckenrode, 1992).

Just as when considering risk factors, the distinction between proximal and distal variables must be made with regard to protective factors. The most proximal variables recognized as protective factors are frequently termed mechanisms. It is essential to identify the effective mechanisms through which protective/vulnerability factors operate and to distinguish these mechanisms from the indicators of the protective factors. Although being female appears to be a protective factor against the adverse effects of family discord, gender is merely a surrogate for the mechanisms that are correlated with gender. Boys are more likely than girls to develop behavior disturbances in response to marked family discord because of such circumstances as sons being more likely to be placed in some form of institutional care and to evoke punitive responses from adults to male-specific disruptive oppositional behavior as opposed to female-specific emotional distress (Rutter, 1990). Similarly, the presence of difficult temperamental characteristics exacerbates the effect of parental discord by increasing the probability that the temperamental characteristics will elicit parental hostility. Further, the apparent protective effects of marital support and positive school experiences may have been mediated by the effect of these variables on self-esteem and self-efficacy.

Rutter (1990) reviewing a number of empirical findings suggests four mechanisms that are implicated in protective processes. The first of these refers to the reduction of risk impact. The impact may be reduced by altering the appraisal of the risk factor or by altering exposure to the risk. In the former case, the meaning of the risk may be mitigated by controlling exposure to the stress so that the individual can successfully cope with smaller doses of the experience. Since the individual can cope successfully in some circumstances, the impact of the greater degree of risk may be mitigated.

Alternatively, a countervailing circumstance may mitigate the impact. If the experience of rejection, bereavement, or separation causes damage to self-esteem, the impact of that event may be neutralized by a new love relationship. The second way in which risk impact may be mitigated is through mechanisms that change the child's exposure to the risk situation. For example, the effect of association with delinquent peers on subsequent delinquent behavior may be mitigated by parental supervision of the child in the environment characterized by high degrees of peer delinquency.

The second type of mechanism refers to the reduction of negative chain reactions that follow exposure to risk and perpetuate the risk effects. For example, early parental loss may lead to greater probability of institutional treatment that has adverse effects on developmental outcomes. The impact of parental loss in producing this chain reaction may be mitigated by adequate functioning of the remaining parent or the provision of alternative care arrangements.

The third mechanism through which protective functions may be served is through the promotion of self-esteem and self-efficacy. Two types of experiences that are influential in the establishment of self-esteem and self-efficacy are the establishment of secure and harmonious love relationships, and opportunities for success in accomplishing tasks that are salient to the individuals. The resultant feeling of self-worth and self-efficacy provides the individual with confidence that he or she can successfully cope with the demands made upon the person.

Finally, protective factors operate through opening up opportunities to obtain experiences that might mitigate the effect of early risk factors. Thus, delay of marriage may increase the range of opportunities available to an individual since it would not be required that the individual cease further education in order to work and support a wife and family.

In addition to·affecting and being affected by other variables, protective factors moderate the influence that each has on the risk-outcome relationship. Smith, Smoll, and Ptacek (1990) distinguish between models characterized by "... *conjunctive moderation, in which multiple moderators must co-occur in a specific combination or pattern to maximize a relation between a predictor and an outcome variable, and disjunctive moderation, in which any one of a number of moderators maximizes the predictor-criterion relation . . ."* (p. 360). The conjunctive operation of protective factors is illustrated by the report (Smith, Smoll, & Ptacek, 1990) that only athletes low in both coping skills and social support manifested a significant stress-injury relationship. The interactive effects among protective factors are also illustrated by the conjunctive effects observed by Cauce, Hannan, and Sargeant (1992) to the effect that school support buffered a number of negative events more strongly for those individuals with an internal locus of control for successes.

Brook and her associates (1990) identified two mechanisms through which protective factors reduce risk for adolescent drug use. A protective mechanism may moderate the effects of exposure to a risk factor. Thus, a strong bond between the parent and the adolescent may reduce the effect of the risk of association with drug-using peers. Further, a protective factor may increase the effectiveness of another protective factor. A strong attachment between the adolescent and the father increased the protective effects of adolescent conventionality and marital harmony in preventing drug use.

Jenkins and Smith (1990) distinguish between protective factors that interacted with parental marriage and those that acted independently in influencing emotional and behavioral problems. Thus, children having a relationship with an adult outside the family (an activity for which they receive positive recognition) and good sibling relationships interacted with the quality of parental marriage while the nature of the parent-child relationship was associated with children s disturbance in both harmonious and disharmonious homes.

Finally, both gender and stage of development together define the likelihood of resiliency in the face of adversity (Werner & Smith, 1982). During the first decade of life more boys than girls had serious physical defects and learning and behavior problems. Factors such as the physical immaturity of the boys, more stringent expectations for male sex-role behavior in childhood, and the predominant feminine environment in which the boys were reared appear to contribute to the greater amount of disordered behavior during childhood among the males than the females. During the second decade of life, however, the number of girls with serious behavior disorders rose while the number of boys with serious learning problems decreased. While the boys appeared to be better prepared for the demands of school and work while remaining involved in antisocial and delinquent behavior, girls were confronted with new social pressures and sex-role expectations that were associated with a higher rate of mental health problems in late adolescence and serious coping problems associated with teenage pregnancies and marriages. As control of aggression was one of the major problems for boys during childhood, dependency was a major problem for the girls in adolescence. Thus, each sex was more vulnerable at a different time. Nevertheless, more high-risk girls than high-risk boys were judged to grow into resilient young adults.

Conceptual and Theoretical Issues

A number of theoretical and conceptual issues lead to a reconsideration of the utility of the constructs "protective factors" and "vulnerability factors." Among the more important of the questions raised is why do the concepts not apply to "well-functioning/low risk" individuals, and is the concept inappropriately applied to so-called "at-risk" individuals. With regard to the former, Richters and Weintraub (1990) express concern over the use of the term protective factors. They note that,

> "... those who study the offspring of psychiatrically ill parents, the search for protective factors seems to stem from surprise at finding high-risk offspring who are doing well—so-called resilient children. The personal and environmental factors that characterize them are assumed to be protective factors. Presumably, children of nondiagnosed parents who are coping as well do not deserve the resilient label, nor are the personal and environmental factors that characterize them labeled protective. Why, then, are these concepts deemed so necessary to explain well-functioning children of psychiatrically ill parents? Or, perhaps more to the point, what is it from which we assume they are being protected" (p. 78).

It may be asked, why should not protective factors be sought as an explanation for well-functioning/low risk subjects? It is possible that these individuals are subject to risks that are not yet identified, or that they would be vulnerable to these risks but the experience of the risks is forestalled by protective factors.

The other side of the coin relates to the question of whether so-called protective factors are in fact protective. It may be that rather than being indicators of protective factors, these factors reflect the absence of high risk. Richters and Weintraub (1990) note that,

> "... positive personality characteristics of the child, a supportive family milieu, and external support systems are associated with lower rates of maladjustment among high-risk offspring... But also it has been demonstrated that the opposite of these—namely common negative personality characteristics, hostile/impoverished family milieu and deficient extrafamilial support systems—may be the very factors that give rise to the association between parental psychopathology and offspring maladjustment... Therefore, high-risk offspring for whom there is no direct evidence of proximal environmental stresses may not truly be at risk; these offspring may have been misplaced in a high risk category as a result of our relatively crude understanding of the parental psychopathology/offspring maladjustment link.
>
> Unfortunately, this possibility seldom receives the attention it deserves. The reason in many cases seems to be that the offspring were expected to manifest adjustment problems as a result of their unspecified yet presumed inherited vulnerabilities. Therefore, when the presence of positive environmental factors is found to be associated with reduced rates of maladjustment in some high-risk offspring, the association is almost always interpreted as evidence for the buffering or protecting influence of those factors. There is a circularity in this de facto strategy

that has at least two unfortunate consequences. First, it perpetuates a belief that there is something inherently bad about being the offspring of a psychiatrically ill parent—an empirically indefensible position with significant negative social consequences. Moreover, it is a strategy that draws attention away from the need to develop a process-level understanding of the factors responsible for maladjustment among the offspring that are somehow affected" (pp. 79–80).

A second issue concerns the nature of the protective factors. It is quite common now to call for an understanding of the causes, consequences, or processes. Thus, Rutter (1990) argues,

"Instead of searching for broadly based protective factors, we need to focus on protective mechanisms and processes. That is, we need to ask why and how some individuals manage to maintain high self-esteem and self-efficacy in spite of facing the same adversities that lead other people to give up and lose hope. How is it that some people have confidants to whom they can turn? What has happened to enable them to have social supports that they can use effectively at moments of crisis? Is it chance, the spin of the roulette wheel of life, or did prior circumstances, happenings, or actions serve to bring about this desirable state of affairs" (pp. 182–183).

The felt need for understanding the mechanisms through which protective factors moderate the influence of other variables is reflected also in the observation (Luthar, 1993) that,

". . . attempts to understand moderating effects in terms of underlying processes, rather than simply as protective or vulnerability factors, is vital to promote understanding of childhood resilience. Accumulating evidence in the field has indicated the need to move from asking simple queries such as. 'What makes for resilience', to questions with far greater specificity, such as, 'What are the types of processes via which a particular attribute might moderate the effects of risk, with reference to a specific aspect of competence?'" (p. 451).

Once these questions are answered, to what does the construct, "protective factor" refer? Do the more proximal moderators of stress represent resiliency and vulnerability factors? That is, do those protective factors that more immediately have an effect upon the strength of the association between risk factors and developmental outcomes constitute resiliency or vulnerability? Does "protective" refer to the total process or to any part of it? What function does the construct serve?

Another issue relates to the definition of the protective factor as serving a moderating function. Whether it is conceived of as a moderator or as exercising a direct effect on individual differences in resiliency depends very much on the nature of the research design. Where adversity or risk was defined as a given, individuals who were characterized as at-risk, under adverse circumstances, or vulnerable were defined as the study group. The purpose was to distinguish between individuals within this group who had positive outcomes from those who had negative outcomes. The variables that distinguished these two groups were defined as protective factors. In the other kind of research design, risk factors were variable. Protective factors were those that moderated the effect of hypothetical risk factors on benign outcomes. Even in instances where statistical interactions are not observed, certain protective factors that have direct effects on outcomes may be conceptualized as moderating variables on the assumption that for any individual a number of life stresses go unmeasured in the study. Thus, the direct effect of the putative protective factor may be taken as an observed effect under conditions of (unmeasured) life stress.

If resilience is defined in terms of individual differences in responses to stressful circumstances, then protective factors may be viewed as direct or indirect causes of the variable responses to stress in terms of approximating more or less desirable outcomes. Stress is taken as a given and the question is asked "Why do people vary in how they respond to stress?" However, if resilience is defined in terms of general characteristics of the individual that interact with the experiences of stress to influence more or less desirable outcomes, then resilience may be regarded as a moderating rather than a direct or indirect influence. The variation in paradigms whereby protective factors are treated in some instances as direct effects and in other instances as moderating influences may be traced to the definitional distinction just elaborated. That is, is resilience a variable that reflects individual differences in response to stress (in which case protective and vulnerability factors may be viewed as directly influencing this variable) or is resilience to be defined in terms of general characteristics of the individual that mitigate or, in the case of vulnerability factors, exacerbate) the relationship between stressful experiences and more or less undesirable outcomes?

A third issue concerns the generality of protective factors. If protective factors are defined as general constructs or processes consisting of or reflected in several variables, the question arises as to why a general construct rather than the several components should be used. As Funk (1992) offered with regard to the concept of hardiness,

> "... the existence of hardiness must be justified. A theoretical rationale detailing why hardiness is more meaningful and important than its component parts is needed. In addition, this rationale should explain why hardiness couldn't be understood by studying commitment, control, and challenge separately. After a theoretical rationale for the existence of har-

diness is provided, the usefulness of hardiness should be demonstrated empirically. For example, studies should test whether hardiness explains more variance in outcomes than its theoretical components. Until the utility of hardiness is established, researchers should report separate results for commitment, control, and challenge" (p. 343).

The use of latent variable/structural equation modeling methodology provides an opportunity for general constructs of protective factors to be employed and evaluated vis a vis their components. A fourth issue is the absence of criteria for defining which elements of interaction terms are to be treated as the protective/vulnerability factors and which are to be treated as stress factors. Which is the risk and which is the protective factor? Does stress moderate the effect of genetic vulnerability? If yes, the stress is the protective/vulnerability factor and genetic makeup is the risk factor. Does genetic vulnerability moderate the effect of life stress? If yes, genetic makeup is the protective/vulnerability factor and stress is the risk factor. Are temperament and activity level risk factors, protective factors, or both? Certainly these variables moderate the effects of other risk factors, and they have direct or indirect effects on outcome measures. Further they are themselves often taken to be outcome measures.

Finally, the incorporation of protective factors into the research process is distressingly atheoretical. The failure to be guided by theoretical frameworks leads to greater and greater dependence upon identifying correlates of resilience. These correlates may have no causal significance. Their identification may lead to dysfunctional focusing on these factors rather than looking for the mechanisms that underlie resilience and the causes of these mechanisms rather than accidental correlates. In any case, neither the search for protective factors, nor the specification of the mechanisms through which they operate is theoretically informed. The atheoretical nature of the process is reflected in both the call for understanding of mechanisms and a description of the process that precedes the search for mechanisms. Regarding the former, Brown and Rhodes (1991) observe:

"Researchers in this area of inquiry are beginning to understand what the resiliency factors are. What is missing in this volume, and appears to be lacking throughout the resiliency literature, is an adequate understanding of how at-risk children integrate these factors to promote resiliency. Knowing that a stable family environment, meaningful relationships, early intervention, average or above intelligence, consistent discipline, and a host of other family, personal, and environmental factors is helpful; but these findings are, for the most part, predictable. What is less predictable is how and why some at-risk children succeed in overcoming the 'odds'" (p. 174).

As Garmezy (1985) describes the process:

"Searching for protective factors in children under stress is a 'catch-as-catch-can' situation. There is no single source or even multiple sources to which one can turn. The search tends to be elusive but gratifying once a study or a project is located that is explicit with regard to children who cope effectively with adversity. But it isn't coping alone that will suffice to provide clues to protective factors. Investigators of children who cope successfully in stressful circumstances must not merely identify such children but also search out the correlates of their adaptive behaviors. These correlates can extend to personality dispositions, parental attributes, situational and cultural contexts, family milieu significant supportive figures and institutions, etc. Stage 1, then, in the search for protective factors would be the identification of children at risk who demonstrate good coping abilities. Stage 2 constitutes the search for the correlates of such adaptive behaviors in the child, the family, and the various situational contexts in which resilient behavior is observed. There is a growing scientific literature of Stage 1 studies, appreciably fewer Stage 2 studies, and fewest of all are the critically important Stage 3 studies. This third stage would involve the systematic search for the processes and mechanisms that underlie the manifestations of stress-resistant behavior in children. So for now one searches for clues to resiliency across diverse studies whatever their heterogeneity with regard to types of stressors, child cohorts, investigative modes, and measures of adaptation. This scarcely seems to have the procedural rigor that would lead one to anticipate a satisfactory identification of protective factors that may be implicated in stress-resistance" (p. 218).

Range of Models

Resilience-related models vary in terms of conceptual frameworks, formal properties of research design, and substantive operationalization of constructs.

Conceptual Frameworks

Causal models overlap greatly in their characteristic features and are distinguished from each other primarily in terms of the degree of emphasis placed on certain of its features. For example, Glantz (1992) puts forth a developmental psychopathology model:

"A developmentally oriented drug abuse etiology model emphasizes the origin of the risk for drug abuse as evolving, particularly during the maturational period of the individual. The factors constituting the risk are

not constant but develop through the interactions of the individual with his or her environment and in the context of that individual's progression through the stages and maturational tasks of growing up. Vulnerability develops, and in this sense it is not just a set of static, predisposing antecedent factors, but rather a dynamic process. No single vulnerability factor is the 'cause' of drug abuse by itself; instead, it is a contributive component in an interactive system that leads to emergent factors that in turn interact and evolve. Any single risk factor must be understood as having its etiological influence in the context of many other factors with which it interacts over time, probably developing through a number of transformations, eventually leading to heightened vulnerability to drug abuse. Thus, a given factor may have a different contributive effect at different developmental periods. Similarly, a factor's contribution will vary in the context of the particular other factors with which it interacts. Particular combinations of characteristics and circumstances interacting over time will differentially predispose an individual to, or protect him or her from, vulnerability to drug abuse.

A developmental psychopathology model of drug abuse emphasizes both the psychopathological nature of drug abuse and its etiology, as well as the developmental character of the etiology. Many forms of psychopathology have identifiable prodromal manifestations during childhood. It is hypothesized that certain patterns of drug (and alcohol) abuse have etiologies that begin in early childhood with detectable and predictable deviations from normal behavior" (p. 401).

Also, illustrative of the view of resilience as process, Egeland, Carlson, and Sroufe (1993) observe:

"Our own research has increasingly led us to view resilience in terms of a transactional process within an organizational framework. From this perspective, developmental outcomes are determined by the interaction of genetic, biological, psychological, and sociological factors in the context of environmental support. According to this view, any constitutional or environmental factors may serve as vulnerability, protective, or risk variables, directly or indirectly influencing behavior. The developmental process is characterized by a hierarchical integration of behavioral systems whereby earlier structures are incorporated into later structures in increasingly complex forms. The individual actively participates in this process, bringing to new experience, attitudes, expectations, and feelings derived from a history of interactions that, in turn, influence the manner in which environmental cues and stimuli are interpreted and organized. In keeping with this view, earlier experience is of critical importance in shaping the way later experience is organized" (pp. 517–518).

Such models allow for changing definitions of resilience as the developmental stage changes:

"Within an organizational-developmental framework, resilience or competence is viewed as the ability to use internal and external resources successfully to resolve stage-salient developmental issues . . . Competence in resolving issues in one developmental period does not predict later competence in a linear deterministic way; rather, competence at one period is thought to make the individual broadly adapted to the environment and prepared for competence in the next period . . . The way in which early developmental tasks are resolved are thought to serve a strong and enduring risk or protective function" (Egeland, Carlson, & Sroufe, 1993, p. 518).

Both the complexity and developmental nature of resilience-related processes are reflected in Murphy's (1987) concluding statement:

"The child shares with other organisms a biological tendency to achieve wholeness not as a static state, but as a dynamic, flexible balance that permits recoil or regression and rebound or progress. Biological rhythms of activity and rest provide a basic pattern for acceptance of restitution from the outside. The whole range of resources may be involved: biochemical factors, including hormones and endorphins; the interaction of cortical, subcortical, autonomic nervous system, and glandular activity; and psychophysiological forces. All these resources interact, mobilizing regenerative power. Residues of experiences of resilience after physical or emotional disturbance contribute both a sense of 'feeling good' and also a consolidation of confidence, optimism, and ability to respond to or seek help when faced with threats in the future. The drive toward integration, then, utilizes selective combinations of other drives and capacities available at a given stage of the child's development" (p. 101).

For Cohler (1987) resilience is influenced by,

". . . constitutionally imposed limitations upon the range of available strategies for solving problems, as well as by the constraints imposed by particular life changes. At least to some extent, variations in resilience during childhood, resulting from temperament and the experience of particular events (e.g. significant losses and extreme poverty), have an impact upon later choice of coping strategies. At the same time, across the adult years, maturational constraints yield to those determined by shared understandings of the course of life, and to expectable life transitions as important determinants of coping strategies" (p. 404).

Some models are organized around explaining positive outcomes that arise out of the challenges presented by life stress in terms of the indirect effects of the person and environmental systems, direct and indirect effects upon each other, life crisis or transition, cognitive appraisal, coping and responses, and feedback loops from positive outcomes of life crises and transitions.

"According to the framework . . . the environmental and personal systems jointly affect the likelihood and characteristics of a life crisis or transition. The environmental system is composed of the individual's ongoing life context, including the relatively stable precrisis aspects of his or her financial, home, and community living situation as well as characteristics of relationships with family members, work associates, and friends. The personal system includes an individual's sociodemographic characteristics and such personal resources as cognitive ability, health status, motivation, and self-efficacy. Life crises or transitions typically reflect changes in ongoing personal factors, such as a physical injury or illness, or environmental factors, such as the death of a spouse.

We organize the coping responses people typically use to manage life crises and transitions . . . into three domains that reflect their primary focus: appraisal-focused coping involves efforts to define, interpret, and understand a situation. Problem-focused coping covers efforts to resolve or master life stressors by seeking information, taking direct action, and finding alternative rewards. Emotion-focused coping involves attempts to manage emotional reactions to life stressors by regulating one's feelings, expressing anger, and accepting the situation. These coping response are affected by environmental, personal, and crisis-related factors; in turn, they may enhance the likelihood of positive outcomes. Overall, the model posits that life crises and the environmental and personal factors that foreshadow them . . . can shape appraisal and coping responses and affect the likelihood of a positive outcome . . ." (Schaefer & Moos, 1992, pp. 151–153).

The paths between these elements of the model are presented as transactions and specify reciprocal feedback at each stage. Other models also focus on the role of challenges in the development of resiliency. For example, building on the work of Anthony (1987a,b), Bandura (1989), Flach (1988), Garmezy (1987), and Werner (1989b), Richardson and his associates (1990) present a model in which,

" . . . the processes of coping with mild to severe disruptions are opportunities for growth, development, and skill building. The products of the resiliency enhancing process are increased protective skills as well as skills that facilitate the coping process. After repeated mild to severe disruptive experiences, the resilient individual does not fall as far following disruption and recovers in a shorter time" (p. 34).

The resilient individual adapts competently to disruptive life events and develops new skills in the process. The development of resiliency as facilitated by those who buffer the adverse effects of adversity, permits development of appropriate protective mechanisms, provides support in the face of failure to negotiate life events successfully, and encourages use of the life event as a challenge to become a better person.

In Werner's (1987) model, major risk factors are viewed as influencing vulnerability with major sources of stress (life events) increasing vulnerability and with protective factors within the child and the caregiving environment increasing stress resistance with regard to the range of probable developmental outcomes. The major risk factors occur at birth, the major sources of stress occur during childhood and adolescence. Protective factors and major sources of support in the caregiving environment refer to various points in the life cycle. Where there are fewer risk factors and stressful events and more protective factors in the child and in the caregiving environment the developmental outcomes are likely to be adaptive. Where there are more risk factors and fewer protective factors in the child and in the caregiving environment, the probability of maladaptive outcomes is increased (Werner & Smith, 1982). The contribution of risk factors, stressful life events, and protective factors appears to differ with the sex of the child and with the stages of the life cycle.

The conceptual framework used by Jessor and his associates (1991) called "Problem-Behavior Theory" postulates four systems of variables: social environment system, personality system, perceived environment system, and behavior system. *"Within each system certain variables represent instigation to engage in problem behavior and others represent controls against problem behavior; . . . it is the balance between instigation and controls that constitutes the level of proneness- or risk- that characterizes that system"* (Jessor, Donovan, & Costa, 1991, p. 20).

Some of the variables, such as friends being models for problem behavior, affect problem behavior directly, while other variables are linked to problem behavior only indirectly (such as parental controls). The personality system and the perceived environment system jointly influence the behavior system. The system presented by Jessor and his associates (1991) is an example of a model that presents countervailing risk and protective factors that exercise direct and indirect linear influences upon negatively evaluated (problem behaviors) or positively evaluated (conventional) behaviors.

Greenbaum and Auerbach (1992) provide a three-dimensional model of risk. The three dimensions are: external risk as opposed to protective factors; vulnerability as opposed to relative invulnerability of the individual; and lack of resilience as opposed to resilience of the individual. Risk factors increase the likelihood that the person will be exposed to an adverse occurrence, while protective factors lower such a probability. Vulnerability factors refer to potentially harmful factors associated with the individual. Vulnerability of the child fefers to the likelihood that if exposed to an adverse event the child will suffer physical of psychological development damage. The degree of constitutional protection possessed by the child which prevents or lessens the extent of damage that would ordinarily occur given certain risk factors is summarized as buffering effects. The root of resilience is to be found in the child's constitutionally based pattern of vulnerability-invulnerability. The environmental input interacting with the roots of resilience affects the child's resilience, that is individual differences in the degree and nature of the ability to cope with and recover from the impact of risk and vulnerability.

Given the three demensional model, Greenbaum and Auerbach (1992) suggest the following assumptions as a conceptual base for theory construction:

1. Early experience of acceptance (as expressed in nurturing behavior toward the child) and age-relevant stimulation will provide protection for the child, lower vulnerability, and increased resilience. Lack of such experiences constitute risk factors and will have opposite effects.
2. The risk-protection factors indicated in assumption 1 will interact with biological and environmental factors in influencing the development of the child; protective factors will augment other protective factors and ameliorate risk factors; and risk factors will augment other risk factors and weaken the effects of protective factors.
3. Vulnerability may be reduced and resilience may be increased by positive (protective) factors at any point in the lifespan. Negative (damaging) factors will have opposite effects.
4. The effectiveness of protective and risk factors is a function of the child's degree of vulnerability, degree of resilience, intensity of the protective or risk experience, duration of the exposure to risk or protective experience, and timing of the experience in the developmental lifespan . . .
5. Within the experience of acceptance and stimulation, some highly limited exposure to risk in the form of stress should result in increased resilience while having no effect or at most a short-term effect on vulnerability. (p. 24)

The multiplicity of conceptual models serves an important function. As Garmezy (1990) argues, *"there is a need for competing models of the development of psychopathology that can serve as the basis for definitive em-pirical tests of their comparative power."* (p. 528). At the same time, the limitations of these models must be recognized. The observation by Richters and Weintraub (1990) regarding the questions left open by the diathesis-stress model of psychopathology are applicable to virtually all models at this level of abstraction. The model leaves open,

> *". . . a host of questions concerning (a) the domains of functioning in which vulnerabilities to particular disorders are likely to be manifest, (b) the types of stressors that might (alone or in combination) influence one's*

vulnerability to a disorder and the eventual onset of the disorder, (c) whether, and when, particular vulnerabilities should be conceptualized as dichotomous or continuous variables, (d) the processes through which distal environmental events might influence or translate into an increase in one's vulnerability, and (e) the processes through which vulnerabilities might interact with subsequent stressors to influence an episode of disorder. In short, the diathesis-stress model itself yields no conclusions about the development of maladjustment and psychopathology. Instead, it provides an important heuristic for the formulation of research questions, while at the same time providing a conceptual structure within which the meaning of research findings can be evaluated" (Richter & Weintraub, 1990, p. 70).

Formal Research Design

A number of models are particularly well noted in the literature of resilience-related research although they by no means exhaust the types of design that exist. In risk models the distinction is drawn between the original identifiers that place the individual at risk and the factors that distinguished those who go on to be disabled from those who do not (Fisher, Kokes, Cole, Perkins, & Wynne, 1987).

"The risk research paradigm has focused on identifying samples of individuals who are at high risk for disability but who, at the point of contact, are symptom-free. These individuals are then followed over time so that the precursors of disability can be identified, the development and course of the disability can be monitored, and outcome data can be related to a host of premorbid and morbid variables" (p. 70).

Risk models vary in the extent to which they are based on a single factor or multiple factors.

"Stated simply, most risk models are based on a single factor that defines child vulnerability, such as parental mental illness . . . , preterm birth of the child with associated medical problems . . . , or parental social status. . . . However, we are becoming increasingly aware that such simple models of vulnerability are inadequate to explain the development of at-risk children who have been studied prospectively during the past two decades What are needed are models that encompass the complexity of developmental processes so that one may properly understand the interplay of risk factors and protective factors in young children" (Seifer & Sameroff, 1987, p. 52).

Within the context of high-risk projects, interaction effects take the form of diathesis-stress or vulnerability models (Richters & Weintraub, 1990). Such models hold that,

". . . individuals may inherit and/or acquire trait like deviations or vulnerabilities that mediate their risk for eventual onset of schizophrenia. These vulnerabilities constitute an individual's diathesis, and are conceptualized broadly as characteristics of functioning that lower one's threshold of susceptibility to environmental stressors that may subsequently trigger the onset of maladjustment or psychopathology" (p. 69).

Stress plays two roles in such models. On the one hand, stress increases vulnerability to a disorder. On the other hand, stress may precipitate psychopathology by interacting with the preexisting diathesis. In the parlance of some investigators, stress would constitute a vulnerability factor that exacerbates the preexisting risk factor (the diathesis). In the absence of the precipitating stress, vulnerability may not be sufficient to elicit psychopathology. However, if stressors are sufficiently intense, the stressors may elicit psychopathological episodes. Paralleling these models, at a higher level of abstraction are two broad categories of models that have been employed in research on resilience. The first of these postulates that the relationship between risk factors and outcome variables are moderated by other variables (including other risk factors). The risk factor (if it is inversely related to a positive outcome variable) or an ameliorative factor (sometimes called a protective factor) has a direct effect on an outcome variable. A second explanatory variable is thought to moderate the effects of the risk or ameliorative or compensatory (or, sometimes, protective) factor on the outcome variable. If the second variable (the moderating variable) is present or has a higher value the effect of the first variable will be different than if the second variable was absent or of a lower value. The second variable may or may not have had direct effect on the outcome variable apart from its effect on the influence of the first independent variable. This model characterized by the related ideas of protective factors and interactive processes, is distinguished from additive, main effect models according to which (Rutter, 1985),

". . . people knuckle under because of the sum of accumulated risk factors minus the sum of accumulated positive experiences. Those who escape the hazards must either have experienced fewer stressors or less severe adversities, or alternatively, these have been counterbalanced by a sufficient weight of compensatory good experiences or happy events" (p. 600).

Luthar (1993) observes,

"In weighing the merits of main effect models and interactive models while studying resilience, it should be noted that the two strategies address different questions, each important. In essence, main effect models ask, 'Among high-risk children, what distinguishes those who do well from

those who do poorly?', whereas interaction models pertain to specific moderating processes, asking, for example, 'Which attributes are associated with differential competence levels at high but not necessarily at low levels of risk?' When possible, the simultaneous exploration of both these sets of issues could provide the most complete understanding of the role of specific variables in childhood resilience" (pp. 448–449).

In point of fact, these and other designs vary along a number of dimensions. First, they may be regarded as single or multiple cause models. The multiple cause models may exert independent effects that are all positive, all negative, or mixed with regard to their positive or negative effects on the outcome. The causal effects of the positive or negative (or sole) causal factor(s) may specify mediating variables or not. The more or less direct positive or negative effect(s) on any specified outcome variable may or may not be moderated by specified variables. The specified moderating variables may all reduce the negative effects or increase the positive effects of the independent variables on the outcome, all of the moderating variables may exacerbate the adverse effects or reduce the ameliorative effects of the independent variables, or some moderating variables may be specified as reducing the adverse effects or increasing the positive effects of the independent variables, while other moderating variables are specified as exacerbating the negative effects or reducing the positive effects of the independent variables on the dependent variable. Where moderating variables are specified (whether positive, negative, or mixed in their moderating influence) the variables may be specified as having their own causes and operating through specified mechanisms or not. The variables specified as distal or proximal risk or resource (compensatory) factors, protective or vulnerability factors, and more or less benign outcomes at an earlier point in a model may or may not be specified as the same and/or different kinds of variables at a later point in the model (an earlier risk factor or outcome variable may later be specified as a protective factor; an earlier protective factor may later be specified as an outcome variable, etc.).

The challenge model, which suggests that stress factors lead to benign outcomes rather than adverse outcomes is a special case of models in which moderating variables are specified. Specific stressors will have a positive effect where the individual is experiencing relatively few demands upon him and has adequate resources to meet those demands, while the outcome of the stressor will be negative to the extent that the individual is already challenged to meet a number of other demands and the availability of resources adequate to meet those demands is problematic. Models in which the effects of multiple risks are multiplicative in their effects are also special cases of moderating variables models whereby one risk factor in the presence of another risk factor has an adverse effect but in the absence of a second risk factor has no effect at all on an outcome. The mixed positive and negative independent variable (or mediating variable) models include those models that have specified compensatory as well as risk factors.

The number of protective/vulnerability factors specified may vary from one to several. Where several are specified the moderating variables may refer to the several contexts in which the individual operates (familial, community, ecological) and/or may refer to individual level characteristics including the several variables that have been specified as independent variables. The independent or mediating variables and the moderating variables may include other outcome variables. Models in which developmental stage is viewed as significant are also special cases of moderating variables. The developmental stage is a short-hand specification of several conditional variables that moderate the effects of the independent variables on the dependent variables.

Substantive Models

The following models appear to be representative of the range of models that embody variability along the dimensions of research design. At the same time they illustrate the range of independent, mediating, moderating, and outcome variables that appear in the literature.

A not atypical model is that described by Luthar (1991) in which the effect of life stress on social competence was moderated by a number of variables. At the same time certain variables counteracted or compensated for risk factors by virtue of having direct effects upon the dependent variable, social competence (defined in terms of peer rating, teacher ratings, and school grades). Ego development was compensatory against stress. Internality and social skills served as protective factors, while intelligence and positive events were involved in vulnerability processes. Scheier, Newcomb, and Skager (1994) offer a model in which a vulnerability latent construct is reflected in three indexes: risk for initiation to drug use, risk for problem drug use, and protection from drug use. The model specifies that vulnerability is related to polydrug use as well as having specific effects on drug use measures. In this model protective factors are countervailing to risk factors rather than being viewed as moderators of the relationships between risk factors and polydrug use. Nakano (1990) estimated models showing main effects of hardiness on both physical symptoms and depression suggesting a protective function for hardiness. Also observed was a marginally significant interaction between hardiness and stressful life events such that hardy individuals reporting high stressful events tended to maintain low physical symptoms. Under conditions of low stressful life events, hardy and non-hardy person's symptoms did not differ. A risk study on a Japanese male sample replicated those of previous studies on American samples regarding the main effects of hardiness on physical and psychological well being. These results are congruent with a model that specifies both direct and moderating effects of protective factors.

Illustrative of models in which indicators of risk and protective factors predicted independently to various outcome variables is the report by Grossman and associates (1992). In multivariate context, family cohesion, good communication with parents, and a more internal locus of control was strongly associated with adaptation in adolescence independently of the predictive value of risk. However, these variables did not moderate the risk factor.

A typical explanatory model reported by Tessier and associates (1992) reported a five variable model accounting for 58.74 percent of the variance of a measure of the experience of stress among mothers following the birth of a first child. The final model is composed of two coping resource variables, a stressor variable, and two interactive variables. The variables predicting to the measure of psychological distress were perceived parental competence in interaction with an index of the frequency of occurrence of daily stressors, the interaction of health-related activity level with ratio of task accomplishment, health-related activity level, index of partner's emotional support, and degree of preoccupation with daily stressors.

A model in which multiple risk and protective factors were used, and in which the protective factors were treated as both main effects and in interaction with risk factors, to predict adjustment in an at-risk population is illustrated by the report of Dubow and Luster (1990) who reported that several risk factors (poverty status, urban residence, mother's self-esteem) were related to children's academic and behavioral adjustment. Increasing the number of risk factors was associated with increased vulnerability to adjustment problems. Several protective factors (intelligence, self-esteem, quality of home environment) were also related to children's adjustment and enhanced the prediction of adjustment beyond that contributed by the risk factors. Among children exposed to risk, protective factors reduced vulnerability to academic and behavioral difficulties. Finally, Dion, Dion, and Pak (1992) reported for a sample drawn from Toronto's Chinese community that the relationship between experienced discrimination and psychological symptoms was stronger among subjects low in hardiness (operationalized in terms of perceived social control and self-esteem) than in those high in hardiness.

Resilience: A Concept Whose Time Has Come and Gone

The concept of resilience and its various implementations in research has become the object of a good deal of criticism in recent years. It has been argued that the use of terms such as invulnerability or resilience is counterproductive in many ways. The terms imply that there is only one dimension rather than multiple dimensions along which individuals vary. The term implies certain constancy rather than permitting variation across time, place, developmental stage, or situational context (Fisher, Kokes, Cole, Perkins, & Wynne, 1987). It has been suggested that the judgment that individuals are resilient, that is, that they have survived in the face of characteristics that would predict failure to survive, reflects an incomplete understanding of the causes of the outcome. That is, the individuals survive or are characterized by other positive outcomes because they were not at-risk in the first place. While they might have been characterized in terms of some predictors, it was the predictors in combination with other circumstances that truly defined risk, and those other circumstances might not have been well known. As Rigsby (1994) observes,

> "For each of the categories of life experiences where resilience has been applied, researchers have made judgments about desirable and undesirable outcomes, about risks and assets (both individual and social), and about assessments of the likelihood of successful adaptations, given the risks and assets. To make and analogy, researchers make value judgments about differences between expected and observed outcomes, where the expectation is based on a prediction equation combining risks and assets. Resilient individuals are those whose adaptations represent extreme positive residuals from a prediction equation where adaptations are predicted from a linear combination of risks and assets. In other words, determination of resilience depends on (a) judgments about outcomes and (b) assumptions about the causes of adaptations that may not have been explicitly described or consciously examined. An incomplete theory gives rise to the possibility of concluding that resilient adaptations have occurred because an incomplete theory explains less well (i.e., produces larger prediction errors) (italics not in the original)" (p. 88).

In a similar vein, Richters and Weintraub (1990) observe:

> "Importantly, our concern here is not with the protective factors concept itself but rather with the practice of automatically invoking it as a quasi explanation for virtually any factor associated with reduced rates of negative outcomes among high-risk offspring. Garmezy rendered an invaluable service to psychology by emphasizing the need to consider protective or buffering factors in any meaningful analysis of the influences of childhood stress. Progress beyond Garmezy's insights to an empirically based understanding of the processes through which protective factors work, however will require a prior understanding of the processes through which stressors themselves exert an influence. Moreover, a necessary (though not sufficient) condition for invoking 'protective factors' as an

explanation for positive outcomes in the high-risk offspring samples should be a demonstration of the proximal stressors to which the offspring are being subjected and from which they are being protected" (pp. 79–80).

To name variables that have linear or negative effects on outcome variable risk factors, ameliorative factors, compensatory factors or some other term does not increase our understanding of the causes of the outcome. Nor does labeling the variables that moderate the direct or indirect effects as protective or vulnerability factors increase our understanding of the causes of the outcome. In fact, often our progress toward understanding the causes is impeded due to the fact that the same terms are frequently applied to factors that have a direct linear influence on the outcome variable as well as to factors that moderate the influence of other variables on the outcome variables. Finally, labeling approximation of an outcome variable in the presence of variables that increase the likelihood of the other end of the pole of the outcome variable "resilience" does not increase our understanding of the causes of the outcome variable, particularly when resilience is sometimes applied to the outcome variable and sometimes applied to the variables that moderate the effects of putative risk factors on the outcome variable.

In a sense everyone is continually under stress. The environment makes constant demands on individuals that they are expected to fill and expect themselves to fulfill. That the significance of these demands varies, and that the resources available to fulfill the demands vary is unquestionable. However, to arbitrarily decide that some point on the continuum of stress constitutes an undue burden and the ability to carry that burden constitutes as special characteristic called resilience is questionable. Perhaps we should recognize (initially, finally, or once again) that people differ in the demands made upon them, and the resources available to them. They differ further in their ability to achieve certain kinds of outcomes (valued and disvalued). Finally, we should recognize, that our purpose is to explain the variability in outcomes taking into account variations in the demands made upon individuals, the resources available to them, and any circumstances (personal or environmental) that might moderate the relationships between demands and resources on the one hand and more or less desirable outcomes on the other. Rigsby (1994) says it well:

"What we really want to understand are the processes of human development in different times and places, for individuals with varying risks and assets, and for individuals developing in a variety of social contexts. Further, we want to understand the causal structures and processes that occur in specific contexts. We need to study the details of the social context

within which children are developing. We resort to concepts like resilience because there is a poverty of theory development in this area. Accumulating more correlates of resilience and failure will not be helpful if it is done outside the context of serious theory building in human development" (p. 91).

Long before the notion of resilience or functionally equivalent terms entered the behavioral science literature, explanations of individual differences in the approximation of desirable or undesirable states were offered. Certain variables were thought to increase the risk of undesirable outcomes or to decrease the likelihood of desirable outcomes. Other variables were believed to decrease the risk of undesirable outcomes or to increase the likelihood of desirable outcomes. In some instances the same variables that were hypothesized to be risk factors, at some level were thought to increase the probability of benign outcomes, as when moderate levels of stress challenge or evoke adaptive patterns. Since then we may have made life too complex. Terms like resilience, vulnerability, protective factors, and risk factors may have muddied the waters rather than served to clarify thought. Perhaps we should go back to basics. Perhaps we should first decide what we are trying to explain. We should be precise about what is the outcome variable of interest. Is it clinical depression, a particular substance abuse pattern, problem drinking, or more positively stated outcomes such as good physical health, positive mental health, self-acceptance, or any of a number of other specified outcomes? As much as possible we should operationalize these constructs in value-free language. While the reasons that we are investigating certain of these outcomes may be due to their evaluative significance for representatives of different segments of the society, the scientific investigation of them can only be hampered by thinking of them as good or bad outcomes. For surely we will find that certain of these outcomes represent the best of all possible adaptations for some segments of society while these adaptations are decried as evil or dysfunctional by other segments of society. The outcome may be the presence or absence of some phenomenon, or a bipolar dimension representing the degrees to which the phenomenon is present or absent.

Having defined the outcome, we should strive to construct a theoretical framework that accounts for the outcome. The theoretical framework will consist of variables that are distantly related to the outcome, variables that are the result of those distantly related variables and that are more closely related to the outcomes, and variables that more or less moderate the effects of the variables that are more distantly or proximally related to the outcome variable of interest.

Insofar as the outcome variables are closely related to each other similar theoretical frameworks may account for the outcomes. To the extent that the outcomes are unrelated different theoretical frameworks will be necessary to account for the outcomes. The task for the future is to distill the many characteristics that are called protective factors, vulnerability factors, or risk factors into their essential elements. It may be that they need to first define a simple model that specifies, for example, that conformity to social expectations is a first cause and factors such as consequent positive responses from others lead to the transmission of conventional skills and self-acceptance which in turn lead to desirable adaptations (Kaplan, 1995). These outcomes in turn moderate age-appropriate or age-inappropriate stresses and other circumstances that in the absence of the moderating variables might have untoward effects. Circumstances that define or influence the initial inability to conform to expectations (including those relating to temperament) may include constitutionally given and genetically transmitted factors. The notion that involuntary deviation from expectations is the beginning of a process by which resources are withheld and needs go unfulfilled provides a good fit to the data from many longitudinal studies. Werner (1989b) states,

> "... we found among the crime resistant delinquents a much smaller proportion considered to be troublesome by their classroom teachers and their parents during middle childhood. Among those who entered an adult criminal career, a significantly higher proportion had been considered dishonest by both teachers and parents, and had exhibited temper tantrums, uncontrolled emotions, and extreme irritability, aggression, and bullying behavior in the classrooms at age ten.
>
> Delinquents who did not commit any adult crimes also had significantly higher scores in early childhood on developmental examinations that assess their sensory-motor and social competence. In addition, they were less frequently considered to be in need of mental health services by age ten than those who went on to commit adult crimes" (p. 79).

The antecedents of the criminal behavior may be thought of as early stages of deviance which evoked negative responses reflecting withholding satisfaction of affectional needs and concomitant withdrawal that resulted in failure to communicate necessary social skills for the negotiation of communal expectations. The deviant behavior during adulthood represents adaptations to the sense of rejection or reflections of the failure to fulfill social expectations and to garner accompanying rewards (Kaplan, 1995).

In sensitizing us to the need to understand the mutual effects of antecedents of more or less positive outcomes, the conditional nature of these effects, and the fact that proximal and conditional variables have their own causes, the concept of resilience has served an important function. The concept has also, more generally alerted us to the fact that we have an incomplete understandings of more or less desirable outcomes. The concept has alerted us to the fact that people who according to conventional wisdom should have experienced adverse outcomes, do not in fact experience them, and that people who should have experienced positive outcomes, given their personal and environmental characteristics do not in fact experience them. Having alerted us to these phenomena, however, resilience may have served its purpose and may be permitted to retire from the field gracefully and with honor. In place of this concept, we must now redirect our attention to creating theoretical structures that take into account individual, environmental, and situational factors that influence each other and interact with each other to influence other variables in different ways at different stages of the developmental cycle and of the evolution of social structures to affect outcomes, the evaluative significance of which is only incidental to the purpose of explaining the phenomenon in question.

References

Anderson, L. (1994). Effectiveness and efficiency in inner-city public schools: Charting school resilience. In M. C. Wang & E. W. Gordon (Eds.), *Educational resilience in inner-city America* (pp. 141–149). Hillsdale, NJ: Erlbaum.

Anthony, E. J. (1987). Risk, vulnerability and resilience: An overview. In E. J. Anthony & B. Cohler (Eds.), *The invulnerable child* (pp. 3–48). New York: The Guilford Press.

Antonovsky, A. (1984). The sense of coherence as a determinant of health. In J. D. Matarazzo, S. M. Weiss, J. A. Herd, N. E. Miller, & S. M. Weiss (Eds.), *Behavioral health: A handbook of health enhancement and disease prevention* (pp. 114–129). New York: Wiley.

Baldwin, A. L., Baldwin, C. P., & Cole, R. E. (1990). Stress-resistant families and stress-resistant children. In J. Rolf, A. S. Masten, D. Cicchetti, K. H. Nuechterlein, & A. S. Weintraub (Eds.), *Risk and protective factors in the development of psychopathology* (pp. 257–280). New York: Cambridge University Press.

Baldwin, A. L., Baldwin, C. P., Kasser, T., Zax, M., Sameroff, A., & Seifer, R. (1993). Contextual risk and resiliency during late adolescence. *Development and psychopathology, 5,* 741–761.

Bandura, A. (1989). Human agency in social cognitive theory. *American Psychologist, 44,* 1175–1184.

Banks, J. K., & Gannon, L. R. (1988). The influence of hardiness on the relationship between stressors and psychosomatic symptomatology. *American Journal of Community Psychology, 16,* 25–37.

Baron, R. S., Cutrona, C. E., Hicklin, D., Russell, D. W., & Lubaroff, D. M. (1990). Social support and immune function among spouses of cancer patients. *Journal of Personality and Social Psychology, 59,* 344–352.

Bartelt, D. W. (1994). On resilience: Questions of validity. In M. C. Wang & E. W. Gordon (Eds.), *Educational resilience in inner-city America* (pp. 97–108). Hillsdale, NJ: Erlbaum.

Block, J. H., & Block, J. (1980). The role of ego-control and ego-resiliency in the organization of behavior. In W. A. Collins (Ed.), *Development of cognition, affect, and social relations* (pp. 39–101). Hillsdale, NJ: Erlbaum.

Bonner, R. L., & Rich, A. R. (1991). Predicting vulnerability to hopelessness: A longitudinal analysis. *Journal of Nervous and Mental Disease, 179*, 29–32.

Bradley, R. H., Whiteside, L., Mundfrom, D. J., Casey, P. H., Kelleher, K. J., & Pope, S. K. (1994). Early indications of resilience and their relation to experiences in the home environments of low birthweight, premature children living in poverty. *Child Development, 65*, 346–360.

Brook, J. S., Brook, D. W., Gordon, A. S., Whiteman, M., & Cohen, P. (1990). The psychosocial etiology of adolescent drug use: A family interactional approach. *Genetic, Social, and General Psychology Monographs, 116 (No. 2)*.

Brown, J. D. (1991). Staying fit and staying well: Physical fitness as a moderator of life stress. *Journal of Personality and Social Psychology, 60*, 555–561.

Brown, W. K., & Rhodes, W. A. (1991). Factors that promote invulnerability and resiliency in at-risk children. In W. A. Rhodes & W. K. Brown (Eds.), *Why some children succeed despite the odds* (pp. 171–178). New York: Praeger.

Carro, M. G., Grant, K. E., Gotlib, I. H., & Compas, B. E. (1993). Postpartum depression and child development: An investigation of mothers and fathers as sources of risk and resilience. *Development and Psychopathology, 5*, 567–579.

Cauce, A. M., Hannan, K., & Sargeant, M. (1992). Life stress, social support, and locus of control during early adolescence: Interactive effects. *American Journal of Community Psychology, 20*, 787–798.

Chandy, J. M., Harris, L., Blum, R. W., & Resnick, M. D. (1994). Disordered eating among adolescents whose parents misuse alcohol: Protective and risk factors. *International Journal of the Addictions, 29*, 505–516.

Cicchetti, D., & Garmezy, N. (1993). Prospects and promises in the study of resilience. *Development and Psychopathology, 5*, 497–502.

Clayton, R. R. (1992). Transitions in drug use: Risk and protective factors. In M. D. Glantz & R. W. Pickens (Eds.), *Vulnerability to drug abuse* (pp. 15–51). Washington, DC: American Psychological Association.

Cohler, B. J. (1987). Adversity, resilience, and the study of lives. In E. J. Anthony & B. Cohler (Eds.), *The invulnerable child* (pp. 363–424). New York: Guilford.

Conrad, M., & Hammen, C. (1993). Protective and resource factors in high- and low-risk children: A comparison of children with unipolar, bipolar, medically ill, and normal mothers. *Development and Psychopathology, 5*, 593–607.

Dion, K. L., Dion, K. K., & Pak, A. W. (1992). Personality-based hardiness as a buffer for discrimination-related stress in members of Toronto's chinese community. *Canadian Journal of Behavioural Science, 24*, 517–536.

DuBois, D. L., Felner, R. D., Brand, S., Adan, A. M., & Evans, E. G. (1992). A prospective study of life stress, social support, and adaptation in early adolescence. *Child Development, 63*, 542–557.

Dubow, E. F., & Luster, T. (1990). Adjustment of children born to teenage mothers: The contribution of risk and protective factors. *Journal of Marriage and the Family, 52*, 393–404.

Egeland, B., Carlson, E., & Sroufe, L. A. (1993). Resilience as process. *Development and Psychopathology, 5*, 517–528.

Felix-Ortiz, M., & Newcomb, M. D. (1992). Risk and protective factors for drug use among Latino and White adolescents. *Hispanic Journal of Behavioral Sciences, 14*, 291–309.

Fisher, L., Kokes, R. F., Cole, R. E., Perkins, P. M., & Wynne, L. C. (1987). Competent children at risk: A study of well-functioning offspring of disturbed parents. In E. J. Anthony & B. Cohler (Eds.), *The invulnerable child* (pp. 211–228). New York: Guilford Press.

Flach, F. F. (1988). Resilience: Discovering new strength at times of stress. New York: Ballantine Books.

Funk, S. C. (1992). Hardiness: A review of theory and research. *Health Psychology, 11*, 335–345.

Garmezy, N. Z. (1985). Stress-resistant children: The search for protective factors. In J. E. Stevenson (Ed.), *Recent research in developmental psychopathology* (pp. 213–233). New York: Pergamon Press.

Garmezy, N. Z. (1987). Stress, competence, and development: Continuities in the study of schizophrenic adults, children vulnerable to psychopathology and the search for stress-resistant children. *American Journal of Orthopsychiatry, 57,* 159–174.

Garmezy, N. Z. (1990). A closing note: Reflections on the future. In J. Rolf, A. S. Masten, D. Cicchetti, K. H. Nuechterlein, & A. S. Weintraub (Eds.), *Risk and protective factors in the development of psychopathology* (pp. 527–534). New York: Cambridge University Press.

Garmezy, N. Z. (1993a). Vulnerability and resilience. In D. C. Funder, R. D. Parke, C. Tomlin-son-Keasey, & K. Widaman (Eds.), *Studying lives through time* (pp. 377–397). Washington, DC: American Psychological Association.

Gentry, W. D., & Kobasa, S. C. (1984). Social and psycholgocial resources mediating stress-illness relationships in humans. In W. D. Gentry (Ed.), *Handbook of behavioral medicine* (pp. 87–116). New York: Guilford Press.

Gerstein, D. R., & Green, L. W. (Eds.). (1993). *Preventing drug abuse: What do we know?* Washington, DC: National Academy Press.

Gest, S., Neemann, J., Hubbard, J. J., Masten, A. S., & Tellegen, A. (1993). Parenting quality, adversity, and conduct problems in adolescence: Testing process-oriented models of resilience. *Development and Psychopathology, 5,* 663–682.

Glantz, M. D. (1992). A developmental psychopathology model of drug abuse vulnerability. In M. D. Glantz & R. W. Pickens (Eds.), *Vulnerability to drug abuse* (pp. 389–418). Washington, DC: American Psychological Association.

Glantz, M. D., & Pickens, R. W. (1992). Vulnerability to drug abuse: Introduction and overview. In M. D. Glantz & R. W. Pickens (Eds.), *Vulnerability to drug abuse* (pp. 1–14). Washington, DC: American Psychological Association.

Glueck, S., & Glueck, E. (1950). *Unraveling juvenile delinquency.* Cambridge: Harvard University Press.

Gordon, E. W., & Song, L. D. (1994). Variations in the experience of resilience. In M. C. Wang & E. W. Gordon (Eds.), *Educational resilience in inner-city America* (pp. 27–43). Hillsdale, NJ: Erlbaum.

Greenbaum, C. W., & Auerbach, J. G. (1992). The conceptualization of risk, vulnerability, and resilience in psychological development. In C. W. Greenbaum & J. G. Auerbach (Eds.), *Longitudinal studies of children at psychological risk: Cross-national perspectives* (pp. 9–28). Norwood, NJ: Ablex Publishing.

Grossman, F. K., Beinashowitz, J., Anderson, L., Sakurai, M., Finnin, L., & Flaherty, M. (1992). Risk and resilience in young adolescents. *Journal of Youth and Adolescence, 21,* 529–550.

Hawkins, J., Catalano, R. F., & Miller, J. Y. (1992). Risk and protective factors for alcohol and other drug problems in adolescence and early adulthood: Implications for substance abuse prevention. *Psychological Bulletin, 112,* 64–105.

Jahoda, M. (1959). *Current concepts of positive mental health.* New York: Basic Books.

Jenkins, J. M., & Smith, M. A. (1990). Factors protecting children living in disharmonious homes: Maternal reports. *Journal of the American Academy of Child and Adolescent Psychiatry, 29,* 60–69.

Jessor, R., Donovan, J. E., & Costa, F. M. (1991). *Beyond adolescence: Problem behavior and young adult development.* New York: Cambridge University Press.

Kaplan, H. B. (1986). *Social psychology of self-referent behavior.* New York: Plenum Press.

Kaplan, H. B. (1995). Drugs, crime and other deviant adaptations. In H. B. Kaplan (Ed.), *Drugs, crime and other deviant adaptations: Longitudinal studies* (pp. 3–46). New York: Plenum Press.

Kernis, M., Grannemann, B. D., & Mathis, L. C. (1991). Stability of self-esteem as a moderator of the relation between level of self-esteem and depression. *Journal of Personality and Social Psychology, 61*, 80–84.

Kessler, R. C., & Magee, W. J. (1994). The disaggregation of vulnerability to depression as a function of the determinants of onset and recurrence. In W. R. Avison & I. H. Gotlib (Eds.), *Stress and mental health* (pp. 239–258). New York: Plenum Press.

Kobasa, S. C. (1979). Stressful life events, personality, and health: An inquiry into hardiness. *Journal of Personality and Social Psychology, 37*, 1–11.

Kumpfer, K. L., & Hopkins, R. (1993). Prevention: Current research and trends. *Recent advances in addictive disorders, 16*, 11–20.

Landerman, R., George, L. K., & Blazer, D. G. (1991). Adult vulnerability for psychiatric disorders: Interactive effects of negative childhood experiences and recent stress. *Journal of Nervous and Mental Disease, 179*, 656–663.

Liddle, H. A. (1994). Contextualizing resiliency. In M. C. Wang & E. W. Gordon (Eds.), *Educational Resilience in Inner-City America* (pp. 167–177). Hillsdale, NJ: Erlbaum.

L"sel, F., Bliesener, T., & K"ferl, P. (1989). On the concept of invulnerability : Evaluation and first results of the Bielefeld project. In M. Brambring, F. L"sel, & H. Skowronek (Eds.), *Children at risk: Assessment, longitudinal research, and intervention* (pp. 186–219). New York: Walter de Gruyter.

Luthar, S. S. (1991). Vulnerability and resilience: A study of high-risk adolescents. *Child Development, 62*, 600–616.

Luthar, S. S. (1993). Annotation: Methodological and conceptual issues in research on childhood resilience. *Journal of Child Psychology and Psychiatry, 34*, 441–453.

Luthar, S. S., & Zigler, E. (1991). Vulnerability and competence: A review of research on resilience in childhood. *American Journal of Orthopsychiatry, 61*, 6–22.

Luthar, S. S., Doernberger, C. H., & Zigler, E. (1993). Resilience is not a unidimensional construct: Insights from a prospective study of inner-city adolescents. *Development and Psychopathology, 5*, 703–717.

MacEwen, K. E., & Barling, J. (1988). Interrole conflict, family support and marital adjustment of employed mothers: A short term, longitudinal study. *Journal of Organizational Behavior, 9*, 241–250.

Maslow, A. (1970). *Motivation and personality*. New York: Harper & Row.

Masten, A. S. (1994). Resilience in individual development: Successful adaptation despite risk and adversity. In M. C. Wang & E. W. Gordon (Eds.), *Educational resilience in inner-city America* (pp. 3–25). Hillsdale, NJ: Erlbaum.

Masten, A. S., Morison, P., Pellegrini, D., & Tellegen, A. (1990). Competence under stress: Risk and protective factors. In J. Rolf, A. S. Masten, D. Cicchetti, K. H. Nuechterlein, & S. Weintraub (Eds.), *Risk and protective factors in the development of psychopathology* (pp. 236–256). New York: Cambridge University Press.

Moran, P. B., & Eckenrode, J. (1992). Protective personality characteristics among adolescent victims of maltreatment. *Child Abuse & Neglect, 16*, 743–754.

Mulholland, D. J., Watt, N. F., Philpott, A., & Sarlin, N. (1991). Academic performance in children of divorce: Psychological resilience and vulnerability. *Psychiatry, 54*, 268–280.

Murphy, L. B. (1987). Further reflections on resilience. In E. J. Anthony & B. Cohler (Eds.), *The invulnerable child* (pp. 84–105). New York: Guilford Press.

Myers, H. F., Taylor, S., Alvy, K. T., Arrington, A., & Richardson, M. A. (1992). Parental and family predictors of behavior problems in inner-city Black children. American Journal of Community Psychology, 20, 557–576.

Nakano, K. (1990). Hardiness, type A behavior, and physical symptoms in a Japanese sample. Journal of Nervous and Mental Disease, 178, 52–56.

Offer, D., & Sabshin, M. (1966). *Normality: Theoretical and clinical concepts of mental health.* New York: Basic Books.

Park, C., Cohen, L. H., & Herb, L. (1990). Intrinsic religiousness and religious coping as life stress moderators for Catholics versus Protestants. *Journal of Personality and Social Psychology, 59,* 562–574.

Radke-Yarrow, M., & Brown, E. (1993). Resilience and vulnerability in children of multiple-risk families. *Development and Psychopathology, 5,* 581–592.

Radke-Yarrow, M., & Sherman, T. (1990). Hard growing: Children who survive. In J. Rolf, A. S. Masten, D. Cicchetti, K. H. Nuechterlein, & S. Weintraub (Eds.), *Risk and protective factors in the development of psychopathology* (pp. 97–119). New York: Cambridge University Press.

Rauh, H. (1989). The meaning of risk and protective factors in infancy. European Journal of Psychology of Education IV, 2, 161–173.

Rhodes, W. A., & Brown, W. K. (1991). Introduction and review of the literature. In W. A. Rhodes and W. K. Brown (Eds.), *Why some children succeed despite the odds* (pp. 1–6). New York: Praeger.

Richardson, G. E., Neiger, B. L., Jensen, S., &. Kumpfer, K. L. (1990). The resiliency model. *Health Education, 21,* 33–39.

Richters, J., & Weintraub, S. (1990). Beyond diathesis: Toward an understanding of high-risk environments. In J. Rolf, A. S. Masten, D. Cicchetti, K. H. Nuechterlein, & S. Weintraub (Eds.), *Risk and protective factors in the development of psychopathology* (pp. 67–96). Cambridge: Cambridge University Press.

Rigsby, L. C. (1994). The Americanization of resilience: Deconstructing research practice. In M. C. Wang & E. W. Gordon (Eds.), *Educational resilience in inner-city America* (pp. 85–92). Hillsdale, NJ: Erlbaum.

Rodin, J., Striegel-Moore, R. H., & Silberstein, L. R. (1990). Vulnerability and resilience in the age of eating disorders: Risk and protective factors for bulimia nervosa. In J. Rolf, A. S. Masten, D. Cicchetti, K. H. Nuechterlein, & S. Weintraub (Eds.), *Risk and protective factors in the development of psychopathology* (pp. 361–383). New York: Cambridge University Press.

Roosa, M. W., Beals, J., Sandler, I. N., & Pillow, D. R. (1990). The role of risk and protective factors in predicting symptomatology in adolescent self-identified children of alcoholic parents. *American Journal of Community Psychology, 18,* 725–741.

Rubenstein, J. L., Heeren, T., Housman, D., Rubin, C., & Stechler, G. (1989). Suicidal behavior in normal adolescents: Risk and protective factors. *American Journal of Orthopsychiatry, 59,* 59–71.

Rutter, M. (1979). Protective factors in children s responses to stress and disadvantage. In M. W. Kent & J. E. Rolf (Eds.), Primary prevention of psychopathology: Vol. 3: *Social competence in children* (pp. 48–74). Hanover, NH: University Press of New England.

Rutter, M. (1985). Resilience in the face of adversity: Protective factors and resistance to psychiatric disorder. British *Journal of Psychiatry, 147,* 598–611.

Rutter, M. (1990). Psychosocial resilience and protective mechanisms. In J. Rolf, A. S. Masten, D. Cicchetti, K. H. Nuechterlein, & S. Weintraub (Eds.), *Risk and protective factors in the development of psychopathology* (pp. 181–214). New York: Cambridge University Press.

Schaefer, J. A., & Moos, R. A. (1992). Life crises and personal growth. In B. N. Carpenter (Ed.), *Personal coping: Theory, research, and application* (pp. 149–170). Westport, CT: Praeger.

Scheier, L. M., Newcomb, M. D., & Skager, R. (1994). Risk, protection, and vulnerability to adolescent drug use: Latent-variable models of three age groups. *Journal of Drug Education, 24,* 49–82.

Schuldberg, D. (1993). Personal resourcefulness: Positive aspects of functioning in high-risk research. *Psychiatry, 56,* 137–152.

Seifer, R., & Sameroff, A. J. (1987). Multiple determinants of risk and invulnerability. In E. J. Anthony & B. Cohler (Eds.), *The invulnerable child* (pp. 51–69). New York: Guilford Press.

Shepperd, J. A., & Kashani, J. H. (1991). The relationship of hardiness, gender, and stress to health outcomes in adolescents. *Journal of Personality, 59,* 747–768.

Smith, R. E., Smoll, F. E., & Ptacek, J. C. (1990). Conjunctive moderator variables in vulnerability and resiliency research: Life stress, social support and coping skills, and adolescent sport injuries. *Journal of Personality and Social Psychology, 58,* 360–370.

Spencer, M. B., Cole, S. P., DuPree, D., Glymph, A., & Pierre, P. (1993). Self-efficacy among urban African American early adolescents: Exploring issues of risk, vulnerability, and resilience. *Development and Psychopathology, 5,* 719–739.

Spencer, S. J., Josephs, R. A., & Steele, C. M. (1993). Low self-esteem: The uphill struggle for self-integrity. In R. F. Baumeister (Ed.), *Self-esteem: The puzzle of low self-regard* (pp. 21–36). New York: Plenum Press.

Staudinger, U. M., Marsiske, M., & Baltes, P. B. (1993). Resilience and levels of reserve capacity in later adulthood: Perspectives from life-span theory. *Development and Psychopathology, 5,* 541–566.

Stevenson, H., & Rhodes, W. A. (1991). Risk and resilience in teenagers who avoid pregnancy. In W. A. Rhodes & W. K. Brown (Eds.), *Why some children succeed despite the odds* (pp. 79–92). New York: Praeger.

Stouthamer-Loeber, M., Loeber, R., Farrington, D. P., Zhang, Q., van Kammen, W., & Maguin, E. (1993). The double edge of protective and risk factors for delinquency: Interrelations and developmental patterns. *Development and Psychopathology, 5,* 683–701.

Swanson, G. E. (1988). *Ego defenses and the legitimation of behavior.* New York: Cambridge University Press.

Tarter, R. E. (1988). The high-risk paradigm in alcohol and drug abuse research. In R. W. Pickens & D. S. Svikis (Eds.), *Biological vulnerability to drug abuse* (pp. 73–86). NIDA Research Monograph 89.

Taylor, R. D. (1994). Risk and resilience: Contextual influences on the development of African-American adolescents. In M. C. Wang & E. W. Gordon (Eds.), *Educational resilience in inner-city America* (pp. 119–137). Hillsdale, NJ: Erlbaum.

Tessier, R., Pich, C., Tarabulsy, G. M., & Muckle, G. (1992). Mothers experience of stress following the birth of a first child: Identification of stressors and coping resources. *Journal of Applied Social Psychology, 22,* 1319–1339.

Topf, M. (1989). Personality hardiness, occupational stress, and burnout in critical care nurses. *Research in Nursing & Health, 12,* 179–186.

Wang, M. C., Haertal, G. D., & Walberg, H. J. (1994). Educational resilience in inner cities. In M. C. Wang & E. W. Gordon (Eds.), *Educational resilience in inner-city America* (pp. 45–72). Hillsdale, NJ: Erlbaum.

Werner, E. E. (1987). Vulnerability and resiliency in children at risk for delinquency: A longitudinal study from birth to young adulthood. In J. D. Burchard & S. N. Burchard (Eds.), *Prevention of delinquent behavior* (pp. 16–43). Newbury Park, CA: Sage.

Werner, E. E. (1989a). Vulnerability and resiliency: A longitudinal perspective. In M. Brambring, F. L"sel, & H. Skowronek (Eds.), *Children at risk: Assessment, longitudinal research, and intervention* (pp. 157–172). New York: Walter de Gruyter.

Werner, E. E. (1989b). High risk children in young adulthood: A longitudinal study from birth to 32 years. *American Journal of Orthopsychiatry, 59,* 71–81.

Werner, E. E. (1993). Risk, resilience, and recovery: Perspectives from the Kauai longitudinal study. *Development and Psychopathology, 5,* 503–515.

Werner, E. E., & Smith, R. S. (1982). *Vulnerable but invincible: A study of resilient children and youth.* New York: McGraw-Hill.

Werner, E. E., & Smith, R. S. (1992). *Overcoming the odds: High risk children from birth to adulthood.* Ithaca, NY: Cornell University Press.

Wiebe, D. J. (1991). Hardiness and stress moderation: A test of proposed mechanisms. *Journal of Personality and Social Psychology, 60,* 89–99.

Wiedenfeld, S. A., O Leary, A., Bandura, A., Brown, S., Levine, S., & Raska, K. (1990). Impact of perceived self-efficacy in coping with stressors on components of the immune system. *Journal of Personality and Social Psychology, 59,* 1082–1094.

Williams, P. G., Wiebe, D. J., & Smith, T. W. (1992). Coping processes as mediators of the relationship between hardiness and health. *Journal of Behavioral Medicine, 15,* 237–255.

Williams, S., Anderson, J., McGee, R., & Silva, P. A. (1990). Risk factors for behavioral and emotional disorder in preadolescent children. *Journal of the American Academy of Child and Adolescent Psychiatry, 29,* 413–419.

Wyman, P. A., Cowen, E. L, Work, W. C., & Kerley, J. H. (1993). The role of children s future expectations in self-system functioning and adjustment to life stress: A prospective study of urban at-risk children. *Development and Psychopathology, 5,* 649–661.

4

Re-Visiting the Validity of the Construct of Resilience

Ralph E. Tarter and Michael Vanyukov

*The tendency has always been strong that whatever received a name must
be an entity or being, having an independent existence of its own. And, if no
real entity answering to the name could be found, men did not for that reason
suppose that none existed, but imagined that is was something peculiarly
abstruse and mysterious.*

John Stuart Mill

Introduction

It is a common observation that some children surmount adversity to
subsequently achieve optimum or even exceptional adjustment. Horatio
Alger, the nineteenth century clergyman, through his inspirational adven-
ture stories about poor and homeless youth elevated to mythic proportion
in American consciousness the belief that hardship can be overcome
through good fortune, a strong will, and hard work. Books having titles such
as *Luck and Pluck, Tattered Tom* and *Sink or Swim* imbued the reader with

Ralph E. Tarter • Center for Education and Drug Abuse Research, Western Psychiatric
Institute and Clinic, University of Pittsburgh Medical School, Pittsburgh, Pennsylvania
15213. **Michael Vanyukov** • Center for Education and Drug Abuse Research, Western
Psychiatric Institute and Clinic, University of Pittsburgh Medical School, Pittsburgh, Pennsylvania 15213.

Resilience and Development: Positive Life Adaptations, edited by Glantz and Johnson. Kluwer
Academic/Plenum Publishers, New York, 1999.

the conviction that inner strength, self-reliance and single-minded individualism constituted the "right stuff." Although Alger's books, totaling over 100, would not be considered a serious contribution to Western civilization literature, the themes struck a responsive chord as indicated by the enduring belief that personal fortitude surmounts adversity. A century later, the widely used term "survivor," whether pertaining to the egregious consequences of living with an alcoholic parent, or an abusive spouse, or remitting from life-threatening disease, reinforces the belief that certain personal attributes distinguish compromised individuals who overcome the odds from those that succumb to emotional disorder and social maladjustment.

Whether the term "survivor" (emanating from the self-help movement) or "resilience" (largely circumscribed to the scientific community) is used, they are intended to denote the same process. In effect, these terms are applied retrospectively to individuals who attain a satisfactory outcome in adolescence and adulthood even though confronted with adverse circumstances during childhood (Masten, Best, & Garmezy, 1991).

Behavioral science, particularly psychology, has a long tradition of borrowing concepts from physics and engineering in the attempt to clarify obscure and complex processes. For example, the terms "energy" and "dynamics" are descriptors of motivation and psychic functioning. The term "resilience" has its most precise meaning in materials science and civil engineering. It is therefore important at the outset to define resilience and determine whether the process is analogous to either psychological or biological functioning.

A common and accepted definition of *resilience* is "the property of a material that enables it to resume its original shape or position after being bent, stretched or compressed" (American Heritage Dictionary, 1978). In engineering, resilience is a property whose attributes include the speed and amount of recovery following *removal* of a known stressor. In the life sciences, individual attributes or characteristics are referred to as phenotypes. The underlying dimension is a trait. Employing the term resilience implies that it is (or will be) possible to predict magnitude of recovery to the pre-stress state upon knowing the properties of the stressor (magnitude, type, duration, etc.) and capacity to measure the resilience trait.

At first glance, materials science would appear to be a good model to help elucidate why some children attain good outcomes despite experiencing severe stress. Traits such as *hardiness, competence, ego resilience*, and *ego strength* have been used synonymously to characterize individuals who have this abstruse attribute of withstanding stress without permanent damage. The range of stressors, although more numerous and more difficult to measure compared to engineering, include factors such as poverty, parental abuse, ethnic discrimination, and physical disability. The fact that some children develop normally despite adversity in these areas has been conducted to suggest that they possess the phenotype of high resilience.

Upon further reflection, however, using the term resilience in biobehavioral science is not only an inaccurate analogy but also is superfluous. The notion that humans and inanimate materials are comparable, and that the latter can serve as a model to understand the former, is simplistic. Consider the following:

1. Resiliency is the extent to which a material returns to the normal state following *removal* of a stressor. In research where the concept of resilience has been invoked, the process implies good outcome *despite the presence* of the stressor. Thus, the term is inappropriately applied, at least with respect to its original intended meaning.

2. The experience of stress not only determines the future quality of response to the same stressor, but also, most importantly, influences future environmental selections. Hence, humans, unlike inanimate objects, are not merely passive recipients of environmental stimuli (e.g. stressors) but instead actively seek out environments consequent to the experience.

3. The analogy between humans and inanimate materials does not hold up because the determinants of resilience are known for inanimate objects. For example, the amount of carbon added to iron to form steel largely determines the magnitude of resilience of the material. A small concentration of carbon results in soft and malleable steel. A high concentration of carbon produces a brittle material. In humans, the "ingredients" comprising the putative trait of resilience are virtually unknown. In other words, no factor has been identified which negatively covaries with liability status to outcome.

4. Although constructs like *hardiness, competence* and *ego resilience* have been advanced to explain individual differences in response to the effects of stress; their predictive validity remains unproven. Unlike inanimate materials, the factors which determine variation in the child's adjustment during or following a stressor are not known. Indeed, the same stressor can either promote or attenuate behavior deviation contingent on the interaction with other factors.

It is consensually recognized that many children who experience extreme or prolonged stress ultimately have good behavioral outcomes, while some of those raised under more auspicious conditions do not. Therefore, the causal factors cannot be simply attributed to having a high or low score on a trait such as resilience. Rather, outcome is determined by the person-environment interactions that enable adaptation. As will be discussed in a later section, this outcome can be conceptualized as the result of the development of the *liability phenotype* within the limits of the *norm of reaction*. The norm of reaction (Dobzhansky, 1951) is the distribution of phenotypic values for a particular trait that is possible for an individual genotype. The term *liability* was introduced to human genetics by Falconer (1965) *"to express not only the individual innate tendency to develop or contract the disease, i.e., his susceptibility in the usual sense, but also the whole combination of external circumstances that make him more or less likely to develop the disease . . ."* If we could quantitatively measure this latent trait, *"it would give us a graded scale of the degree of affectedness or of normality and we should find that all individuals above a certain value exhibited the disease and all below it did not"* (p. 52). Phenotypic values surpassing a certain point on the scale of the liability (e.g., defined by DSM-IV diagnostic criteria), the *threshold*, are ascribed a diagnostic label and the person is deemed "affected." Obviously, the notion of liability can be applied both to so-called non-Mendelian and Mendelian disorders, with, respectively, normal and dichotomous phenotypic distributions corresponding to the differences in the mode of inheritance. Mendelian, or single-locus, disorders have only one genetic polymorphism contributing to the liability variation (if we disregard the variation in the severity of the disorder which may depend both on the genetic and environmental factors). Liabilities to polygenic (or multifactorial) disorders vary due to multiple genetic polymorphisms, environmental factors, and their interactions. It should be pointed out that terms "polygenic" and "multifactorial" do not indicate, as is often assumed, that the number of factors participating in the *etiology* of the disorder is higher than one. It would be tautological, since any disorder develops as a function of the whole organism interacting with the environment. Rather, these terms indicate the existence of multiple sources of *variation*, genetic and non-genetic, in the liability. Genetic causes of the phenotypic variation can be summarily termed *genetic predisposition* to the disorder. Variation in the liability is expressed, in subthreshold phenotypes, in individual differences in the risk for the disorder, and, in suprathreshold phenotypes, in the variation in the severity of the disorder. The individual phenotype for the liability to a behavioral disorder such as substance abuse changes during the lifetime, along with the changes in drug use behavior and severity of dependence. The cardinal assumption in this framework is that understanding the quality of interaction between the organism and the environment in psychosocial development is central to explaining individual differences on biopsychological traits. The notion of *resilience* in this perspective is superfluous as well as too amorphous to facilitate clarification of the ontogenetic trajectory culminating in either favorable or unfavorable outcomes.

The Basis of Individual Differences

A phenotype can be defined as an individual value on any observed characteristic (trait) of the organism. Figure 1 depicts the determinants of phenotypes. From birth onward, the individual manifests phenotypes for manifold traits spanning biological and psychological processes. Research into the antecedents of psychopathology and substance abuse has intensively explored a wide range of biochemical, physiological, cognitive, emotional and motivational traits as contributors to the variation in liability or covarying with it. It is noteworthy that it is population variation in a liability (e.g., to drug abuse) rather than an individual phenotype (e.g., drug abuse) which is, in fact, targeted in all such studies, even though the goal may be formulated as evaluating the relationship between a particular characteristic and "drug abuse." In other words, the main aim of research is to elucidate the mechanisms of phenotypic variation in the liability, which would allow us to influence these mechanisms using efficient preventive and treatment interventions resulting in under-the-threshold liability phenotypes.

To review the heuristic value of the notion of resilience in solving this problem, let us consider causes of phenotypic differences between individuals in more detail.

With the exception of monozygotic twins, everyone's genetic makeup or genotype is unique. As the result of differential exposure to environments occurring from the *in utero* period onward, even monozygotic twins become phenotypically different on numerous traits. This is evidenced most dramatically by the consistent observation that the concordance rate for monozygotic twins for all psychiatric and behavioral disorders is far less

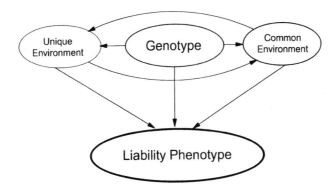

Figure 1. Genetic and environmental determinants of liability phenotypes.

than 100%. In the general population, therefore, phenotypic variation on the majority of traits results from both genotypic and environmental differences. This corresponds to a less-than-100% *heritability* of the trait—a measure of the contribution of differences between individual genotypes in the phenotypic variation in this trait in a given population at a certain time. Importantly, heritability estimates obtained in one population cannot be automatically assumed to be the same in another population and cannot be used to explain phenotypic differences *between* populations (even if heritability in each population were unity, phenotypic differences between populations could be totally environmental). It should be emphasized that heritability as well as its environmental complement in phenotypic variation (sometimes termed *environmentality*) does not have any direct relation to the causes of phenotypes (e.g., etiology of a disorder). By definition, heritability and environmentality refer only to the causes of phenotypic variation and covariation in the population. Clearly, if *"it is important to avoid such shorthand expressions as 'height is genetic' when really we mean 'individual differences in height are mainly genetic'"* (Neale & Cardon, 1992, p. 4), it is even more important when we consider psychological traits. For instance, even if heritability of the liability to substance abuse were in fact 100%, it would neither give us information about the causes of a particular individual's drug dependence nor tell us how to treat (or, as some might think, not to treat, because it is "genetic") this person's addiction. Specifically, preventing an individual from exposure to drugs would prevent his/her drug use and abuse regardless of heritability. Such a heritability would tell us, however, that, in the population where this estimate was obtained, variation in relevant environmental conditions is negligible compared to relevant genotypic variation (this situation could probably be observed, for instance, if everybody was getting the same exposure to a drug as a matter of everyday routine). In other words, within the range of *natural* environmental conditions varying between individuals, no difference between them is influential enough to influence variation in liability. However, for many disorders, when the liability is far from being 100% heritable, efficient treatment means and measures are not encountered within the range of natural environmental conditions (e.g., synthetic antibiotics). Conversely, the treatment of a disorder, when the liability has a heritability close to 100%, can be environmental. For instance, the natural variation in the liability to phenylketonuria (PKU) is almost entirely due to variation in one gene encoding an enzyme (phenylalanine hydroxylase, PAH) which converts phenylalanine into thyrosine. In individuals homozygous for the defective allele of this gene, the enzyme is inactive, and phenylalanine is accumulated and metabolized through an alternative pathway into neurotoxic phenylpyruvate. As all natural foods contain phenylalanine at a level sufficient to produce the disorder in such individuals, *natural* environment does not influence the phenotypic variation. Nonetheless, PKU is prevented environmentally, with an *artificial* diet low in phenylalanine.

Under natural conditions, the PKU liability distribution is dichotomous (presence/absence of the disorder) and strictly corresponds to the dichotomous distribution of the genetic predisposition to the disorder: no predisposition (homozygotes for the normal PAH allele and heterozygotes) and the presence of the predisposition (homozygotes for the mutant PAH allele). As can be seen, the notion of resilience is inapplicable in this situation since phenylalanine is either not a stressor (without the predisposition), or there is no successful adaptation. With the introduction of a low-phenylalanine diet, the liability in the genetically predisposed individuals decreases inasmuch as the PAH deficiency is diagnosed in time, and the formula is available and used. In addition, the *in utero* form of PKU has to be prevented: PAH-deficient women have to resume using the formula during pregnancy to preclude the harmful effect of their high phenylalanine levels on their offspring's development. Obviously, the notion of resilience is still inapplicable in this situation, where phenylalanine is simply removed from the environment when it can be an "adversity" or "stressor." Therefore, the notion of resilience, in contrast to liability, does not have universal applicability. This makes the usage of the concept of resilience questionable at best. Let us, however, consider its utility in more complex cases, particularly where attempts are made to apply this notion to psychosocial development.

Unlike monogenically inherited liabilities (e.g., to PKU, hemophilia, etc.), liabilities to psychopathology, behavior disorder, and substance abuse involve a number of genes as well as environmental factors contributing to the phenotypic variation. Accordingly, in keeping with the central limit theorem, phenotypes for these liabilities and other behavioral traits (sensation seeking, social conformity, IQ, etc.) are normally distributed in the population. The phenotypes that are described as resilient are, in fact, subthreshold on the liability scale while being high on the traits (or environmental characteristics, stressors, adversities) statistically associated with high liability. It should be noted that while the liability phenotype is the actual *individual* phenotype, individual resilience is evaluated *post hoc* as an *individual* outcome under conditions considered to be adversities based on *population* data. Arguably, an extreme phenotype (high IQ, low sensation seeking disposition) can be construed to convey resilience; however, as noted above, this is only when the outcome is favorable in spite of adversities. The term resilience by itself in this context does not capture the salient feature of surmounting adversity but merely denotes the person's position on the liability axis.

A person's liability phenotype is determined by the interaction among

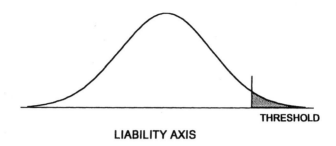

THRESHOLD

LIABILITY AXIS

Figure 2. Liability axis depicting threshold for a disorder.

the individual's phenotypes for all traits and environmental factors contributing to the variation in the liability to a particular disorder. Their combination is thus a multidimensional liability trait. This is depicted in Figure 2. Upon surpassing a threshold, such as DSM-IV criteria, the person is classified as affected, thereby qualifying for a diagnosis.

How does the construct of resilience fit in this multivariate schema? The person's position on the liability axis is the conjoint influence of factors that augment liability as well as factors that reduce liability. It is superficially plausible to invoke the construct of resilience for those influences that are liability reducing; however, as noted previously, this does not capture the central concept of the process–namely the capacity to rebound from stress. With respect to substance abuse, liability phenotypes appear to be associated with EEG pattern, stress reactivity, behavioral self-regulation, cognitive capacity, information processing efficiency, physique, and quality of affect (see Tarter & Vanyukov, 1994 and Tarter, Moss, & Vanyukov, 1995 for reviews). How phenotypes for these and other characteristics interact to determine the person's position on the liability axis is poorly understood but is arguably the most important task confronting researchers concerned with elucidating the etiology of psychopathology and behavior disorder. Although it can be argued that particular phenotypes for some traits can offset the influence of other factors to reduce liability (e.g., high IQ may offset the negative influence of high impulsivity), there is no advantage to invoke the term *resilience* to distinguish these liability-reducing phenotypes as a special category. Not only will this be contradictory to parsimony, but, additionally, it has no obvious heuristic value. Instead, it is more accurate and simple in practical settings to employ objective and affectively neutral terminology such as *liability augmenter* and *liability reducer* to describe the determinants of the person's position on the liability axis. Even this would require the knowledge that at least the direction of the influence of these factors is unconditional, otherwise the conditions (individual values on other characteristics) have to be elucidated.

Resilience and Development

The person's phenotype for multifactorial traits, particularly liability to a behavioral disorder may not be fixed throughout life. It may be alterable concomitant to individual variation in rate of maturation and transaction with a continually changing environment. The overarching aim of etiological research in developmental psychopathology is to delineate the interaction between the person's phenotypic characteristics and environmental influences so as to quantify the person's risk of experiencing an adverse outcome at specific times in life.

The construct of resilience is proposed to depict the scenario in which a person, by having experienced an adversity that resulted in putatively high liability at Time 1, manifests a satisfactory outcome at Time N. This developmental pathway is illustrated in Figure 3 as *pathway A*. These individuals are presented as role models, and commonly elevated to the status of heroes, to reaffirm the shared societal belief that is possible to succeed in a democracy despite adversity. It is, however, possible that the presumed stressor, instead of being a liability promoter based on population estimates, actually serves to decrease liability *in the particular person*. This situation was observed, for instance, when the frequency of alcoholism in the sons of alcoholics who had been raised by their alcoholic parents was found to be somewhat lower compared to the adopted away sons of alcoholics (Goodwin, Schulsinger, Hermansen, Guze, & Winokur, 1973). An increase, on the average, in genetic predisposition to alcoholism may thus be offset in some children who live with an alcoholic parent due perhaps to the aversive effect of observing the consequences of parental drinking rather than the offspring's presumed resilience. Other individuals under the same conditions, on the contrary, could imitate parental behavior, which would increase their already elevated risk.

An equally important developmental pathway which cannot be studied at all within the resilience framework pertains to the scenario in which no appreciable adversities can be found but the person develops an adverse outcome (*pathway B*). These individuals often become topics of fascination in the media. Why a seemingly well-adjusted person having social and economic advantages manifests a bad outcome is perplexing. These are the notorious criminal trials of the rich and famous as well as the good kid gone bad. This unexpected scenario challenges assumptions about our capacity to conceptualize the reasons for this developmental pathway apart from simplistically and incorrectly assigning negative attributions to the person, the person's parents, socioeconomic factors, or demographic factors as *the* cause for the unfavorable outcome.

The link between the presence of adversity to result in high initial liability and good outcome, *Pathway A*, as all other individual developmental trajectories, can be readily understood within the framework of developmental behavior genetics. There is no need to impute the presence of a resiliency trait to understand this pathway provided that two well-established notions are taken into consideration: the *unique (nonshared) environment* and *epigenesis*.

Figure 3 (*pathway A*) presents the developmental scenario in which a child having high initial liability due to "adversities" experiences a good outcome. A good outcome is defined herein as the absence of a diagnosable condition at a particular age (e.g., Time 1, Time 2, etc.). Another,

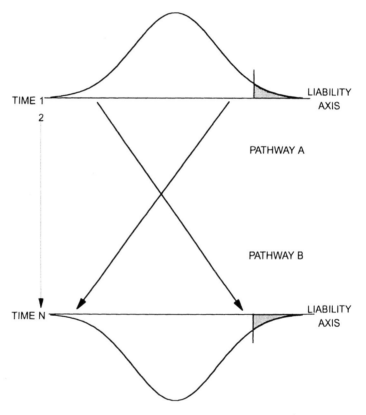

Figure 3. Differential outcomes based on outset position on the liability axis.

equally pertinent scenario, is when the initial liability is low (e.g., due to a low genetic predisposition) and does not change much despite adversities. The fact that these two completely different scenarios can both be interpreted as manifestations of resilience further illustrates the low heuristic value of this notion.

In Figure 4, the factors influencing the shape of the developmental trajectory are illustrated in a hypothetical scenario. As can be seen, beginning at age one, a constellation of liability augmenting and liability reducing factors ($V_1, V_2 \ldots V_n$, etc.) interact among each other to comprise an overall resultant vector. This composite vector (R), having by definition both a quantity and direction, initially shifts the person's position on the liability axis such that when measured at age one, the child has greater liability; that is, moves closer to the threshold for diagnosis. At age two in this hypothetical scenario, the resultant vector has the effect of slightly deflecting the child toward the normative side of the liability distribution. Ultimately, in the example presented in Figure 4, the changing combination of vectors occurring during ontogeny culminates in a negative outcome. By connecting the phenotypic values on the liability axis at multiple ages during development, it is theoretically possible to chart the trajectory to outcome.

Clearly, there are liability augmenting and reducing factors that affect the person's position on the liability axis (e.g., family, school, peer influences). Hence, the shape of the trajectory linking outset liability to outcome has infinite variations in the population. The fact that the trajectory is unique for each individual will have to be eventually dealt with in studies concerned with elucidating etiology of psychopathology and substance abuse. To date, researchers have not emphasized the importance of clarifying the relationship between the individual liability phenotype and organism-environment interactions. This is due in large part to the fact that the liability is a latent trait on which the variation has yet to be accounted for by observed indices. Another important reason may be the characterization of the set of the relevant environmental variables that could comprise an *envirotype* (analogous to genotype) of the person is difficult. The ability of such a set to account for the environmental component of the liability variation will need testing employing genetically informative designs.

The scenario illustrated in Figure 4 is only one of an infinite number of potential developmental pathways. In keeping with the fact that liability is modifiable and the environment is continually changing, the developmental pathway is not linear. Consequently, it is an extremely difficult task to predict distal outcomes. The complexity of this problem notwithstanding, it is important to emphasize that primary prevention consists of reducing liability by implementing an intervention that fosters normative

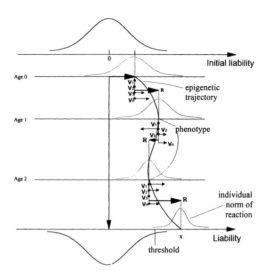

Figure 4. Hypothetical developmental trajectory culminating in a disorder.

behavior. Typically, the format involves applying the same intervention to all individuals. In view of the above discussion, it is clear why no prevention program has yet been, or likely will be, impressively successful. Without accounting for the individual based factors that determine liability in conjunction with specific environmental factors capable of shifting liability phenotype to the more normative side of the distribution, robust lasting liability reduction is not possible.

Nonshared Environment

As shown in Figure 1, phenotypes are the product of genetic influences interacting with two types of environments. The shared environment refers to those aspects, which are common to members of the family. These facets may include features like crime rate in the neighborhood, the characteristics of the domicile, and socioeconomic status. However, the perplexing enigma confronting researchers and practitioners alike is the common observation that siblings, including monozygotic twins, often have divergent outcomes even though they have the same genotype and shared environment.

How then does one explain the emergence of a good outcome in a person having a potential for the development of high liability, as can be presumed, for instance, when the monozygotic co-twin has severe substance dependence? Since monozygotic twins have identical genotypes, the answer lies in the important effects of the nonshared environment. These facets of the environment are unique to the individual. There are obviously numerous unique environmental factors that could alter the person's position on the liability axis. These include, for example, a particular quality of relationship with another member of the nuclear or extended family, peer affiliation patterns, recreational environment, classroom, and quality of interaction with a teacher.

Resilience is the construct or trait that has been proposed to explain the development of a positive outcome despite the presence of adversities. Based on the above discussion, rather than impute a new trait, it is suggested herein that this process could be parsimoniously understood as the product of phenotype-environment interactions. In this context, the unique environment is especially salient since, by definition, important components of the shared environment may be liability augmenting for the whole population deemed to be at risk (e.g., poverty, high crime neighborhood, etc.). How then does the unique environment offset the effects of the adverse shared environment and/or high genetic predisposition to reduce liability?

The answer resides in the innumerable, idiosyncratic, and chance opportunities to engage in interactions with facets of the environment that are particular to the person's liability phenotype. Being the favorite child in a dysfunctional family, having athletic talent and winning a college scholarship and a neighbor who serves as a surrogate parent are several examples. Perhaps the most common, albeit untested, nonshared environmental factors that can deflect high liability youths to a good outcome are bonding with a normative adult and connecting to a socially normative best friend. Whatever the specific nonshared environmental influence, the effect is the same; namely, a child having high initial liability ultimately achieves a good outcome.

Epigenesis

It is well established that prior phenotypes influence the acquisition of successive phenotypes concomitant to environmental interaction. This process is referred to as epigenesis. Behavior concomitant to person-environment interactions that reduce liability can be positively reinforced, ignored, or punished. Where positive reinforcement occurs, an epigenetic process can be set in motion that produces more normative phenotypes that in turn biases the developmental trajectory toward a good outcome. Just as success begets success, reinforcing normative behavior begets normative

behavior. Ignoring or punishing the person having high liability concomitant to normative environmental interactions on the other hand augments
liability. Thus, in order to understand the link between high liability and
good outcome, it is essential to elucidate how the repertoire of phenotypes
is successively acquired such that each prior phenotype influences reactions
to environments (e.g., coping) as well as selection of environments (e.g.
joining in sports instead of a gang). In this framework, there is no need to
posit a construct of resilience.

Are There Practical Implications of the Resilience Construct?

The most prudent and cost-effective allocation of resources in prevention is to target intervention to those individuals in the population who
have high initial liability (due to high genetic predisposition to the disorder and/or unfavorable family environment). Considering that making
alterations in genotype, even if it were possible, is hardly ethical, three types
of strategies can be implemented. First, intervention can be directed at
changing the person by changing his/her individual environment. Prevention strategies using this approach attempt to improve self-esteem, coping
skills and social skills (Botvin & Tarter, 1988). Imparting knowledge about
the potentially harmful effects of drugs is perhaps the most common type
of intervention. Pharmacological approaches aimed at ameliorating psychiatric disturbance and behavioral disorder may be effective in lowering
liability, although empirical investigations have yet to be conducted.
Second, prevention can be directed at changing the global environment.
Interventions typifying this approach include establishing policy and laws
to regulate access to, and use of, abusable substances. And third, interventions can focus on modifying the covariation between specific facets of liability with specific environmental influences. Preventions of this type are
oriented to modifying the quality of interaction between specific attributes
(phenotypes) of the person and factors in the environment which augment
liability. Despite the well-accepted fact that outcome is the product of
person-environment interaction, the science and practice of preventions
have not embraced an interactional framework that emphasizes the importance of *interaction* between individual characteristics and environmental
characteristics. The reasons for this are difficult to comprehend apart from
the fact that most intervention oriented researchers and practitioners may
not be informed about the importance of individual differences as a determinant of liability variation, or lack an appreciation of the mechanisms
underlying person-environment interactions.

For the reasons discussed above, it would appear important in an interactional framework to modify components of environment that are related to the variation in liability. For example, high sensation seeking, affective disturbance, high aggressivity, and difficult temperament are among the phenotypes that are well known to be associated with increased liability to substance abuse (Tarter & Vanyukov, 1994). In certain environmental contexts, these phenotypes may not culminate in an adverse outcome. Upon identifying the environments that are liability reducing, effective preventions can be implemented. The goal of prevention, therefore, is to marshal the components of the environment that are able to deflect the developmental trajectory toward normative outcome and incorporate them into a comprehensive program of intervention. Within this perspective, there is no need to hypothesize a resilience trait. More importantly, the perspective proposed herein avoids the need to apply negative labels. For example, an unfavorable outcome, or a failed intervention, cannot be attributed to low resilience in the person. This type of counter-productive thinking approaches a "blame the victim" perspective. Successful or poor adjustment does not ultimately reside in some abstruse property of the person such as resilience but instead emanates from the interaction between the person's phenotype and environment. The label or attribute of resilience does not enhance understanding of etiology or guide the strategy for prevention.

Absence of Validity of the Construct of Resilience

As noted earlier, the attribute or label of resilience is applied on a *post hoc* basis. Hence, its heuristic value and practical usefulness are at best dubious. Prediction is extraordinarily difficult because of the nonlinear developmental pathway linking liability to outcome. Surmounting adversity at one time in life does not portend success at another time. Successful coping with combat during war does not portend adjustment in peacetime society. Surmounting the emotional trauma of early age physical or sexual abuse is not necessarily innocuous to mid-life depression, cause for divorce, or drug abuse even though there is an extended hiatus of successful adjustment. The reason for this unpredictability is simply that the epigenetic trajectory is continually being modified, biasing the person toward favorable or unfavorable outcome, concomitant to interactions with manifold aspects of the physical and social environment. In effect, the lack of capacity for long-term prediction inevitably results in a high rate of false positives and false negatives. The notion of resilience is thus overly simplistic by assuming that a personal attribute or complement of attributes at one time has substantial and lasting effects at another time in life. For example, who would have predicted that Bruno Bettelheim, the renowned child psychologist, would commit suicide in a nursing home after having surmounted the unimaginable horrors of a concentration camp? Does his suicide imply a lack of resilience? Simply stated, the construct of resilience has neither construct validity nor predictive validity, and there is no scientifically justifiable reason to assume the existence of this trait. Clearly, the term has substantial connotative meaning. As pointed out in the introduction of this discussion, it evokes sentiments that are collectively shared as part of our beliefs and social values. Based on both theoretical and practical considerations presented herein, it is becoming increasingly evident that this construct not only lacks denotative meaning but has obscured thinking about the etiology and prevention of psychopathology, behavior disorder, and substance abuse.

ACKNOWLEDGMENTS.   This work was supported by a center grant from the National Institute on Drug Abuse to the consortium of the University of Pittsburgh and St. Francis Medical Center.

References

American Heritage Dictionary. (1978). Boston: Houghton Mifflin.

Botvin, G., & Tortu, S. (1988). Preventing adolescent substance abuse through life skills training. In R. Price (Ed.), *Fourteen Ounces of Prevention: A Casebook for Practitioner*. Washington, DC: American Psychological Association, 98–110.

Dobzhansky, T. G. (1951). *Genetics and the Origin of Species*. New York: Columbia University Press.

Falconer, D. (1965). The inheritance of liability to certain diseases estimated from the incidence among relatives. *Annals of Human Genetics, 29*, 51–86.

Goodwin, D. W., Schulsinger, F., Hermansen, L., Guze, S. B., & Winokur, G. (1973). Alcohol problems in adoptees raised apart from alcoholic parents. *Archives of General Psychiatry, 28*, 238–243.

Masten, A. S., Best, K. M., & Garmezy, N. (1991). Resilience and development: Contributions from the study of children who overcome adversity. *Development and Psychopathology, 2*, 425–444.

Neale, M., & Cardon, L. (1992). *Methodology for Genetic Studies of Twins and Families*. Boston: Kluwer Academic Publishers.

Tarter, R., & Vanyukov, M. (1994). Alcoholism: A developmental disorder. *Journal of Consulting and Clinical Psychology, 62*, 1096–1107.

Tarter, R., Moss, H., & Vanyukov, M. (1995). Behavior genetics and the etiology of alcoholism. In H. Begleiter & B. Kissin (Eds.), *The Genetics of Alcoholism* (pp. 294–326). New York: Oxford University Press.

5

Drug Use, Resilience, and the Myth of the Golden Child

Fred Beauvais and Eugene R. Oetting

Introduction

Kaplan (1999), in this volume, questions whether the concept of resilience is useful. He notes that the definitions tend to be vague, that it is not clear whether definitions relate to outcomes or processes, and that resilience is likely to be confused with protective factors. A frequent stereotype illustrates some of Kaplan's points. It assumes that resilience is innate, that there are resilient children who simply resist the effects of adverse environments, i.e., the myth of the "golden child." The image is of a ghetto or barrio, visualized as a sea of muck and grime. Standing in the midst of this fetid squalor is a pristine, clean and shining "golden child", a resilient child with the built in ability to resist temptation and shed off the effects of poverty and prejudice. But all three elements of this stereotype are false, the squalid ghetto, the "golden child" and the idea that this represents resilience. Resilience is not an innate characteristic that magically prevented the negative environment from influencing this child. The real causes of the child's success are protective factors that provide attitudes and skills that allow the child to resist the effects of the environmental risk factors that are present. These protective factors led to the child's prosocial

Fred Beauvais • Tri-Ethnic Center for Prevention Research, Colorado State University, Fort Collins, Colorado 80523.   **Eugene R. Oetting** • Tri-Ethnic Center for Prevention Research, Colorado State University, Fort Collins, Colorado 80523.

Resilience and Development: Positive Life Adaptations, edited by Glantz and Johnson. Kluwer Academic/Plenum Publishers, New York, 1999.

attitudes and resistance skills and were developed through positive learning experiences, so if the "golden child" stands in the ghetto, it is because the ghetto is not a purely negative environment. It is, instead, a rich and complex mixture of family dysfunction and family support, of the breakdown of values and of strong traditions, of both antisocial and prosocial attitudes and beliefs. The resources to produce success are available in the ghetto or barrio, so it is not surprising to find successful children in those environments.

The "golden child" may appear magical because it is not always obvious why one child is successful and another is not. Given what we know about risk and protective factors, if we studied these children in detail, we would probably find at least one personal interaction where a combination of the child's personal traits and those of a significant adult allowed that child to learn prosocial attitudes and life skills. Where the family is dysfunctional or the neighborhood provides predominantly negative influences, we would likely find that there was some special person in the successful child's life, the influential grandmother, a committed teacher, or a special friend who provided the prosocial interactions that created the "golden child." The concept of resilience is not needed to explain what happened to this child; the balance of risk and protective factors provides an adequate explanation. Nevertheless, the idea of resilience can add a further dimension to understanding the etiology of drug use and other problems. But first it is necessary to define resilience so that it avoids false stereotypes and so that the definition distinguishes resilience from risk and protective factors.

Risk Factors

Risk factors for drug use include such characteristics as poor neighborhood environments, family dysfunction, school dropout, drug use by friends, traits such as high anger or sensation seeking, and many other social and psychological characteristics. A thorough review of risk and protective factors is provided by Hawkins, Catalano, and Miller (1992). Risk factors can differ depending on the problem, but usually a risk factor for drug use operates through increasing the probability of incorporation of deviant norms, generally by increasing the chances of involvement with deviant peers (Oetting & Beauvais, 1986, 1987a, 1987b). The total number of different risk factors may be important. There is research evidence of a linear relationship, with increasing risk of drug use for each additional risk factor (Maddahian, Newcomb, & Bentler, 1986).

Protective Factors

Protective factors against drug use include characteristics such as strong family sanctions against drugs, religious identification, school success, etc. Some risk and protective factors are defined as opposite poles of the same dimension, but this is not essential; being in the lowest quartile for trait anger, for example, might not protect against drug use, but being in the upper quartile is a risk factor. A protective factor against drug abuse usually operates by increasing the chances of incorporation of prosocial norms, reducing the chances of involvement with deviant peers, and reducing the probability of drug involvement. There is evidence that the balance of risk and protective factors is important; that if more risk factors are present, more protective factors are needed to compensate (Werner, 1989).

Resilience

In order to contribute to the understanding of drug use, resilience has to be defined differently from risk and protective factors. Resilience, therefore, is defined here as the ability to tolerate, to adapt to, or to overcome life crises. Resilience reduces the chances of drug use because, under some circumstances, the inability to deal with a crisis can place a person at greater risk for drug involvement. This definition distinguishes resilience from protective factors. A protective factor helps set a trajectory that reduces the probability of getting involved with deviant peers and of subsequent drug use. It tends to operate consistently and all the time. In contrast, resilience consists of those personal and social resources for dealing with the problems and crises that are bound to appear in life, and resilience becomes important *only* when those problems appear. Protective factors save you from disaster; resilience lets you bounce back. For example, an adolescent crisis, such as the breakup of a relationship, can lead to negative feelings, among them a sense of rejection and possibly self-derogation. Kaplan (1986) has shown that self-derogation can increase the chances that a child will bond with deviant peers and therefore get involved with drugs. The resilient youth, however, when meeting the same crisis, may have the personal and social resources that help deal with the crisis, reducing the probability of negative emotional and behavioral consequences.

A protective factor may or may not produce resilience. A high level of parental monitoring is usually a protective factor for drug use. But in the extreme, while families that severely restrict peer contacts can prevent drug use because children from those families have no contact with peers who might use drugs, those overprotected and restricted youth may not develop resilience. They may lack confidence in peer relationships and may not develop the social skills that could help them deal with crises and problems that occur later in life. When the youth leaves the protective family circle, the youth may lack resilience.

Resilience is often defined as a personal characteristic, but there are also resilience factors that exist outside of the person. These are external resources that help a person deal with crises. Some are both protective and resilience factors. A closely linked extended family can make family/child bonding stronger and therefore be a protective factor. The extended family can also provide emotional support and advice in a crisis, particularly if that crisis involves illness or other problems in the primary family, and therefore it can also become a resilience factor. There are resilience factors that are outside of the person, but do not serve as protective factors. They help the person deal with crises. Examples would include legal services, rape counseling services and the availability of treatment for sexually transmitted diseases. Personal resilience can include the attitudes and skills needed to identify and make sure of these external resources.

Resilience and Cultural Identification

A high level of cultural identification can be a resilience factor. When the family has a high level of cultural identification, it means that the family is functioning in a cultural context where its members are meeting cultural demands successfully and where its members are being strongly reinforced by that culture in ways that are meaningful to family members; the family is successful in that culture (see Oetting, 1993; Oetting & Beauvais, 1990–1991). The child in that family lives in a secure and stable environment and has a chance to learn competencies, develop strengths, and incorporate norms that provide a basis for personal resilience. That family is also likely to provide a protective and secure base for exploration of life alternatives; when a crisis occurs, the family provides support and assistance. Further, the family's success in the culture means that the child has access to cultural resources to deal with crises. In western culture these might involve legal assistance, counseling or psychotherapy, in some ethnic minority cultures methods for dealing with crises might include a network of connections ("pala", in Puerto Rico), access to folk medicine or, among American Indians, healing ceremonies.

Resilience and Drug Use

A strong family, with prosocial values and beliefs, and with strong sanctions against using drugs, provides a foundation that is both a protective factor and that helps produce personal resilience. Schools and peers are other sources, both of protective factors and for development of resilience. Success in school serves as a protective factor, because successful youth tend to form peer clusters that are more likely to have prosocial norms and avoid drugs. School success also provides youth with self-confidence and a belief in their ability to solve problems, both factors in resilience. Peer acceptance can actually be a risk factor for drug use, since much of adolescent drug use is social and peer involvement can include social use of drugs. But if the association is with peers who are only involved in drug use as a social activity and who are not involved in other crime and delinquency, those peer associations are a risk factor for drug use, but they may, at the same time, be resilience factors. Peer acceptance can involve development of self-esteem and learning of skills for successfully dealing with peer problems, skills that may produce resilience when peer relationships, later on, create a serious problem. Further, the peers themselves may be supportive in time of need, for instance, when a family or other personal crisis occurs.

The actual links between resilience and drug use may be hard to measure. Resilience has an effect when a life crisis emerges, until then it is only a potential. Resilience, therefore, does not directly influence drug use; it has an effect only where inadequate handling of a life crisis might lead to problems that increase the potential for drug use. But all crises do not increase the potential for drug use, so even when crises do appear, resilience may not influence drug use.

These indirect and partial effects of resilience on drug use may provide some portion of an explanation for the failure to find strong relationships between some personal traits and drug use when logic would suggest there should be a relationship. Self esteem self confidence, lack of depression, cultural identification, and internal locus of control should all be personal assets and should, therefore, prevent drug involvement, but they tend to have only weak relationships with drug use. That may occur because the influence of these traits on drug use occurs predominantly through their contribution to resilience. These traits may increase resilience, but resilience only comes into play at times of crises, so they can only inoculate against drug use in limited circumstances. Resilience may be more important when predicting outcomes other than drug use. While there may be only small correlations between resilience and drug use, resilience may be a very important factor in prevention of problems that arise from crises such as situational depression or post traumatic stress disorder.

Summary

Resilience can take its place with risk factors and protective factors in understanding drug use and other problems. It adds a dimension that can be important for understanding how a few youth avoid drug involvement despite exposure to serious life crises. This suggested role of resilience also indicates that approaches to prevention should include attention to developing personal resilience, the attitudes and skills needed for dealing with crises. It also suggests that attention be paid to external resilience factors, resources that assist in crises. Further, developing resilience is likely to be valuable for young people even though it does not influence drug use. All lives include crises, and the resources and the abilities to deal with them are useful. Since resilience is probably related to self esteem and to cultural identification, it suggests that prevention programs probably should incorporate elements aimed at improving self esteem and increasing cultural identification despite past failures to demonstrate that they have a strong direct influence on drug use. But if resilience is to be included as an element in prevention, it must be remembered that the role played by resilience is complex and is likely to be indirect, and that resilience may come into play only in the resolution of crises. Even programs that successfully increase resilience may not reduce drug use except in individual cases where lack of resilience prevents resolution of a crisis and leads to circumstances that place the person at risk. On the other hand, increasing resilience can provide protection not only for the moment, and not only for one incident, but for an extended future. Since no life is crisis free, resilience could be one of the more important assets in life.

References

Hawkins, J. D., Catalano, R. F., & Miller, J. Y. (1992). Risk and protective factors for alcohol and other drug problems in adolescence and early adulthood: Implications for substance abuse prevention. *Psychological Bulletin, 112*(1), 64–105.
Kaplan, H. B. (1986). *Social psychology of self-referent behavior.* New York: Plenum Press.
Kaplan, H. (1999). Toward an understanding of resilience: A critical review of definitions and models. In M. Glantz & J. Johnson (Eds.), *Resilience and development: Positive life adaptations.* New York: Plenum Press.
Maddahian, E., Newcomb, M. D., & Bentler, P. M. (1986). Risk factors for drug use among adolescents: Concurrent and longitudinal analyses. *American Journal of Public Health, 76*(5), 525–531.

Oetting, E. R. (1993). Orthogonal cultural identification: Theoretical links between cultural identification and substance use. In M. Delarosa & J. L. Reicio Adrados (Eds.), *Drug abuse among minority youth: Methoological issues and recent research advances* (pp. 32–56). National Institute on Drug Abuse, #130 (NIH #93-3479).

Oetting, E. R., & Beauvais, F. (1986). Peer cluster theory: Drugs and the adolescent. *Journal of Counseling and Development, 65*(1), 17–22.

Oetting, E. R., & Beauvais, F. (1987a). Common elements in youth drug abuse: Peer clusters and other psychosocial factors. *Journal of Drug Issues, 17*(1&2), 133–151.

Oetting, E. R., & Beauvais, F. (1987b). Peer cluster theory, socialization characteristics, and adolescent drug use: A path analysis. *Journal of Counseling Psychology, 34*(2), 205–213.

Oetting, E. R., & Beauvais, F. (1990–1991). Orthogonal cultural identification theory: The cultural identification of minority adolescents. *The International Journal of the Addictions, 25*(5A & 6A), 655–685.

Werner, E. E. (1989). Vulnerability and resilience: A longitudinal perspective. In M. Brambring, F. Lösel, & H. Skowronek (Eds.), *Children at risk: Assessment, longitudinal research, and intervention* (pp. 158–172). New York: Aldine de Gruyter.

6

Analysis and Reconceptualization of Resilience

Meyer D. Glantz and Zili Sloboda

Introduction

The concept of resilience has strong intuitive appeal. Although the label, the denotations and the connotations of the concept vary (for a comprehensive review, see Kaplan, this volume, 1999), the basic notion has persisted in both scientific and non-scientific views of human behavior. Resilience, which has been defined as "the process of, capacity for, or outcome of successful adaptation despite challenging or threatening circumstances" (Masten, Best, & Garmezy, 1990, page 426) seems to describe a quality that is often attributed to people and is a common interpretation and explanation of behavior. However, whether resilience is a quality (or a trait) at all and whether it is a useful explanatory concept are open questions. It is not the intention of this paper to review the literature on resilience; this has ably been done by others, (Kaplan, this volume, 1999; Masten, Best, & Garmezy, 1990; Rutter, 1990; Cowan, Cowan, & Schulz, 1996; Mrazek & Haggerty, 1994; Gore & Eckenrode, 1994; Anthony, 1987).

Meyer D. Glantz • Division of Epidemiology and Prevention Research, National Institute on Drug Abuse, National Institutes of Health, Bethesda, Maryland 20892. **Zili Sloboda** • Division of Epidemiology and Prevention Research. National Institute on Drug Abuse, National Institutes of Health, Bethesda, Maryland 20892.

Resilience and Development: Positive Life Adaptations, edited by Glantz and Johnson. Kluwer Academic/Plenum Publishers, New York, 1999.

The goal of this paper is to analyze the concept of resilience and propose a reconceptualization which may be useful[1].

Resilience describes a prevalent attribution and even a common subjective phenomenon or self-attribution. It is often the case that we observe that someone resists, overcomes, or recovers from major, if not seemingly, insurmountable problems, obstacles, failures, disabilities, self-destructive characteristics or weaknesses. When we see someone triumph over a strongly negative circumstance it is not unusual to feel that something special and inherent in that person or his/her environment was responsible. Similarly, most people have had the experience themselves of inner strength, resolve, persistence, or difficult sacrifice. This type of determinative model is pervasive in the way we view events, even those involving non-sentient organisms. If one tree in a grove resists a hurricane we attribute a quality of strength to the tree. If a plant recovers despite severe damage, we make an attribution of durability or hardiness. We even make similar attributions about inanimate objects that endure despite long or hard use; for example, we believe there is something special about an old car that keeps on running long after its expected functional life.

Resilience or some variation of this idea is a concept that is explicitly if not tacitly implicit in almost all explanatory models of behavior ranging from the biological to the social. It may be an inextricable part of the ways in which we define and explain not only human behavior but virtually all phenomena with variable outcomes. However, while the stresses and the qualities that determine the endurance of an inanimate object or a non-sentient organism are often tangible, consensually agreed on, fairly constant over time and circumstances and probably measurable, the same is rarely true in attempts to understand human behavior.

Problems with the Concept

Unfortunately, the concept of resilience is heavily laden with subjective often unarticulated assumptions and it is fraught with major logical, measurement, and pragmatic problems. Serious concerns have been raised by researchers in the field about the value of the concept of resilience and how it has been measured in behavior research studies and how it has been

---

[1]The analytic observations and recommendations made here build on the previous work of others. When we have adopted a concept that has previously been suggested by others, we have cited these works. We apologize if we have failed to recognize or cite any relevant previous contributions. Readers are strongly encouraged to refer to the many excellent publications cited in this chapter.

used in the explanation of behavior and outcomes (e.g., Tarter & Vanyukov, this volume, 1999; Rutter, 1990; Richters & Weintraub, 1990; Kaplan, this volume, 1999; Luthar & Cushing, this volume, 1999; Beauvais & Oetting, this volume, 1999; Fisher et al., 1987). We share many of these concerns. We find that there is great diversity in the use of the concept; it is used variously as a quality, a trait, a process or an outcome. We have identified few attempts to assess resilience in which measurement problems do not cloud or eclipse the findings. There is no consensus on the referent of the term, standards for its application, or agreement on its role in explanations, models and theories. In sum, the problems and inconsistencies in measurements, findings, and interpretations in the published literature raise serious questions about the utility and heuristic value of the concept of resilience.

Despite the assertion that "resilience" has both significant conceptual and methodological problems, we are not recommending that the concept be abandoned. The phenomenon which Garmezy and his colleagues found so striking 50 years ago is just as compelling when observed today. There certainly are people who seem to have resisted or overcome presumably overwhelming problems, obstacles or stresses and most individuals report having had this experience at least to some degree. While the pure empiricist might be inclined to say that these are simply instances of incomplete information or failed predictions on the part of the observer, most people are inclined to make an attribution of some special "quality", effort or circumstance to the "resilient" person. In any case, given the history and appeal of the concept of resilience, it seems unlikely that either the scientific or lay communities would be willing to totally abandon its use. A reasonable approach is to salvage the useful aspects of the concept.

The attraction to the concept of "resilience" is captured by Cicchetti and Garmezy in their introduction to a series of articles in the 1993 special issue of *Development and Psychopathology* focusing on resilience (page 497). They state:

> "... it is especially refreshing to explore the more optimistic component of the psychopathology-risk equation, namely, resilience. What individual, familial, or societal factors stem the trajectory from risk to psychopathology, thereby resulting in adaptive outcomes even in the presence of adversity?"

The history of the "resilience movement" grows out of a literature that explores individuals' responses to major and often devastating stresses, experiences and conditions such as schizophrenia, poverty, and extreme physical and psychological trauma. For instance, natural history studies of schizophrenic patients usually focused on the typical modal negative outcomes while ignoring the positive, more adaptive outcomes of a small subset of the study populations. Because of this focus, the seemingly inevitable deterioration was considered so overwhelming that there was virtually no hope for the schizophrenic patients. When a small number of schizophrenics did not have the anticipated highly negative outcome, it seemed that there must be something special about these individuals and/or their circumstances. This was the beginning of the more scientific espousal of "resilience" (see Garmezy & Rutter, 1983). Some later investigations found that this more adaptive group of patients had a premorbid history that showed evidence of higher social and personal competence. Studies of children who experienced severe biological problems or extreme social and economic deprivation further demonstrated adaptive subgroups (Mrazek & Haggerty, 1994). These groups, evidencing unexpected positive outcomes and competencies, became the focus of several later studies that further influenced the development of "resilience models" that guided research on populations emerging from other stressor situations. The findings about "resilient" subgroups have fueled the hope that whatever enabled these individuals to overcome their problems might be helpful to other individuals facing extreme negative circumstances and the hope that research on resilience may lead to the development of more effective preventive and treatment interventions.

The concept of resilience not only reflects an important observation about unpredicted outcomes for some people but also a consensual recognition of a phenomenon. Even detractors of the concept of resilience generally agree that in some cases, at least some individuals who appear to be subject to extreme stressors or harmful influences and/or who appear themselves to demonstrate characteristics associated with dysfunctional, pathological or antisocial behaviors, do not follow the expected negative course. Instead they avoid what appears to be the likely outcome of the negative antecedents and function in a relatively healthy and adaptive manner. Even if it is unclear what led to the positive outcome or if different mechanisms may be operating, understanding the phenomenon is necessary (see Garmezy, 1985). We believe that this phenomenon should not just be discounted as being merely an incorrect prediction about a subgroup that was the result of poor data or overly pessimistic expectations. However, we are not recommending that the concept be maintained simply for the hope and optimism that it may offer. First, it should not be discarded because it encourages an important focus on a real and important phenomenon. Second, we believe that many unsupported hypotheses and much problematic research related to this phenomenon are the consequence of a logical weakness that is common in attempts to understand behavior. To simply discard the term "resilience" and adopt a synonym is to perpetuate a common conceptual flaw.

It is important to note that our concerns about the concept of resilience are not primarily semantic and do not relate to simple differences in definitions or usage of the word. The definition proposed by Masten et al (see above) is a reasonable one. Even if this definition were universally adopted, we would still maintain that the concept must be rethought and revised. The associated empirical problems relate to the difficulties in operationalizing and measuring the current application of the concept regardless of the definition used and to the failure to identify in research any universal quality, process or outcome which could consistently be construed as "resilience". As will be discussed in greater detail later, "resilience" does not have a consistent meaningful referent.

Fundamental to many models of human behavior is the tacit assumption that "normal" function and behavior is by nature basically healthy and adaptive and that negative outcomes must therefore be the product of negative influences. According to these types of "normal positive" views, positive outcomes are to be generally expected unless there are intervening negative influences (which would include absent positive ones). For example, it is not "normal" to abuse drugs, to commit crimes, to be depressed, etc. It follows that if there "should" have been a positive outcome and there was not, the logical question to ask is "why, what intervened? What altered the 'normal' trajectory"? To understand negative outcomes and behaviors, the primary task then becomes to identify the negative determinative factors. Positive outcomes only need to be accounted for when significant negative determinative factors are present and the predicted negative outcomes do not manifest. For the most part, these models tacitly assume that adequate positive influences are usually if not "naturally" present. Since most "normal positive" models are not designed to account for positive outcomes in the face of negative determinative factors, the result is often the invocation of a vaguely conceived conceptualization of "resilience".

Part of the essential character of "resilience" seems to be that the positive outcome was unexpected. If someone is expected to overcome a significant problem, the positive outcome is typically not attributed to resilience but attributed instead to a lesser severity of the stressor or to some positive quality or circumstance. Resilience is often hypothesized when a model or theory fails to accurately predict behavior for some individuals. In these cases, it is a band-aid concept for inadequate or misapplied models.

For the most part the "normal positive" model is a "medical" or "disease" model of behavior (see Sameroff & Seifer, 1990). This type of model predisposes investigators to ignore or minimize the importance of positive determinative factors, leads to poor predictions, and provides limited if not misleading insight into behavior. Models of behavior that do not presume a positive outcome, that have a systems orientation, and that postulate the interaction of positive and negative influences leading to variable outcomes are more heuristically useful. This is the fundamental principle of what we propose.

Research on Risk and Resilience

A reading of the research literature on resilience as well as on the overlapping literature on risk and protective factors indicates the following, (see Mrazek & Haggerty, 1994, chapter 6; Rolf et al., 1990; Haggerty et al., 1994; Robins and Rutter, 1990; Masten, Best and Garmezy, 1990; Werner, 1989, Masten et al., 1990):

1. Any major disruption of the physical, cognitive, self and/or social developmental process disables or impairs the individual in some way
2. The extent of the disability or impairment depends on:
   a. the particular process that is affected, i.e., whether physical, cognitive, self or social developmental, etc.
   b. the chronological age and developmental level of the individual
   c. the duration of the disruption
   d. the severity of the disruption and how proximate the impact is; (for example, the death of a parent of a child would presumably be more disruptive than an adolescent's loss of a friend)
   e. mitigating factors which include the positive characteristics of the individual and the compensating and supportive influences in the environment
   f. the cumulation of stresses and negative circumstances and of positive and buffering influences over time and as they interact at a given point in time
3. Recovery is possible and is associated at least in part with the factors listed under Number 2 above, i.e., recovery is more difficult if there is physical impairment, particularly organic brain damage, and if cognition is impaired as opposed to a disruption of self or social development; there are greater chances of recovery in a younger than an older child; there is a greater probability of recovery if the duration of the disruption is short-lasting

4. Some factors seem to have positive influence for a large number of individuals, for individuals with a wide range of qualities and circumstances and in relation to a large number of potential negative outcomes; these factors include:

  a. positive characteristics of the individual such as intelligence, social skills, an easy disposition, and a good natured temperament

  b. positive influences in the environment such as strong attachments to parents and involvement with good schools and other pro-social institutions

5. Some factors seem to have negative influence for a large number of individuals, for individuals with a wide range of qualities and circumstances and in relation to a large number of potential negative outcomes; these factors include:

  a. characteristics of the individual such as neurological disorders, difficulties with emotional regulation and expressiveness, aggression and difficulty in controlling impulses and behavior, social incompetence and impaired or limited social relationships, antisocial personality and behaviors, and other psychiatric dysfunctions and difficulties

  b. influences in the environment such as poverty (i.e., severe deprivation and associated factors), severe parental and family dysfunction, and severe traumatic life events (e.g., child maltreatment)

There is relatively little in the literature about those individuals who experienced major stressors but do not appear to have experienced the difficult sequelae from which others must recover. It seems likely however that much of what is known about resilience would apply to this group as well. Clearly, given the broad nature of the studies conducted to date, it is important to take what can be gleaned from them and begin rebuilding an approach to the very compelling issue of determining what processes and factors are associated with successful life adaptation in the face of negative influences.

Based on our reading of the scientific literature and reviews conducted by others (e.g., Kaplan, this volume, 1999; Masten, Best, & Garmezy, 1990) there does not appear to be any credible evidence that there is a single quality or circumstance, and certainly not a single universal factor of resilience that is beneficial in most if not all circumstances. In fact, at least in some cases, it seems that the qualities and circumstances which contribute to a positive outcome in one situation may be irrelevant or even counterproductive in another. For example, a child's strong family identification can be either beneficial or harmful depending on the values and behavior of the family. The same inflexibility and rigidity which may be disastrous in some circumstances may be the unyielding focus and strength of beliefs and purpose which is crucial to success in other circumstances. Relatedly, it seems extremely unlikely that there are "invulnerable" people. While some qualities and influences almost always contribute to an individual's well being and ability to overcome difficulties (e.g., intelligence and problem solving ability, social facility and healthy relationships, positive self esteem, effective affect regulation, a supportive and loving family, positive role models, etc.), none of these factors is "resilience." It may be possible to create an index of resilience based on a set or sets of characteristics, but even this would address only some conceptual problems.

A number of researchers in the field have written about some of these issues; many of their discussions focus on the definition of resilience as either a factor, a characteristic or a process. Garmezy and his associates (Garmezy, 1993; Masten, Best, & Garmezy, 1990) have described resilience as a "capacity" for successful adaptation in face of hardship while Rutter (1990) describes resilience as a positive outcome. Cicchetti and Schneider-Rosen (1986) and Egeland, Carlson and Sroufe (1993) consider resilience to be a "transactional process within an organizational framework ... developmental outcomes are determined by the interaction of genetic, bio-logical, psychological, and sociological factors in the context of environ-mental support." While we would lean toward this last usage, our proposal takes a somewhat different approach.

"Resilience" is not useful merely as a statement of a positive status or outcome. Individuals who faced no particularly severe problems or devel-opmental disruptions and had ample support and opportunities would not usually be considered to be resilient no matter how positive their status (see Rutter, 1990). Resilience denotes that a person has faced and overcome severe problems or resisted strongly negative circumstances and/or charac-teristics. Therefore, any attempt to understand resilience must include a determination of that to which the individual is being resilient. The more specific the statement of the negative circumstances, stressor, etc., the more useful the attribution and the more the heterogeneity and mechanisms of resilience can be understood. Ultimately, resilience is a concept, which is meaningful only in the context of particular problems, stressors, etc.

Masten, Best and Garmezy (1990) point out that the concept of resilience has been used in different ways and may refer to a positive outcome despite an individual's demonstrating characteristics and circum-stances associated with high risk for negative outcomes, continued positive status and function despite adverse circumstances, or to recovery from detrimental and/or damaging experiences and influences. In addition, it is not always clear from the literature as to what constitutes a resilient outcome. Outcomes are often viewed as dichotomies–either one has a negative outcome or not. In reality, it is probably the case that outcomes are a matter of degree and that whereas a person may be resilient in terms of one type of outcome, he or she may not be resilient for another (see Luthar, Doernberger, & Zigler, 1993). For example, a study that narrowly focused on resilience related to drug abuse or drug initiation may not consider that a person may not be a drug user but may abuse alcohol, be clinically depressed, or manifest other negative outcomes. Resilience should be construed and assessed not by one behavior or outcome alone but by a multifaceted approach. Further, it is important to consider that many influences and outcomes are neither completely positive nor completely negative and understanding their non-absolute character may help in the understanding of subsequent outcomes.

Anthony (1974) observed that individuals who appear to be "invulnerable" at earlier stages of their life may develop negative outcomes during later stages, particularly during periods of increased stress. Studies by Vaillant (e.g., Felsman & Vaillant, 1987) and others indicate that the appearance of resilience may manifest at any point in an individual's life. For example, someone who may have been designated at age 20 to be a non-resilient person, i.e. to manifest significant negative outcomes, may be functioning well by age 50. Someone else facing similar stressors may appear to cope well for several years but then succumb to the stressors and/or to the problems inherent in their coping response and have an even more negative outcome in the long run than the other person did initially. Clearly, the determination of an individual's resilience is at least in part a product of the time points of measurement. Assessments of resilience may be reasonable only through long term longitudinal observations and measurements (e.g., Glantz, 1992). This is particularly true since even individuals diagnosed with severe psychiatric disorders and those identified as engaging in serious anti-social behaviors typically have extensive periods when the symptoms or the problem behaviors are not evident.

Furthermore, as Kaplan points out in his discussion of definitions and models of resilience (this volume, 1999), researchers conducting studies on resilience often make value judgements about desirable and undesirable outcomes mostly from their own cultural backgrounds. Even "mental illness" is defined by behaviors that in some cultures are accepted, tolerated, or even venerated. Cultural variation makes it difficult to conceive of resilience as a consistent concept (e.g., Burton, 1996). "Resilience" readily takes on a political meaning that may have as much to do with beliefs about societies and environments as it does about individuals; blaming those who do not demonstrate "resilience" when some of their peers do is an example of this. Certainly, in a plural culture society such as the United States, this leads to much confusion and some conflict, which in itself can lead to negative adaptational outcomes. Resilience must go beyond the concept of an outcome or state that is bound either temporally or culturally; at the very least, explicit, concrete definitions which may be reviewed and evaluated are necessary.

Proposals

We propose altering the common concept of resilience from that of the often hypothesized basically undefined inner personal trait to the concept of resilience as adaptive or compensating (positive) behaviors and factors. Relatedly, we propose that models of problem behaviors and negative outcomes attempt to account for outcomes not merely by identifying and tallying negative influences but by investigating the ways in which different sets of positive and negative factors interact leading to different outcomes. This will improve the utility of the concept of resilience and will help researchers to find better ways to examine and understand resilient individuals' "success" and to develop better methods for assessing the "resilience status" of those under stress. The ultimate goal of such efforts is to develop interventions to help a much greater number of people overcome the barriers to positive adaptations. Prevention and treatment interventions based on poorly conceptualized notions of resilience or ill-conceived versions of the somewhat related notions of coping and/or adaptation are likely to be very limited in their effectiveness.

To further elaborate our basic position, we would like to make five specific proposals regarding research and theory on resilience. The first proposal is that studies and theories of resilience incorporate concretely identified (preferably assessable) statements of problems or stresses to which the "resilience" is a response. It may be helpful to use the more focused concept of "adaptation to" or "coping with" a particular problem, stress, lack, etc. rather that the more general notion of "resilience". The advantage would be to emphasize the importance of considering the particular problem. Regardless of which word is chosen, the identification of the stressor is necessary. Similarly, concrete operationalized definitions of as many positive and negative influences as possible are also necessary.

Just as the nature of the negative circumstances varies, so does the nature of positive influence and effective resilience to those negative circumstances. A given problem or stressor may be successfully coped with in a variety of ways and different means and styles may be differentially effective for different people under different situations. Some "resilience" factors may be general positive influences or circumstances while others may have an effect primarily in relation to specific negative factors. It is important for research and theory on resilience to recognize the multiplicity of positive influences and of the ways in which people adapt to problems, and for the most part this is accepted by the field. Also, as Cicchetti and Garmezy note (1993), resilience is not static and is likely to evolve and change over time. However, researchers and theorists too often narrowly focus on the outcome rather than the factors and mechanisms of resilience; for example some researchers have considered environmental factors as being the stressors, and have not given equal consideration to the role of other environmental factors as compensating, protective and/or facilitative forces.

Taking this idea a step further, resilience may be a useful concept not only when applied to individuals but also when applied to some groups. It may well be the case that some social systems, such as some families, cultural groups and/or communities, for example, may have qualities and processes which are comparable or parallel to resilience characteristics usually thought of only in the context of individuals. Protective or coping functions may be served by some social systems or groups in ways that go beyond individuals or even individuals in the contexts of their environments. In these cases, the social structure, roles, mutual support, activities, values, circumstances, etc. may serve a "resilience" function, i.e. a protective, adaptive coping function for the group members and this function may not be greatly dependent on the particular members or their situations at any given time. One of the hoped for possibilities of resilience research is that understanding the resilience of some individuals will provide the necessary information to make it possible to facilitate greater resilience in others. It may be that there is a greater practical potential for increasing people's resilience if the intervention operates through or targets these potentially resilient social groups than if it focuses on individuals. It may be easier to enhance the resilience of families or communities than to enhance the resilience of individuals.

The second proposal relates to the role of resilience in explanations of behavior. It is not really useful to assert that an individual overcame a severe problem because he or she was "resilient." This is the logical equivalent of stating that someone must be resilient because they had an unexpected positive outcome and then explaining the outcome as resulting from the individual's resilience. Therefore, it is proposed is that the concept of resilience be used as a descriptive concept and *not* be considered explanatory. To maximize its usefulness, researchers and theorists should attempt to apply the concept of resilience incorporating depictions of the mechanisms and/or processes by which it was achieved (see Rutter, 1990). An additional advantage of adopting this proposal would be that there would be less inclination to "blame the victims" of severe negative circumstances for not being adequately resilient.

Two other dichotomies in conceptualizations of resilience are important to note. Some tend to think of resilience more in terms of the characteristics of the individual (e.g., intelligence) and some think of resilience more as a factor or set of factors in the environment (e.g., a healthy family); this latter view more often refers to "protective" factors rather than resilience, as the terms are often used. It seems most reasonable to assume that resilience varies, sometimes being more intra-personal and sometimes being more environmental but most often being an interaction of both. In terms of the second dichotomy, some views of resilience are based more on attributions of qualities or some form of competence while others are based more on attributions of motivation or will power. Again it seems most reasonable to assume that resilience varies, sometimes being more an issue of competence and sometimes more an issue of motivation, but most often being an interaction of both. This also argues for a terminology and an orientation based on systems of positive and/or adaptive factors rather than simple resilience factors.

An increasingly prevalent belief is that if some members of a group could overcome a given adversity then other members can as well and if they do not, it is because they were unmotivated or put in too little effort. At the other extreme, there are some views of behavior in which individual effort, sacrifice and persistence are discounted as factors in overcoming severe problems. This view usually incorporates the tacit assumption that outside remediation is an inevitable necessity, that extraordinary effort should not be expected of those facing severe adversity and that individual effort is not a factor in resilience. Both of these extreme views are based on questionable assumptions and a more middle of the road perspective seems most reasonable. However, a rarely considered developmental issue is important to note. This leads to the third proposal.

Some stressors exert a particularly pernicious influence in that they interfere with or diminish the development of the individual's coping repertoire, abilities, expectations and potential resilience. Interfering with an individual's development of adaptive, effective coping functions and abilities may be one of the most harmful effects of some major stresses and negative influences. This potential consequence of early traumas, deprivations and other severe negative influences may at least partially account for the severe problems and the maladaptive or ineffective coping and functioning which characterize some seemingly dysfunctional individuals. Incorporating a consideration of whether an individual has been affected in a way that prevents the development of coping and resilience and, when relevant, the level of an individual's pre-stress abilities and function would enhance an understanding of many aspects of resilience.

Other developmental issues are also important to consider in investigating resilience. For example, some limited stress and negative experience may be necessary to help a child to learn to successfully meet challenges and develop coping abilities (Anthony, 1974; Werner & Smith, 1982). Attempts to understand responses to strongly negative circumstances and the development or avoidance of problems and pathologies would be greatly strengthened by including considerations of developmental phenomena, stages and transitions. Thus the third proposal is that both research and theoretical investigations of resilience and response to severe problems, stresses, etc., utilize a developmental framework and incorporate not only information about the age of the individuals but also information about their developmental level and function and the interaction of developmental factors with predisposing and protective (or positive and negative) factors (see Murphy, 1987).

An additional implication of adopting more developmentally oriented models is the recognition that particular outcomes are rarely final endpoints. Most outcomes are themselves positive and/or negative influences contributing to subsequent outcomes and stages. Behavior, function and experience are continuously evolving states of being and models which recognize this will be considerably more valid and useful. In other words, outcomes or consequences are themselves contributors to subsequent situations and events. For example, drug use, so often treated as a terminal outcome variable, is not a final endpoint. The use of drugs occurs over a long period of time and at each point, the behaviors and experiences of using drugs influences the individual and their subsequent behaviors and events. If drug abuse, clinical depression or other outcomes are considered as terminal states, then understanding, prediction and the potential to intervene after the designated outcome will be unnecessarily limited.

The fourth proposal espouses a systems approach to resilience (see Garmezy, 1985; Rutter, 1990; Haggerty et al., 1994). Perhaps the most important contribution of research and theory on resilience is to draw attention to the positive, protective and beneficial characteristics and influences which are involved with individuals' function and what the outcome will be when a severe negative circumstance is faced by a person. "Resilient" outcomes may not be as rare and remarkable a phenomenon as is often thought. In fact, most outcomes are positive for most people and most are probably the result of the interaction of positive and negative influences. As we have stated, there is a tendency by both theory and research to focus on risk factors and problems and neglect positive characteristics, influences and outcomes. While it is easy to understand how the attempt to understand negative outcomes predisposes toward a focus on the negative, we reiterate that it is unrealistic and incomplete. The fourth proposal is that research and theoretical attempts to understand resilience and the development or avoidance of problems and pathologies routinely adopt a systemic approach considering both positive and negative circumstances and both predisposing and protective characteristics and the ways in which they interact in the relevant situations.

Relatedly, many research investigations have focused on only a single stressor and/or protective factor. As Emery and Forehand (1994) note, "single variables do not operate in isolation" (p. 93); they give the example that even the usually beneficial characteristic of an easy temperament may operate to facilitate resilience only in the context of adequate supports. Further, there is a tendency to view factors as mono-directional influences rather than considering that seemingly deterministic factors are themselves influenced interactively. Bi-directional approaches have demonstrated more validity in research (e.g., Hetheringon & Blechman, 1996) and systemic models where all variables are recognized as being influences, mediators and outcomes tied in varying degrees to the entire system of variables are likely to be significantly more powerful.

A part of the fourth proposal recommending a more systemic or transactional approach to resilience is the corollary that a broad range of both positive and negative factors from multiple domains must be considered in order to understand the "resilience" of individuals. It is also critical to consider influences from different domains including the biological, psychological, psychiatric, social, familial and environmental. Additionally, as Masten, Best and Garmezy (1990) point out, the cumulation of factors and the influences of both proximal and distal factors must be considered. It is important to stress that the fourth proposal is for a comprehensive multifactorial systems oriented approach which investigates the interaction of factors and recognizes the diversity and variability of the influences of both positive and negative influences. Simple linear approaches that list and add up numbers of protective and risk factors make a very limited contribution. We acknowledge that a multifactorial systemic approach significantly increases the difficulty, complexity and resource demands of research, but unfortunately, it is necessary.

The fifth proposal relates to the ways in which outcomes are characterized. What constitutes a positive outcome is frequently a subjective matter of perspective based on often controversial values, cultural biases and/or the vantage and the particular time of observation. For example, is someone who overcomes the obstacles of poverty, discrimination and lack of employment opportunity by becoming a wealthy drug dealer a "resilient" person? Is a child who resists the emotional stresses of abuse by closing him or herself off from emotion and interpersonal bonding more "resilient" than the child who is devastated but slowly learns to deal with the pain over time and eventually is able to experience emotions normally and have normal relationships? Viewed at a time close to the abuse, the insulated child may appear to have a more positive outcome; given a longer time span for perspective, the reactive child appears to have the healthier outcome. Is a person with severe depression or bipolar disorder who self-medicates and achieves some higher level of function by abusing alcohol or illegal drugs being "resilient"? Would the same judgement be made if it were known that the self-medicator avoided suicide by the self-medication and would the judgement change when the effects of the substance abuse subsequently exacerbated the original problems?

The fifth proposal is that specific, concrete operationalized definitions of positive and negative outcomes be included in research on resilience and that collateral consequences of the "resilience" response to severe negative consequences also be considered in evaluating outcomes. Sometimes, the "cost" or harm of an adaptation to a strongly negative circumstance may be greater in the long run than the positive benefit. Also, a longer term more developmental assessment of the outcome is necessary. Defining and taking a more comprehensive and long term view of outcomes will avoid at least some invalid inferences, controversial value judgements and the consideration of Pyrrhic victories as desirable resilient outcomes.

Ultimately then, we are not proposing a new or different definition for "resilience". We would accept the definition proposed by Masten, Best & Garmezy (1990) (see above), but we would be open to alternatives. Neither are we proposing that resilience merely become a synonym for a positive influence that facilitates overcoming a negative one, or that it become a simple designation for a positive outcome achieved by overcoming negative factors. "Resilience" might meaningfully refer to certain positive or adaptational influences, characterize some types of outcomes, or designate particular transactional processes. Though more rigorous use of the term would be highly desirable, this is not the primary point of our proposals. Rather, we are recommending that in addition to the requirement of more comprehensive and measurable definitions for the term, that the use of the concept of "resilience" be embedded within the structure of the above proposals and the approach to explanatory models from which they were derived. A statement referring to resilience would then have a meaningful referent and would imply that certain conceptual concerns had been satisfied.

An important corollary to our reconceptualization of resilience and the related proposals is that the exact same concerns and recommendations apply to the concept of "risk," "risk" factors and "at risk" individuals, and factors and circumstances that are determinative of negative, including unexpected negative outcomes. Although the focus of the discussion here has been on the concept of "resilience," "resilience" factors and "resilience" outcomes, our primary concern is the broader advocacy of models, theories and research approaches that are developmental, transaction or systems based, focus on the interactions of a wide range of positive and negative influences, and presume the complexity, relativity and variability of both influences and outcomes.

NOTE. The opinions expressed herein are the views of the authors and do not necessarily reflect the official policy or position of the National Institute on Drug Abuse or any other part of the U.S. Department of Health and Human Services.

References

Anthony, E. J. (1974). The syndrome of the psychologically invulnerable child. In E. J. Anthony & C. Koupernik (Eds.), *The child and his family: Children at psychiatric risk. Volume 3*, (pp. 99–121). New York: John Wiley and Sons.

Anthony, E. J. (1987). Risk, vulnerability, and resilience: An overview. In E. J. Anthony & B. Cohler (Eds.), *The invulnerable child* (pp. 3–48). New York: Guilford Press.

Beauvais, F., & Oetting, E. (1999). Drug use, resilience, and the myth of the golden child. In M. Glantz & J. Johnson (Eds.), *Resilience and development: Positive life adaptations*. New York: Plenum Press.

Burton, L. (1996). The timing of childbearing, family structure, and the role responsibilities of aging black women. In E. M. Hetherington & E. Blechman (Eds.), *Stress, coping, and resiliency in children and families* (pp. 155–172). Mahwah, New Jersey: Lawrence Erlbaum Associates.

Cowan, P., Cowan, C. P., & Schulz, M. (1996). Thinking about risk and resilience in families. In E. M. Hetherington & E. Blechman (Eds.), *Stress, coping, and resiliency in children and families* (pp. 1–38). Mahwah, New Jersey: Lawrence Erlbaum Associates.

Cicchetti, D., & Garmezy, N. (1993). Prospects and promises in the study of resilience. *Development and Psychopathology, 5*, 497–502.

Egeland, B., Carlson, E., & Sroufe, L. A. (1993). Resilience as process. *Development and Psychopathology, 5*, 517–528.

Emery, R., & Forehand, R. (1994). Parental divorce and children's well-being: A focus on resilience. In R. Haggerty, L. Sherrod, N. Garmezy, & M. Rutter (Eds.), *Stress, risk, and resilience in children and adolescents: Processes, mechanisms, and interventions* (pp. 64–99). Cambridge: Cambridge University Press.

Felsman, J. K., & Vaillant, G. (1987). Resilient children as adults: A 40 year study. In E. J. Anthony & B. Cohler (Eds.), *The invulnerable child* (pp. 289–314). New York: Guilford Press.

Fisher, L., Kokes, R., Cole, R., Perkins, P., & Wynne, L. (1987). Competent children at risk: A study of well-functioning offspring of disturbed parents. In E. J. Anthony & B. Cohler (Eds.), *The invulnerable child* (pp. 211–228). New York: Guilford Press.

Garmezy, N. (1985). Broadening research on developmental risk. In W. Frankenburg, R. Emde, & J. Sullivan (Eds.), *Early identification of children at risk: An international perspective* (pp 289–303). New York: Plenum.

Garmezy, N., & Rutter, M. (Eds.). (1983). *Stress, coping, and development in children*. New York: McGraw-Hill.

Glantz, M. D. (1992). A developmental psychopathology model of drug abuse vulnerability. In M. Glantz & R. Pickens (Eds.), *Vulnerability to drug abuse*, (pp. 389–418). Washington D. C.: American Psychological Association Press.

Gore, S., & Eckenrode, J. (1994). Context and process in research on risk and resilience. In R. Haggerty, L. Sherrod, N. Garmezy, & M. Rutter (Eds.), *Stress, risk, and resilience in children and adolescents: Processes, mechanisms, and interventions*, (pp. 19–63). Cambridge: Cambridge University Press.

Haggerty, R., Sherrod, L., Garmezy, N., & Rutter, M. (Eds.). (1994). *Stress, risk, and resilience in children and adolescents: Processes, mechanisms, and interventions*. Cambridge: Cambridge University Press.

Hetherington, E. M., & Blechman, E. A. (Eds.). (1996). *Stress, coping, and resiliency in children and families*. Mahwah, New Jersey: Lawrence Erlbaum Associates.

Kaplan, H. (1999). Toward an understanding of resilience: A critical review of definitions and models. In M. Glantz & J. Johnson (Eds.), *Resilience and development: Positive life adaptations*. New York: Plenum Press.

Luthar, S., & Cushing, G. (1999). Measurement issues in the empirical study of resilience: An overview. In M. Glantz & J. Johnson (Eds.), *Resilience and development: Positive life adaptations*. New York: Plenum Press.

Luthar, S., Doernberger, C., & Zigler, E. (1993). Resilience is not a unidimensional construct: Insights from a prospective study of inner-city adolescents. *Development and Psychopathology*, 5, 703–717.

Masten, A., Best, K., & Garmezy, N. (1990). Resilience and development: Contributions from the study of children who overcame adversity. *Development and Psychopathology*, 2, 425–444.

Masten, A., Morison, P., Pellegrini, D., & Tellegen, A. (1990). Competence under stress: Risk and protective factors. In J. Rolf, A. Masten, D. Cicchetti, K. Nuechterlein, & S. Weintraub (Eds.), *Risk and protective factors in the development of psychopathology* (pp. 236–256). Cambridge: Cambridge University Press.

Mrazek, P. J., & Haggerty, R. (Eds.). (1994). *Reducing risks for mental disorders: Frontiers for preventive intervention research*. Washington, DC: National Academy Press.

Murphy, L. B. (1987). Further reflections on resilience. In E. J. Anthony & B. Cohler (Eds.), *The invulnerable child* (pp. 84–105). New York: Guilford Press.

Richters, J., & Weintraub, S. (1990). Beyond diathesis: Toward an understanding of high-risk environments. In J. Rolf, A. Masten, D. Cicchetti, K. Nuechterlein, & S. Weintraub, (Eds.), *Risk and protective factors in the development of psychopathology* (pp. 67–96). Cambridge: Cambridge University Press.

Robins, L., & Rutter, M. (1990). *Straight and devious pathways from childhood to adulthood*. Cambridge: Cambridge University Press.

Rolf, J., Masten, A., Cicchetti, D., Nuechterlein, K., & Weintraub, S. (Eds.). (1990). *Risk and protective factors in the development of psychopathology*. Cambridge: Cambridge University Press.

Rutter, M. (1990). Psychosocial resilience and protective mechanisms. In J. Rolf, A. Masten, D.

Cicchetti, K. Nuechterlein, & S. Weintraub (Eds.), *Risk and protective factors in the development of psychopathology* (pp. 181–214). Cambridge: Cambridge University Press.

Sameroff, A., & Seifer, R. (1990). In J. Rolf, A. Masten, D. Cicchetti, K. Nuechterlein, & S. Weintraub (Eds.), *Risk and protective factors in the development of psychopathology* (pp. 52–66). Cambridge: Cambridge University Press.

Tarter, R., & Vanyukov, M. (1999). Re-visiting the validity of the construct of resilience. In M. Glantz & J. Johnson (Eds.), *Resilience and development: Positive life adaptations.* New York: Plenum Press.

Werner, E. (1989). High-risk children in young adulthood: A longitudinal study from birth to 32 years. *American Journal of Orthopsychiatry, 59*(1), 72–81.

Werner, E., & Smith, R. (1982). *Vulnerable but invincible: A longitudinal study of resilient children and youth.* New York: McGraw Hill.

II

THE MEASUREMENT OF
RESILIENCE

7

Measurement Issues in the Empirical Study of Resilience
An Overview

Suniya S. Luthar and Gretta Cushing

Introduction

This paper provides a broad appraisal of measurement issues in empirical research on resilience. The measurement strategies reviewed here are based on a compilation of studies that specify a focus on resilience, or equivalents such as stress-resistance, located via a search on PsycINFO. Rather than striving for a comprehensive review of the literature, the aim in this paper was to arrive at a "representative sample" of methods that have been used in psychosocial studies of resilience. Having identified the approaches used by different investigative teams, the objective then was to appraise the major types of measurement strategies, in terms of the specific advantages, limitations, and precautions associated with each.

As will be evident, the bulk of empirical studies surveyed here have been based on work with children; the literature contains relatively few research studies involving resilience among adults. Many of the measurement issues examined here, however, generalize across age groups: while the specific instruments used would vary, the salient approaches to measurement discussed here are applicable across the life span.

Suniya S. Luthar • Department of Human Development, Teachers College, Columbia University, New York, New York 10027   **Gretta Cushing** • University of Utah, Salt Lake City, Utah 84102.

Resilience and Development: Positive Life Adaptations, edited by Glantz and Johnson. Kluwer Academic/Plenum Publishers, New York, 1999.

Pivotal Constructs in Measuring Resilience

Although definitions of resilience have varied, two central constructs are subsumed in every definition of the term, that is, risk or adversity, and positive adaptation or competence. Whether resilience is conceived of as (a) good outcomes despite adversity, (b) sustained competence under stress, or (c) recovery from trauma (Masten, Best, & Garmezy, 1990), risk and competence are the two key constructs that recur as pivotal components embedded in the overall construct of resilience. In the existing research, a range of strategies have been used to measure each of these constructs.

Risk

Three broad approaches have been used to measure psychosocial risk in empirical studies on resilience. The first involves multiple-item questionnaires on adverse influences or experiences, exemplified in checklists of negative life events. The second involves single stressors of a chronic or acute nature, such as child abuse, parental divorce, or parental psychopathology. The third approach utilizes a collection of specific, discrete risk indices primarily of a sociodemographic nature, such as poverty status or large family size, that are aggregated to derive an overall estimate of adversity experienced.

Multiple-Item Measures of Risk

In studying resilience, a common approach to measuring risk involves the use of multiple item instruments—presented either in a questionnaire or interview format—that reflect a collection of adverse events or influences in a child's life. This measurement strategy is reflected, most commonly, in the use of scales of *negative life events* (Baldwin et al., 1993; Cowen, Work, & Wyman, 1992; Egeland & Kreutzer, 1991; Garmezy, Masten, & Tellegen, 1984; Gest, Neemann, Hubbard, Masten, & Tellegen, 1993; Herrenkohl et al., 1994; Luthar, Doernberger & Zigler, 1993; Grossman, Beinashowitz, Sakurai, Finnin, & Flaherty, 1992; Holahan & Moos, 1991; Pianta, Egeland, & Sroufe, 1990; Wyman, Cowen, Work, & Kerley, 1993; Wyman, Cowen, Work, & Parker, 1991). Less frequently, questionnaires have been used to assess other more circumscribed risk domains as well, such as *parental symptomatology* (Baldwin et al., 1993; Carro, Grant, Gotlib, & Compas, 1993); quality of *family relations* (Baldwin et al., 1993; Neighbors, Forehand

& McVicar, 1993), and level of *exposure to community violence* (Richters & Martinez, 1993).

From a measurement perspective, a primary concern with such strategies involves the validation of the instruments as measures of risk. As Masten and colleagues (1990) have noted, risk factors in resilience research are those which show statistical correlations with poor or negative outcomes. This assertion echoes central tenets in measurement theory regarding construct validity: Empirical evidence of associations between scores on a certain measure, and other theoretically related indices, are imperative for inferences that the measure does in fact represent its intended theoretical concept (Anastasi, 1982; Carmines & Zeller, 1987).

In resilience research, then, assumptions that an instrument does in fact capture the theoretical construct of "high adversity" necessitate, at the very least, evidence of associations with relevant outcomes (in the sample under study or in comparable others). The forced reliance on statistical links to infer validity is associated with at least three potential problems, issues that have been addressed to varying degrees in the existing studies on resilience.

First, judgements on the validity of risk measurement require attention not only to the statistical significance of relations with outcomes, but also to the magnitude of these associations. In several recent studies on resilience, links between risk measures and outcomes—although statistically significant—have been in the range of .10 to .20. An effect that accounts for less than four percent of variance in adjustment outcomes must raise concern about whether the measure does, in fact, capture "high adversity" in the empirical study of resilience.

The second consideration presents the obverse of the first. Within a particular sample, a *low* statistical correlation between a risk scale and adjustment does not necessarily indicate poor validity of the instrument as a measure of risk. Low associations could arise, for example, due to the presence of curvilinear rather than linear associations, or as a result of a truncated range of either or both variables concerned within that sample (whereas the constructs concerned might, in fact, have robust associations in the general population).

Finally, even when relatively high correlations are obtained for multiple-item measures of risk, resilience researchers need to provide anchors of some sort, indicating where on the scale of potential life stressors the distribution of scores in the sample under study might fall. While investigators typically indicate means and standard deviations of scores on multiple-item measures, an average score of four or eight on a particular instrument conveys little about the magnitude or severity of the specific risks confronted. Put differently and borrowing from the erstwhile classification of psychosocial stressors in the Diagnostic and Statistical Manual, it is not clear what proportion of subjects in a particular sample faced stressors that could be categorized as mild, moderate, extreme, or catastrophic. Such ambiguities could be partly reduced by providing brief descriptions of the range and types of adversities experienced by the most highly stressed subset within a particular sample.

Since life events measures are the most commonly used within the multiple-item approach to measuring risk in resilience research, central methodological concerns specific to this strategy are addressed briefly. Typically, life event instruments (e.g., Coddington, 1972; Holmes & Rahe, 1967; Johnson & McCutcheon, 1980; Swearingen & Cohen, 1985) consist of a list of items judged to be experienced frequently by children, adolescents, or adults, and respondents are asked, in a questionnaire or interview, to indicate the specific events experienced in the recent past. There is a large literature on the methodological issues associated with measures of life events (Cohen, 1988; Dohrenwend & Dohrenwend, 1978; Johnson, 1986; Thoits, 1983; Zimmerman, 1983). A brief overview of salient issues—most of which pertain to the heterogeneity of events sampled—is presented here.

In resilience research, potential measurement confounds constitute among the most serious concerns about the use of life events measures. Several instruments in this category include not only "uncontrollable" items (e.g., death of a parent), but also events which themselves could be indices of maladjustment, such as failing a grade, or losing a job. The inclusion of such "controllable" incidents in life events measures artificially inflates associations between stress and outcomes (Gersten, Langner, Eisenberg, & Simcha-Fagan, 1977; Masten et al., 1988). On the other hand, some researchers have argued for the inclusion of both types of events given the intention to sample the major domain of stressful occurrences, since even those events partially under the person's control could be stressful when experienced (Johnson, 1986).

From a methodological perspective, in resilience research, the most stringent strategy is to explore central hypotheses with life event measurements that are free of confounds (only uncontrollable incidents). As and when appropriate, replicative analyses might then be conducted including different types of negative events.

A second commonly noted concern about life events measures pertains to the heterogeneity of items in terms of potential impact. The question here is whether it is appropriate to treat as equivalent events that vary in seriousness such as suicide by a parent or financial difficulties in the family. On the face of it, the failure to account for varying degrees of seriousness seems problematic from a measurement perspective. Several studies, on the other hand, have examined weighted negative events based on the respondent's estimation of relative impact, and have shown little difference in overall scores involving "raw" scores (each event with unit weight) and scores with weighting by impact (Johnson, 1986; Swearingen & Cohen, 1985; Thoits, 1983).

The need to distinguish between chronic and acute stressors has been demonstrated in recent research on life events and adjustment. Masten and colleagues have demonstrated that effects associated with chronic negative events can differ from those linked with discrete stressors, and that separate examination of each of these categories can yield important information about underlying processes in stress-adjustment associations (Masten, Neemann, & Adenas, 1994).

The many complexities associated with using life events measures in resilience research must be weighed against the several advantages linked with their use. Anthony (1987), for example, has commented that life stress measures provide controlled, quantitative assessments of various negative events across different individuals' lives. Additional advantages in using this method are seen in its pragmatic value in terms of ease of data collection, and the in-built provision of control group data. Since stress scores are on a continuous scale, comparisons between high and low stress groups are possible without the need to locate specific high-risk and control samples (Luthar & Zigler, 1991).

In conclusion, in resilience research, the use of multiple-item measures to assess risk necessitates validation of the instruments (at the very least), in terms of significant associations with relevant outcomes. The magnitude of statistical associations with adjustment indices must be interpreted with caution, and researchers need to indicate descriptively where on the broad continuum of severity, the stressors faced by their particular subject population might fall. In using checklists involving negative life events, investigators must be attentive to potential measurement confounds in such instruments, as well as to the heterogeneity of types of events sampled.

Specific Life Stresses

A second approach to measuring high-risk conditions in research on resilience has been based on specific stressful life circumstances. In recent empirical studies, a wide variety of life occurrences have been utilized within this approach, including severe disasters such as *war* (Casella & Motta, 1990; Elder & Clipp, 1989; Hobfall, London, & Orr, 1988), *hospitalization/chronic illness* (Hobfall & Lerman, 1988; Wells & Schwebel, 1987), and sociodemographic and familial stressors including *economic deprivation* (Baldwin et al., 1993); *institutionalization* (Quinton, Pickles, Maughan,

& Rutter, 1993; Rutter & Quinton, 1984), *child abuse or neglect* (Cicchetti, Rogosch, Lynch, & Holt, 1993; Crittendon, 1985; Herrenkohl, Herrenkohl, & Egolf, 1994), *parental divorce* (Mulholland, Watt, Philpott, & Sarlin, 1991), and *parental psychopathology* such as drug addiction (Johnson, Glassman, Fiks, & Rosen, 1990), alcoholism (Werner, 1986) and depression (Beardslee & Podorefsky, 1988; Conrad & Hammen, 1993; Radke-Yarrow & Brown, 1993).

As with multiple-item instruments, the validation of single life occurrences as measures of adversity often rests on significant links between these and outcomes, and again, there are a host of potential difficulties. Even in instances where maladjustment has been documented in a substantial proportion of those facing a global risk, questions can remain about the specific life circumstances of different individuals in a particular sample. Single risk indices studied in resilience research—such as parental psychopathology, divorce, or low SES—are of a "distal" nature; they do not impinge on the child directly but are mediated by sundry proximal variables such as affective unavailability of parents, or lack of resources within the family (Baldwin, Baldwin, & Cole, 1990; Richters & Weintraub, 1990). It has been argued that when considering distal risk factors, some well-functioning children within the sample may not be resilient at all, but may actually have faced low proximal risks (Richters & Weintraub, 1990).

Interpretive dilemmas in this regard are illustrated using recent research findings on children of drug abusers. Among offspring of treatment-seeking individuals addicted to cocaine or opioids—frequently with comorbid psychopathology—65% of the children themselves were found to have a major psychiatric disorder (Luthar, Cushing, Merikangas, & Rounsaville, 1994). While the 35% disorder-free children might be seen as "resilient", it is possible, too, that their particular families provided relatively healthy environments. Many of the mothers, for example, could have had supportive spouses or extended family members, which as several investigators (Brown & Harris, 1978; Quinton, Rutter, & Liddle, 1984; Rutter & Quinton, 1984) have shown, can be considerable assets. This hypothetical scenario leads, then, to the question of whether all children in such ostensibly high-risk groups are really at risk, or alternatively, whether the "measure" of adversity—simply, parental drug abuse—is faulty.

Individual differences in proximal processes do not necessarily indicate flawed measurement of distal risk indices. Returning to the findings noted earlier (Luthar et al., 1994), for example, the 65%–35% split indicates that considering just one risk factor—parental drug abuse with comor-

---

[1]Obvious exceptions are indices with manifestly high "face validity", such as exposure to armed combat.

bid psychopathology—the odds are six out of ten that a particular offspring will be disturbed (assuming that the data were derived from a fairly representative sample). Admittedly, an unusually well-functioning mother in one family, or the presence of a nurturing grandparent in another, may buffer the child against the risk. This, however, is precisely what the search for protective factors is about, i.e., the location of a set of processes that might systematically distinguish a substantial proportion of the healthy children from the maladjusted ones. Therefore, whereas in some situations it may be more appropriate to see the *family* as resilient rather than conferring labels of stress-resistant on well-functioning offspring (Baldwin et al., 1990), the fact remains that the odds were high that children in this group would develop psychiatric difficulties.

In short, uncertainty regarding the presence or nature of proximal risks in the lives of individual children does not automatically fault distal measures as indices of risk. In using such instruments, typically, what is implied is simply that the statistical odds of adjustment difficulties are high in the presence of a certain global risk; this does not necessitate any assumptions about the specific proximal risks that confront individual children.

Having said this, we turn to the other side of this issue, i.e., arguments in favor of scrutinizing proximal processes potentially underlying measures of distal risk. As several major theorists have noted (Bronfenbrenner, 1986; Zigler, Lamb, & Child, 1982), psychologists tend to remain uneasy with associations between sociological variables, such as social class membership, and behaviors. Reduction of the sociological variable into psychological terms is critical for understanding processes via which the environmental variable might operate.

Arguments such as this apply not only to sociodemographic distal risks, but even to single risk indices of a psychological nature. Maternal mental illness, for example, might be seen as a relatively straightforward psychological risk factor. Two complications in the use of this variable were outlined, however, by Seifer and Sameroff (1987) in their research. The authors noted, first, the need to identify which aspects of the global variable represented risk factors. Severity and chronicity of maternal mental illness were found to be better predictors of clinical symptoms in children than was any particular diagnosis. Second, a variable tapping subclinical aspects of mental health, i.e., maternal anxiety, was also found to be strongly related to child competence. Based on these data, Seifer & Sameroff (1987) concluded that even factors generally treated as simple indices of risk have their own complex internal structures which must be considered.

From a measurement perspective, findings such as these must inevitably provoke uneasiness among resilience researchers, in terms of uncertainty regarding what precisely is measured while using global distal risk indices. Emphasizing this equivocality, several investigators have focused on an in-depth study of the specific processes most strongly implicated in an at-risk child's adjustment (e.g., Baldwin et al., 1993; Spencer et al., 1993). Richters and Martinez (1993), for example, have empirically examined several proximal processes—such as family environment—that might mediate the effects of children's exposure to dangerous environments. Research of this nature not only enriches our understanding of the specific processes associated with global risk factors, but in addition and as a consequence, can be of great help in intervention planning.

Considered together, the preceding discussions indicate that in the study of resilience, the diverse approaches to examining distal risks might each be appropriate or useful depending on the specific aims of the research. As Zigler and Child (1969) asserted, notwithstanding psychologists' typically greater comfort with constructs essentially of a psychological nature, there is no single "correct" level of analysis of behavior. "Psychogenic" and "sociogenic" approaches can each be useful in attempting to explain inter-group variations in psychosocial outcomes, depending on the orientation and aims of the researcher.

By the same token, then, in studying resilience, when the central objective is to understand the dynamics underlying a particular sociodemographic or other distal risk, it is clearly critical to scrutinize the mediating proximal processes. On the other hand, there are several invaluable studies on resilience that have used distal risk variables, with all their attendant "fuzziness" in terms of what precisely is measured in psychological terms. Unquestionably, there are times when it can be very profitable to examine "who beats the odds", even if the "odds" themselves—represented, simply, by distal risk indices—remain incompletely understood in terms of the specific mechanisms via which adversity may be conferred.

A final issue to be confronted with the use of single life circumstances as risk indices is that of potential confounds of measurement. Although possibly less so than in research involving controllable life events, confounds could plague even research using single life circumstances, particularly in cross-sectional designs. Consider, for example, research on child abuse. Several investigators (Gelles, 1973; Parker & Collmer, 1976) have suggested that abused children can be particularly difficult to care for. It is not clear, therefore, whether abuse is necessarily a stressor that results in maladjustment, or, at least in some instances, whether having difficult temperaments might cause children to be abused (Farber & Egeland, 1987). In short, as with multiple life event scales, investigators need to ensure that measures of single risk indices have little overlap with assessments of adjustment.

In summary, there are several issues to be considered in using single indices to measure risk in resilience research. Measures involving distal risk factors, or those that do not directly affect the child, convey little about the proximal processes by which they operate. The empirical scrutiny of proximal processes underlying specific distal risks is invaluable. At the same time, resilience research involving global measures of distal risks can yield critical insights on successful adaptation in the face of adversity. Finally, as with multiple-item measures of risk, the use of single life circumstances necessitates attention to the validity of the measure as an assessment of adversity, as well as to the possibility of confounds with adjustment outcomes.

Constellations of Multiple Risks

A third increasingly utilized approach to measuring risk in resilience research involves the simultaneous consideration of multiple sociodemographic and familial indices, such as low parental occupation and income, absence of a parent in the household, minority group membership, crowding in the household, and poor emotional/physical health of the mother (Egeland & Kalkoske, 1993; O'Grady & Metz, 1987; Osborn, 1990; Sameroff, Seifer, Barocas, Zax, & Greenspan, 1987; Spencer et al., 1993; Werner & Smith, 1982). The increasing use of measures of "risk constellations" in resilience research reflects cognizance of the co-occurrence of serious adversities in the real world; typically, biological and psychosocial risks do not act in isolation but tend to coexist (e.g., Meyer-Probst, Rosler, & Teichmann, 1983).

When multiple aspects of risk are used in studies on resilience, typically, measures of "overall" risk have been derived via simple additive strategies. In research by Sameroff and colleagues (Sameroff & Seifer, 1990; Sameroff et al., 1987), for example, a series of indices previously established to be high risk in nature were selected, such as minority group status, large family size, low maternal education, and high maternal anxiety. Using simple counts of one versus zero, those risk indices faced by a particular child were added to compute the overall risk encountered. A similar additive strategy has been adopted with continuous data (Masten, Morison, Pellegrini, & Tellegen, 1990). In this case, scores on different risk scales were standardized, and these z scores were added to indicate total risk faced.

From a measurement perspective, summative approaches to assessing risk might be questioned on various grounds. It may be argued, for instance, that the items added have high overlap (e.g., poverty and minority group status), and/or that they differ dramatically in their seriousness as risk factors. Problems such as these, however, are inherent in most psychological scales. For example, in questionnaires on life events, or even on symptoms or personality, multiple items on a scale are added; the items have high shared variance (they must, in the interest of internal consistency); and the items often vary considerably in how strongly they are related to a particular outcome.

From a conceptual perspective, it might be argued that summated risk scores convey nothing about the specific processes via which these factors might affect adjustment. This harkens back to previous discussions on distal versus proximal risks. The indubitable value of understanding psychological processes mediating a single risk—or a collection of risks—does not mitigate the contributions of research focusing on protective forces (such as those related to personal attributes), rather than on the specific dynamics underlying the adversity studied.

On the positive side of the coin, several factors argue in favor of using summative approaches to assessing risk. Summated risk measures are likely to be more reliable than measurements involving individual risk factors since in general, increasing the number of items on a scale increases its reliability (Carmines & Zeller, 1979). Similarly, "scales" involving summated risks have high face validity, given the coexistence of multiple psychosocial stressors in the real world. Empirical support for the validity of such measures is seen in unequivocal research evidence that the simultaneous consideration of multiple stressors accounts for far more variance in outcomes than any one stressor considered individually (Masten, 1989; Meyer-Probst et al., 1983; Rutter & Quinton, 1977; Sameroff et al., 1987; Seifer & Sameroff, 1987).

While summated risk scales have several advantages, a critical issue to be appraised by researchers considering this approach pertains to the "riskiness", within particular populations, of component variables within the composite. The importance of this concern is illustrated with data on large family size, a sociodemographic risk that has frequently been used within composite measures while studying resilience. Particularly in low-income households, a high ratio of children to adults tends to be associated with relatively poor child outcomes, reflecting, for example, the high demands on adults' caregiving resources in terms of both time and energy (see Garfinkel & McLanahan, 1986; Garret, Ng'andu, & Ferron, 1994; Heer, 1985). On the other hand, a recent study involving young, low-income African-American mothers (Chase-Lansdale, Brooks-Gunn, & Zamsky, 1994) found that the co-residence of another adult, the maternal grandmother, was significantly *negatively* associated with the quality of parenting *both* by grandmothers and by the mothers themselves. In discussing these findings, the authors speculate on various underlying processes, e.g., conflict between mothers and their own mothers, and/or uncertainty among the women regarding who held primary responsibility for the child.

One might argue that trends found by Chase-Lansdale and colleagues were possibly specific to the group studied—i.e., poor, minority group, single mothers—and that given other research findings, a high child to adult ratio should in fact be seen as "generally" constituting risk. A major difficulty with such arguments is that *all* populations studied in resilience research are potentially deviant not only from normative groups, but also, frequently, from each other. As the preceding discussions show, myriad ways have been used to measure or define high stress in resilience research; each of the approaches, by definition, strives to capture deviance in some sense. Therefore, cognizance that psychosocial processes and associations can differ drastically across different high risk groups is critical in considering composite risk measures. The "riskiness" of the individual items must be examined before deriving composite measures in resilience research.

In summary, the use of multiple indices is an approach to operationalizing risk that merits further examination in studying resilience. The simultaneous consideration of several indices may provide the most comprehensive assessment of the overall risk experienced by individuals facing adverse life circumstances. In using this measurement approach, however, it is critical that researchers carefully attend to whether components integrated within a composite risk constellation, each do, in fact, represent high risks within the sample under consideration.

Competence

As with the study of risk, concerns around measuring competence vary depending on the approach used to operationalize the construct. There are three broad approaches that have been used to assess competence in resilience research, which are somewhat analogous to the strategies employed to measure risk. The first approach involves continuous data on multiple-item scales, such as those assessing competent behaviors in school, or symptomatology. A second strategy is a categorical one that is based on the presence or absence of serious psychopathology. The third approach to measuring competence involves the addition or integration of diverse aspects of adjustment.

Multiple-Item Measures of Competence/Maladjustment

In resilience research, a widely used approach for measuring competence rests on multiple-item instruments, typically with well documented psychometric properties, that provide assessments on the continuum between adjustment and maladjustment. Most often, this strategy has involved ratings of behavioral indicators of *emotional health and/or success at meeting salient developmental tasks*, based on information sources other than just the target individual. In studying resilience among children and adolescents, for example, adjustment has frequently been assessed via *ratings by parents, teachers, and peers*, as well as by level of *academic success* or performance on *standardized achievement tests* (Carro et al., 1993; Egeland & Kalkoske, 1993; Egeland & Kreutzer, 1991; Garmezy et al., 1984; Gest et al., 1993; Grossman et al., 1992; Hobfall et al., 1988; Holohan & Moos, 1991; Luthar, 1991; Luthar et al., 1993; Mulholland et al., 1991; O'Grady & Metz, 1987; Osborn, 1990; Richters & Martinez, 1993; Spencer et al., 1993; Wyman et al., 1991, 1993).

As with multiple-item measures of risk, there are often problems of interpreting what is connoted by "high competence" on continuous measures, since reference groups are frequently the samples themselves and not any larger normative group. Behavioral ratings by peers or teachers, for example, are commonly used in resilience research, and the use of such measures precludes reference to any normative data; the reference group has to be the one under study. Yet there are considerable ambiguities inherent in reports indicating, for example, that average peer acceptance ratings for the resilient group were one standard deviation above the sample mean. By definition, in every sample, some children must be rated as better accepted than others by their peers. The unanswered question remains: might the most competent (resilient) of the high-risk individuals, within a particular sample, simply be the best of a generally poorly functioning group?

The importance of this issue is illustrated in findings from studies that have contrasted overall levels of competence achieved by high-risk individuals versus comparable low-risk controls. In comparing grade point average trends among children in divorced versus intact families, for example, Mulholland and colleagues (1991) found that high achievers in the divorce group performed significantly more poorly, over time, than high achieving children in the control group. Similar relative deficits in performance over time were found among low-achieving children of divorce as well; these youngsters performed at a significantly lower level than low achieving children from intact families. The implications of such findings for empirical research on resilience are clear: good adjustment relative to others within a particular high risk group does not necessarily translate into high competence in any absolute sense.

In studies lacking a quantitative "yardstick" against which competence levels within a particular high-risk sample might be judged, descriptive characterizations could help reduce interpretive ambiguities. Researchers might provide simple anchors to characterize high and low levels of competence achieved by individuals within their samples, patterned, for example, after Werner and Smith's (1992) descriptions of the behavioral profiles associated with labels of resilience among children, adolescents, and adults within their high-risk research.

A word, now, about the validity of competence measures: while studying resilience, selection of competence indices must be tied in to the particular risk domain being studied. In the research literature, there exist almost as many psychometrically sound measures of adjustment as there are theoretically distinct facets of competence and adjustment. In studying resilience, the selection of measures of competence has to be based on theoretical links with the specific risk under study. Stated differently, with reference to the particular type of risk confronted, a "critical" set of outcomes must be identified. The maintenance of socially responsible behaviors might be targeted, for instance, among children at risk for conduct disorder, while the absence of clinically significant internalizing symptomatology may be the focus among children at familial risk for affective disorders. In each case, other outcome variables could provide additional information on children's adjustment levels.

While these may seem like self-evident exhortations, our own data have indicated several subtleties in this regard that make this issue worthy of comment. In a study of inner-city adolescents (Luthar et al., 1993), a subset of 25 apparently resilient inner-city teens were identified, i.e., those with frequent negative life events, who also excelled on any one of four indices of school-based behavioral competence (derived from grades and teacher- and peer-ratings). More than half of these youngsters ($n = 15$) were found to have significant difficulties in a behavioral competence domain other than the one(s) on which they were initially identified as resilient. With additional "exclusionary criteria" applied, e.g., relatively high levels of self-reported symptoms, this proportion went up to 84%. Put differently, of the children who seemed resilient based on excellence in one domain of functioning, only 16% had managed to evade significant adjustment difficulties in other areas of behavioral competence/symptomatology, over the course of a six-month period.

It should be emphasized that in this research (Luthar et al., 1993), we started out with a fairly circumscribed approach to defining resilience, that is, primarily in terms of school-based behavioral competence. Even just considering grades, teacher-ratings, and peer-ratings, however, we found that frequently, children who seemed resilient in one behavioral domain showed significant difficulties in others. These findings, along with others (Farber & Egeland, 1987; Luthar, 1991; Radke-Yarrow & Sherman, 1990), indicate that when research designs involve multiple competence measures, definitions of resilience must be based on *a priori*, theoretically-derived "hierarchies" of adjustment indices. Apropos the specific type of risk under scrutiny, a particular adjustment domain—that most likely to be affected—must be designated as the "primary" criterion for labels of resilience. Other indices examined might then be explored to provide additional information on the adjustment profiles of at-risk individuals.

Specificity of competence measures is critical not only in terms of validity vis-a-vis the particular risk measured, but is also a crucial concern in the presentation of research findings on resilience. As illustrated in the preceding discussion, resilience is not a unidimensional construct: high risk individuals can function extremely well in one behavioral domain yet display significant difficulties in other areas of overt competence. Thus, when trends on resilience are based on two or three circumscribed domains of competence, it is imperative that findings are discussed in equally circumscribed terms, and do not imply resilient functioning in some sweeping, across-the-board sense (Luthar, 1993).

In summary, when competence is measured via multiple-item scales (such as those involving behavior ratings), it is often difficult to ascertain how the highest levels of competence within the high-risk sample under study might compare with those in low-risk groups, or in the general population. Ambiguities in this context can be partially addressed by providing qualitative characterizations of a subset of high- and low-functioning individuals within the group being examined. Other concerns with using this approach to measuring competence include the need for specificity in selection of competence indices vis-a-vis the particular risk under scrutiny, and specificity, as well, in the discussion of findings in terms of the particular domains in which resilience is identified.

Absence of Maladjustment

Measures based on the *absence versus presence of psychiatric diagnoses* are most commonly employed in resilience research involving individuals at high risk for serious psychopathology, e.g., offspring of individuals with major psychiatric disorders (Conrad & Hammen, 1993; Luthar et al., 1994; Radke-Yarrow & Brown, 1993); or war veterans (Casella & Motta, 1990) (see also Quinton et al., 1993; Stouthamer-Loeber et al., 1993). In such instances, measurement has typically been based on semi-structured or structured interviews such as the Schedule for Affective Disorders and Schizophrenia—Lifetime Version (SADS-L) (Endicott & Spitzer, 1978) and associated Research Diagnostic Criteria (RDC) (Spitzer, Endicott,

& Robins, 1978); the Kiddie-Schedule for Affective Disorders and Schizophrenia—Epidemiologic version (K-SADS-E) (Puig-Antich, Orvaschel, & Tabrizi, 1980); and, the Diagnostic Interview for Children and Adolescents (DICA) (Reich & Welner, 1988).

From a research perspective, one of the most commonly encountered difficulties with using such measurement approaches concerns the choice of respondent(s), particularly when the target individual is a child. Empirical evidence indicates generally low to moderate levels of agreement among different respondents—such as teachers, parents, and children themselves—on the presence of symptomatology among children (Achenbach, McConaughy & Howell, 1987; Hart, Lahey, Loeber, & Hanson, 1994; Kazdin, 1990; Reynolds & Graves, 1989). Similarly, studies with adults have shown that as respondents regarding psychopathology among their family members, spouses and children are generally better informants than are parents or siblings, and that frequently, female relatives are more accurate diagnosticians than male relatives (Gershon & Guroff, 1984; Kosten, Anton, & Rounsaville, 1992; Orvaschel et al., 1982; Thompson et al., 1982).

In view of such differences across respondents, a commonly employed research strategy is to use what has been called the "best estimate" diagnosis (Leckman et al., 1982). This strategy involves the derivation of psychiatric diagnoses based on the collective appraisal of multiple sources of information on a particular individual (e.g., parents, spouses, siblings, etc., as well as medical records). In instances where contradictions across reporters occur, judgements about whose account to consider "correct" can vary depending, for example, on the relationship of the respondent to the target individual, as well as on the particular diagnosis under consideration. For example, adolescents may tend to underreport their own conduct problems as compared to their parents, whereas parents may be less reliable than their children about teenage offsprings' feelings of depression (see Kazdin, 1990; Reynolds & Graves, 1989). In a similar vein, research with adults has suggested that consideration of family members' reports, beyond just those of the target individual, enhances the accuracy of diagnosis more so for some psychiatric disorders such as antisocial personality disorder, than for others, such as depressive disorders (Leckman et al., 1982).

Problems of reliability of measurement arise not only because of differences across respondents, but also potentially because of differences among interviewers conducting the assessments, as well as those deriving the "best estimate" diagnoses. As Weismann et al. (1986) indicate in their review of methodology in psychiatric epidemiology, some diagnostic assessment interviews such as the K-SADS require more clinical training of interviewers, as compared to others such as the DISC. Regardless of which instrument is used, however, the authors note the need not only for a period of training for all interviewers, but also for tests of interrater reliability, as well as periodic tests for reliability to avoid rater drift.

When viewed against measures based on the presence of behavioral competence, those requiring simply the absence of maladjustment may appear to represent less stringent criteria for labels of resilience; however, this is not necessarily the case. In point of fact, the absence of psychiatric disorders may often be the *more* stringent of the two approaches. If a given high-risk individual were found to have no psychiatric diagnoses, based on an instrument such as the SADS or K-SADS, in effect, the entire range of maladjustment possibilities would have been sampled and ruled out. Such an across-the-board appraisal would be impossible with measuring competence; there is no resource equivalent to the Diagnostic and Statistical Manual, that might allow a researcher to classify individuals, considering all possible adjustment domains, as essentially competent or not.

A second reason that the absence of diagnoses is not necessarily a lax criterion for labels of resilience is that in the real world, baseline rates of most psychiatric disorders, among even low-risk groups or the population at large, are not zero. Epidemiological research has shown, for example, that among individuals less than thirty years old, *thirty-seven percent* reported prevalence of one or more psychiatric disorders across their lifetimes (Robins & Regier, 1991). In effect, then, when criteria for labels of resilience are that individuals are disorder-free across their lifetimes—at whatever stage in the life cycle they maybe—the standards set may considerably exceed the "performance level" achieved by the population at large.

In summary, in using interview-based tools that assess the presence versus absence of psychiatric disorders, major measurement issues concern potential threats to reliability of information, given the frequently high variability across respondents as well as among those arriving at diagnoses. In the study of adaptation in the face of adversity, the absence of psychiatric disorders may appear to be a less stringent criterion for labels of resilience, as compared to the presence of competence. In reality, however, this is not necessarily the case: evasion of all psychiatric disorders can be relatively high standard even for individuals in low-risk life situations.

Summative Approaches: Multiple Indices of Adjustment

A third approach that has been used in measuring competence in resilience research rests on the integration of scores across different domains of adjustment or competence. Two strategies have been used within this broad category, one largely based on theory, and the other empirically based.

The theoretical approach to measuring multiple facets of social competence is reflected in the development of the Premorbid Social Competence Index by Zigler and Phillips (1960). This instrument involves assessments on different dimensions that represent salient stage-specific developmental tasks in adulthood. Various behavioral indices reflecting effective coping in adult life are considered, including education, occupation, employment history, and marital status. The rationale is that while each of these domains taken individually captures only a small part of what is considered successful coping in adulthood, when considered together, they provide a broad benchmark of personal and social maturity (Zigler & Glick, 1986).

Instead of/in addition to this, another approach has been to apply empirical data reduction strategies to a collection of indices, which themselves are selected on the basis of theoretical or conceptual considerations (e.g., Baldwin et al., 1993; Cicchetti et al., 1993; Egeland, Carlson, & Sroufe, 1993; Hobfall & Lerman, 1988; Johnson et al., 1990; Spencer et al., 1993). Examples are seen in the Project Competence research by Garmezy, Masten, and colleagues. Given the major developmental tasks confronting school age children, these investigators assessed competence in terms of academic achievement as well as behavioral competence in the classroom as rated by both classmates and teachers. Data reduction procedures applied to peer- and teacher-rated dimensions led to the development of composite scores on different aspects of behavioral competence in the classroom (Garmezy et al., 1984; Masten et al., 1988).

Such composite scores based on multiple domains, can be invaluable; yet there are some dangers associated. This has been illustrated in resilience research by our group involving school-based behavioral competence among inner-city adolescents. Based on data-reduction strategies, peer ratings in our studies have been examined within two composite constructs, one involving acceptance (high popularity and low rejection/isolation), and the other, prosocial leadership (high prosocial behaviors, and low aggressiveness/disruptiveness) (Luthar, 1991; Luthar et al., 1993). Recently, the separate examination of these four component peer-rated dimensions has brought to light a critical trend that was obscured while using the composite constructs: popularity in the inner-city teenage peer group can characterize *disruptive bullies* as much as it does prosocial leaders (Luthar & MacMahon, 1994). Findings such as these indicate that although peer acceptance is generally viewed as a sought-after or desirable attribute, popularity in the inner-city group cannot necessarily be seen as connoting "high social competence". It could be a mistake, therefore, to include such a construct in deriving a composite measure of behavioral competence in this population.

As with other approaches to measuring both risk and competence, researchers face the question of what exactly is connoted by high scores on a particular composite competence construct. In this instance too, there is a need to indicate—using qualitative characterizations and/or quantitative comparisons, for example—how an ostensibly resilient high-risk subset might compare with comparable low-risk groups in terms of overall levels of adaptation achieved.

In summary, in resilience research, the use of composite competence scores based on multi-method, multiple informants are valuable: such "broad-band" assessment strategies buttress the validity of measurement of the competence construct. At the same time, however, researchers must carefully examine the component domains that are aggregated in deriving overall competence indices. Even constructs that seem fairly unequivocal in terms of representing positive versus negative adjustment, can show unexpected trends in populations other than the mainstream. And the mainstream, it must be underscored, is what has formed the basis of most current theories and empirically based understanding of psychosocial development.

Resilience

While risk and competence have often been noted as being the two "critical" components of resilience, there is a third that has been relatively neglected in discussions on definitions/measurement, i.e., the nature of the associations between these two constructs. Research strategies in this context fall in two broad categories. Several studies have involved variable-based analyses, which rely on statistical links across measures of risk, competence, and "vulnerability or protective factors" in studying resilience (Baldwin et al., 1993; Carro et al., 1993; Garmezy et al., 1984; Gest et al., 1993; Grossman et al., 1992; Luthar, 1991; O'Grady & Metz, 1987; Osborn, 1990; Richters & Martinez, 1993; Spencer et al., 1993). Other investigations have used individual-based analyses, which involve the isolation of specific individuals who have experienced high risk and demonstrate high competence (e.g., Wyman et al., 1993; Werner & Smith, 1992; Radke-Yarrow & Brown, 1993).

Variable-Based Approaches

In the context of variable-based strategies, perhaps the most perplexing issue from a measurement perspective, is that resilience itself is rarely measured as a construct but is indirectly inferred. The many studies that have used this approach have been aimed not at studying resilience in itself, but at examining (vulnerability/protective) factors linked with a certain pattern of stress-competence associations. Resilience is then inferred based on a certain pattern of these statistical associations.

The specific patterns of associations used to infer resilience, most commonly, have been based on interactive theoretical models of resilience, such as those outlined by Rutter (1987), Masten et al., (1988), and others (Carro et al., 1993; Conrad & Hammen, 1993; Garmezy et al., 1984; Luthar, 1991; Masten et al., 1988; O'Grady & Metz, 1987; Wyman et al., 1993; see Rutter, 1987 for a review of additional studies involving interactive models). These models, illustrated in Figure 1, involve interactions between stress and particular protective attributes—such as intelligence or internal locus of control—in relation to a competence outcome. Trends such as those in Figure 1 have commonly been viewed as reflecting the protective role of the attribute examined in resilience, since they suggests some sort of "engagement" with high stress, wherein the trajectory of competence is altered from a relatively negative to a positive one (Luthar, 1993; Masten et al., 1988; Rutter, 1987).

While this approach to studying resilience carries considerable conceptual and theoretical appeal, there are two problems from a measurement perspective, both of which relate to the forced reliance on statistical interactions to "detect" such interactive processes. The first difficulty pertains to the lack of information on the actual numbers of individuals who faced high risk and were highly competent within the sample concerned, and the second concerns the instability of findings involving such interactive trends.

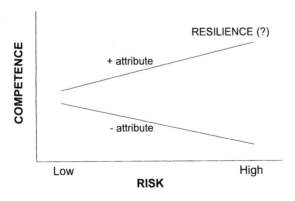

Figure 1. Illustration of an interactive model of resilience.

In discussing the first issue, it would be useful to comment briefly on the mechanics underlying graphs such as Figure 1, which are commonly seen in the resilience literature. The first step in deriving such figures typically rests on the detection of a statistically significant interaction effect (e.g., within hierarchical multiple regression analyses). In these analyses, the measure of risk and the protective factors are predictor variables, and the competence index is an outcome variable. Once statistical significance of the interaction term is obtained, the regression equation is solved illustratively for high and low levels of the two predictor variables concerned, using cutoffs such as one standard deviation above and below the various group means. Solutions such as these yield illustrative values that are used as endpoints of the slopes such as those in Figure 1.

A major problem with this strategy is that it conveys nothing about the number of individuals who actually faced high levels of both risk and competence, or how deviant their scores might be vis-a-vis the sample means (let alone the population means). This problem is illustrated with a hypothetical example. Assume a sample of $n = 200$, a sample size fairly representative of resilience studies employing this technique. Assume, further, normal distributions of both risk and competence. The number of individuals with scores greater than one standard deviation above *both* sample means might range anywhere between 0 and 32. This number would approximate 32 if stress and competence had a near-perfect *positive* association (clearly an impossibility); it would approach zero with increasingly strong *negative* correlations between the two constructs (a definitional stipulation).

The preceding discussions illustrate, then, potential fallacies in viewing illustrations such as Figure 1 as necessarily implying that a certain attribute "fosters resilience". Solving interaction terms in statistical analyses will inevitably yield numbers that might be plotted on such graphs. In reality, however, there may be very few individuals in the sample—or none—who actually meet the stated criteria for resilience implied in these graphs, i.e., of being in the top 16% of the sample on both risk and competence.

Aside from conveying nothing about how many individuals within a particular sample actually meet the dual criteria of high risk and high competence, another problem with using this strategy is its instability as a "measure" of resilient processes. Interaction effects in statistical models are

---

[2]If two normally distributed variables in a sample of 200 were perfectly positively correlated, the number of individuals at +1SD above both sample means would be 16%, or $n = 32$. If the two distributions were perfectly orthogonal, this proportion would be (.16)(.16), which is $n = 5$. If the two variables were negatively correlated, the likelihood of finding *no* individuals with scores at +1SD on both distributions would progressively increase, as correlation coefficients increased in magnitude.

typically associated with small effect sizes, and as a result, are notoriously unstable (see Luthar (1993) and Rutter (1983) for detailed discussions on this issue). Without replication of such effects across comparable samples, with comparable measures of all constructs involved, the credibility of such figures, as potential evidence of resilience, remains limited at best.

Individual-Based Measurement in the Study of Resilience

There is considerable methodological variability within existing individual-based empirical research on resilience, studies that have involved the isolation of a subset of individuals based on high risk and high competence (e.g., Beardslee & Podorefsky, 1988; Cicchetti et al., 1993; Cowen et al., 1992a,b; Egeland et al., 1993; Luthar, 1991; Luthar et al., 1993; Neighbors et al., 1993; Osborn, 1990; Radke-Yarrow & Brown, 1993; Stouthamer-Loeber et al., 1993; Werner & Smith, 1992; Work, Parker, & Cowen, 1990; Wyman, Cowen, Work, & Raoof, 1992). Stipulations for categorizing high-risk individuals as resilient, for example, have varied in stringency. To illustrate, whereas some researchers have accorded labels of resilience only to those high-risk individuals with adjustment scores in the top 16% (+1 SD) of the sample distributions (Cicchetti et al., 1993; Luthar, 1991), others have used competence cutoffs based on quartiles or thirds of distributions (Luthar et al., 1993; Neighbors et al., 1993; Stouthamer et al., 1993; Wyman et al., 1991), and still others have required functioning that is better than the average or median within the sample (e.g., Egeland & Kreutzer, 1991; Osborn, 1990).

Variations in stringency are apparent, as well, in the breadth of domains across which "resilient" individuals are required to show at least adequate functioning. Some investigators have defined resilience based on overall high scores on a global competence index, that combines several discrete areas of adjustment (e.g., Cicchetti et al., 1993; Egeland & Kreutzer, 1991). Others have scrutinized different domains of adjustment individually; they have required that to be labeled as resilient, individuals should not only function well in one or more areas but in addition, should not display *poor* adjustment in any of the domains examined (Luthar, 1991; Osborn, 1990; Wyman et al., 1991).

Individual-based approaches are not prone to the fallacies of measurement previously discussed vis-a-vis variable-based strategies, since a subset of resilient individuals is actually identified, whatever the criteria for high adversity and positive adjustment. Not all research designs, however, lend themselves to such approaches. The isolation of specific groups of high risk, high competence individuals is most straightforward when both constructs involved are studied in a categorical form (e.g., presence versus absence of maternal psychopathology, and presence versus absence of psychiatric disorders). As discussed in preceding sections, many resilience researchers use continuous measures of both risk and competence, and in doing so, confront the well-accepted dictum that continuous data should generally not be converted to categorical form, to avoid the loss of potentially valuable information (Aiken & West, 1991).

As argued elsewhere in this review, in the study of resilience, descriptive profiles of individuals can considerably reduce ambiguities sometimes inherent in quantitatively based measurements. Discussing various individualized approaches to studying behavioral development such as the "idiographic approach" (Rutter, 1980), a biopsychosocial model (Engel, 1977), a life-span developmental perspective (Baltes, Reese, & Lipsitt, 1980), a system-theory model (Marmor, 1983), as well as their own goodness-of fit model in studying temperament, Chess and Thomas (1990) argue persuasively for the use of qualitative analyses in the empirical study of complex psychological phenomena. In the study of resilience, the value of supplementing quantitative empirical data with quantitative insights is indicated in the works of Werner and Smith (1982, 1992), and of Radke-Yarrow and colleagues (Radke-Yarrow & Brown, 1993; Radke-Yarrow & Sherman, 1990). The descriptive profiles provided by these authors are invaluable in reifying, or making meaningful to the reader, what precisely is meant by quantitatively delineated resilience among the high risk cohorts they studied.

In summary, in the many variable-based approaches that have been used to study resilience, resilience itself has not been measured but has been inferred via statistical interaction terms; this strategy can sometimes be misleading. Comparatively, individual-based approaches may be less prone to statistically artifactual insights in studying resilience. In instances where variable-based analyses are essential due to the continuous nature of measures in the research, qualitative analyses of exemplar resilient individuals can be a valuable addition.

Diversity of Measurement in Resilience: Comments on the "State of the Science"

The tremendous diversity of measurement approaches used in resilience research, which have been discussed in this review, compels us to confront a difficult question: what exactly does the term resilience mean, in contemporary social science? The perplexity of this issue is underscored in the equivocality inherent in the pivotal constructs. Any researcher would undoubtedly be nonplussed if asked to comment on "what makes for good adjustment", without further qualifiers attached to the request. Similarly, researchers would seek clarification at the outset if asked to provide an overview of "high psychosocial risk"; the question, inevitably, would be, risk of what kind? Given these ambiguities in the component constructs, it is not entirely clear why resilience has come to be a term that is relatively rarely questioned, in terms of what exactly it might connote.

The seriousness of this issue is reflected in Pedhazur and Schmelkin's (1991) eloquent discussions on definition and measurement concerns in the development of a scientific discipline. The authors state, *"In part, the state of theory in a given field or discipline determines the scope of problems and difficulties in defining dispositional concepts, and the degree of agreement among scientists with respect to such definitions. In addition . . . the state of measurement in a given discipline affects the degree of agreement attainable among researchers. . . . (In sociobehavioral sciences, there are many concepts) about which definitions abound and agreement is nowhere in sight"* (Pedhazur & Schmelkin, 1991, p. 169).

Pursuing this issue and borrowing further from Pedhazur and Schmelkin (1991), these authors allude to what they call "jingle and jangle fallacies" in psychosocial research. Jingle fallacies refer to the assumption that because we call many different things by the same name, they represent the same thing. Considering the enormous diversity of approaches that have been used in measuring risk, competence, and the associations between them, the phrase jingle fallacies resonates uncomfortably with the term resilience.

There is also cause for concern regarding jangle fallacies, which reflect beliefs that things vary from each other because they are called by different names (Pedhazur & Schmelkin, 1991). The empirical literature contains an impressive array of methodologically rigorous studies that do not refer specifically to resilience, yet examine different aspects of adjustment under high-risk conditions. Considering just the domain of substance abuse, for example, there have been great strides over the last five years in empirically-based understanding of vulnerability and protective processes among at-risk youth (Blackson, Tarter, Martin, & Moss, 1994; Brook, Cohen, Whiteman, & Gordon, 1992; Brunswick, Lewis, & Messeri, 1991; Chassin, Pillow, Curran, & Molina, 1993; Hops, Tildesley, & Lichenstein, 1990; Johnson & Pandina, 1993; Kandel & Davies, 1992; Kaplan, Johnson, & Bailey, 1988; Newcomb & Bentler, 1990; Peterson, Hawkins, Abbott, & Catalano, 1994; Schuckit, 1994; Stice, Barrera, & Chassin, 1993; Swaim, Oetting, Edwards, & Beauvais, 1989; Windle, 1990).

Having weighed some of the more disconcerting issues, we turn to the considerable reasons for optimism inherent in the current research scenario. While the breadth of approaches spawned within recent resilience research may suggest a bewildering lack of consensus within the field, this very breadth is critical for the future refinements in the search for protective forces. For the maturation of any scientific discipline, juxtaposed with the stipulation of consensual agreement across researchers, is the requirement that central tenets be examined across a variety of research circumstances. Such diversity of applications is critical for the identification of what Lakatos (1978) has termed the "hard core" of a theory, that is, a set of central principles that are impervious to challenge.

In short, then, it is only with accumulated empirical evidence employing varying research strategies that we can seek out generalizations, and exceptions to these, in the processes associated with resilient functioning. The melange of empirical approaches used across the last two decades allows for a more fine-grained scrutiny than has been heretofore possible, in honing in on central principles—that might eventually form the core of integrative yet parsimonious theories—regarding risk, competence, and the associations between these and protective forces.

Summary

There has been a range of measurement approaches used in empirically studying the different components embedded with the construct "resilience", i.e., risk, competence, and the association between them. High risk conditions have been studied in terms of multiple-item measures such as those of negative life events, by single negative life experiences such as child abuse, and by aggregations of a variety of sociodemographic risks. From a measurement perspective, issues of potential concern with all three of these approaches pertain to where, on some absolute "real-world" scale, high risk as assessed within a particular sample might fall. Other potential problems, which may apply more to some of these approaches than to others, concern confounds of measurement, uncertainties regarding underlying processes, and the validity of the measures used as indices of risk.

Analogous to the measurement of risk are three broad approaches that have been used to measure competence in resilience research. The first involves continuous measures of different domains of functioning, each examined separately. In studies using this approach, the reference group for gauging "high competence" has often been the high-risk sample itself; little is known about how the resilient individuals within these samples compare with individuals in the general population. The second strategy rests on the absence of psychiatric disorders. Measurement issues in this regard pertain essentially to reliability concerns, that is, levels of agreement across respondents as well as among those conducting psychiatric diagnoses. The third major strategy for assessing competence involves aggregation across several different domains of adjustment, on a theoretical and/or empirical basis. A critical precaution in using this approach is that before aggregating different scores, individual domains of functioning must each be validated carefully as, in fact, connoting high competence within the particular "deviant" (high-risk) sample under study.

Finally, variable-based and individual-based analyses have both been used in applying the joint criteria of high risk and high competence, in empirically studying resilience. Variable-based analyses have chiefly been based on statistical interactions between risk and a particular "protective/ vulnerability" factor with competence as outcomes; there are several potential biases associated with the sole reliance on statistics to test interactive theoretical models of resilience. Individual-based approaches in studying resilience have involved both quantitative and qualitative measurement. The richness of information yielded by qualitative approaches argues for their use in supplementing variable-based strategies to examining resilient phenomena.

In conclusion, this review of measurement of resilience has indicated an impressive range of approaches in empirical research. The breadth and diversity of approaches used in recent research makes it possible, far more so than two decades ago, to identify protective and vulnerability processes that might generalize across, or be idiosyncratic to, different aspects of high risk and of competence. Clearly, the task ahead is challenging. Its complexity, however, is more than offset by the potential gains in further understanding a construct of tremendous theoretical and practical importance.

References

Achenbach, T. M., McConaughy, S. H., & Howell, C. T. (1987). Child/adolescent behavioral and emotional problems: Implications of cross-informant correlations for situational specificity. *Psychological Bulletin, 101*, 213–232.

Aiken, L. S., & West, S. G. (1991). *Multiple regression: Testing and interpreting interactions.* Newbury Park, CA: Sage.

Anastasi, A. (1982). *Psychological Testing* (Fifth edition). New York: Macmillan.

Anthony, E. J. (1987). Risk, vulnerability, and resilience: An overview. In E. J. Anthony & B. J. Cohler (Eds.), *The invulnerable child* (pp. 3–48). New York: Guilford Press.

Baldwin, A. L., Baldwin, C., & Cole, R. E. (1990). Stress-resistant families and stress resistant children. In J. Rolf, A. S. Masten, D. Cicchetti, K. H. Nuechterlein & S. Weintraub (Eds.), *Risk and protective factors in the development of psychopathology* (pp. 257–280). New York: Cambridge University Press.

Baldwin, A. L., Baldwin, C. P., Kasser, T., Zax, M., Sameroff, A., & Seifer, R. (1993). Contextual risk and resiliency during late adolescence. *Development and Psychopathology, 5*(4), 741–761.

Baltes, P. B., Reese, H. W., & Lipsitt, L. P. (1980). Life-span developmental psychology. *Annual Review of Psychology*, 65–110.

Beardslee, W. R., & Podorefsky, D. (1988). Resilient adolescents whose parents have serious affective and other psychiatric disorders: Importance of self-understanding and relationships. *American Journal of Psychiatry, 145*(1), 63–69.

Blackson, T. C., Tarter, R. E., Martin, C. S., & Moss, H. B. (1994). Temperament mediates the effects of family history of substance abuse on externalizing and internalizing child behavior. *American Journal on Addictions, 3*(1), 58–66.

Brown, G. W., & Harris, T. O. (1978). *Social origins of depression: A study of psychiatric disorders in women.* London: Tavistock Publications.

Bronfenbrenner, U. (1986). Ecology of the family as a context for human development: Research perspectives. *Developmental Psychology, 22*, 723–742.

Brook, J. S., Cohen, P., Whiteman, M., & Gordon, A. S. (1992). Psychosocial risk factors in the transition from moderate to heavy use or abuse of drugs. In M Glantz & R. Pickens (Eds.), *Vulnerability to drug abuse* (pp. 211–253). Washington, DC: American Psychological Association.

Brunswick, A. F., Lewis, C. S., & Messeri, P. A. (1991). A life span perspective on drug use and affective distress in an African-American sample. *Journal of Community Psychology, 19*, 123–135.

Carmines, E. G., & Zeller, R. A. (1979). *Reliability and validity assessment.* In *Sage University Paper Series on Quantitative Applications in the Social Sciences* (pp. 7–17). Beverly Hills: Sage Publications.

Carro, M. G., Grant, K. E., Gotlib, I. H., & Compas, B. E. (1993). Postpartum depression and child development: An investigation of mothers and fathers as sources of risk and resilience. *Development and Psychopathology, 5*(4), 567–579.

Casella, L., & Motta, R. W. (1990). Comparison of characteristics of Vietnam veterans with and without posttraumatic stress disorder. *Psychological Reports, 67*, 595–605.

Chase-Lansdale, P. L., Brooks-Gunn, J., & Zamsky, E. S. (1994). Young African-American multigenerational families in poverty: Quality of mothering and grandmothering. *Child Development, 65*(2), 373–393.

Chassin, L., Pillow, D. R., Curran, P. J., & Molina, B. S. (1993). Relation of parental alcoholism to early adolescent substance use: A test of three mediating mechanisms. *Journal of Abnormal Psychology, 102*(1), 3–19.

Chess, S., & Thomas, A. (1990). Continuities and discontinuities in temperament. In L. Robins & M. Rutter (Eds.), *Straight and devious pathways from childhood to adulthood* (pp. 205–220). Melbourne, Australia: Cambridge University Press.

Cicchetti, D., Rogosch, F. A., Lynch, M., & Holt, K. D. (1993). Resilience in maltreated children: Processes leading to adaptive outcome. *Development and Psychopathology, 5*(4), 629–647.

Coddington, R. D. (1972). The significance of life events as etiologic factors in the diseases of children. II: A study of a normal population. *Journal of Psychosomatic Research, 16*, 205–213

Cohen, L. H., (1988). Measurement of life events. In L. H. Cohen (Ed.), *Life events and psychological functioning: Theoretical and methodological issues* (pp. 11–30). Newbury Park, CA: Sage Publications.

Conrad, M., & Hammen, C. (1993). Protective and resource factors in high and low-risk children: A comparison of children with unipolar, bipolar, medically ill, and normal mothers. *Development and Psychopathology, 5*(4), 593–607.

Cowen, E. L., Work, W. C., & Wyman, P. A. (1992a). Resilience among profoundly stressed urban school children. In M. Kessler, S. E. Glodston & J. M. Joffe (Eds.), *The present and future of prevention* (pp. 155–168). Newbury Park, CA: Sage.

Cowen, E. L., Work, W. C., Wyman, P. A. (1992b). Similarity of parent and child self-views in stress-affected and stress-resilient urban families. *Acta Paedopsychiatrica: International Journal of Child & Adolescent Psychiatry*, *55*(4), 193–197.

Crittendon, P. (1985). Maltreated infants: Vulnerability and resilience. *Journal of Child Psychiatry and Psychology*, *26*(1), 85–96.

Dohrenwend, B. P., & Dohrenwend, B. S. (1978). Some issues in research on stressful life events. *Journal of Nervous and Mental Diseases*, *166*, 7–15.

Egeland, B., & Kreutzer, T. (1991). A longitudinal study of the effects of maternal stress and protective factors on the development of high risk children. In A. Greene, E. Cummings & K. Karaker (Eds.), *Life-span developmental psychology: Perspectives on stress and coping* (pp. 61–84). Hillsdale, N. J.: Erlbaum.

Egeland, B., Carlson, E., & Sroufe, L. A. (1993). Resilience as process. *Development and Psychopathology*, *5*(4), 517–528.

Egeland, B., & Kalkoske, M. (1993). *Continuity as a function of risk status: Infant attachment to the early school years.* Paper presented at the biennial meeting of the Society for Research in Child Development, New Orleans.

Elder, G. H., & Clipp, E. C. (1989). Combat experience and emotional health: Impairment and resilience in later life. *Journal of Personality*, *57*(2), 311–341.

Emshoff, J. G. (1989). A preventive intervention with children of alcoholics. *Prevention in Human Services*, 225–253.

Endicott, J., & Spitzer, R. L. (1978). A diagnostic interview: The Schedule for Affective Disorders and Schizophrenia. *Archives of General Psychiatry*, *137*, 837–844.

Engel, G. L. (1977). The need for a new medical model: A challenge for biomedicine. *Science*, *196*, 129–135.

Farber, E., & Egeland, B. (1987). Abused children: Can they be invulnerable. In J. Anthony & B. Cohler (Eds.), *The invulnerable child* (pp. 253–288). New York: Guilford Press.

Garfinkle, I., & McLanahan, S. S. (1986). *Single mothers and their children: A new American dilemma.* Washington, DC: Urban Institute Press.

Garmezy, N., Masten, A. S., & Tellegen, A. (1984). The study of stress and competence in children: A building block for developmental psychopathology. *Child Development*, *55*, 97–111.

Garrett, P., Ng'andu, N., & Ferron, J. (1994). Poverty experiences of young children and the quality of their home environments. *Child Development*, *65*(2), 331–345.

Gelles, R. (1973). Child abuse as psychopathology: A sociological critique and reformulation. *American Journal of Orthopsychiatry*, *43*, 611–621.

Gershon, E. S., & Guroff, J. J. (1984). Information from relatives. *Archives of General Psychiatry*, *48*, 173–180.

Gersten, J. C., Langner, T. S., Eisenberg, J. G., & Simcha-Fagen, O. (1977). An evaluation of the etiologic role of stressful life-change events in psychological disorders. *Journal of Health and Social Behavior*, *18*, 228–244.

Gest, S. D., Neemann, J., Hubbard, J. J., Masten, A. S., & Tellegen, A. (1993). Parenting quality, adversity, and conduct problems in adolescence: Testing process-oriented models of resilience. *Development and Psychopathology*, *5*(4), 663–682.

Grossman, F. K., Beinashowitz, L., Sakurai, M., Finnin, L., & Flaherty, M. (1992). Risk and resilience in young adolescents. *Journal of Youth and Adolescence*, *21*(5), 529–550.

Hart, E. L., Lahey, B. B., Loeber, R., & Hanson, K. S. (1994). Criterion validity of informants in the diagnosis of disruptive behavior disorders in children: A preliminary study. *Journal of Consulting and Clinical Psychology*, *62*(2), 410–414.

Heer, D. M. (1985). Effects of sibling number on child outcome. *Annual Review of Sociology, 11*, 27–47.

Herrenkohl, E. C., Herrenkohl, R. C., & Egolf, B. (1994). Resilient early school-age children from maltreating homes: Outcomes in late adolescence. *American Journal of Orthopsychiatry, 64*(2), 301–309.

Hobfall, S. E., & Lerman, M. (1988). Personal relationships, personal attributes, and stress resistance: Mothers' reactions to their child's illness. *American Journal of Community Psychology, 16*(4), 565–589.

Hobfall, S. E., London, P., & Orr, E. (1988). Mastery, intimacy, and stress resistance during war. *Journal of Community Psychology, 16*, 317–331.

Holahan, C. J., & Moos, R. H. (1991). Life stressors, personal and social resources, and depression: A 4-year structural model. *Journal of Abnormal Psychology, 100*(1), 31–38.

Holmes, T. H.,& Rahe, R. H. (1967). The social readjustment rating scale. *Journal of Psychosomatic Research, 11, 213–218.*

Hops, H., Tildesley, E., & Liechtenstein, E. (1990). Parent-adolescent problem-solving interactions and drug use. *American Journal of Drug and Alcohol Abuse, 16*, 239–258.

Johnson, H. L., Glassman, M. B., Fiks, K. B., & Rosen, T. S. (1990). Resilient children: Individual differences in developmental outcome of children born to drug abusers. *Journal of Genetic Psychology, 151*(4), 523–539.

Johnson, J. H., & McCutcheon, S. M. (1980). Assessing life stress in older children and adolescents: Preliminary findings with the Life Events Checklist. In I. G. Sarason & C. D. Spielberger (Eds.), *Stress and anxiety* (pp. 111–125). Washington, DC: Hemisphere.

Johnson, J. H. (1986). *Life events as stressors in childhood and adolescence.* Beverly Hills, CA: Sage.

Johnson, V., & Pandina, R. J. (1993). Affectivity, family drinking history, and the development of problem drinking: A longitudinal analysis. *Journal of Applied Social Psychology, 66*, 2055–2073.

Kandel, D. B., & Davies, M. (1992). Progression to regular marijuana involvement: Phenomenology and risk factors for near-daily use. In M Glantz & R. Pickens (Eds.), *Vulnerability to drug abuse* (pp. 211–253). Washington, DC: American Psychological Association.

Kaplan, H. B., Johnson, R. J., & Bailey, C. A. (1988). Explaining adolescent drug use: An elaboration strategy for structural equation modeling. *Psychiatry, 51*(2), 142–163.

Kazdin, A. E. (1990). Childhood depression. *Journal of Child Psychiatry and Psychology, 31*, 121–160.

Kosten, T. A., Anton, S. F., & Rounsaville, B. J. (1992). Ascertaining psychiatric diagnoses with the family history method in a substance abuse population. *Journal of Psychiatric Research, 26*(2), 135–147.

Lakatos, I. (1978). *The methodology of scientific research programs: Philosophical papers* (Vol. I). J. Morrall & G. Currie (Eds.), New York: Cambridge University Press.

Leckman, J. F., Sholomskas, D., Thompson, W. D., Belanger, A., & Weissman, M. M. (1982). Best estimate of lifetime psychiatric diagnosis: A methodological study. *Archives of General Psychiatry, 39*, 879–883.

Loo, C., Tong, B., & True, R. (1989). A bitter bean: Mental health status and attitudes in Chinatown. *Journal of Community Psychology, 17*(4), 283–296.

Luthar, S. S. (1993). Annotation: Methodological and conceptual issues in research on childhood resilience. *Journal of Child Psychiatry and Psychology, 34*(4), 441–453.

Luthar, S. S., (1991). Vulnerability and resilience: A study of high risk adolescents. *Child Development, 62*, 600–616.

Luthar, S. S., Cushing, G., Merikangas, K. R., & Rounsaville, B. J. (1994). *Psychiatric disorders among children of addicts.* Paper to be presented at the 1995 annual meetings of the American Psychiatric Association, Miami.

Luthar, S. S., & MacMahon, T. (1994). Doing well in whose eyes? Peer reputation among inner-city teens [Submitted.].

Luthar, S. S., & Zigler, E. (1991). Vulnerability and competence: A review of research on resilience in childhood. *American Journal of Orthopsychiatry, 61*, 6–22.

Luthar, S. S., Doernberger, C. H., & Zigler, E. (1993). Resilience is not a unidimensional construct: Insights from a prospective study of inner-city adolescents. *Development and Psychopathology, 5*(4), 703–717.

Marmor, J. (1983). Systems thinking in psychiatry: Some theoretical and clinical implications. *American Journal of Psychiatry, 140*, 833–838.

Masten, A. S., Morison, P., Pellegrini, D., & Tellegen, A. (1990). Competence under stress: Risk and protective factors. In J. Rolf, A. S. Masten, D. Cicchetti, K. H. Nuechterlein & S. Weintraub (Eds.), *Risk and protective factors in the development of psychopathology* (pp. 236–256). New York: Cambridge University Press.

Masten, A. S. (1989). Resilience in development: Implications of the study of successful adaptation for developmental psychopathology. In D. Cicchetti (Ed.), *Rochester symposium on developmental psychopathology: Vol. 1. The emergence of a discipline* (pp. 261–294). Hillsdale, NJ: Erlbaum.

Masten, A. S., Best, K. M., & Garmezy, N. (1990). Resilience and development: Contributions from the children who overcome adversity. *Development and Psychopathology, 2*, 425–444.

Masten, A. S., Garmezy, N., Tellegen, A., Pellegrini, D. S., Larkin, K., & Larsen, A. (1988). Competence and stress in school children: The moderating effects of individual and family qualities. *Journal for Child Psychiatry and Psychology, 29*(6), 745–764.

Masten, A. S., Neemann, J., & Adenas, S. (1994). Life events and adjustment in adolescents: The significance of event independence, desirability, and chronicity. *Journal of Research on Adolescence, 4*(1), 71–97.

Meyer-Probst, B., Rosler, H., & Teichmann, H. (1983). Biological and psychosocial risk factors and development during childhood. In D. Magnusson & V. L. Allen (Eds.), *Human development: An interactional perspective* (pp. 243–259). New York: Academic Press.

Mulholland, D. J., Watt, N. F., Philpott, A., & Sarlin, N. (1991). Academic performance in children of divorce: Psychological resilience and vulnerability. *Psychiatry, 54*, 268–280.

Neighbors, B., Forehand, R., & McVicar, D. (1993). Resilient adolescents and interparental conflict. *American Journal of Orthopsychiatry, 63*(3), 462–471.

Newcomb, M. D., & Bentler, P. M. (1990). Antecedents and consequences of cocaine use: An eight-year study from early adolescence to young adulthood. In Robins. L. & M. Rutter (Eds.), *Straight and devious pathways from childhood to adulthood* (pp. 158–181). Melbourne, Australia: Cambridge University Press.

O'Grady, D., & Metz, J. R. (1987). Resilience in children at high risk for psychological disorder. *Journal of Pediatric Psychology, 12*(1), 3–23.

Orvaschel, H., Thompson, W. D., Belanger, A., Prusoff, B. A., & Kidd, K. K. (1982). Comparison of the family history method to direct interview: Factors affecting the diagnosis of depression. *Journal of Affective Disorders, 4*, 49–59.

Osborn, A. F. (1990). Resilient children: A longitudinal study of high achieving socially disadvantaged children. *Early Child Development and Care, 62*, 23–47.

Parker, R., & Collmer, C. (1976). Child abuse: An interdisciplinary analysis. In E. M. Hetherington (Ed.), *Review of child development research (Vol. 5)*. Chicago: University of Chicago Press.

Pedhazur, E. J., & Schmelkin, L. P. (1991). *Measurement, design and analysis: An integrated approach*. Hillsdale, NJ: Lawrence Erlbaum Associates, Inc.

Peterson, P. L., Hawkins, D. J., Abbott, R. D., & Catalano, R. F. (1994). Disentangling the effects of parental drinking, family management, and parental alcohol norms on current drinking by black and white adolescents. *Journal of Research on Adolescence, 4*(2), 203–227.

Pianta, R., Egeland, B., & Stroufe, A. (1990). Maternal stress and children's development: Prediction of school outcomes and identification of protective factors. In J. E. Rolf, A. S. Masten, D. Cicchetti, K. Nuechterlein & S. Weintraub (Eds.), *Risk and protective factors in the development of psychopathology* (pp. 215–235). New York: Cambridge University Press.

Puig-Antich, J., Orvaschel, H., & Tabrizi, M. A. (1980). *The schedule for affective disorders and schizophrenia for school- age children-epidemiologic version (Kiddie-SADS-E), ed 3.* New York: New York State Psychiatric Institute.

Quinton, D., Pickles, A., Maughan, B., & Rutter, M. (1993). Partners, peers, and pathways: Assortative pairing and continuities in conduct disorder. *Development and Psychopathology, 5*(4), 763–783.

Quinton, D., Rutter, M., & Liddle, C. (1984). Institutional rearing, parenting difficulties, and marital support. *Psychological Medicine, 14,* 107–124.

Radke-Yarrow, M., & Sherman, T. (1990). Hard growing: Children who survive. In J. Rolf, A. S. Masten, D. Cicchetti, K. H. Nuechterlein & S. Weintraub (Eds.), *Risk and protective factors in the development of psychopathology* (pp. 97–119). New York: Cambridge University Press.

Radke-Yarrow, M., & Brown, E. (1993). Resilience and vulnerability in children of multiple-risk families. *Development and Psychopathology, 5*(4), 581–592.

Reich, W., & Welner, Z. (1988). *Diagnostic interview for children and adolescents.* Unpublished manuscript, Washington University, St. Louis, MO.

Reynolds, W. M., & Graves, A. (1989). Reliability of children's reports of depressive symptomatology. *Journal of Abnormal Child Psychology, 17,* 647–655.

Richters, J. E., & Martinez, P. E. (1993). Violent communities, family choices, and children's chances: An algorithm for improving the odds. *Development and Psychopathology, 5*(4), 609–627.

Richters, J. E., & Weintraub, S. (1990). Beyond diathesis: Toward an understanding of high risk environments. In J. E. Rolf, A. S. Masten, D. Cicchetti, K. Nuechterlein & S. Weintraub (Eds.), *Risk and protective factors in the development of psychopathology* (pp. 67–96). New York: Cambridge University Press.

Robins, L. N., & Regier, D. A. (1991). *Psychiatric disorders in America: The epidemiologic catchment area study.* New York: Free Press.

Rutter, M. (1987). Psychosocial resilience and protective mechanisms. *American Journal of Orthopsychiatry, 57*(3), 316–331.

Rutter, M. (1980). Introduction. In M. Rutter (Ed.), *Scientific foundations of developmental psychiatry* (pp. 49–62). London: Heinemann.

Rutter, M. (1983). Prevention of children's psychosocial disorders: Myth and substance. *Annual Progress in Child Psychiatry & Child Development,* 271–295.

Rutter, M., & Quinton, D. (1977). Psychiatric disorder: Ecological factors and concepts of causation. In *Ecological factors in human development.* Amsterdam: North-Holland.

Rutter, M., & Quinton, D. (1984). Long-term follow-up of women institutionalized in childhood: Factors promoting good functioning in adult life. *British Journal of Developmental Psychology, 2*(3), 191–204.

Sameroff, A. J., Seifer, R., Barocas, R., Zax, M., & Greenspan, S. (1987). Intelligence quotient scores of 4-year-old children: Social-environmental risk factors. *Pediatrics, 79*(3), 343–350.

Sameroff, A. J., & Seifer, R. (1990). Early contributors to developmental risk. In J. Rolf, A. S. Masten, D. Cicchetti, K. H. Nuechterlein & S. Weintraub (Eds.), *Risk and protective factors in the development of psychopathology* (pp. 52–66). New York: Cambridge University Press.

Seifer, R., & Sameroff, A. J. (1987). Multiple determinants of risk and invulnerability. In E. J. Anthony & B. J. Cohler (Eds.), *The invulnerable child* (pp. 51–59). New York: Guilford Press.

Spencer, M. B., Cole, S. P., DuPree, D., Glymph, A., & Pierre, P. (1993). Self-efficacy among urban African American early adolescents: Exploring issues of risk, vulnerability, and resilience. *Development and Psychopathology, 5*(4), 719–739.

Shuckit, M. A. (1994). Low level of response to alcohol as a predictor of future alcoholism. *American Journal of Psychiatry, 151*(2), 184–189.

Spitzer, R. L., Endicott, J., & Robins, E. (1978). Research diagnostic criteria: Rationale and reliability. *Archives of General Psychiatry, 36*, 733–782.

Stice, E., Barrera, M., & Chassin, L. (1993). Relation of parental support and control to adolescents' externalizing symptomatology and substance use: A longitudinal examination of curvilinear effects. *Journal of Abnormal Child Psychology, 21*(6), 609–629.

Stouthamer-Loeber, M., Loeber, R., Farrington, D. P., Zhang, Q., van Kammen, W., & Maguin, E. (1993). The double edge of protective and risk factors for delinquency: Interrelations and developmental patterns. *Development and Psychopathology, 5*(4), 683–701.

Swaim, R. C., Oetting, E. R., Edwards, R. W., & Beauvais, F. (1989). Links from emotional distress to adolescent drug use: A path model. *Journal of Consulting and Clinical Psychology, 57*(2), 227–231.

Swearingen, E. M., & Cohen, L. H. (1985). Life events and psychological distress: A prospective study of young adolescents. *Developmental Psychology, 21*, 1045–1054.

Thoits, P. (1983). Dimensions of life events that influence psychological distress: An evaluation and synthesis of the literature. In H. Kaplan (Ed.), *Psychosocial stress: Trends in theory and research* (pp. 33–103). New York: Academic Press.

Thompson, W. D., Orvaschel, H., Prusoff, B. A., & Kidd, B. A. (1982). An evaluation of the family history method for ascertaining psychiatric disorders. *Archives of General Psychiatry, 39*, 53–58.

Weissman, M. M., Merikangas, K. R., John, K., Wickramaratne, P., Prusoff, B. A., & Kidd, K. K. (1986). Family-genetic studies of psychiatric disorders. *Archives of General Psychiatry, 43*, 1104–1116.

Wells, R. D., & Schwebel, A. I. (1987). Chronically ill children and their mothers: Predictors of resilience and vulnerability to hospitalization and surgical stress. *Developmental and Behavioral Pediatrics, 8*(2), 83–89.

Werner, E. E. (1986). Resilient offspring of alcoholics. *Journal of Studies on Alcohol, 47*(1), 34–40.

Werner, E. E., & Smith, R. S. (1992). *Overcoming the odds: High risk children from birth to adulthood.* Ithaca, NY: Cornell University Press.

Werner, E. E., & Smith, R. S. (1982). *Vulnerable but invincible.* New York: McGraw-Hill.

Windle, M. (1990). A longitudinal study of antisocial behaviors in early adolescence as predictors of late adolescent substance use: Gender and ethnic group differences. *Journal of Abnormal Psychology, 99*, 86–91.

Work, W. C., Parker, G. R., & Cowen, E. L. (1990). The impact of life stressors on childhood adjustment: Multiple perspectives. *Journal of Community Psychology, 18*(1), 73–78.

Wyman, P. A., Cowen, E. L., Work, W. C., & Kerley, J. H. (1993). The role of children's future expectations in self-system functioning and adjustment to life stress: A prospective study of urban at-risk children. *Development and Psychopathology, 5*(4), 649–661.

Wyman, P. A., Cowen, E. L., Work, W. C., & Parker, G. R. (1991). Developmental and family milieu correlates of resilience in urban children who have experienced major life stress. *American Journal of Community Psychology, 19*(3), 405–426.

Wyman, P. A., Cowen, E. L., Work, W. C., & Raoof, A. (1992). Interviews with children who experienced major life stress: Family and child attributes that predict resilient outcomes. *Journal of the American Academy of Child & Adolescent Psychiatry, 31*(5), 904–910.

Zigler, E. F., Lamb, M. E., & Child, I. L. (1982). *Socialization and personality development* (pp. 97–119). New York: Oxford University Press.

Zigler, E., & Child, I. L. (1969). Socialization. In G. Lindzey & E. Aronson (Eds.), *Handbook of social psychology (2nd ed.)* (pp. 450–589). Reading, MA: Addison-Wesley.

Zigler, E., & Phillips, L. (1960). Social effectiveness and symptomatic behaviors. *Journal of Abnormal and Social Psychology, 61*, 231–238.

Zigler, E., & Glick, M. (1986). *A developmental approach to adult psychopathology.* New York: Wiley.

Zimmerman, M. (1983). Methodological issues in the assessment of life events: A review of issues and research. *Clinical Psychology Review, 3*, 339–370.

8

Critical Conceptual and Measurement Issues in the Study of Resilience

Michael Windle

Introduction

In their overview article in this volume, Luthar and Cushing, 1999, identified a number of salient measurement issues in resiliency research that merit serious consideration to further advance the field. Some of the measurement issues raised by Luthar and Cushing have origins in other research literatures, such as the measurement of stressful life events in psychiatric epidemiology (e.g., Dohrenwend & Dohrenwend, 1978, 1981), whereas others were more specific to resiliency research. Examples of those specific to resiliency research included limitations of interaction-based statistical models to evaluate risk-protective factor relations because of potential sampling restrictions on the distributions of risk and protective factors, and tradeoffs in measurement by selecting individual or summated (aggregated) scores to optimally assess risk and protective factors. In this article, I elaborate on some of the issues identified by Luthar and Cushing and expanded on some additional conceptual and measurement issues pertinent to resiliency research. The article consists of four components: (1) a brief presentation of some strengths of resiliency research; (2) a general orientation toward risk and protective factors and resiliency research that may, at a general level, clarify alternative conceptual models and measurement

Michael Windle • Department of Psychology, University of Alabama at Birmingham, Birmingham, Alabama 35294.

Resilience and Development: Positive Life Adaptations, edited by Glantz and Johnson. Kluwer Academic/Plenum Publishers, New York, 1999.

traditions; (3) an enumeration of some measurement weaknesses in risk and protective factor research; and (4) the consideration of systematic ways to maintain the vitality and promote the longevity of resiliency research. This last issue is of particular importance lest the resiliency concept fade into obscurity as have other psychological concepts where at least some level of conceptual and methodological consensus has not been attained.

Strengths of Research on Resiliency

Research on resiliency research has been a contributor to and constituent member of a broader Zeitgeist of human functioning characterized by active human agency and a prevention and health promotion orientation. This orientation may be contrasted with narrow-range medical model approaches that have emphasized passive human agency, reductionism, and inevitable disease progression. This more recent health promotion approach is evidenced in resiliency research by a focus on protective factors and biopsychosocial processes that contribute to ongoing healthy adaptation in the face of either initial (e.g., low birthweight, poverty) or ongoing (e.g., stressful life events) adverse circumstances. Thus, rather than focusing exclusively on those risk factors that contribute to the manifestation of psychiatric disturbances, substance abuse disorders, or criminality, equal (or perhaps more) weight has been directed toward the study of factors that may mitigate or eliminate problematic or disturbed manifestations in the face of disadvantaged or adverse circumstances.

Given this more general health promotion orientation toward the identification of protective factors and resiliency processes, the emerging resiliency literature has made significant contributions in four ways. First, it has identified a broad range of background conditions (e.g., poverty, family history of psychopathology), personal characteristics (e.g., temperament, cognitive functioning), social relations (e.g., with family members, peers), and community resources (e.g., teachers, clergymen) that are essential to understanding healthy adaptation in face of adversity. Second, resiliency research has helped ignite interest across the fields of child and adult psychology and psychiatry and to the adoption of a more integrationist, developmental psychopathology model (e.g., Sroufe & Rutter, 1984). Third, resiliency research has stimulated research in a wide variety of disciplines, including epidemiology, sociology, education, psychology, and psychiatry, and from more specialized areas related to alcohol and substance abuse and delinquency/criminology. Fourth, resiliency research has contributed to new ideas and insights in prevention and treatment programs. That is, there is more of a focus on the facilitation and enhancement of skills and competencies (e.g., social skills, problem solving, peer refusal skills) that involve the development of prosocial, and potentially protective skill-related factors, rather than sole reliance on reactive treatment strategies (i.e., insight-oriented or pharmacologic treatment *after* the individual is manifesting serious problems).

General Orientation toward Risk and Protective Factors and Resilience

There is often ambiguity in the literature regarding the conceptual definitions of, and distinctions between, risk and protective factors and resilience, and the use of statistical models that correspond to these concepts. At a general level, perhaps the most agreed upon definition of resilience is the "successful" adaptation to life tasks in the face of social disadvantage or highly adverse conditions. Resiliency is *inferred* on the basis of significant interactions between risk and protective factors to the extent that protective factors are associated with healthy adaptation (e.g., Rutter, 1987). There are a number of oblique conceptual and measurement issues associated with this seemingly straightforward definition of resilience that are the focus of many of the contributions to this volume, including some that are identified and discussed subsequently in this article.

However, at the general level, this interactive resiliency model needs to be distinguished from a broader, more encompassing orientation that focuses on risk and protective factors largely independent of the resiliency concept. That is, advocates of a health promotion model have often sought to identify protective factors that decrease the probability of undesirable behaviors (e.g., aggression, early onset substance use, high risk sex) *independent* of the occurrence of social disadvantage or adverse circumstances. This orientation assumes that all individuals are at some level of risk for undesirable outcomes and that the prevention focus should be on those elements of behavior (e.g., positive parent-child relations, peer refusal skills) that reduce or eliminate the expression of problematic behaviors.

Note that this more general risk and protective factors orientation is not incompatible with the interactive resiliency model; in fact, the interactive resiliency model may be viewed as a restricted version, or class of model, underlying the more general model. However, it is argued in this article that this distinction between the restricted and general model is critical for the viability and utility of the resiliency concept. At issue here are the boundary conditions to be identified to characterize the phenomenon of resilience; if the boundaries are defined in an overly "loose" fashion, then resiliency may be a superfluous concept to a more general concept of adaptive coping (independent of risk-defining contextual features, e.g., social disadvantage). It is argued that the resilience model must include the identification of salient (and empirically established) risk factor(s) (e.g., parental psychopathology, social disadvantage) and that an interactive (risk x protective factor) measurement model (either implicitly or explicitly specified) is appropriate to investigate implied resiliency processes. Such restrictions are not essential components of the more general health promotion model as no salient risk factor need be identified and effects may be evaluated via additive or interactive statistical models.

Measurement Weaknesses

Within the context of the conceptualization provided above regarding the distinction between the general health promotion orientation and the more specific interactive resiliency model, several weaknesses of existing research on resiliency are now discussed. In some ways, these weaknesses reflect both conceptual and measurement limitations of a domain of research that has been largely descriptive, but now seeks toward a consensual, explanatory paradigm.

Absence of a Unifying Conceptual Framework

There has been an absence of a unifying conceptual framework to accommodate the integration of findings across disciplines and specialized research areas. Risk status has been defined by a range of characteristics, including socioeconomic indicators (e.g., poverty), neighborhood crime statistics, family discord, parental deviance, child maltreatment, family history of alcoholism, substance abuse, or mental illness, institutional rearing environment, childhood psychiatric status (e.g., ADHD, learning disabilities) or homeless status, perinatal stress and low birthweight, and cutoff scores for high levels of stress (e.g., Garmezy, 1993; Hechtman, 1991; Herrenkohl, Herrenkohl, & Egolf, 1994; Keough & Weisner, 1993; Neiman, 1988; Rutter & Quinton, 1984). Given the diversity of risk status factors to evaluate protective factors and resiliency processes, a larger, more encompassing, framework may facilitate comparisons across studies for general and specific processes, and may assist in some level of integration of findings across disciplines and specialty areas. It may turn out that there are a limited number of common resiliency processes that operate across risk status variables, or that a more comprehensive understanding of resiliency may be facilitated by a knowledge of both common and unique aspects. Lifespan models of developmental psychopathology (e.g., Cicchetti, 1994; Sroufe & Rutter, 1984; Windle & Searles, 1990) have implicitly, if not explicitly, been adopted by some resiliency researchers; however, such a framework has not been consistently or systematically utilized to integrate findings across age groups and across studies that differ with respect to risk status definition. The adoption and utilization of such an orientation may enhance efforts to integrate findings across diverse risk and protective factors, facilitate the investigation of age-related resiliency processes, and provide guidance for the identification of age-appropriate, optimal targets for preventive interventions.

Attention to Causal Time-Lagged Structure

There has been insufficient attention to causal time-lagged features of longitudinal research designs (e.g., Gollob & Reichardt, 1987) that may be essential to the understanding of (causal) dynamic processes associated with resilience. While some notable prospective research has been completed with regard to resilience (e.g., Rutter & Quinton, 1984; Werner & Smith, 1992), many prospective studies have often relied on long-term follow-up periods of assessment (e.g., across several years) that may impose limitations on drawing inferences about time-ordered causal effects. For example, the identification of some presumed protective factors (e.g., locus of control, extra-familial support) that differentiate successful adjustment in adulthood by children with a risk status designation (e.g., parental psychopathology, poverty status, ADHD) may provide highly useful descriptive information. The identified factors may simultaneously provide quite limited information with regard to the dynamic causal processes underlying the successful adaptation, or with regard to the identification of resiliency mechanisms or processes. The protective triad factors of personal characteristics (e.g., temperament), familial influences, and community resources have consistently been identified as salient moderators of developmental outcomes associated with adverse circumstances (e.g., Garmezy, 1983; Werner & Smith, 1992), but the proximal causal factors contributing to resilience (or the lack thereof) remain largely unknown (though, of course, reasonable explanations regarding causal mechanisms have been proffered).

Under ideal circumstances, it would be desirable to have longitudinal assessments that corresponded to the causal event structure as it is manifested in the unfolding of multivariate processes across time. The attainment of these ideal circumstances is typically very difficult for numerous reasons, two of which are mentioned here. *First*, the timing of the causal lagged structure for the phenomenon under study is often unknown or is variable in influence across the lifespan. For example, a family history of alcoholism may be a potent risk factor in childhood via influences on disruptive parenting, childhood physical or sexual abuse, and marital conflict, whereas it may function more as a risk factor for alcoholism in adulthood via more biologically-based stress dampening or alcohol tolerance mechanisms (e.g., Schuckit, 1994; Sher & Levenson, 1982). *Second*, there may be variable timing, or heterogeneity, with regard to periods of maximal risk and protectiveness for different age groups or different individuals, contingent on the "initial conditions" (e.g., developmental level) of subjects. With longitudinal, multivariate correlational research designs, or quasi-experimental designs, one generally cannot control for some of these subject heterogeneity factors (e.g., one cannot control the occurrence or sequence of stressful life events) that may contribute to alternative time-lagged causal processes for different individuals or different subsets (clusters) of individuals.

Despite the considerable difficulties encountered in pursuing the appropriate causal time-lagged structure in prospective research designs on resiliency (e.g., Pickles, 1988; Rutter, 1988), it is proposed that a focus on the cross-temporal relations among risk and protective factors and problem behaviors are, nevertheless, valuable to study (and confirm) behavioral regularities in human functioning. These dynamic behavioral regularities may then form the basis of making inferences about resilience and dynamic resiliency processes. By dynamic resiliency processes, reference is made to explication of time-ordered relations of multivariate change among specific risk and protective factors, and specific behavior problems. The understanding of such dynamic resiliency processes would greatly facilitate the targeting of preventive interventions for children and adolescents by incorporating both risk and protective factors, and by including temporal data pertinent to time course characteristics (i.e., timing, duration). The investigation of such dynamic resiliency processes may require prospective research designs with both more occasions of measurement and shorter intervals between occasions of measurement.

Bidirectionality of Effects

Most studies of resilience have adopted unidirectional, rather than bidirectional, models of dynamic relations. That is, risk and protective factors have often been viewed as static variables whose influences increase, decrease, or negate (i.e., cancel out) one another in relation to outcome variables, as well as to ongoing stressors. Note, that there has been a general recognition in the literature that risk and protective factors may function in alternative ways for different age groups, and in alternative ways for the same individual at different periods in the lifespan. Nevertheless, this recognition has not been adequately translated into the research literature to address issues pertinent to dynamic, bidirectional relations. For example, the expression of various emotional and behavioral problems may have direct and indirect influences on potential risk and protective factors. Early onset deviant behaviors such as high levels of aggression or early onset substance use may influence and be influenced by a range of risk factors (e.g., difficult temperament, parental deviance, poor parental monitoring and a lack of nurturance). However, the expression of these deviant behaviors has consequences that may impact the escalation, maintenance, and severity of problematic behaviors via multiple aspects of human functioning. Early onset heavy substance use may contribute to deviant social labeling, to affiliations with other more deviant peers, to alienating self-identification processes, and to fluctuating mood states resultant from the pharmacologic properties of the substances used.

As the entry and progression of children/adolescents into deviant peer contexts continues, the probability that some protective factors will emerge to counteract the risk factors and problematic behaviors may be decreased; as such, children identify with deviant peer group norms and are alienated from possible protective factor sources, such as teachers, counselors, clergymen, family members, etc. Furthermore, because of the manifestation of these problem behaviors, adults find interactions with such children undesirable (e.g., Pelham & Lang, 1993). As such, there needs to be an additional emphasis on the *consequences of problem behaviors on risk and protective factors across time* to complement the current emphasis on problem behaviors as outcomes. In essence, it is important to study the bidirectional relations and cross-temporal linkages of risk and protective factors and problem behaviors to comprehend differential individual trajectories across the lifespan (e.g., Lerner, 1991; Windle & Searles, 1990).

From a somewhat different perspective, Kendler, Neale, Kessler, Heath, & Eaves (1993) have emphasized a similar point with regard to self-perpetuating, negative cycles of person-environment relations on the basis of findings from a twin study of recent life events. Kendler et al., (1993) reported that correlations for life events among monozygotic twins consistently exceeded those of dizygotic twins, with familial-environmental and genetic factors each accounting for approximately 20% of the total variance. While not suggesting that the variance estimates associated with genetic and familial environment components directly "cause" the life events, Kendler et al. (1993) concluded that: (a) life events are not random; and (b) genetically-influenced temperament attributes (e.g., impulsivity, risk taking propensity) may contribute to the occurrence and persistence of life events in a dynamic, bidirectional, rather than unidirectional manner.

In sum, the study of resilience and resiliency processes may be facilitated by prospective, longitudinal models that incorporate a dynamic, bidirectional approach, in contrast to a static, unidirectional approach. By viewing children/adolescents as active agents who contribute to their own development via their actions and inactions (e.g., Lerner, 1991), dynamic person-environment processes associated with the fostering of risk or protective factors across time may be investigated to evaluate resilience processes.

Restrictions on Measurement of Dependent Variables

Many studies of resilience have included a restricted range of outcome variables, and have not used a multivariate approach in conceptualizing or measuring the domains under study. For example, many studies of children and adolescents have focused on aspects of depression and disturbed family functioning, but have not assessed externalizing symptomatology or substance use, whereas other studies have concentrated solely on externalizing symptomatology and substance use to the exclusion of internalizing symptomatology. The failure to adequately assess both internalizing and externalizing problem domains is problematic for three reasons. First, as duly described by Luthar and Cushing (1996), incorrect conclusions regarding resilient functioning may be drawn if too narrow of a focus is used with respect to the measurement of outcome variables. For example, children from adverse circumstances (e.g., poverty, parental deviance) may not be engaging in high levels of delinquent activity, but may, nevertheless, be suffering from depression and anxiety disorders. If one only measured externalizing behavior problems, resilient functioning may (incorrectly) be inferred. Second, there is increasing evidence of the need to study comorbid childhood conditions related to internalizing and externalizing symptomatology (e.g., Windle & Windle, 1993) that may be relevant for etiology, time course, and treatment. To the extent that comorbid childhood internalizing/externalizing problems represent a unique risk for the subsequent development of disorders, general and specific protective factors need to be identified to reduce or eliminate the progression to disorder status. Third, it is important to measure both internalizing and externalizing problems because of possible gender-specific differences in the expression of disorders (e.g., Horwitz & White, 1987), and importantly, the possible gender-specific role of protective factors and resiliency processes in overcoming risk factors associated with these disorders.

Operationalization of Risk and Protective Factors

There has been a lack of consensus about the optimal way to measure risk and protective factors. Luthar and Cushing (1996) identified some significant issues with regard to the measurement of stressful life events, for example to issues related to the use of single versus multi-item (aggregate) stress indexes. Three additional issues are briefly discussed now: (1) ways to identify risk and protective factors that exist within the same (bipolar) variable (e.g., low verus high school motivation, good versus poor peer relations); (2) ways to combine multiple risk and protective factor indexes; and (3) issues pertinent to method (e.g., informant) bias.

Identification of Risk and Protective Factors with Bipolar Variables

The identification of some variables as "risk only" has a precedent in high-risk studies associated with dichotomous characterizations based on family history of mental illness, alcoholism, or drug abuse. That is, a rearing environment characterized by parental non-psychopathology is not necessarily considered protective to offspring development. However, there is often much less certainty regarding risk or protectiveness associated with other variables where both effects may occur along different portions of the variates distribution. For example, high levels of maternal nurturance may be protective for children living in adverse circumstances; similarly, low levels of maternal nurturance may be a risk factor for children living in adverse circumstances by contributing to poor mother-child bonding and to an insecure or avoidant attachment style. To further complicate matters, some variables may manifest curvilinear relations with problem behaviors and thus be risk factors at the two tails of the distribution, but protective in some middle portion of the distribution. An example of this stems from family systems theory notions regarding negative outcomes at the two poles of family relations (chaotic or rigid disengagement and enmeshment), but higher levels of positivity along the middle range of the distribution (e.g., Olson, Lavee, & McCubbin, 1988).

This conceptual and measurement issue surrounding bipolar variables is central to the study of risk and protective factors and resilience, yet it remains largely unaddressed in the literature. Stouthamer-Loeber et al., (1993) proposed an empirical approach to identifying risk and protective factors. Briefly, they formed 3 × 3 contingency tables for each of a large number of independent variables and delinquency (their dependent variable of interest, though other variables, e.g., depressive symptoms, could be substituted). Empirically derived splits based on the trichotomization of each of the independent variables and the delinquency variable were made with distributions corresponding to 25%, 50%, and 25% for each variable. Various cells of the 3 × 3 table were then systematically collapsed to obtain contingency coefficients and odds ratios to determine empirically (i.e., via statistical tests) whether each independent variable functioned as a risk factor, a protective factor, or both in relation to delinquency (for details of this approach, see Southamer-Loeber et al., 1993). The findings indicated that most of the independent variables investigated manifested both risk and protective effects (e.g., trustworthiness, school motivation, peer delinquency). That is, high trustworthiness, high school motivation, and low peer delinquency were significantly associated with lower delinquency, and low trustworthiness, low school motivation and high peer delinquency were significantly associated with higher delinquency. A few variables had predominantly risk effects (e.g., attention deficit/hyperactivity and oppositional defiant behavior) and none of the variables had protective effects only.

One could quibble over specific features of the Stouthamer et al., (1993) approach, for instance with regard to why the 25th percentile was selected to define risk and protective factors rather than the 10th or 20th percentile or some normed referenced split. Similarly, one could express concerns about the failure to simultaneously consider multiple risk and multiple protective factors. Nevertheless, the issues raised by Stouthamer et al. and the empirically-based solution proposed highlight a significant gap in the field. That gap, of deciding on how to identify risk and protective factors within the same variable, provides a formidable challenge that needs to be on the "front burner" of the resiliency research agenda. If we are simply referring to opposite ends of a single, bipolar variable to identify risk and protective factors, then the relations of these factors to the concept of resilience as successful adaptation in the face of adversity needs to be rethought. That is, resilience implies an interactive relationship between protective factors and adverse circumstances, not simply the addition of some positively scored dimensions (e.g., low peer delinquency).

Multiple Risk and Multiple Protective Factor Indexes

In addition to the importance of evaluating methods to identify individual risk and protective factors, another prominent measurement issue pertains to the way(s) to combine risk and protective factors to construct composite indexes. One possibility is to simply treat each risk and protective factor as separate variates and to enter each of these variates in linear regression models along with (2-way) interaction terms to evaluate risk ×

protective factor interactions. Limitations of this approach are both statistical (e.g., multicollinearity of predictors) and pragmatic (the sheer number of risk and protective factors may substantially reduce statistical power). Two alternative proposals for constructing composite risk and protective factors have been formulated by Newcomb (1992; also see Newcomb & Felix-Ortiz, 1992). These proposals were designed to accommodate bipolar factors, i.e., factors that reflected protection at one end of the continuum and risk at the other end.

The first alternative proposal was to assign each bipolar factor to *either* the risk or protective factor domain contingent on the relative strength of the empirical relations between the poles in relation to the outcome variable (drug abuse in this instance). For example, if a variable such as parental monitoring was negatively associated with substance use, it was defined as a protective factor, whereas a variable such as peer deviance was specified as a risk factor due to the positive association with substance use. Separate, unit weighted, summated scores were then derived for risk and protective factors for subsequent analyses. Because each independent variable was specified as *either* a risk or protective factor, there was no statistical dependence between the derived indexes as an intrinsic component of the scoring method.

The second alternative proposal was to assign each bipolar factor a risk and a protective factor score (using lower and upper 20% cutoffs); thus if there were 10 bipolar factors, 20 scores were derived (10 risk and 10 protective scores). This second approach therefore captured potentially meaningful variance at both ends of the spectrum for bipolar variables, but also introduced a certain level of empirical, statistical dependence for the constructed indexes. Unit weighted, summated scores were then calculated for risk and protective factor indexes. These two indexes were then used by Newcomb (1992) and Newcomb and Felix-Ortiz (1992) as manifest indicators of a general latent variable referred to as vulnerability (or extreme vulnerability), with low scores reflective of high protection/minimal risk, and high scores reflective of low protection/high risk. This vulnerability latent factor was then used in structural equation modeling applications to evaluate cross-sectional and longitudinal relations with other constructs (e.g., alcohol, marijuana, and cocaine abuse).

The use of summated scores for risk factors has a precedent in the work Bry, McKeon, and Pandina (1982); furthermore, unit weighting appears plausible, at least based on some prior research regarding alternative weighting for the stressfulness of life events (e.g., Newcomb, Huba, & Bentler, 1981). Despite the parsimony and potential utility of this approach, it is important to consider three points that may restrict its widespread adoption. First, for research purposes relevant to descriptive analyses or to cutoff-scores for clinical screening objectives, the summated score approach may be useful; however, for purposes of causal, or plausible, explanation, such a summated index, or vulnerability latent variable, may be quite limited with regard to *which* (specific) risk or protective factors are contributing to what resiliency process, when, and how. This is particularly problematic for evaluating resiliency models that incorporate interactions (i.e., risk × protective factor interactions) in that it is difficult to isolate which risk and protective factors are contributing to the interaction and to the inferred resiliency process. Risk and protective factors may span multiple institutional (e.g., school, work), social (family, peers), and individual (e.g., temperament) level variables. The lack of specificity associated with summated risk and protective factor indexes may undermine attempts to investigate explanatory resiliency processes, and may limit the usefulness of findings for targeted behaviors for preventive interventions (i.e., limit the identification of specific risk and/or protective factors).

A second point is that the use of latent variables with manifest indicators represented by summated risk and protective factor indexes assumes the unidimensionality and additivity of the respective risk and protective factor scores. Both of these assumptions are testable and may indeed be false, as the derived indexes may be multidimensional and the interrelations among risk and protective scores may be nonlinear (i.e., multiplicative interactions may occur within, or between, sets of risk or protective factors such that the occurrence of one factor exacerbates or attenuates the influence of a second factor on outcome variables). A third point is that the use of summated indexes may restrict the study of risk and protective factors as disjunctive (i.e., having an effect on the dependent variable independent of the influence of other moderator variables) or conjunctive (i.e., having an effect on the dependent variable only in combination with other moderator variables) (Smith, Smoll, & Ptacek, 1990). The investigation of risk and protective factors as disjunctive or conjunctive moderators may be highly relevant to the study of processes underlying resilience by moving toward multiple-variable relation models, and by including the systematic evaluation and classification of variables according to their moderating influences, rather than by a priori "clumping".

Method (Informant) Bias

A final measurement issue that is not unique to resiliency research, but nevertheless merits greater attention pertains to method (e.g., rater) effects associated with the identification of risk and protective factors, and the choice of outcome variables. Kaufman, Cook, Arny, Jones, and Pittinsky

(1994) reported considerable heterogeneity in the prevalence of resilience (ranging from 5 to 64%) for a sample of maltreated children contingent on alternative operational definitions. For example, if teacher (rather than child) ratings were used to define cut-off points and variables of interest, fewer children were identified in the resilient range on measures of academic achievement. Thus, concerns over heterogeneity contributed by alternative raters (e.g., children, teachers, mothers, fathers) or methods of assessment (report measures, physiological indexes, observational procedures) needs to be addressed in subsequent research. Furthermore, Kaufman et al. reported that rates of resilience varied as a function of the criteria imposed with regard to non-problematic outcomes in one versus multiple domains. That is, the number of children identified as resilient was reduced to 5% if non-problematic functioning was required in all three domains of social competence, academic achievement, and (trivial) clinical symptomatology. Clearly, more attention to operational definitions is required for assessments associated with method effects and with the comprehensiveness of healthy functioning for an individual to be identified as resilient (or perhaps resilient with respect to particular domains of functioning).

The Validity and Longevity of Resilience Research

In this article, a number of limitations and challenges confronting the field of resiliency research have been identified. Many of the conceptual and methodological issues pertinent to the identification of dynamic causal relations via bidirectional, cross-temporal linkages in prospective research designs are not unique to resiliency research. However, they do have implications for research design (e.g., spacing of observational points to capture causal time lagged processes) and breadth of assessment (e.g., multiple domain) that are relevant to an explanatory account of risk and protective factors, and resiliency processes.

Summary

In conclusion, I am going to briefly present two major challenges that confront the resiliency research community. First, it would be beneficial to the field if greater effort were directed toward some empirically-based taxonomy of risk and protective factors and resiliency processes that would serve as an organizational tool for existing (and ongoing) research findings across disciplines and specialty areas. The research literature on resilience is proliferating at an exponential rate, yet there is no organizing framework for integrating studies, for evaluating common and unique findings across different subject populations, variable domains, or spacing intervals, or for studying the impact of alternative operational definitions and classification procedures on the identification of resilient individuals. Conceivably, with at least some initial, elementary taxonomic organizational scheme, and a heretofore unparalleled level of cooperation among investigators, it would be possible to develop a large database of studies to conduct systematic meta-analyses. Such meta-analyses could be of enormous value in identifying common and unique risk and protective factors associated with the wide range of problems currently under investigation. Although there would obviously be numerous logistical issues and details to be addressed in embarking on such an endeavor (e.g., who decides on the initial categories, who has access to the data, etc.), the Internet provides a potent technological tool to be exploited to share information across research laboratories worldwide. There may be clear integrationist advantages to entertaining such a notion to organize and maximally utilize the existing (and expanding) body of literature in the resiliency domain.

Second, and more concretely, additional effort needs to be focused on the multi-variable measurement issues surrounding the construction of risk and protective factor indexes, and the associated trade-offs in using "clumped" summated indexes versus alternative scoring methods. Similarly, greater attention needs to focus on the solo, or combination, influences of moderator variables (e.g., Smith et al., 1990), and how such combined or conjoint influences contribute to resiliency processes. These resiliency processes, in turn, may provide a stronger empirical basis for targeted prevention and intervention programs, which will provide the ultimate tests for the usefulness of the resiliency concept and its application to lifespan development.

References

Bry, B. H., McKeon, P., & Pandina, R. J. (1982). Extent of drug use as a function of number of risk factors. *Journal of Abnormal Psychology, 91*, 273–279.

Cicchetti, D. (1994). Integrating developmental risk factors: perspectives from developmental psychopathology. In C. A. Nelson (Ed.), *Threats to optimal development: Integrating biological, psychological, and social risk factors* (pp. 285–325). Hillsdale, NJ: Erlbaum.

Dohrenwend, B. P. (1978). Some issues in research on stressful life events. *Journal of Nervous and Mental Disease, 166*, 7–15.

Dohrenwend, B. S., & Dohrenwend, B. P. (Eds.) (1981). *Stressful life events and their contexts.* New Brunswick, NJ: Rutgers University Press.

Garmezy, N. (1983). Stressors of childhood. In N. Garmezy & M. Rutter (Eds.), *Stress, coping, and development in children* (pp. 43–84). New York: McGraw-Hill.

Garmezy, N. (1993). Children in poverty: Resilience despite risk. *Psychiatry, 56*, 127–136.

Gollob, H. F., & Reichardt, C. S. (1987). Taking account of time lags in causal models. *Child Development, 58*, 80–92.

Hechtman, L. (1991). Resilience and vulnerability in long term outcome of attention deficit hyperactive disorder. *Canadian Journal of Psychiatry, 36*, 415–421.

Herrenkohl, E. C., Herrenkohl, R. C., & Egolf, B. (1994). Resilient early school-age children from maltreating homes: Outcomes in late adolescence. *American Journal of Orthopsychiatry, 64*, 301–309.

Horwitz, A. V., & White, H. R. (1987). Gender role orientations and styles of pathology among adolescents. *Journal of Health and Social Behavior, 28*, 158–170.

Kaufman, J., Cook, A., Arny, L., Jones, B., & Pittinsky, T. (1994). Problems defining resiliency: Illustrations from the study of maltreated children. *Development and Psychopathology, 6*, 215–229.

Keough, B. K., & Weisner, T. (1993). An ecocultural perspective on risk and protective factors in children's development: Implications for learning disabilities. *Learning Disabilities Research & Practice, 8*, 5–10.

Kendler, K. S., Neale, M., Kessler, R., Heath, A., & Eaves, L. (1993). A twin study of recent life events and difficulties. *Archives of General Psychiatry, 50*, 789–796.

Lerner, R. M. (1991). Changing organism-context relations as the basic process of development: A developmental contextual perspective. *Developmental Psychology, 37*, 27–32.

Luthar, S. S., & Cushing, G. (1999). Measurement issues in the empirical study of resilience: An overview. In M. D. Glantz & J. Johnson (Eds.), *Resilience and development: Positive life adaptations*. New York, Plenum Press.

Neiman, L. (1988). A critical review of resiliency literature and its relevance to homeless children. *Children's Environment Quarterly, 5*, 17–25.

Newcomb, M. D. (1992). Understanding the multidimensional nature of drug use and abuse: The role of consumption, risk factors, and protective factors. In M. Glantz & R. Pickens (Eds.), *Vulnerability to drug abuse* (pp. 255–297). Washington, DC: American Psychological Association.

Newcomb, M. D., & Feliz-Ortiz, M. (1992). Multiple protective and risk factors for drug use and abuse: Cross-sectional and prospective findings. *Journal of Personality and Social Psychology, 63*, 280–296.

Newcomb, M. D., Huba, G. J., & Bentler, P. M. (1981). A multidimensional assessment of stressful life events among adolescents: Derivation and correlates. *Journal of Health and Social Behavior, 22*, 400–415.

Olson, D. H., Lavee, Y., & McCubbin, H. I. (1988). Types of families and family response to stress across the family life cycle. In D. M. Klein & J. Aldous (Eds.), *Social stress and family development* (pp. 16–43). New York: Guilford Press.

Pelham, W. E., & Lang, A. R. (1993). Parental alcohol consumption and deviant child behavior: Laboratory studies of reciprocal effects. *Clinical Psychology Review, 13*, 763–784.

Pickles, A. (1988). Statistical modeling of longitudinal data. In M. Rutter (Ed.), *Studies of psychosocial risk: The power of longitudinal data* (pp. 62–76). Great Britain: Cambridge University Press.

Rutter, M. (1987). Psychosocial resilience and protective mechanisms. *American Journal of Orthopsychiatry, 57*, 316–331.

Rutter, M. (1988). Longitudinal data in the study of causal process: Some issues and some pitfalls. In M. Rutter (Ed.), *Studies of psychosocial risk: The power of longitudinal data* (pp. 1–28). Great Britain: Cambridge University Press.

Rutter, M. & Quinton, D. (1984). Long-term follow-up of women institutionalized in child-hood: Factors promoting good functioning in adult life. *British Journal of Developmental Psychology, 2,* 191–204.

Schuckit, M. A. (1994). A clinical model of genetic influences in alcohol dependence. *Journal of Studies on Alcohol, 55,* 5–17.

Sher, K. J., & Levenson, R.W. (1982). Risk for alcoholism and individual differences in the stress-response-dampening effect of alcohol. *Journal of Abnormal Psychology, 91,* 350–368.

Smith, R. E., Small, F. L., & Ptacek, J. T. (1990). Conjunctive moderator variables in vulnera-bility and resiliency research: Life stress, social support and coping skills, and adolescent sport injuries. *Journal of Personality and Social Psychology, 58,* 360–370.

Sroufe, L. A., & Rutter, M. (1984). The domain of developmental psychopathology. *Child Development, 55,* 17–29.

Stouthamer-Loeber, M., Loeber, R., Farrington, D. P., Zhang, Q., van Kammen, W., & Maguin, E. (1993). The double edge of protective and risk factors for delinquency: Interrelations and developmental patterns. *Development and Psychopathology, 5,* 683–701.

Werner, E. E., & Smith, R. S. (1992). *Overcoming the odds: High risk children from birth to adulthood.* Ithaca: Cornell University Press.

Windle, M., & Searles, J. S. (1990). Summary, integration, and future directions: Toward a lifes-pan perspective. In M. Windle & J. S. Searles (Eds.), *Children of alcoholics: Critical per-spectives* (pp. 217–238). New York: Guilford.

Windle, M., & Windle, R. C. (1993). The continuity of behavioral expression among disinhib-ited and inhibited childhood subtypes. *Clinical Psychology Review, 13,* 741–761.

III

THE APPLICATION OF
RESILIENCE

9

Factors and Processes Contributing to Resilience

The Resilience Framework

Karol L. Kumpfer

Introduction

Resilience is becoming an increasingly popular concept for research and application in the field of prevention. Because of reduced funding for services to help at-risk children and families, information on low cost methods for increasing resilience to negative life events is critically needed. A better understanding of ways to increase resilience in all children holds great promise for improving the effectiveness of preventive community, school, and family services.

A shift in focus from risk to resilience, according to Turner (1995), has developed partially from a frustration with such a pervasive emphasis on the identification of risk factors. While a risk-focused approach has been very helpful in the public health field in the reduction of infectious diseases, more complex diseases of life style require a more comprehensive approach including protective and resilience mechanisms (Rutter, 1993). A paradigm-shift appears to be occurring towards an increasing emphasis on optimism and hope as opposed to the frustration and despair that can occur from an emphasis on risk processes.

Karol L. Kumpfer • Center for Substance Abuse Prevention, Substance Abuse and Mental Health Services Administration, Rockville, Maryland 20857.

Resilience and Development: Positive Life Adaptations, edited by Glantz and Johnson. Kluwer Academic/Plenum Publishers, New York, 1999.

Prevention programs, whether *universal* programs serving all youth and families, *selective* programs for at-risk youth or *indicated* prevention interventions for identified youth (Mrazek & Haggerty, 1994), could be strengthened by a conscious attempt to promote resilience. Unfortunately, despite an increasing research literature on resilience mechanisms (Kumpfer, in press; Rutter, 1993), the systematic application of existing knowledge about resilience to prevention services is almost non-existent. Fortunately for the delivery of youth and family services, many of the resilience mechanisms being discovered by research are already being applied on an intuitive basis. A systematic application of methods for increasing resilience could improve child outcomes and prevent future problem behaviors and poor life adjustment, which are becoming increasingly costly to treat.

Few prevention programs are based on resilience theory or are specifically designed to increase resilience. One such program specifically designed to increase resiliency is the Iowa Strengthening Families Program (Kumpfer, Molgaard, & Spoth, in press). This family skills training program for 11- to 14-year-olds specifically focuses on motivating at-risk youth towards positive life adaptations by encouraging dreams, goals, problem solving, and academic and social skills. Issues in developing and conducting research on interventions designed to promote resilience are addressed in Rolf and Johnson's chapter in this book.

Purpose and Content of Chapter

Understanding resilience is a very difficult task. Despite recent interest in etiological factors and processes leading to resilience in high risk individuals, resilience remains an illusive construct. The goal of this chapter is to review resilience processes and factors predictive of successful life adaptation in resilient children who, because of multiple environmental risk factors, should not be so successful. Because resilience has been such a loose, broadly defined construct, this paper attempts to organize variables found related to increased resilience into a dynamic framework that allows for interactions between the resilient person and his/her high risk environment. This transactional model includes: 1) environmental precursors commonly called risk and protective factors, 2) characteristics of the resilient person, 3) his/her resilient reintegration or positive outcome after a negative life experience as well as dynamic processes that mediate between the person and their environment and the person and the outcome. Relevant research on etiological factors and dynamic processes within each of these areas of the proposed resilience framework is discussed. Without a clear differentiation of the stimuli, the person, and the outcome, resilience can become a tautology—a concept that predicts itself. This paper ends with implications of these resilience research findings for increasing positive life adaptation and reducing drug use in high-risk youth.

Defining Resilience

According to many developmental psychopathologists, who constitute the major group conducting resilience research: *"Resilience in an individual refers to successful adaptation despite risk and adversity"* (Masten, 1994, p. 3). More specifically, resilience has been broadly defined as a *"process, capacity or outcome of successful adaptation despite challenges or threatening circumstances. . . . good outcomes despite high risk status, sustained competence under threat and recovery from trauma"* (p. 426, Masten, Best, & Garmezy, 1990). Most researchers have defined resilience more narrowly by focusing on "resiliency factors" or protective personality traits (see Wolin & Wolin, 1993 for a review). Often these shorthand "factor labels" mask a more complex interaction between a resilient youth and his/her environment. It is increasingly recognized that resilient youth are active participants in creating their own environment (Scarr & McCarty, 1983)— a reasonably radical concept that transcends stimulus-response behaviorism and smacks of human agency (Bandura, 1989). Some researchers have attempted to describe these transactional person/person interplays that buffer negative life events, such as between a caring adult and a child (Rutter, 1992; Radke-Yarrow & Sherman, 1990; Werner, 1993). Few resilience researchers have stressed resilience processes that help an individual develop resilient reintegration after disruption by stressors or challenges, yet these are commonly recognized by therapists (Richardson, Neiger, Jensen, & Kumpfer, 1990).

Research Issues in Studying Resilience

A number of major stumbling blocks make research on resilience a formidable task for anyone, whether a seasoned veteran or newcomer to the field, because of a lack of agreement on: 1) operationalization of the resilience concept, 2) gender, age or culturally unbiased definitions of the successful outcomes indicative of a resilient person, 3) definitions of environmental risk protection, and 4) the primary self characteristics of a resilient person. Additionally, research in this field suffers from difficulties separating cause and effect, locating good measures for resiliency variables, simultaneously studying large numbers of variables needed to determine which are most salient or predictive of positive outcomes despite high risk status, and finding non-linear, transactional data analytic methods capable of accurately summarizing bi-directional, transactional data. Each of these resilience research issues is covered in more detail in Kumpfer (in press).

Operationalization of Resilience

A review of the resilience research demonstrates that resilience has been defined by different researchers as virtually all internal and external variables or transactional and moderating or mediating variables capable of affecting a youth's life adaptation. The only focusing concept appears to be the search for positive protective factors or processes (as opposed to negative risk factors) that are predictive of successful life adaptation in high-risk children. In most longitudinal studies focusing on determining resilience factors or processes, the concept of resilience is *operationalized* as the positive end of a distribution of *outcomes* in samples of high-risk children (Egeland, Carlson, & Sroufe, 1993). This important point means that resilience has been equated with virtually any direct or indirect variable correlated or predictive of positive outcomes in high-risk children. According to Staudinger and associates (1993), *"the distinction between the protective factors and mechanisms underlying resilience and resilience as an outcome can be quite arbitrary"* (p. 545).

Because research output has not matched the popularity of resilience as an explanatory construct for children's behavior, resilience risks losing credibility within the scientific community (Cicchetti & Garmezy, 1993). As mentioned by many researchers in this field (Cicchetti & Garmezy, 1993; Liddle, 1994; Luthar, 1993; Gordon & Song, 1994) additional theoretical clarity would promote research precision and improve communication. Different operational definitions of resilience result in disparate findings in summarizing the critical components of resilience or determining estimates of the rate of resilience in similar target populations of high-risk youth. Gordon and Song (1994) suggest that definition may be difficult because resilience may not be a single construct, but *"a complex of related processes that deserve to be identified and studied as discrete constructs"* (p. 30). Nevertheless, according to Cicchetti and Garmezy (1993): *"Depending on how broad or conservative the definition of resilience, vastly different conclusions can be drawn"* (p. 499). To summarize outcome or predictive research results across many different foci of resilience research using different definitions, the following broad framework was developed. This framework is preliminary and should be considered a starting point for organizing factors and processes predictive of positive outcomes in high-risk children.

Organization of Multiple Resilience Constructs into a Framework for Resilience Research

Because predictive longitudinal studies discuss resilience factors or processes as many different constructs, the following organizational framework or model of resilience has been developed. Bronfenbrenner and Crouter (1983) recommended the use of social ecology models or person-process-context models to study the relationship of contextual risk and protective factors, intervening processes, and individual characteristics. Rutter (1987) has also argued that resilience be understood in terms of processes rather than just identifying static factors. Therefore, this resilience framework includes both process and outcome constructs.

Six major constructs are specified. Four are domains of influence and two are transactional points between two domains. The four influence domains are: the acute stressor or challenge, the environmental context, the individual characteristics, and the outcome. Points for transactional processes are the confluence between the environment and the individual and the individual and choice of outcomes. Therefore, resilience research on predictors discussed in this paper are organized into these six major predictors of resilience, namely:

1. Stressors or Challenges—These incoming stimuli activate the resilience process and create a disequilibrium or disruption in homeostasis in the individual or organizational unit (e.g., family, group, community) being studied. The degree of stress perceived by the individual depends on perception, cognitive appraisal and interpretation of the stressor as threatening or aversive.
2. The External Environmental Context includes the balance and interaction of salient risk and protective factors and processes in the individual child's external environment in critical domains of influence (i.e., family, community, culture, school, peer group). These change with age and are specific to culture, geographic location, and historical period.
3. Person–Environment Interactional Processes include transactional processes between the child and his or her environment as the child

or caring others either passively or actively attempt to perceive, interpret and surmount threats, challenges or difficult environments to construct more protective environments.

4. Internal Self Characteristics include internal individual spiritual, cognitive, social/behavioral, physical and emotional/affective competencies or strengths needed to be successful in different developmental tasks, different cultures, and different personal environments.

5. Resilience Processes include unique short-term or long-term resilience or stress/coping processes learned by the individual through gradual exposure to increasing challenges and stressors that help the individual to bounce-back with resilient reintegration (Richardson, Neiger, Jensen, & Kumpfer, 1990).

6. Positive Outcomes or successful life adaptation in specific developmental tasks which are supportive of later positive adaptation in specific new developmental tasks culminating in a higher likelihood of reaching a global designation in adulthood as a "resilient child or adult". While this is an outcome, in a dynamic model, a positive outcome suggesting resilience is also predictive of later resilient reintegration after disruption or stress.

All six of these major cluster variables or constructs are needed to organize predictors of resilient outcomes in high-risk youth because research studies have reviewed these different constructs as predictive of resilience in an individual. Organizing research findings by these six areas would help to clarify the differences between environmental stimuli, transactional environment buffering processes, internal mediating self factors, resilience processes used to bounce-back after a challenge, and the final developmental outcomes of resilient children. Because it is a daunting task to simultaneously test multicausal models (Sameroff, Seifer, & Barocas, 1983), most of the predictive research cited in this review includes only parts of this framework in a single study. This resilience framework has been empirically tested in doctoral dissertations at the University of Utah using structural equation models in simultaneous measures of multiple domains in college students (Neiger, 1991), working mothers (Dunn, 1994), and children of alcoholics (Walker, 1995). As highlighted by Egeland, Carlson, & Sroufe (1993), an organizational approach or framework for the study of resilience provides a means of integrating findings on risk and protective factors in individuals and environments and focuses attention on processes of adaptation. *"From such an organizational view, the capacity for resilience is seen as developing over time through an integration of constitutional and experiential factors in the context of a supportive environment"* (p. 525).

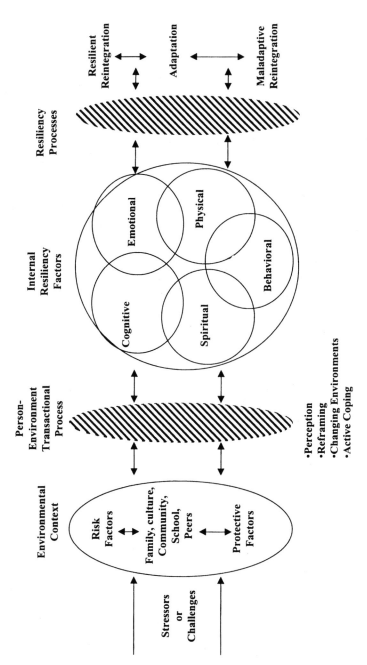

Figure 1. Resilience Framework.

Types of Resilience Research

Different research designs have been used to study resilience or related concepts (e.g., stress-coping, ego-resilience, personality, motivation, and health). Each of these different research methodologies can produce discrepant, but perhaps eventually converging, results concerning the most critical elements predicting resilience to negative life events or high-risk environments. Five major types of resilience research were reviewed.

Retrospective, Single Sample, or Cross-Sectional Studies

This type of research design is used primarily by life events researchers and some other resilience researchers. Because of time constraints, this design is popular with graduate students. Life events researchers, typically limit their collection of data to determining the relationship of negative life events and adaptation. If children or adolescents are studied, they are generally asked to rate stressful life events experienced in the recent past and whether they perceive the event as positive or negative (Swearingen & Cohen, 1985). Simple correlational data analyses suggest that major life stressors impact life adjustment, but these relationships are more complicated in individual cases and appear to be moderated by daily hassles and stressors (DeLongis, Coyne, Dakof, Folkman, & Lazarus 1982). Retrospective, small sample studies are also conducted using qualitative, in-depth interview studies of successful adults who have "made it despite the odds" (Gordon & Song, 1993). Life events analysis is used to develop grounded theory for later hypothesis testing (Strauss & Glaser, 1967).

Retrospective, Cross-Sectional, Multivariate Studies

Resilience researchers using cross-sectional designs tend to include intervening variables (i.e., daily hassles, personality traits, environmental context, and interactive processes with significant others). In adults, a retrospective rating of major negative life events occurring at any time in their lives combined with daily hassles has been used to determine "high-risk" status (Dunn, 1994). High and low risk groups have been created post-hoc or chosen in advance. General population comparison groups are sometimes compared to high-risk populations–children of alcoholics, schizophrenics, and families living in poverty. More sophisticated multivariate statistics are used, such as multiple regression and structural equation modeling. Including multiple variables from environmental, individual, and adjustment domains, researchers increased correlation coefficients to between .60 to .80, in contrast to the usual .30 or .40 found in studies that include environmental stressors and adjustment outcomes but exclude individual characteristics (Garmezy, Masten & Tellegen, 1984; Luthar, 1991). While helpful in linear model development and testing, these cross-sectional studies cannot ascertain the impact of resilience on life adjustment. Longitudinal studies are needed for such conclusions.

Short-Term, Transactional, Longitudinal Studies

Transactional models of the reciprocal influence of people with their environment are considered more powerful in accounting for variance in developmental outcomes than are simple linear models (Bronfenbrenner, 1986; Sameroff & Chandler, 1975). Some researchers are using three month to several year longitudinal designs to determine the impact of risks and protective factors and processes. Different statistical methods have been used ranging from cross-lagged correlations to cross-lagged structural equation models (Roosa, 1991). Using longitudinal designs, researchers have discovered bi-directional relationships between environmental precursors, individual competence, and adjustment. Specifically, adjustment problems at Time 1 are related to increased negative life events (Compas, Howell, Phares, Williams, & Giunta, 1989).

Long-Term Prospective Developmental Studies— No Control Group

Some researchers are conducting very long-term studies of general populations of children, occasionally from birth, such as Werner and Smith's (1992) 30-year study or White, Moffitt, and Silva's (1989) New Zealand cohort. Some studies focus on presumed high-risk groups, such as those from low-income schools. The longitudinal study of Project Competence is a good example of this (Gest, Neeman, Hubbard, Masten, & Tellegen, 1993), as is the 20 year longitudinal Mother-Child Project of 267 children of young, poor, pregnant women (Egeland, Carlson, & Sroufe, 1993). Frequently, these studies do not include a comparison group, but create post-hoc comparisons of children high in risk factors and compare them to children lower in the targeted risk factors. Sometimes these studies select children from very high-risk populations, such as children of alcoholics (Werner, 1986), children of depressed mothers (Radke-Yarrow & Brown, 1993), children of schizophrenics (Garmezy, 1974), institutionalized children (Rutter & Quinton, 1994) for study. Longitudinal studies without normal comparison groups are limited in their ability to determine whether resilient children from high-risk samples function comparably to well-functioning children in general population samples (Luthar & Zigler, 1991). Occasionally these prospective studies begin after the occurrence of a specific traumatic event, such as child abuse or parental divorce. Such studies can be criticized for not having data on the child's adjustment prior to the onset of the major stressor or risk factor. Causality is difficult to determine since these children may have poor life adjustment or behaviors prior to the trauma.

Prospective, Multiple Sample Studies

This type of design is used by developmental researchers interested in comparing children in the general population with a high-risk population over time (Conger et al., 1992; Kumpfer, Molgaard, & Spoth, in press). Matched pairs or families are sometimes used as control groups (Johnson, Glassman, Fiks, & Rosen, 1990). This design could be used with many prevention studies where one group is given an intervention, another is not, and a general population sample exists for comparison. Using this type of design, Abelson, Zigler, & DeBlasi (1974) and Mulholland and associates (1991) discovered that the resilient children in high-risk groups did not equal the attainment of the normal, low-risk groups. This type of design is encouraged by Luthar and Cushing (1996) to answer the question of whether the most resilient individuals of a high-risk group truly resilient or are simply the best of a generally poorly functioning group.

Outcome Research Pertaining to the Six Resiliency Predictor Areas of the Resilience Framework

Outcome research on resilience was organized into the six predictor areas of the proposed resiliency framework, namely: 1) the acute stressor or challenge, 2) the external environmental context, 3) person–environment interactional processes, 4) internal self characteristics or resiliency factors, 5) resiliency processes, and 6) the positive outcome. Research on each of these six resilience predictor areas are discussed below in their own sections.

The Acute Stressor or Challenge

The resiliency framework or process begins with an initiating event and ends with an outcome, hopefully a successful one that demonstrates resilience. The stimulus in any resiliency situation should be some type of stressor or challenge, because by definition, resilience can only be demonstrated when the person experiences some type of stressor or challenge. Measuring life stressors and challenges is discussed by Luthar and Cushing (1996) in this book and presents it's own challenges. The initiating stimuli or event can be selected by the person with more or less anticipated stressors. Challenges help a person to face new stressors and to grow from the experience. This is the essence of resilience. For instance, a youth may decide to train and enter a marathon, try out for the basketball team, or sign up for a theater class. Both parents and youth are constantly balancing the successes and failures of challenges in an attempt to have positive healthy development. Unanticipated negative experiences are the other side of stressors. Most people don't choose the have them happen, but never the less, they can also learn valuable lessons in coping successfully from negative life events.

External Environmental Risk and Protective Factors

The environmental context within which a child operates is very influential on risk and resilience processes. Aspects of the family, neighborhood, school, and peer group impact the socialization process of the child. When acute or chronic stressors occur, this environmental context can buffer or exacerbate the negative impact on the child. High-risk youth often live in high-risk environments that are, by definition, not as supportive of positive life adaptation as they should be. Many of these high-risk environments are determined by the family circumstances. Poverty often reduces opportunities for some children and leads to an impoverished environment (Dunst, 1995). Resilient youth are those who find micro-niches of support with adequate growth opportunities even within high-risk environments (Garmezy, 1993).

Research on resilience requires the ability to define "high-risk" environments and high-risk children who adapt amazingly well. Some youth can be high-risk because of personal biological, genetic, or personality dysfunctions, such as cognitive or biological damage due to in utero drug exposure, hyperactivity, anti-social personality, or biological differences in endocrine or metabolic functioning (Kumpfer, 1987; Tarter & Mezzich, 1992). Most high-risk youth are categorized in resilience research on the basis of a high-risk environment, rather than internal high-risk characteristics. Demographic factors are often used, such as poverty, minority status, high-crime neighborhoods, single parent family, and other indicators of risk status. Hence, considerable attention should be focused on how to define "high risk". Merely assuming that a child is high risk because of belonging to a high-risk category has been questioned. This review of environmental risk and protective factors will not attempt an exhaustive list of the most critical risk and protective factors because 1) many existing reviews of risk and protective factors for different adjustment problems exist, and 2) the most important risk and protective factors differ for each field. For reviews of risk factors for substance abuse, the reader is referred to Kumpfer (1987) for a review that includes biological risk factors. Hawkins, Arthur and Catalano (1994) or Hawkins, Catalano and Miller (1992) provide more recent summaries of risk factors for substance abuse as well. What is discussed in this section are dimensions of risk and protective factors that must be considered when attempting to determine the most predictive risk or protective factors for positive life outcomes.

In most research "high-risk" means children from high-risk environments, such as children from dysfunctional families. However, some researchers also include personal risky behaviors (i.e., substance use, conduct disorders, attention deficit disorder, and delinquency) in their definition of high risk samples (Stouthamer-Loeber et al., 1993). According to Luthar and Zigler (1991), it is important to differentiate risk factors or stressors that the individual can influence (e.g., failing in school) and those generally out of their control (e.g., death of a parent, war, being born to a dysfunctional parent). If this is not done, predictive results are confounded by having maladjustment predict maladjustment or the converse.

In this review, risk factors are defined primarily by chronic adversity in the environment of the child. Acute stressors are considered the stimuli for disruption and integration, thus beginning the resiliency process (Richardson, Neiger, Jensen, & Kumpfer, 1990) towards maladaptation or resilient reintegration. The environmental context of stressors and supports can help the child through psychosocial facilitation processes. Critical dimensions of risk factors and processes must be considered in resilience research in defining risk, namely:

1. Whether the child actually experiences the risk factors (Plomin & Daniels, 1987; Werner & Smith, 1992),
2. Perception or attribution of risk or threat by child (Gordon & Song, 1994),
3. Degree of direct or indirect effects on the child because of proximal or distal status in a chain of causal variables,
4. Degree of transactional buffering by child or caring others (Radke-Yarrow & Brown, 1993),

5. The balance of the accumulation of risk and protective factors (Radke-Yarrow & Brown, 1993),
6. Presence of salient or powerful protective factors (e.g., supportive home life) in counterbalancing risk factors (Richters & Martinez, 1993),
7. General or specific risk or protective factors for different developmental outcomes,
8. Different risk factors or protective factors critical for different ages, developmental tasks, cultures, geographic locations, and historical periods.

For a more complete review of these conditions for defining risk the reader is referred to the original NIDA resilience conference paper (Kumpfer, 1994) which was shortened and revised for this chapter. A number of researchers (Bry, 1983; Magnusson, 1988; Rutter, 1993) have found that youth can adjust reasonably well to one or two risk factors or processes, but beyond two risk factors they are the damage increases rapidly. Research suggests that increasing the number of protective processes can help to buffer those risk mechanisms (Dunst, 1995; Rutter, 1993; Sameroff & Chandler, 1975).

Person–Environment Interactional Processes

The second juncture of the Resiliency Framework (see Figure 1), includes important transactional processes that mediate between a person and his/her environment. Better understanding of ways that people consciously or unconsciously modify their environment or selectively perceive their environment, holds promise for prevention programs. In some cases, youth living in high-risk environments may actively seek better environments for themselves by going to a different school or choosing to live with a relative in a better neighborhood, seeking positive prosocial friends. However, most youth don't have the option to leave a negative environment or neighborhood. Resilient youth living in high drug and crime communities seek ways to reduce environmental risk factors by seeking the prosocial elements in their environment. They maintain close ties with prosocial family members, participate in cultural and community events, seek to be school leaders, and find non-drug using friends and join clubs or youth programs that facilitate friendships with positive role models or mentors.

Unfortunately, much less resiliency research has been focused on person-environment transactional processes than on internal self resiliency factors (Masten, 1994). Considerable person-person or person-environment research is potentially relevant, but it must be gleaned from applicable research within psychology, anthropology, sociology and other related fields. Potentially useful resiliency building processes have already been summarized in more depth in Kumpfer and Bluth (in press). Some interactional processes that help these youth transform a high-risk environment into more protective environment include: 1) selective perception, 2) cognitive reframing, 3) planning and dreaming, 4) identification and attachment with prosocial people, 5) active environmental modifications by the youth and 6) active coping. Caring others sought out by resilient youth facilitate positive life adaptations and enhancement of protective processes by positive socialization or caregiving through: 1) role modeling, 2) teaching, 3) advice giving, 4) empathetic and emotionally responsive caregiving, 5) creating opportunities for meaningful involvement, 6) effective supervision and disciplining, 7) reasonable developmental expectations and 8) other types of psychosocial facilitation or support. As suggested by Coie and associates (1993) family prevention and intervention research can be used to better understand these complex person-environment processes by systematically varying transactional processes within the program variations and testing the impact on youth.

Internal Individual Resiliency Factors

Children are not born equal. Some children are physically stronger and more intellectually and physically endowed. Such physical and biological strengths help to make a youth more resilient to life stresses. Biological invulnerability variables do play a major role in resiliency. Temperament variables have been found associated with risk and resiliency to drug use. According to the Biopsychosocial Model of Vulnerability to Drug Use (Kumpfer & DeMarsh, 1985), there are three major categories of biological characteristics to consider in susceptibility to drug use: 1) genetic and biological factors, 2) in utero factors, and 3) temperament and personality factors.

Genetic and Biological Invulnerability Factors

Intelligence. Intellectual capacity (I.Q.) has been widely studied in predicting resilience. In general, most studies have found a protective effect of higher cognitive levels (Kandel et al., 1988; Long & Vaillant, 1984; Werner & Smith, 1982) or a risk effect for low cognitive levels. Most researchers propose a unidirectional, linear model in which low IQ predicts adjustment difficulties directly or through intervening variables (White, Moffitt, & Silva, 1989). The St. Louis Risk Research Project found the childhood intelligence measures predicted mental health in children of mentally ill parents (Anthony, 1987; Worland, Weeks, & Jones, 1987). Other studies with children of mentally ill parents support this relationship (Bleuler, 1984; Garmezy, 1985; Long & Vaillant, 1984).

Increased intellectual capabilities, particularly verbal skills, have been found in resilient children of schizophrenic and depressed parents (Garmezy, 1985; Masten, Best, & Garmezy, 1990) and children of alcoholics (COAs) (Werner, 1985). This latter study found that none of the resilient COAs were judged below average at two years in intellectual development, compared to 16% of COAs who later manifested adaptive problems. Verbal capabilities and aptitude were significantly higher by age 10 as well as scholastic aptitude and educational achievement tests in grades 5, 8–10, and 12 in COAs who did not develop serious coping problems compared to those who did. The resilient COAs also had fewer errors on the Bender-Gestalt Test, considered a measure of central nervous system integrity.

A recent study by Luthar and Zigler (1992) examined the role of intelligence looking for interaction effects with level of stressors and personal characteristics. They found that I.Q. can be a vulnerability factor in high stress situations for high IQ children. Inner-city, multi-cultural ninth grade students with higher intelligence showed considerably more variation in school-based performance depending on locus of control and impulse control (ego development). Hence, youth with higher levels of internal locus of control and impulse control were more likely to be motivated to use their intelligence to achieve academically. However, if these youth have learned powerlessness through social and educational inequities leading them to believe that school success does not lead to life success (Fordham & Ogbu, 1986), they tended to underachieve dramatically. Possibly, their achievement motivation is directed to other areas where they perceive greater chances of successfully applying their talents and intelligence, such as illegal activities and drug dealing (Myers, 1990).

Gender.   Another major genetic factor related to increased resiliency in high-risk children is female gender. Repeatedly, developmental studies of children living in at-risk environments and families have found girls to be more resilient than boys (Werner, 1985). Boys appear to be more vulnerable to out-of-home care (Gamble & Zigler, 1986). Some researchers (Rutter 1982) suggest that boys react emotionally and behaviorally in more negative ways than girls to negative family situations.

Temperament and Personality. Most resiliency researchers (Garmezy, 1985; Rutter, Maughan, Mortimore, Ouston, & Smith, 1979) regardless of their discipline, agree that constitutional and temperamental disposition is a major factor in resilience. Both Garmezy (1985) and Rutter (1979) have discussed positive temperament or positive personality disposition as one of the three major precursors of resilience; the other two factors are supportive family milieu (family cohesion and warmth) and the availability and use of external support systems by parent and child. In their 14-year study of ego resilience from pre-school to late adolescence, Block and Block (1980) found precursors of resilience in children to be positive temperament traits, such as responsiveness to environmental change, ability to be comforted after stress, and ability to maintain physiological equilibrium, as well as to modify sleep-wakefulness states. Wertlieb and associates (1989) found three temperament traits related to effects of stress: distractibility, stimulus threshold sensitivity, and response to novel stimuli.

A number of studies have supported the hypothesis that "difficult" temperament is associated with alcohol and other drug use in later life. A "difficult" temperament as defined by frequent negative moods and withdrawal was found by Lerner and Vicary (1984) as correlated with later drug problems in a longitudinal study that tracked kindergartners until adulthood. Children characterized as "easy" children, defined by greater adaptability and happier dispositions, were significantly less likely than "difficult" children to become adult regular users of tobacco, alcohol, and marijuana.

As described by Lerner and Vicary (1984), as well as Brook and associates (1990), two major temperament traits in children who later used drugs are: 1) negative mood states (anxiety, irritability, sadness, emotional upset, anger and crying) and 2) social withdrawal. These are very similar to the two major temperament characteristics—aggression and shyness—found in the Kellam and Brown (1982) longitudinal study of adolescents who later used drugs. If youth continue aggressive behaviors until 13 years of age, they have a strong likelihood of developing alcoholism (Loeber, 1988) or drug abuse (Barnes & Welte, 1986) and delinquency (Stouthamer-Loeber et al., 1993). Hyperactivity, attention deficit disorder and oppositional defiant behavior in junior high school aged children have been found to increase odds ratios for delinquency (Stouthamer-Loeber et al., 1993).

Neurotransmitter Imbalances. Because of the consistent finding of temperament differences in negative life adjustment, temperament should be considered a significant risk factor leading to risk processes involving parents, teachers, and peers. Youth with difficulty, unpleasant, or aggressive temperaments are often rejected by other prosocial peers. The role of biological chemical imbalances (neurotransmitter or hormonal imbalances) should be more thoroughly investigated in this powerful risk process. Such chemical imbalances can be due to genetic inheritance, *in utero* chemical exposure, and postnatal exposure. The use of alcohol, tobacco, and other drugs also leads to neurotransmitter imbalances that can increase craving for drugs (Goodwin, 1986). In addition to complex interactional processes between external environmental variables, internal self factors have complex relationships.

Internal Psychological Self Resiliency Factors

Organization of Internal Personal Traits or Self Factors. To develop a categorical framework for improving understanding of self factors to resilience, the internal individual factors have been reviewed in the child development and child psychopathology literature. Following traditional wisdom, they have been organized into five major overlapping domains: spiritual, cognitive, social/behavioral, emotional, and physical.

This organization maps reasonably well on the mind, body, and spirit division of traditional wisdom. The "Four Worlds" Native American tradition consider four major developmental tasks for youth—namely physical, emotional, cognitive, and spiritual. An additional cluster variable of social/behavior competencies has been added because of the large number of resilience studies that equate resilience with social competencies. Luthar (1993) has distinguished three of these five domains in her longitudinal study, namely social, emotional and physical. It is of interest that very few researchers have focused on the spiritual or affective domain which is critical to the concepts of flexibility, perseverance, hopefulness, optimism and the ability to bounce back after failure.

Individual characteristics within each of these five internal domains will be discussed in detail including those that are more determined by genetics or biological, *in utero* environment effecting biology or temperament, and the five types of self factors. In addition, resilience processes will be discussed although few researchers currently focus their research on these unique processes despite resilience specifically being considered the ability to bounce back after failure. A number of longitudinal studies of positive life adaptation despite stressful or high-risk environments (Garmezy, 1985; Luthar, 1991; Radke-Yarrow & Brown, 1993; Werner & Smith, 1982, 1992) indicate that strength, hardiness and competence are predictive of successful interactions with their environments.

Resilience as Internal Capacity or Competence. Resilient children have coping skills and competencies to minimize stress of negative impacts, maintain self-esteem and gaining access to opportunities. In studying resilience, researchers have often focused on the internal characteristics of

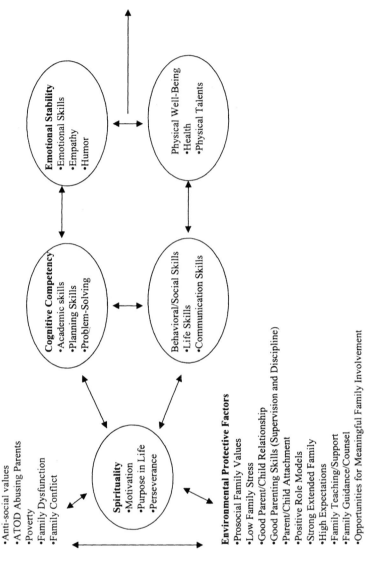

Environmental Risk Factors
•Anti-social values
•ATOD Abusing Parents
•Poverty
•Family Dysfunction
•Family Conflict

Emotional Stability
•Emotional Skills
•Empathy
•Humor

Physical Well-Being
•Health
•Physical Talents

Cognitive Competency
•Academic skills
•Planning Skills
•Problem-Solving

Behavioral/Social Skills
•Life Skills
•Communication Skills

Spirituality
•Motivation
•Purpose in Life
•Perseverance

Environmental Protective Factors
•Prosocial Family Values
•Low Family Stress
•Good Parent/Child Relationship
•Good Parenting Skills (Supervision and Discipline)
•Parent/Child Attachment
•Positive Role Models
•Strong Extended Family
•High Expectations
•Family Teaching/Support
•Family Guidance/Counsel
•Opportunities for Meaningful Family Involvement

Figure 2. Internal Self Resiliency Characteristics.

"resilient" children. Comparing outcomes in successful and unsuccessful high risk children, many different personal characteristics have been found to be predictive of resilience in diverse at-risk populations (Rolf, Masten, Cicchetti, Nuecherlein, & Weintraub, 1990), such as children of mentally ill mothers (Garmezy, 1985); children of depressed mothers (Conrad & Hammen, 1993; Radke-Yarrow & Brown, 1993); children of poverty (Garmezy, 1991); children of alcoholics (Werner & Smith, 1989, 1992); children addicted to drugs (Newcomb & Bentler, 1990); children exposed to inner city violence and stress (Luthar, Doernberger, & Zigler, 1993; Richters & Martinez, 1993; Wyman, Cowen, Work, & Kerley, 1993); and children of divorced parents (Wallerstein, 1983). While these researchers are looking for unique characteristics predictive of the ability to beat the odds, many of the personal traits or learned capabilities are helpful to any child.

Internal Self Resiliency Factors

Review of Internal Psychological Resiliency Factors

A review of the literature produced many overlapping resiliency traits or factors within a child associated with successful adaptation under negative life circumstances or stressors. Individuals considered more resilient in research studies have been found to have significantly more of the characteristics mention below. It should, however, be mentioned that because these characteristics were examined in many different studies, resilient individuals do not necessarily possess all of the following mentioned cognitive styles and coping skills (see Figure 3). These internal personality or cognitive capabilities have been organized according to the prior mentioned resilience framework for self factors into five major cluster variables: (1) Spiritual or Motivational Characteristics, (2) Cognitive Competencies, (3) Behavioral/Social Competencies, (4) Emotional Stability and Emotional Management, (5) Physical Well-Being and Physical Competencies. Each of these areas of internal competencies and related coping or life skills will be discussed below in separate sections in depth because they constitute the core of the resilient traits which most prevention specialists are attempting to foster in their high-risk youth.

Spiritual or Motivational Characteristics

The spiritual or motivational cluster of resiliency characteristics include primarily cognitive capabilities or belief systems which serve to motivate the individual and create a direction for their efforts. Success depends on direction or focus. Hence, the variables hypothesized for inclusion are the following:

* Dreams and Goals (Bandura, 1989; Quinton et al., 1993; Rutter & Quinton, 1984)
* Purpose in Life (Neiger, 1992)
* Existential Meaning for Life (Frankel, 1959)
* Spirituality (Dunn, 1994; Gordon & Song, 1994).
* Belief in Uniqueness or in Oneself (Gordon & Song, 1994).
* Internal Locus of Control (Luthar, 1991a; Murphy & Moriarty, 1976; Parker, Cowen, Work, & Wyman, 1990; Werner & Smith, 1992).
* Hopefulness and Optimism (Seligman, 1975)
* Determination and Perseverance (Bandura, 1989; Werner, 1986)

Dreams/Goals and Purpose in Life. One very important psychological characteristic of resilient children living in high-risk environments is their ability to dream (Bandura, 1989; Rutter & Quinton, 1984; Quinton, Pickeles, Maughan, & Rutter, 1993), create plausible fantasies for themselves and to develop a mission or purpose for their lives (Bernard, 1991; Richardson, Neiger, Jensen, & Kumpfer, 1990). Surviving difficult childhoods often was achieved by a sense of uniqueness or specialness and spiritual belief that they are here for some cosmic purpose—often a general commitment to making the world a better place for similar types of children.

This purpose in life or existential meaning (Frankel, 1959), helps these resilient individuals to endure hardships, because they believe they must survive to complete their mission. Beardslee's research (1983; 1989) on civil rights workers in South and Segal's research (1986) on prisoners of war discovered that a predominant characteristic of resilient individuals was having a purpose in life related to helping others. Creating a perceived purpose for their pain and suffering (Beardslee, 1989; Segal, 1986) and healing through helping or caring for others (Werner, 1986; Segal, 1986) helps individuals to regain environmental mastery and perceived control (Taylor, 1983) which has been found critical to maintaining hope in adverse life threatening situations (e.g., concentration camps, prisons, war zones, acute care hospital units, and abusive families). Neiger (1991) confirmed in a structural equations modeling study of college students in South Carolina that resiliency was the final pathway to positive life adaptation. The most predictive variable in his multifactorial resiliency cluster was life purpose, next was problem solving, followed by self-efficacy.

Spirituality. Hypothesizing that purpose in life may be part of a larger latent construct called spirituality, Dunn (1994) used structural equation modeling procedures, but a much more comprehensive testing battery to test a variation of Kumpfer's Resiliency Model. The results confirmed that "spirituality" (including life purpose) was a major predictor of resilience and later positive life adaptation in a large national sample of working and non-working mothers. Using the same testing battery, Walker (1995) was able to replicate these results with a national sample of adult children of alcoholics. For all three of these samples, spirituality has been highly predictive of positive life adaptation.

Based on a review of longitudinal and cross-sectional studies, Masten (1994) concluded that an important individual resilience factor is religious faith or affiliation. Qualitative, retrospective studies of successful adults from very high risk environments frequently mention the importance of a strong religious belief system in positive life adaptation. Being adopted or having foster parents with strong religious beliefs, when lacking in the biological family, were mentioned by some resilient subjects as helpful. More than half of the Gordon and Song (1994) sample mentioned following strong religious beliefs that significantly impacted their lives positively. According to Gordon and Song (1994), *"A belief system seems to provide anchorage and stability in the face of faith-challenging experiences. When questioned about religion, most of the subjects expressed the sense of community, direction, and fellowship typically associated with African Americans, and a traditional affiliation with religiosity"* (p. 38).

Belief in Uniqueness or in Oneself. Additional cognitive processes or traits that tend to motivate resilient individuals towards positive achievement is belief in oneself and one's uniqueness or specialness (Gordon & Song, 1994). Religious instruction or parental/other adult support tend to reinforce this specialness. Cameron-Bandler (1986) found that the critical variable for resilient children of alcoholics was their "sense of a compelling future", which helps these high-risk youth to "subordinate immediate gratification for a more fulfilling later gratification, or to save ourselves from some intensely unpleasant future experience."

Independence. Success against the odds was also found to be related to an autonomous, self-directedness in resilient subjects in Gordon and Song's (1994) retrospective, qualitative study. They describe them as autonomous/maverick types who would avoid negative peer pressure so as to participate in goal-directed activities, such as going to a museum or library and saving illegal earnings to buy real estate rather than go partying.

Internal Locus of Control, Hopefulness, and Optimism. Related to life purpose and planning ability is the concept of internal locus of control or the perception of being able to influence their current environment and future destiny (Rotter, 1954). Resilient individuals have more internal locus of control (Campbell, Converse & Rodgers, 1976; Luthar, 1991; Murphy & Moriarty, 1976; Parker, Cowen, Work, & Wyman, 1990; Werner & Smith, 1992) and are more hopeful about their ability to create positive outcomes for themselves and others. This sense of hopefulness and optimism is a direct contrast from Seligman's (1975) learned helplessness concept so often found in high-risk youth lacking in positive experiences. These positive life experiences and adaptation are dependent on congruence between objective life circumstances and control beliefs (Christensen, Turner, Smith, Holman, & Gregory, 1991). Hence, the ability to give up attempts to control that which is not controllable is also characteristic of resilient individuals. The "ability to know the difference" is a major recovery goal in Alcoholics Anonymous and for children of alcoholics.

An external locus of control or unknown locus of control can result when infants or children experience powerlessness due to unresponsive caregiving. In such children, failure is attributed to self, but success is attributed to chance or powerful others. Baldwin and associates' (1993) regression analysis results suggest that low unknown locus of control, intelligence, and self-esteem predict mental health, but could also be considered alternative measures of mental health. Possibly, one of the most powerful predictors of positive life adaptation against environmental odds is a sense of powerfulness and an ability to modify one's negative life circumstances through direct actions or soliciting help from others. Past successes lead to increased hopefulness and optimism, versus hopefulness. Therefore, increasing opportunities for youth to demonstrate self-direction and to be successful is important in prevention programming. A self-efficacy cycle includes multiple achievements developed by *"building on small steps with high probability for success."* (p. 14). With time resilient children develop with time an "optimistic bias" and latch "on to any excuse for hope and faith in recovery" (Murphy, 1987).

Determination and Perseverance. In order to be successful in their chosen mission or direction, resilient youth are described as being perseverant (Bandura, 1989) and determined (Werner, 1986) in their cognitive style. Coping skills needed to achieve their goals include practicality, and life skills or many competencies and talents (Garmezy, 1985). They are also creative (Flach, 1988) and street smart (Wolin, 1989). While long-range planning abilities and determination are important to resilient individuals in achieving their mission in life (Bandura, 1989; Wolin, 1989), flexibility in planning and the ability to create new or alternative plans also character-izes resilient individuals. If it appears that original plans are not likely to be successful given new information or changes in the environment, resilient youth rebound by developing new goals and plans.

Cognitive Competencies

This cluster of individual resiliency characteristics include cognitive abilities that help a person to achieve their dreams or goals, namely:

- Intelligence (Masten, 1988; Kandel et al., 1988; Kaufman & Zigler, 1989; Kolvin, Miller, Fleeting, & Kolvin, 1988; Long & Vaillant, 1984; White, Moffit, & Silva, 1989).
- Academic Achievement and Homework Skills (Masten, Garmezy, Tellegen, Pellegrini, Larkin, & Larsen, 1988).
- Ability to Delay Gratification (Garmezy & Masten, 1991; Rutter & Quinton, 1984)
- Reading Skills (Luthar & Zigler, 1992)
- Moral Reasoning (Coles, 1989; Wolin & Wolin, 1993)
- Insight (Flach, 1988; Wolin & Wolin, 1993)
- Interpersonal Awareness (Luthar, 1991; Doernberger, 1992).
- Self-esteem and the Ability to Restore Self-esteem (Bandura, 1989).
- Planning Ability (Anthony, 1987; Rutter & Quinton, 1984)
- Creativity (Jacobs & Wolin, 1991)

Intellectual Competence and Academic and Job Skills. As mentioned earlier, many studies have found more resilient children generally have higher intellectual and academic abilities than less resilient children (Garmezy, 1985; Masten, Garmezy, Tellegen, Pellegrini, Larkin, & Larsen, 1988; Werner, 1985). Intelligence is a major protective factor (Garmezy & Masten, 1991) that is influenced by both genetics, postnatal biological vari-ables, such as nutrition, physical trauma, drug abuse, and learning experi-ences. Intelligence helps to buffer or reduce life stress (Masten et al., 1988). In addition, resilient children generally do better in school academically than their intelligence scores will predict. Hence, they tend to be more over-achievers than underachievers. They are described as being achievement oriented (Werner, 1986) and capable of delaying gratification (Rutter & Quinton, 1994) in order to be successful. School or achievement motivation serves as a protective factor and major pathway to later job and life success (Masten, 1994; Werner & Smith, 1982, 1992; Stouthhamer-Loeber, et al., 1993).

As mentioned earlier, some high-risk youth in inner cities with high intelligence dramatically underachieve in school performance if they have a low internal locus of control or poor ability to delay gratification (Luthar & Zigler, 1992). Unfortunately, some ethnic youth (particularly African-American boys) equate academic achievement to "acting White", because of few concrete role models of success through the traditional academic achievement (Fordham & Ogbu, 1986). High verbal skills are critically important for success in early grades of elementary school, unfortunately, children of substance abusers and children of deprived families tend to have lower verbal scores on standardized tests (Kumpfer, 1987). Increasing verbal competence by teaching phonetic reading, spelling, and encouraging reading will help disadvantaged youth. High verbal and reading skills tend to help resilient children to learn about the world outside of their family and neighborhoods (Luthar & Zigler, 1992). Fairy tales and children's stories frequently portray disadvantaged children overcoming the odds, hence exposing children to these cultural stories can increase dreams and belief in achievement against the odds. Girls, however, often experience a downward academic performance trajectory in middle school related to sex-role socialization processes sometimes promoted by traditional cultural stories, teacher's differential response to girls, and an increasing social orientation that sometimes overwhelms academic priorities. Maternal educational achievement and role modeling tends to help girls to achieve.

Moral Reasoning. A product of higher intellectual thought is the higher moral reasoning levels these children are capable of attaining and demonstrating. Jacobs and Wolin (1991) suggest that resilient children separate themselves from the value systems of their families by becoming their own moral guardians. Coles (1989) has also discussed the importance of "moral energy" in resilient children from impoverished homes around the world. Moral energy creates a life-sustaining force that can move resilient children towards positive lives. Wolin and Wolin (1993) consider morality as one of seven resiliencies in their Resilience Mandala, which defines morality as an informed conscience that extends wishes of a good personal life to all of humankind. Cognitive aspects of morality include judging right and wrong, developing internal images or standards for the way things should be or what is normative, valuing compassion, fairness and decency, and serving others. Kagan's (1984) research suggests that children develop by two years of age internal images or standards about how things or events should be. By age seven, Selman (1980) reports children have a good idea about how parents should treat them—with sensitivity to their feelings and with generosity.

Insight and Intrapersonal Reflective Skills. Resilient children have been described as "mini-psychologists" capable of a quality of "early knowing" (Wolin, 1989) and personal insight (Flach, 1988). According to Wolin and Wolin (1993), insight is the number one resiliency. Insight is the mental habit of asking penetrating questions of oneself and subsequently, providing honest answers. Resilient children from dysfunctional parents often are aware very early in life that they are different from and stronger than their sick parent. While empathetic and caring, they develop "adaptive distancing" to protect their sense of healthy separation from the parent's maladaptive coping skills and life patterns. This failure to identify with their dysfunctional parent and to find more successful role models is adaptive for these children (Beardslee & Podorefsky, 1988). Adaptive distancing has been found to be a crucial mechanism in children of alcoholics (Bennett, Wolin, Reiss, & Teitelbaum, 1987; Berlin & Davis, 1989).

The capability to analyze one's psychological and physical strengths and compare them to others takes a certain level of intrapersonal and interpersonal reflective skill, which not all children possess. For some reason only a few children excel in analyzing their intrapersonal skills and judging their strengths and limitations, whereas others living in similar family and peer environments are completely unaware of these psychological differences. Possibly, the early development of certain conceptual centers in the brain make this type of relational thinking possible in resilient youth.

Self-Esteem and Ability To Restore Self-Esteem. Resilient youth have higher self-esteem associated with an accurate appraisal of their increased strengths and capabilities. They have resilient self-efficacy (Bandura, 1977; 1989) and the ability to restore self-esteem (Flach, 1988) after failure or disruption in homeostasis. Self-efficacy is a self-perception about competence to perform specific behavioral tasks (Bandura, 1977) and influences choice of tasks or challenges attempted, the degree of effort employed, and emotional reactions to threat of failure (Lawrence & McLeroy, 1986).

Youth who avoid opportunities to master challenges because of low self-esteem or specific task self-efficacy will have a more difficult time developing resilience (Schunk & Carbonari, 1984). Bandura (1989) believes that overcoming stressors or taking on challenges is necessary for the development of self-efficacy. Children who are overprotected or shy in accepting challenges are hindered in developing self-efficacy and competencies. He has written: *"If people experience only easy successes, they come to expect quick results and their sense of efficacy is easily undermined by failure"* (p. 1179). Perseverance and determination are possible by-products of resilient self-efficacy that in turn lead to increased self-efficacy when youth are successful in *"sticking it out through tough times"* (p. 1179).

Planning Ability. Another cognitive skill probably related to intelligence is planning ability, which has been found related to resilience in high-risk youth (Anthony, 1987; Rutter & Quinton, 1984). Ability to foresee consequences of choices and to plan a bright future are characteristics of individuals who successfully overcome negative environments. According to Quinton and associates (1993), planful competence is the ability to think ahead and consider the future. Planful competence effects the direction of the life course from adolescence onward and maintains a certain continuity in personality features (Clausen, 1991). Studies (Mann, Harmoni, & Powers, 1989) suggest that planful behavior can be successfully taught. Youth are less likely to succumb to negative peer pressure to engage in behaviors with life long negative consequences, such as teen sexuality, early marriage, and drug use, if they have planning abilities and internal locus of control to use these abilities. A recent study by Quinton and associates (1993) found plannful behavior was the primary internal cognitive characteristic of individuals that helped them to avoid assortative pairing with conduct disordered mates. Resilient, institutionally-reared women had been found in earlier studies (Rutter & Quinton, 1984) to demonstrate planning in their choice of supportive partners and careers.

Creativity. Creativity in children at risk allows them the opportunity of improving their self-esteem through creating new things (ideas, objects, music, tools, software) which others value or prize. Jacobs and Wolin (1991) believe that creativity in children of alcoholics allows them to express and resolve inner conflicts through painting, photography, dance, music and writing. Freud (1908) interprets the creative urge as individual ability to control a troubled past. Wolin and Wolin (1993) *state "In adolescence, many resilient survivors dabble in writing, music, painting, or dance to break the constraints of their troubled families and their own hurt feelings"* (p. 163).

Behavioral/Social Competencies

While very similar to cognitive competencies because they build on them, behavioral and social competencies differ because they require behavioral action, not just thoughts. Cognitively competent youth may know what they need to do to become popular, but lack the necessary social skills or talents to accomplish these aims. Aspects of the behavioral and social competencies domain or cluster to be discussed in this review are:

• Social Skills (Platt, Belding, & Husband, in press)
• Street Smarts (Garmezy & Masten, 1986)
• Problem Solving Skills (Platt, Belding, & Husband, in press)
• Communication Skills (Wolin, 1991)
• Peer Resistance Skills (Pentz et al., 1989)

- Multi-cultural Competencies (Burial, Classed, & Vasquez, 1982; Oetting & Beauvais, 1990).
- Bi-gender Competencies (Dunn, 1994)
- Talents (Garmezy, 1985)
- Capacity for Intimacy (Wolin & Wolin, 1993)

Social Skills and Street Smarts. Social and behavioral competence or effective functioning within different environments, sometimes called "street smarts" (Garmezy & Masten, 1986) has been found to be associated with resilience. A number of behavioral skills or life skills are related to resilience, including problems solving skills, communication skills, and peer resistance skills which are frequently addressed in substance abuse prevention programs.

Problem-Solving Skills. Many researchers have reported that problem-solving ability is a component of resilience (Anthony, 1987; Neiger, 1991; Rutter & Quinton, 1994). It is likely that individuals who are more confident in their plans or direction are those who have experienced considerable success in the past due to excellent problem solving abilities. Wolin and Wolin (1993) provide an example of the importance of problem solving in increasing self-efficacy and willingness to tackle challenges in their description of the enjoyment in solving each life threatening problem arising for a Mt. Everest climber. Ability to focus on the goal and chip away at each problem as they arise leads to increased initiative, belief in personal control, and optimism.

Two types of problem solving have been found effective in increasing resilience to AOD use in high-risk youth: 1) general problem solving skills useful in any new problem situation and 2) specific problem solving skills that relate primarily how to solve specific types of problems related to alcohol and drug use.

General problem solving involves the ability to: 1) be interested and motivated to solve problems through a generalized cognitive-affective-behavioral response set, 2) accurately identify the problem, 3) generate a wide variety of possible solutions, 4) consider the consequences of each possible solution and consider all possible resources, 5) choose the best solution, and 6) implement the best solution and verify the results to learn better strategies for later problems (D'Zurilla & Nezu, 1990; Spivack, Platt, & Shure, 1976). Flexibility, originality and creative problem solving have been considered a hallmark of resilient children (Flach, 1988; Demos, 1989; Cohler, 1987; Murphy & Moriarty, 1976). Halverson and Waldrup's (1974) research on pre-schoolers found the children who are capable change agents from an early age tend to be successful in grade school.

Prevention programs that explicitly teach general problem-solving have found increased positive outcomes in their participants, including reductions in precursors of substance use (DeMarsh & Kumpfer, 1986; Kumpfer, 1991; Spivack & Shur, 1982). Botvin and associates (1990) have also reported reductions in tobacco use (Botvin & Tortu, 1988) and alcohol use (Botvin, Baker, Renick, Filazzola, & Botvin, 1984) following a generic life skills or social problem solving skills program including advertising analysis, decision making, goal-setting, stress management, communication and dating skills. Follow-up studies (Botvin, Baker, Dusenbury, Tortu, & Botvin, 1990) replicated these positive effects in seventh to ninth graders by providing booster sessions over three years. The exception to positive findings of the study was that, although the prevalence of self-reported intoxication was reduced, the quantity and frequency of alcohol use was not.

Specific problem solving strategies for the resistance of alcohol and other drugs, such as peer refusal skills, assertiveness training, advertising or peer appeal analysis, consequences analysis have been popular substance abuse prevention interventions. Specific problem solving skills are often scripted and taught through cognitive behavioral techniques involving modeling, role playing, behavioral reversal often involving repeated practice, audio or video feedback and reinforcement for new skills.

Increased resilience to initiation to tobacco (Biglan et al., 1985) and lower prevalence rates for weekly tobacco, alcohol and marijuana use (Pentz, 1983; Pentz et al., 1989) were found after two years of intervention using these specific skill training strategies in combination with other multicomponent education, parent and community strategies. After three years, the positive results for reduced alcohol use in participants was no longer supported (Johnson et al., 1989), which is a common finding for many specific skills training programs. Reducing alcohol use in youth appears to be much more difficult. However, Dielman and associates (Dielman, Schope, Leech, & Butchard, 1989) have had success in reducing the increasing rate of alcohol misuse in students who began using alcohol with their peers in unsupervised settings. Their specific skills training program also reduced the rate of increase in susceptibility to peer pressure.

Unfortunately, many of the specific substance abuse resistance skill training programs do not directly and independently test the efficacy of the skills training in reducing alcohol and other drug use. Several exceptions are the Ketchel and Bieger (1989) study and the Kim, McLeod, and Palmgren (1989) study which both found increased intentions to not use alcohol and other drugs, and decreased substance use. It has been hypothesized that these positive drug use changes may be due more to reinforcement of the existing school or peer non-use norms (Kumpfer, Moskowitz & Klitzner, 1986), or to recent changes in the social climate towards tobacco and other drug use or the informal social control climate (Moskowitz, 1983). Hansen and Graham (1991) have empirical evidence that changing the perceptions of AOD norms is more salient than specific resistance skills training in reducing AOD use in youth.

Multi-Cultural and Bi-Gender Competencies. Research studies have also found multicultural or bicultural competence as related to less substance use in youth (Oetting & Beauvais, 1990; Buriel, Calzada, & Vasquez, 1982). Youth who are capable of acting competently in several cultures if needed are more successful. Additionally, bi-gender competence is related to increased resilience and life success in women (Dunn, 1994).

Empathy and Interpersonal Social Skills. Another hallmark of resilient children is their sense of responsibility for others, willingness to care for others, and ability to be empathetic of the needs of others (Werner, 1985; 1986). Related coping skills include interpersonal social skills (Platt, Belding, & Husband, in press), an engaging personality, good listening and communicating skills (Wolin, 1991), and politeness (Kumpfer, 1990a,b). Resilient children are responsive and active in their relationships with others and elicit more positive responses from their associates even from infancy (Demos, 1989; Werner & Smith, 1982). Because of their increased social skills, resilient children are popular and have increased choice of friends allowing them to establish friendships with positive, prosocial peers if they desire (Berndt & Ladd, 1989).

When combined with the availability of social support (Rutter, 1987) and the willingness to use external supports (Schwartz, Jacobson, Hauser, & Dornbush, 1989), resilient children are capable of getting the social supports they need to buffer stressors and teach them even more coping skills. Jacobs and Wolin (1991) report that resilient children of alcoholics even as young children sought *"oases of health in interacting with the healthiest parts of their troubled families"* (p. 111). By middle childhood, these children are connecting with neighbors, teachers, and other substitute parents. Werner (1985) also identified attachment to community institutions and positive role models of youth leaders as important. Felsman (1989) found in his study of resilient Colombian street children that they were skillful in locating existing social supports and using them to their advantage. Children of mothers who are willing to use social agency support are reported to have more competencies (Musick, Scott, Spencer, Goldman, & Cohler, 1984), possibly because of the effective role modeling of the mother, increased resulting resources or increased social contact.

Wolin and Wolin (1993) report resilient individuals have a capacity for intimacy. In addition, they are careful in their choice of intimates. Rutter and Quinton (1994) found the more resilient females living in institutions married better than their less successful cohorts. They choose more prosocial and supportive spouses and friends.

Emotional Stability and Emotional Management

Characteristics of resilient individuals that could be considered primarily within the domain of emotional characteristics and skills would be:

- Happiness (versus Depression)
- Recognition of Feelings
- Emotional Management Skills and Ability to Control Anger and Depression
- Ability to Restore Self-Esteem
- Humor (Masten, 1982; Wolin & Wolin, 1993)
- Hopefulness

Happiness. Resilient individuals are characterized as reasonably happy people, at least they are not prone to depression or negative appraisals of reality characteristic of depressed individuals. The ability to be hopeful and optimistic may occur because of mastery experiences but also because of good mental health practices, avoiding psychotropic drugs, eating well, reducing stress and getting exercise. After all, Garmezy (1974) has noted that resilient people work well and play well.

Emotional Management Skills. A primary characteristic of resilient children is their optimism and positiveness about life. Resilient individuals recognize feelings and can control undesirable feelings such as fear, anger and depression. For children of alcoholics and drug abusers, learning to recognize feelings may be more difficult. Special exercises are developed in prevention programs to help these children learn to recognize their feelings, however, nothing is as effective as having parents who daily discuss feelings with the child. Learning to recognize and control destructive impulses based on these feelings are learned through role modeling and transactions between a parent and a child.

Humor. Many clinical and research descriptions of resilient individuals mention them as happy, energetic people who frequently use humor as a coping strategy. The ability to use humor to reduce tension and stress and restore perspective is a skill of many resilient children. The ability to find the comic in the tragic, to make themselves and others laugh, is considered by Wolin and Wolin (1993) as one of several basic resiliencies in children of alcoholics. Humor is also a useful interpersonal skill that helps to establish and maintain social standing and friendships. Masten (1982) found highly stressed, but resilient kids had higher scores on humor generation than less competent, but high stress kids. Werner (1991) has found in her longitudinal study that a positive temperament, including an optimistic outlook on life, is one of five major clusters of resiliency characteristics. These children have "faith that the odds could be overcome." Happiness is related to good neurotransmitter balance, good nutrition, and exercise. Hence, genetic and biological factors can influence whether a youth has a generally happy disposition.

Physical Well-Being and Physical Competencies

Variables that have been included in resilience studies that correlate with resilience include the following:

- Good Health (Werner & Smith, 1982, 1992)
- Health Maintenance Skills (exercise, good diet, sleep)
- Physical Talent Development (Masten, 1994)
- Physical Attractiveness (Kaufman & Zigler, 1989)

Studies have demonstrated that good physical status is predictive of resiliency. Children with few physical problems, good sleep patterns, and physical strength may internalize this physical strength and interpret themselves as "strong" psychologically as well. Better physical health during infancy and childhood has been found related to resilience in the children of Kauai (Werner, 1989; Werner & Smith, 1982, 1992). In the St. Louis Risk Research Project (Anthony, 1987) childhood measures of visual-motor coordination predicted mental health.

The development of physical talents or accomplishments valued by others and the child are considered by Masten (1994) as three or four resilience factors that can be impacted by the child rather than by others. Becoming an excellent athlete, dancer, musician or artist increases self-efficacy and self-worth. Additionally, having a teacher or a coach increases the child's opportunities for role modeling and support.

Physical attractiveness has been found related to positive life adaptation, particularly if associated with charm and social skills (Kaufman & Zigler, 1989). The mechanism for this effect is not difficult to predict. Children who are more attractive are generally more liked and valued by parents or find it easier to attract caring others. In the Oakland Growth Study (Elder, Caspi, & van Nguyen, 1986), fathers were more supportive and less harsh with more attractive daughters.

Risk researchers have discovered that the more risk factors youth have, the more likely they are to use drugs (Bry, 1983; Bry, McKeon, & Pandina, 1982; Newcomb, Maddahian, Skager, & Bentler, 1987; Rutter, 1979; Rutter, 1990). Just as with risk factors, future research is likely to discover that the more resiliency traits youth have, the more resilient they are likely to be over time. Actually, a more probable scenario is that those youth with many risk factors and few resiliency factors are those with increased likelihood of becoming drug abusers.

Resiliency Processes

The final process that occurs to predict a positive outcome associated with resilient youth is the interaction between the internal characteristics of the person and the final outcome. Most resiliency researchers (Rutter, 1987; Werner, 1993) agree that the final stage of resilience research, sometimes called Stage Three research, must address those processes that develop resiliency in youth. It will never be enough simply to identify protective factors in the environment or resiliency factors in the youth; we need to know how to create these resiliency factors through designing and encouraging resiliency building processes in the transaction of the youth with his or her environment.

Resilience as Ability to Bounce Back

Garmezy (1991) has defined resilience as *"the capacity for recovery and maintained adaptive behavior that may follow initial retreat or incapacity upon initiating a stressful event"* (p. 459). Despite an early emphasis on studies that focused on this process of recovering from stressful events, little research except in the stress-coping literature addresses the ability to bounce-back. More resilience research focuses on predictive factors in the environmental context (risk and protective factors) and individual resiliency traits or competencies.

Resilience Process Model

Most of the resiliency field agrees that we need to understand better the processes that help to develop resiliency characteristics or ego-strength in individuals. Part of that process is modifying the environment to remove stressors and find a better goodness-of-fit. People, however, will always experience acute stressors that are not predictable or they may actually choose to face challenges at which they might fail. Baldwin and associates (1993) write: *"Children develop in a dialectical process of meeting challenges, resolving them, and then meeting new ones. If the challenge is too severe, the developmental process breaks down. Resilience is a name for the capacity of the child to meet a challenge and use it for psychological growth."* (p. 743). When a person does fail, but develops as a stronger person in the process, some type of resiliency process is occurring. As a beginning step to understanding the micro concept of a resiliency process, Richardson elaborates on the application of a Resiliency Process Model (Richardson, Neiger, Jensen, & Kumpfer, 1990) for use in the resilience field. This process model is useful in conceptualizing the stress-diathesis model discussed by Tarter and Mezzich (1992).

The Resiliency Model shows that stressors or life challenges not balanced by external envirosocial protective processes or biopsychospiritual resiliency factors within the individual can lead to imbalances in homeostasis or disruption (Flach, 1988). Disorganization of the individual occurs which can be relieved and result in reintegration of homeostasis if envirosocial supportive processes occur. This model also proposes several different levels of reintegration can occur based on envirosocial reintegrating processes:

1. Resilient reintegration, or a higher state of resiliency and strength
2. Homeostatic reintegration or the same state before the stressor
3. Maladaptive reintegration, or a lower state of reintegration
4. Dysfunctional reintegration or a major reduction in positive reintegration

This model proposes that the positiveness of the level of homeostasis does change over time, which should match any clinician's observations of clients who have experienced a crisis in their lives. Some clients appear to grow from the experience and look on the positive nature of the disruption, whereas others decompensate into depression and negativism.

Another way that this model is useful to the prevention field is that it proposes four different intervention points in the resiliency process. The first point, envirosocial protective processes, help to prevent the youth from ever experiencing disruption. The other three processes:

1. Envirosocial enhancing processes
2. Envirosocial supportive processes
3. Envirosocial reintegrating processes support resilient integration

Conducting research on the mini-processes or transactions between the child and the environment that encourage resilient reintegration is the basis for designing more effective prevention programs. This is the wave of the future in the prevention business. Every parent, teacher and youth worker struggles with what they can do to help youth to learn competencies or skills and to become stronger or more resilient. Increased research on how much to challenge youth and how much to support them would help these people dedicated to creating youth with more self-esteem, confidence, self-efficacy and psychological hardiness to better judge what is in the best interest of the child.

Responsible parents are continually struggling with decisions on how much to challenge their children. Should they push their children into activities or challenges which they are not inclined to choose themselves? Conversely, if their children want to undertake an experience, which the parents think they are likely to fail at, should they be given the opportunity anyway? Often caretakers must make decisions on the basis of intuition, traditional family child rearing practices, and resource available. It would be useful to have basic scientific research to help inform these critical child rearing decisions.

Positive Life Outcomes

Defining a successful outcome that demonstrates resilience can be difficult because this judgement is so value-laden and culturally-relative. Resilience research generally begins with a search for resilient children who are successful despite the odds. Conducting this research outside of one's culture is fraught with differences in the definition of successful across cultures. For instance, resilience research being conducted with Native American youth has had to begin with ethnomethodological research on people that the local tribe consider "successful" despite negative life events. Preliminary results suggest a very different definition of success that does not involve competence in schools and jobs, but more in family and tribal relations (Evans, 1996). Similarly, resilience and coping research with African-American children suggest culturally different definitions of success or definitions of success adapted to stressful environments (Barbarin, 1993).

Implications for Prevention Strategies

Because research on resilience is relatively new, principles for guiding the design and implementation of prevention programs are just being summarized (Bernard, 1993; Turner, 1995; Kumpfer, in press). The research literature suggest there are many opportunities to increase resilience in a plannful manner in designing more supportive environments for children.

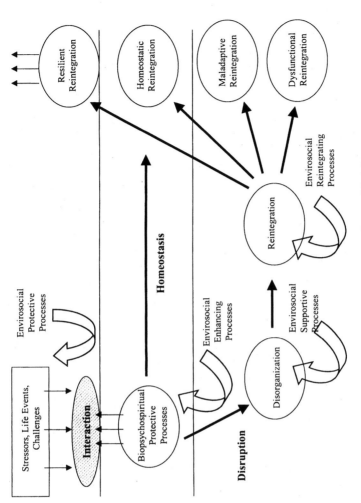

Figure 3. The Resiliency Process Model.

The primary implication of resiliency research for prevention programming with high-risk youth is that prevention programs should focus more directly on the development of the primary resilient characteristics identified in this review. These resilient traits can be developed by modifying the external environment to increase protective processes, employing small challenges, creating opportunities for involvement and the demonstration of competence, and increasing involvement, bonding and attachment to prosocial groups. Interventions should strive to improve the quality of caregiving, teaching parents and youth workers how to increase resiliency characteristics in children, reducing environmental inequities and stressors for children in high-risk or unhealthy environments. Some interventions should work directly with children and youth to increase personal power and resilience. Assessments of personal and academic competence could provide information for tailored resilience interventions, possibly through computer interactive programs or video tapes for caretakers and families.

Summary

Why is it that we have invested so much into material and scientific technology to build better material goods, yet we know so little about how to build better children? The future success of our country depends on increasing our technology and interest in building better children. For this reason, increased research into this field of resilience and child development is critical to the prevention field and our nation's prosperity and well being. Promoting resilience in youth holds promise for creating more effective prevention programs. As can be concluded from this extensive review of research, there are no simple formulas for instilling resilience. Research on resilience, while holding much promise for the alcohol and drug prevention field, is also plagued by a number of definitional issues and research limitations. This review suggests that virtually all aspects of a child's personality and environment as well as transactional relationships between the child and his/her environment influence positive life adaptation. Determining the most salient variables is complicated by gender, culture, history, local environmental issues and developmental appropriateness. A number of caveats on the quality of the research have been discussed including issues in theoretical paradigms, definitions, measurement, designs and statistical analysis procedures. Because of the increasing willingness to see behaviors of individuals as influenced by dynamic transactions with significant others and the environment, studying the predictors of resilience have become much more complicated. Additional transactional, cross-lagged prospective studies are needed including multivariate data collections strategies and advanced statistical methodologies capable of analyzing transactional data.

The Resilience Framework is discussed to organized the findings of many cross-sectional and longitudinal resilience studies. This theoretical framework includes *six major predictors of resilience*: initiating stressors, environmental risk and protective mechanisms, person-environmental transactional processes, internal individual resiliency factors (spiritual, cognitive, behavioral, emotional, and physical), resiliency processes, and the positive outcome. The results of this review suggest that there are many opportunities or possible targets for increasing resilience in a plannful manner in designing more supportive environments for children living in at-risk families.

In order to increase drug prevention effectiveness with high-risk youth, selective and indicated prevention interventions, as recently defined by the Institute of Medicine (Mrazek & Haggerty, 1994), should be designed with a special focus on promoting resilience. The prevention field is not far from this goal. By and large prevention programs currently focus on increasing protective processes and factors. They use risk factor assessments primarily to determine high-risk status only. While prevention interventions often focus on increasing protective and resilience processes, the evaluations often primarily assess reductions in risk factors. While increasing protective factors and resilience theoretically should reduce risk factors, the degree of change in resilience and protective processes should also be measured. Empirically tested etiological models including both risk and protective/resilience factors and processes should be developed through prevention studies. Such multivariate studies should increase the field's information about protective and resilience building processes and hence, better inform prevention program methodology on ways to increase effectiveness with high-risk youth.

References

Abelson, W. D., Zigler, E., & DeBlasi, C. L. (1974). Effects of a four-year follow through program on economically disadvantaged children. *Journal of Educational Psychology, 66*, 756–771.

Anthony, E. J. (1987). Risk, vulnerability and resilience: An overview. In E. J. Anthony & B. Cohler (Eds.), *The invulnerable child* (pp. 3–48). New York: The Guilford Press.

Baldwin, A. L., Baldwin, C. P., Kasser, T., Zax, M., Sameroff, A., & Seifer, R. (1993). Contextual risk and resiliency during late adolescence. *Development and Psychopathology, 5*, 741–761.

Bandura, A. (1977). Self-efficacy: Toward a unifying theory of behavior change. *Psychological Review, 84*, 191–215.

Bandura, A. (1989). Human agency in social cognitive theory. *American Psychologist, 44*(9), 1175–1184.

Barbarin, O. (1993). Coping and Resilience: Exploring the inner lives of African-American Children. *Journal of Black Psychology.*

Barnes, G. M., & Welte, J. W. (1986). Patterns and predictors of alcohol use among 7–12th grade students in New York State. *Journal of Studies on Alcohol, 47,* 53–62.

Beardslee, W. R. (1983). Commitment and endurance: A study of civil rights workers who stayed. *American Journal of Orthopsychiatry, 53,* 34–42.

Beardslee, W. R. (1989). The role of self-understanding in resilient individuals: The development of a perspective. *American Journal of Orthopsychiatry, 59*(2), 266–278.

Beardslee, W. R., & Podorefsky, D. (1988). Resilient adolescents whose parents have serious psychiatric disorders: Importance of self-understanding and relationships. *American Journal of Psychiatry, 145*(1), 63–69.

Bennett, L. A., Wolin, S. J., Reiss, D., & Teitelbaum, M. A. (1987). Couples at risk for alcoholism transmission: Protective influences. *Family Process, 26,* 111–129.

Berlin, R., & Davis, R. B. (1989). Children from alcoholic families: Vulnerability and resilience. In Timothy F. Dugan and Robert Coles (Eds.), *The Child in Our Times: Studies in the Development of Resiliency* (pp. 81–105). New York: Brunner/Mazel.

Benard, B. (1991). Fostering resilience in kids: *Protective factors in family, school, and community.* San Francisco: Western Center for Drug-free Schools and Communities, August 1991.

Benard, B. (1993, April). [Discussion during conference on "Putting Resiliency into Substance Abuse Prevention for Adolescents."] Unpublished presentation, New York.

Berndt, T., & Ladd, G. (1989). *Peer Relationships in Child Development,* New York: John Wiley & Sons (Ed.).

Biglan, A., Severson, H. H., Ary, D. V., Faller, C., Thompson, R., Nautel, C., Lichtenstein, E., & Weissman, W. W. (1985). Refusal skills training and the prevention of adolescent cigarette smoking. *Preventative Medicine, 11,* 199–211.

Bleuler, M. (1984). Different forms of childhood stress and patterns of adult psychiatric outcome. In N. F. Watt, E. J. Anthony, & J. E. Rolf (Eds.), *Children at risk for schizophrenia* (pp. 537–542). Cambridge: Cambridge University Press.

Block, J. H., & Block, J. (1980). The role of ego-control and ego-resiliency in the organization of behavior. In W. A. Collins (Ed.), *Development of cognition, affect, and social relations: The Minnesota Symposia on Child Psychology, 13,* 39–101. Hillsdale, NJ: Lawrence Erlbaum Associates.

Botvin, G. J., Baker, E., Dusenbury, L., Tortu, S., & Botvin, E. M. (1990). Preventing adolescent drug use through a multimodal cognitive-behavioral approach: Results of a 3-year study. *Journal of Consulting and Clinical Psychology, 58,* 437–446.

Botvin, G. J., Baker, E., Filazzola, A. D., & Botvin, E. M. (1990). A Cognitive-Behavioral Approach to Substance Abuse Prevention: One-year follow-up. *Addictive Behaviors, 15,* 47–63.

Botvin, G. J., & Tortu, S. (1988). Peer relationships, social competence, and substance abuse prevention: Implications for the family. *Journal of Social Work and Human Sexuality, 6*(2), 105–119.

Botvin, G. J., Baker, E., Renick, N. L., Filazzola, A. D., & Botvin, E. M. (1984). A cognitive behavioral approach to substance abuse prevention. *Addictive Behaviors, 9,* 137–147.

Bronfenbrenner, U. (1986). Ecology of the family as a context for human development: Research perspectives. *Developmental Psychology, 22,* 723–742.

Bronfenbrenner, U., & Crouter, A. C. (1983). The evolution of environmental models in developmental research. In P. H. Mussen (Ed.), *Handbook of child psychology* (4th edition). New York: Wiley.

Brook, J. S., Brook, D. W., Gordon, A. S., Whiteman, M., & Cohen, P. (1990, May). The psychological etiology of adolescent drug use: A family interactional approach. *Genetic, Social, and General Psychology Monographs, 116,* (Whole No. 2).

Bry, B. H. (1983). Predicting drug abuse: Review and reformulation. *The International Journal of the Addictions, 18*(2), 223–233.

Bry, B. H., McKeon, P., & Pandina, R. J. (1982). Extent of drug use as a function of number of risk factors. *Journal of Abnormal Psychology, 91*(4), 273–279.

Buriel, R., Calzada, S., & Vasquez, R. (1982). The relationship of traditional Mexican American culture to adjustment and delinquency among three generations of Mexican American male adolescents. *Hispanic Journal of Behavioral Sciences, 1*(4), 41–55.

Cameron-Bandler, L. (1986). Strategies for creating a compelling future. *Focus on Family and Chemical Dependency,* July/August 1986, 6–7, 37, 44.

Campbell, A., Converse, P. E., & Rodgers, W. L. (1976). *The quality of American life.* New York: Russell Sage Foundation.

Christensen, A. J., Turner, C. W., Smith, T. W., Holman, J. M., & Gregory, M. C. (1991). Health locus of control and depression in end-stage renal disease. *Journal of Consulting and Clinical Psychology, 59*(3), 419–424.

Cicchetti, D., & Garmezy, N. (1993). Prospects and promises in the study of resilience. *Development and Psychopathology, 5,* 497–502.

Clausen, J. S. (1991). Adolescent competence and the shaping of the life course. *American Journal of Sociology, 96,* 804–842.

Cohler, B. J. (1987). Adversity, resilience, and the study of lives. In E. J. Anthony & B. J. Cohler (Eds.), *The invulnerable child* (pp. 363–424). New York: Guilford.

Coie, J. D., Watt, N. F., West, S. G., Hawkins, J. D., Asarnow, J. R., Markman, H. J., Ramey, S. L., Shure, M. B., & Long, B. (1993). The science of prevention: A conceptual framework and some directions for a national research program. *American Psychologist, 48*(10), 1013–1022.

Coles, R. (1989). Moral energy in the lives of impoverished children. In T. F. Dugan & R. Coles (Eds.), *The child in our times: Studies in the development of resiliency* (pp. 45–55). New York: Brunner/Mazel.

Compas, B. E., Howell, D. C., Phares, V., Williams R. A., & Giunta, C. T. (1989). Risk factors for emotional/behavioral problems in young adolescents: A prospective analysis of adolescent and parental stress and symptoms. *Journal of Consulting and Clinical Psychology, 57,* 732–740.

Conger, R. D., Conger, K. J., Elder, G. H., Lorenz, F. O., Simons, R. L., & Whitbeck, L. B. (1992). A family process model of economic hardship and adjustment of early adolescent boys. *Child Development, 63,* 526–541.

Conrad, M., & Hammen, C. (1993). Protective and resource factors in high- and low-risk children: A comparison of children with unipolar, bipolar, medically ill, and normal mothers. *Development and Psychopathology, 5,* 593–607.

DeLongis, A., Coyne, J. C., Dakof, G., Folkman, S., & Lazarus, R. S. (1982). Relationship of daily hassles, uplifts, and major life events to health status. *Health Psychology, 1,* 119–136.

DeMarsh, J. P., & Kumpfer, K. (1986). Family-oriented interventions for the prevention of chemical dependency in children and adolescence. In Ezekoye, S., Kumpfer, K., & Bukoski, W. (Eds.), *Childhood chemical abuse: Prevention and intervention* (pp. 117–152). The Haworth Press, New York, NY, 117–151.

Demos, E. V. (1989). Resiliency in infancy. In T. F. Dugan & R. Coles (Eds.), *The child in our times: Studies in the development of resiliency* (pp. 3–22). New York: Brunner/Mazel.

Dielman, T. E., Shope, J. T., Leech, S. L., & Butchart, A. T. (1989). Differential effectiveness of an elementary school-based alcohol misuse prevention program by type of prior drinking experience. *Journal of School Health, 59*(6), 255–263.

Doernberger, C. H. (1992). *Aspects of competence: resilience among inner-city adolescents.* Unpublished Masters' Thesis, Yale University, New Haven, CT.

Dunn, D. (1994). Resilient reintegration of married women with dependent children: Employed and unemployed. (Doctoral Dissertation, Department of Health Education, University of Utah, Salt Lake City, Utah.)

Dunst, C. (1995). Risk and opportunity factors influencing child and family behavior and development. Presentation, 4th National Early Intervention Meeting. Coimbra, Portugal, June, 1995.

D'Zurilla, T. J., & Nezu, A. M. (1990). Development and preliminary evaluation of the social problem-solving inventory. *Psychological Assessment: A Journal of Consulting and Clinical Behavior, 2,* 156–163.

Egeland, B., Carlson, E., & Sroufe, A. (1993). Resilience as process. *Development and Psychopathology, 5,* 517–528.

Elder, G. H., Caspi, A., & Van Nguyen, T. (1986). Resourceful and vulnerable children: Family influence in hard times. In R. K. Silbereisen & K. Eyferth (Eds.), *Development as action in context* (pp. 167–186). Berlin: Springer-Verlag.

Evans, C. (1996). Resilience in Native Americans: A Qualitative Study. (Doctoral Dissertation, Department of Health Education, University of Utah, Salt Lake City, Utah 84112.)

Felsman, J. K. (1989). Risk and resiliency in childhood. In T. F. Dugan & R. Coles (Eds.), *The child in our times: Studies in the development of resiliency,* 56–80. New York: Brunner/Mazel.

Flach, F. F. (1988). *Resilience: Discovering new strength at times of stress.* New York: Ballantine Books.

Fordham, S., & Ogbu, J. U. (1986). Black students' school success: Coping with the "burden of 'acting white.'" *Urban Review, 18,* 176–206.

Frankel, V. E. (1959). *Man's Search for Meaning: An Introduction to Logotherapy.* Preface by Gordon W. Allport. Boston: Beacon Press.

Freud, S. (1908). On the sexual theories of children.

Gamble, T. J., & Zigler, E. (1986). Effects of infant day care: Another look at the evidence. *American Journal of Orthopsychiatry, 56,* 26–42.

Garmezy, N. (1974). Children at risk: The search for antecedents of schizophrenia. I. Conceptual models and research methods. *Schizophrenia Bulletin, 8,* 14–90.

Garmezy, N. (1985). Stress-resistant children: The search for protective factors. In J. E. Stevenson (Ed.), Recent research in developmental psychopathology (pp. 213–233). *Journal of Child Psychology and Psychiatry, 4* (Book Supplement).

Garmezy, N. (1991). Resiliency and vulnerability to adverse developmental outcomes associated with poverty. *American Behavioral Scientist, 34*(4), 416–430.

Garmezy, N. (1993). Vulnerability and resilience. In D. C. Funder, R. D. Parker, C. Tomlinson-Keesey, & K. Widaman (Eds.), *Studying lives through time: Approaches to personality and development* (pp. 377–398). Washington, DC: American Psychological Association.

Garmezy, N., & Masten, A. S. (1986). Stress, competence, and resilience: Common frontiers for therapist and psychopathologist. *Behavior Therapy, 57*(2), 159–174.

Garmezy, N., & Masten, A. S. (1991). The protective role of competence indicators in children at risk. In E. M. Cummings, A. L. Greene, & K. H. Karraker (Eds.), *Life-span developmental psychology: Perspectives on stress and coping* (pp. 151–174). Hillsdale, NJ: Lawrence Erlbaum Associates.

Garmezy, N., Masten, A. S., & Tellegen, A. (1984). The study of stress and competence in children: A building block for developmental psychopathology. *Child Development, 55,* 97–111.

Gest, S. D., Neemann, J., Hubbard, J. J., Masten, A. S., & Tellegen, A. (1993). Parenting quality, adversity, and conduct problems in adolescence: Testing process-oriented models of resilience. Special Issue: Milestones in the development of resilience. *Development and Psychopathology, 5*(4), 663–682.

Goodwin, D. W. (1986). Alcoholism and genetics. *Archives of General Psychiatry, 42*, 171–174.

Gordon, E. W., & Song, L. D. (1994). In M. C. Wang & E. W. Gorden (Eds.), *Educational resilience in inner-city America* (pp. 27–43). Hillsdale, NJ: Erlbaum.

Halverson, C. F., & Waldrup, M. P. (1974). Relations between preschool barrier behaviors and early school measures of coping, imagination and verbal development. *Developmental Psychology, 10*, 716–720.

Hansen, W. B., & Graham, J. W. (1991). Preventing alcohol, marijuana and cigarette use among adolescents: Peer pressure resistance training versus establishing conservative norms. *Preventative Medicine, 20*, 414–430.

Hawkins, J. D., Arthur, M. W., & Catalano, R. F. (1994). Preventing substance abuse. *Crime and Justice, 8*(24), 197–277.

Hawkins, J. D., Catalano, R. F., & Miller, J. Y. (1992). Risk and protective factors for alcohol and other drug problems in adolescence and early adulthood: Implications for substance abuse prevention. *Psychological Bulletin, 112*(1), 64–105.

Jacobs, J., & Wolin, S. (1991, October). *Resilient Children Growing Up in Alcoholic Families.* Paper presented at National Consensus Symposium on Children of Alcoholics and Co-Dependence.

Johnson, H. L., Glassman, M. B., Fiks, K. B., & Rosen, T. S. (1990). Resilient children: Individual differences in developmental outcome of children born to drug abusers. *Journal of Genetic Psychology, 151*(4), 523–539.

Johnson, J. L., Rolf, J. E., Tiegel, S., & McDuff, D. (1991, October). *Developmental assessment of children of alcoholics.* Paper presented at National Consensus Symposium on Children of Alcoholics and Co-Dependence.

Johnson, C. A., Pentz, M. A., Weber, M. D., Dwyer, J. H., MacKinnon, D. P., Flay, B. R., Baer, N. A., & Hansen, W. B. (1989). *The relative effectiveness of comprehensive community programming for drug abuse with risk and low risk adolescents.* Unpublished manuscript, University of Southern California, Pasadena.

Kagan, J. (1984). *The nature of the child.* New York: Basic Books.

Kandel E., Mednick, S. A., Kirkegaard-Sorensen, L., Hutchings, B., Knop, J., Rosenberg, R., & Schulsinger, F. (1988). IQ as a protective factor for subjects at high risk for antisocial behavior. *Journal of Consulting and Clinical Psychology, 56*, 224–226.

Kaufman, J., & Zigler, E. (1989). The intergenerational transmission of child abuse. In D. Cicchetti & V. Carlson (Eds.), *Child Maltreatment: Theory and research on the causes and consequences of child abuse and neglect* (pp. 129–150). Cambridge: Cambridge University Press.

Kellam, S. G., & Brown, H. (1982). *Social adaptational and psychological antecedents of adolescent psychopathology ten years later.* Baltimore: John Hopkins University.

Ketchel, J. A., & Bieger, G. (1989, April). *The efficacy of a psychosocially based drug prevention program for young adolescents.* Paper presented at the New England Educational Research Corporation Annual Meeting, Portsmouth, NH.

Kim, S., McLeod, J., & Palmgren, C. L. (1989). The impact of the "I'm Special" program on student substance abuse and other related student problem behavior. *Journal of Drug Education, 19*, 83–95.

Kolvin, I., Miller, F. J. W., Fleeting, M., & Kolvin, P. A. (1988). Social and parenting factors affecting criminal-offense rates: Findings from the Newcastle Thousand Family Study. *British Journal of Psychiatry, 152*, 80–90.

Kumpfer, K. L. (1987). Special populations: Etiology and prevention of vulnerability to chemical dependency in children of substance abusers. *In B. Brown and A. Mills (Eds.), Youth at High Risk for Substance Abuse.* NIDA Monograph. Rockville, MD: Office for Substance Abuse Prevention.

Kumpfer, K. L. (1990a). *Resiliency and the ecology of drug abuse.* Presentation at the Quarterly Research Symposium at Toronto Addiction Research Foundation, Toronto, Canada, June 27, 1990.

Kumpfer, K. L. (1990b). Resiliency and AOD use prevention in high risk youth. Unpublished manuscript submitted to CSAP, Dept. of Health Education, University of Utah, Salt Lake City, Utah.

Kumpfer, K. L. (1991). *Risk factors in children of alcoholics.* Paper presented at the National Consensus Symposium on Children of Alcoholics and Co-Dependence, Warrenton, Virginia, October 1991.

Kumpfer, K. L. (1994). Predictive validity of resilience for positive life adaptations. Paper presented at the National Institute on Drug Abuse Resilience Conference. Dec. 13–15, 1994.

Kumpfer, K. L. (in press). Mechanisms for increasing drug abuse resilience and positive life adaptations in at-risk youth. *International Journal of Addictions.*

Kumpfer, K. L., & Bluth, B. (in press). The links between prevention and treatment for drug abusing women and their children.

Kumpfer, K., & DeMarsh, J. (1985). Family, environmental, and genetic influences on children's future chemical dependency. In S. Ezekoye, K. Kumpfer, & W. Bukoski (Eds.), *Childhood and Chemical Abuse: Prevention and Intervention.* New York: Hayworth Press.

Kumpfer, K. L., Molgaard, V., & Spoth, R. (1996). Strengthening families for the prevention of delinquency and drug use. In R. DeV. Peters & R. McMahon (Eds.), *Preventing Childhood Disorders, Substance Abuse, and Delinquency.* Thousand Oaks, CA: Sage Press.

Kumpfer, K., Moskowitz, J., & Klitzner, M. (1986). Future issues and promising directions in the prevention of chemical dependency. *Journal of Children in Contemporary Society.*

Lawrance, L., & McLeroy, K. R. (1986). Self-efficacy and health education. *Journal of School Health, 56,* 317–321.

Lerner, J. V., & Vicary, J. R. (1984). Difficult temperament and drug use: Analyses from the New York longitudinal study. *Journal of Drug Education, 14,* 1–8.

Liddle, H. A. (1994). Contextualizing resiliency. In M. C. Wang & E. W. Gordon (Eds.), *Educational resilience in inner-city America* (pp. 167–177). Hillsdale, NJ: Erlbaum.

Loeber, R. (1988). Natural histories of conduct problems, delinquency, and associated substance use: Evidence for developmental progressions. In B. B. Lahey and A. E. Kazdin (Eds.), *Advances in clinical child psychology, 11,* (pp. 73–124). New York: Plenum Press.

Long, J. V. F., & Valliant, G. E. (1984). Natural history of male psychological health XI: Escape from the underclass. *American Journal of Psychiatry, 141,* 341–346.

Luthar, S. (1991). Vulnerability and resilience: A study of high-risk adolescents. *Child Development, 62,* 600–616.

Luthar, S. S. (1993). Annotation: Methodological and conceptual issues in research on childhood resilience. *Journal of Child Psychology and Psychiatry, 34,* 441–453.

Luthar, S. S., & Zigler, E. (1991). Vulnerability and competence: A review of research on resilience in childhood. *American Journal of Orthopsychiatry, 61,* 6–22.

Luthar, S. S., & Zigler, E. (1992). Intelligence and social competence among high-risk adolescents. *Development and Psychopathology, 4,* 287–299.

Luthar, S. S., Doernberger, C. H., & Zigler, E. (1993). Resilience is not a unidimensional construct: Insights from a prospective study of inner-city adolescents. *Development and Psychopathology, 5,* 703–717.

Luthar, S. S., & Cushing, G. (1996). Measurement issues in the empirical study of resilience:

An overview. Paper presented at a conference by the National Institute of Drug Abuse on "The role of resilience in drug abuse, alcohol abuse, and mental illness." December 5–6, 1994. Washington, D.C.

Magnusson, D. (1988). *Individual development from an interactional perspective.* Hillsdale, NJ: Erlbaum.

Mann, L., Harmoni, R., & Power, C. (1989). Adolescent decision-making: The development of competence. *Journal of Adolescence, 12,* 265–278.

Masten, A. S. (1982). Humor and creative thinking in stress-resistant children. Unpublished doctoral dissertation, University of Minnesota.

Masten, A. S. (1994). Resilience in individual development: Successful adaptation despite risk and adversity. In M. C. Wang & E. W. Gorden (Eds.), *Educational resilience in inner-city America* (pp. 3–25). Hillsdale, NJ: Erlbaum.

Masten, A. S., Best, K. M., & Garmezy, N. (1990). Resilience and development: Contributions from the study of children who overcome adversity. *Development and Psychopathology, 2,* 425–444.

Masten, A. S., Garmezy, N., Tellegen, A., Pellegrini, D. S., Larkin, K., & Larsen, A. (1988). Competence and stress in school children: The moderating effects of individual and family qualities. *Journal of Child Psychology and Psychiatry, 29,* 745–764.

Moskowitz, J. M. (1983). Preventing adolescent substance abuse through drug education. In T. J. Glynn, C. G. Leukefeld, & J. P. Ludford (Eds.), *Preventing adolescent drug abuse: Intervention strategies* (pp. 233–249). National Institute on Drug Abuse Research Monograph No. 47 (DHHS Publication No. ADM 83–1280). Rockville, MD: National Institute on Drug Abuse.

Mrazek, P. J., & Haggerty, R. J. (1994). *Reducing Risks for Mental Disorders: Frontiers for Preventive Intervention Research.* Institute of Medicine (IOM), (1994). Washington, D.C.: National Academy Press

Mulholland, D. J., Watt, N. F., Philpott, A., & Sarlin, N. (1991). Academic performance in children of divorce: Psychological resilience and vulnerability. *Psychiatry, 54*(3), 268–280.

Murphy, L. B. (1987). Further reflections on resilience. In E. J. Anthony & B. Cohler (Eds.), *The invulnerable child* (pp. 103–104). New York: Guilford Press.

Murphy, L. B., & Moriarty, A. E. (1976). *Vulnerability, coping and growth: From infancy to adolescence.* New Haven, CT: Yale University Press.

Musick, J., Scott, F., Spencer, K., Goldman, J., & Cohler, B. (1984). The capacity for enabling mentally ill mothers. *Zero to Three, 4*(4), 1–6.

Myers, L. M. Jr. (1990). Crime, entrepreneurship and labor force withdrawal. Paper presented at the 65th Annual Western Economic Association Conference. June 29–July 3, San Diego.

Neiger, B. (1991). *Resilient reintegration: Use of structural equations modeling.* Unpublished doctoral dissertation, University of Utah, Salt Lake City.

Neiger, B. L. (1992). *Resilient reintegration: Use of structural equations modeling.* Doctoral dissertation, University of Utah, Salt Lake City.

Newcomb, M. D., & Bentler, P. M. (1990). Antecedents and consequences of cocaine use: An eight-year study from early adolescence to young adulthood. In L. Robins & M. Rutter (Eds.), *Straight and devious pathways from childhood to adulthood* (pp. 158–181). Melbourne, Australia: Cambridge University Press.

Newcomb, M. D., Maddahian, E., Skager, R., & Bentler, P. M. (1987). Substance abuse and psychosocial risk factors among teenagers: Associations with sex, age, ethnicity, and type of school. *American Journal of Drug and Alcohol Abuse, 13,* 413–433.

Oetting, E. R., & Beauvais, F. (1990). Orthogonal cultural identification theory: The cultural identification of minority adolescents. Colorado State University, Fort Collins, CO. In press: *International Journal of the Addictions.*

Parker, G. R., Cowen, E. L., Work, W. C., & Wyman, P. A. (1990) Test correlates of stress affected and stress resilient outcomes among urban children. *Journal of Primary Prevention, 11,* 19–35.

Pentz, M. A. (1983). Prevention of adolescent substance abuse through social skills development. In T. J. Glynn, C. G. Leukefeld, & J. P. Ludford (Eds.), *Preventing Adolescent Drug Abuse: Intervention strategies* (pp. 195–232). National Institute on Drug Abuse Research Monograph 47 (DHHS Publication No. ADM 83-1280). Washington, DC: U. S. Government Printing Office.

Pentz, M. A., Johnson, C. A., Dwyer, J. H., MacKinnon, D. P., Hansen, W. B., & Flay, B. R. (1989). A Comprehensive Community Approach to Adolescent Drug Abuse Prevention: Effects of cardiovascular disease risk factors. *Annals of Medicine, 21,* 219–222.

Platt, J. J., Belding, M. A., & Husband, S. D. (in press). Competency building in adolescents. In K. L. Kumpfer (Ed.), *Promoting AOD Resiliency in High Risk Youth.* Submitted to Office 'of Substance Abuse Prevention, Rockville, MD.

Plomin, R., & Daniels, D. (1987). Why are children in the same family so different from one another? *Behavior and Brain Sciences, 10,* 1–60.

Quinton, D., Pickeles, A., Maughan, B., & Rutter, M. (1993). Partners, peers, and pathway: Assortative pairing and continuities in conduct disorder. *Development and Psychopathology, 5,* 763–783.

Radke-Yarrow, M., & Brown, E. (1993). Resilience and vulnerability in children of multiple-risk families. *Development and Psychopathology, 5,* 581–592.

Radke-Yarrow, M., & Sherman, T. (1990). Hard growing: Children who survive. In J. E. Rolf, A. S. Masten, D. Cicchetti, K. Nuechterlein, & S. Weintraub (Eds.), *Risk and Protective Factors in the Development of Psychopathology* (pp. 97–119). New York: Cambridge University Press.

Richardson, G. E., Neiger, B. L., Jensen, S., & Kumpfer, K. (1990). The Resiliency Model. *Health Education, 21*(6), 33–39.

Richters, J. E., & Martinez, P. E. (1993). Violent communities, family choices, and children's: An algorithm for improving the odds. *Development and Psychopathology, 5,* 609–627.

Rolf, J. E., Masten, A. S., Cicchetti, D., Nuechterlein, K., & Weintraub, S. (1990). (Eds.), *Risk and protective factors in the development of psychopathology.* New York: Cambridge University Press.

Roosa, M., Beals, J., Sandler, I. N., Pillow, D. R. (1990). The role of risk and protective factors in predicting symptomatology in adolescent self-identified children of alcohol parents. *American Journal of Community Psychology, 18*(5), 725–741.

Rotter, J. B. (1954). *Social learning and clinical psychology.* Englewood Cliffs, NJ: Prentice-Hall.

Rutter, M. (1979). Protective factors in children's responses to stress and disadvantage. In M. W. Kent and J. Rolf (Eds.), *Primary Prevention of Psychopathology, Vol. III: Social Competence in Children* (pp. 49–74). Hanover, N. H., University Press of New England.

Rutter, M. (1982). Epidemiological-longitudinal approaches to the study of development. In W. A. Collins (Ed.). *The concept of development. The Minnesota Symposia on Child Psychology (Vol. 15)* (pp. 105–144). Hillsdale, NJ: Lawrence Erlbaum.

Rutter, M. (1987). Psychosocial resilience and protective mechanisms. *American Journal of Orthopsychiatry, 57*(3), 316–331.

Rutter, M. (1990). Psychosocial resilience and protective mechanisms. In J. Rolf, A. S. Masten, D. Cicchetti, K. H. Neuchterlein, & S. Weintraub (Eds.), *Risk and protective factors in the development of psychopathology* (pp. 181–214). New York: Cambridge University Press.

Rutter, M. (1992, December). Transitions and turning points in development. Paper presented at the British Psychological Society Conference, London.

Rutter, M. (1993). Resilience: Some conceptual considerations. *Journal of Adolescent Health, 14*, 626–631.

Rutter, M., & Quinton, D. (1994). Long-term follow-up of women institutionalized in childhood: Factors promoting good functioning in adult life. *British Journal of Developmental Psychology, 18*, 225–234.

Rutter, M., Maughan, B., Mortimore, P., Ouston, J., & Smith, A. (1979). *Fifteen thousand hours: Secondary schools and their effects on children.* Cambridge, MA: Harvard University Press.

Sameroff, A. J., & Chandler, M. J. (1975). Reproductive risk and the continuum of caretaking casualty. In F. D. Horowitz (Ed.), *Review of child development research 4,* (pp. 187–244). Chicago: University of Chicago Press.

Sameroff, A. J., Seifer, R., & Barocas, R. (1983). Impact of parental psychopathology: Diagnosis, severity, or social status effects. *Infant Mental Health Journal, 4*(3), 236–249.

Scarr, S., & McCarty, K. (1983). How people make their own environments: A theory of genotype environment effects. *Child Development, 54*, 424–435.

Schunk, D. H., & Carbonari, J. P. (1984). Self-efficacy models. In J. D. Matarazzo, S. M. Weiss, J. A. Herd, and N. E. Miller (Eds.), *Behavioral health: A handbook of health* (pp. 230–247). New York: Wiley.

Schwartz, J. M., Jacobson, A. M., Hauser, S. T., & Dornbush, B. B. (1989). Explorations of vulnerability and resilience: Case studies of diabetic adolescents and their families. In T. F. Dugan & R. Coles (Eds.), *The child in our times: Studies in the development of resiliency* (pp. 134–156). New York: Brunner/Mazel.

Segal, J. (1986). *Winning life's toughest battles: Roots of human resilience.* New York: McGraw-Hill.

Seligman, M. (1975). *Helplessness: On Depression, Development, and Death.* San Francisco: Freeman.

Selman, R. L. (1980). *The growth of interpersonal understanding: Developmental and clinical analysis.* New York: Academic Press.

Spivack, G., & Shure, M. B. (1982). The cognition of social adjustment: Interpersonal cognitive problem-solving thinking. In B. B. Lahey & A. E. Kazdin (Eds.), *Advances in Clinical Child Psychology* (pp. 323–372). New York: Plenum Press.

Spivack, G., Platt, J. J., & Shure, M. (1976). *The problem-solving approach to adjustment.* San Francisco: Jossey-Bass.

Staudinger, U. M., Marsiske, M., & Baltes, P. B. (1993). Resilience and levels of reserve capacity in later adulthood: Perspective from life-span theory. *Development and Psychopathology, 5*, 541–566.

Stouthamer-Loeber, M., Loeber, R., Farrington, D. P., Zhang, Q., Van Kammen, W., & Maguin, E. (1993). The double edge of protective and risk factors for delinquency: Interrelations and developmental patterns. *Development and Psychopathology, 5*, 683–701.

Strauss, B. G., & Glaser, A. L. (1967). *The Discovery of Grounded Theory.* Chicago: Aldine.

Swearingen, E. M., & Cohen, L. H. (1985). Measurement of adolescents' life events: A Junior High Life Experiences Survey. *American Journal of Community Psychology, 13*, 69–85.

Tarter, R., & Mezzich, A. (1992). Ontogeny of substance abuse: Perspectives and findings. In M. Glantz and R. Pickens (Eds.), *Vulnerability to drug abuse.* American Psychiatric Association.

Taylor, S. E. (1983). Adjustment to threatening events: A theory of cognitive adaptation. *American Psychologist, 38*, 1161–1173.

Turner, S. (1995). Family variables related to adolescent substance misuse: Risk and resiliency factors. In T. R. Gullotto, G. R. Adams, & R. Montemayor (Eds.), *Substance Misuse in Adolescence.* Thousand Oaks, CA: Sage.

Walker, R. J. (1995). *Resiliency in adult children of alcoholic parents: Use of structural Equation Modeling.* Dissertation submitted to The University of Utah.

Wallerstein, J. (1983). Children of divorce: The psychological tasks of the child. *American Journal of Orthopsychiatry, 53*(2), 230–243.

Werner, E. E. (1985). Stress and protective factors in children's lives. In A. R. Nicol (Ed.), *Longitudinal studies in child psychology and psychiatry* (pp. 335–355). New York: John Wiley and Sons.

Werner, E. E. (1986). Resilient offspring of alcoholics: A longitudinal study from birth to age 18. *Journal of Studies on Alcohol, 47,* 34–40.

Werner, E. E. (1989). High-risk children in young adulthood: a longitudinal study from birth to 32 years. *American Journal of Orthopsychiatry, 59,* 72–81.

Werner, E. E. (1993). Risk, resilience, and recovery: Perspectives from the Kauai Longitudinal Study. *Development and Psychopathology, 5,* 503–515

Werner, E. E., & Smith, R. S. (1989). *Vulnerable but invincible: A longitudinal study of resilient children and youth.* New York: Adams-Bannister-Cox. (Original work published 1982).

Werner, E. E., & Smith, R. S. (1992). *Overcoming the odds: High risk children from birth to adulthood.* Ithaca, New York: Cornell University Press.

Wertlieb, D., Weigel, C., Springer. T., & Feldstein, M. (1989). Temperament as a moderator of children's stressful experiences. In S. Chess, A. Thomas, & M. E. Hertzig (Eds.), *Annual progress in child psychiatry and child development: 1988.* New York: Brunner/Mazel.

White, J. L., Moffitt, T. E., & Silva, P. A. (1989). A prospective replication of the protective effects of IQ in subjects at high risk for juvenile delinquency. *Journal of Consulting and Clinical Psychology, 57,* 719–724.

Wolin, S. J. (1989). Resiliency in children of alcoholics. Paper presented at the American Academy of Child and Adolescent Psychiatry Institute on Substance Abuse, New York, New York, October 13, 1989.

Wolin, S. J. (1991). Paper presented at the Protecting Vulnerable Children Project, Children of Alcoholics Foundation, Inc. Princeton University, Princeton, New Jersey, November, 1991.

Wolin, S. J., & Wolin, S. (1993). *Bound and Determined: Growing up resilient in a troubled family.* New York: Villard Press.

Worland, J., Weeks, D. G., & Janes, C. L. (1987). Predicting mental health in children at risk. In E. J. Anthony & B. J. Cohler (Eds.), *The invulnerable child* (pp. 185–210). New York: Guilford Press.

Wyman, P. A., Cowen, E. L., Work, W. C., & Kerley, J. H. (1993). The role of children's future expectations in self-system functioning and adjustment to life stress: A prospective study of urban at-risk children. *Development and Psychopathology, 5,* 649–661.

10

Commentary
Resilience as Transactional Equilibrium

Jeannette L. Johnson

Introduction

Kumpfer (1999, this volume) writes a provocative and comprehensive chapter on the factors and processes that contribute to resilience. Her review, along with the others in this book, provides an exhaustive accounting of how we have come to speak of resilience and the possibilities this new language holds for our thinking about how lives can be lived more fully than biological or environmental circumstances might allow.

The concept of resilience, as a paradigm shift, is in direct contrast to the public health risk-focused approach. The public health approach encouraged us to focus on the reduction of infectious diseases but did not assist our understanding of how one can live a productive, happy life, despite the actual or looming presence of physiological disease or social plight. According to Kumpfer, it is not the fault of the public health model, but more inherent in the notion of resilience itself. Resilience, as a concept, remains illusive and broadly defined.

Elusiveness aside, Kumpfer deftly catalogues the research that influences successful adaptation to life in resilient children. By organizing these variables into a dynamic framework, she promotes a transactional

Jeannette L. Johnson • Department of Psychiatry, Division of Alcohol and Drug Abuse, University of Maryland, Baltimore, Maryland 21201.

Resilience and Development: Positive Life Adaptations, edited by Glantz and Johnson. Kluwer Academic/Plenum Publishers, New York, 1999.

model that argues that the individual negotiates his or her environment with or without the benefit of resilience. Resilience becomes a complex of related processes instead of a list of external or internal "things" that will predict the way a person thinks, feels, or acts.

The transactional model proposed by Kumpfer includes environmental precursors (commonly referred to as risk and protective factors), personal characteristics of the individual, and the dynamic processes that mediate between the person and their environment or the person and their outcome. In her model, she specifies six major constructs: (1) the stressor or challenge, (2) environmental contexts, (3) individual characteristics, (4) outcomes, (5) the confluence between the environment and the individual, and (6) the individual and his or her choice of outcomes. Each cluster of these variables are needed to understand how to predict resilience.

Kumpfer's transactional model is similar to other models proposed by Rutter (1982, 1987, 1993), Wolin and Wolin (1993), and Masten and her colleagues (1990, 1994). Most researchers recognize that resilience changes across time, circumstance, and context. For example, it is not clear whether or not shyness is a risk factor, a protective factor, or could serve as a generalized construct of "resilience", depending on the context in which the shyness occurs. A shy girl who lives in a neighborhood that promotes drug activity or other deviant acts will be protected from deviance by her shyness because she is unlikely to engage in peer interaction in her neighborhood. On the other hand, a shy girl who goes to a private girls school brimming with opportunities to engage in prosocial activities might not engage in peer interaction that could be of a potential benefit to her. Similarly, shyness coupled with a fast developing girl going through precocious puberty at an earlier rate than her same age cohort would be protected from engaging in early sexual activity that puts her at risk for STDs or pregnancy.

Resilience, therefore, is not just a construct, but becomes a complex of constructs that move across time. No wonder it is hard to measure and hard to grasp. Depending upon who you are, where you live, what intrinsic or extrinsic "opportunity structures" are available to you, resilience becomes a personal negotiation through life. To think about resilience in didactic terms, i.e., one is either resilient or not-resilient, might be too simple. Resilience, viewed as a personal transaction and occurs because each one of us is not only governed by what we're born with, what we acquire along the way, and all the random acts in-between, but also how we think about it.

Piaget takes this into account with his theory of equilibrium and disequilibrium. Best known for his theory of cognitive developmental stage sequencing, Piaget was not only concerned about the characteristics of each stage, but also how we move from one stage to the other. Given that we have what we have at each cognitive developmental stage, how do we move to another stage that is qualitatively and quantitatively different? Such is a similar question in trying to understand resilience. Given that we have what we're born with (and this might be bad), how do we turn it into something that is useful, that moves us on to live a better life?

Kumpfer's transactional model helps us to understand the psychological movement individuals need to make lemonade out of lemons. Her model is much like the one used by Piaget to explain movement across cognitive developmental stages. Piaget's theory of how we move from stage to stage centers on the process of equilibration. We are in a state of equilibrium, much like homeostasis, when the status quo is not interrupted. When it is perturbed, disequilibrium ensues, and it is this state of disequilibration that provides the opportunity for us to move from stage to stage. Kumpfer's transactional model likens the movement needed to negotiate resilience to what she terms "resilient reintegration", or a higher state of resiliency and strength. Her model proposes several different levels of reintegrating processes: (1) resilient reintegration, or a higher state of resiliency and strength, (2) homeostatic reintegration, the same state before the stressor, (3) maladaptive reintegration, or a lowered state of reintegration, and (4) dysfunctional reintegration, or a major reduction in positive reintegration. Homeostasis changes over time.

Kumpfer, as well as others in this volume, give us some clues as to how resilience creates an opportunity for a disequilibrating, yet growth inducing and protecting event, to occur. Listing traits that can be considered protective factors, such as insight and humor, is the start. These traits might be, as in Piaget's words, necessary, but not sufficient to understand the process of resilience. Kumpfer moves us a step along by suggesting that it is the transaction between the person and their environment that creates an "atmosphere" for resilience to occur. To be resilient, one doesn't merely give and receive. Risk and protective factors are filtered through the thoughts about what this giving and receiving means, what it meant in the past, and what it might mean in the future. Thus, resilience becomes a personal negotiation through the complexities of the risk and protective factors available to individuals.

The problem in understanding the transactional character of resilience is much like understanding psychological movement. It may not be that resilience is elusive, but that it is invisible. What if it is something you feel, but you can't describe? What if resilience is something that happens, but you can't see? What if resilience is something that creates music in a life born deaf? What if resilience is something that warms you in your thoughts, but there is no language to share it? What if resilience is the poetry of life, and we are now just learning the alphabet?

Our research models must take this poetry and put it into scientific language, testable theories, lists of dependent and independent variables, and make it readable to statistical programs that only work with numbers. What a task, and yet it must be done if resilience is to be credible to our minds born into Western thinking and governed by medical models of disease. Kumpfer's transactional model does not lose this meter or rhyme, however, as she recognizes the complexity of the task. It is when the task is simplified by language that reduces resilience to a trait that we lose what the meaning of resilience could be in the lives of individuals who were born into abject poverty, or without adequate parenting, or with potentially debilitating handicaps. Resilience is all of what we have said it is, but Kumpfer's model tells us what it could be if we were to understand the significance of its' deeper meaning.

References

Kumpfer, K. (1999). Factors and processes contributing to resilience: The resilience framework. In M. Glantz & J. Johnson (Eds.), *Resilience and development: Positive life adaptations.* New York: Plenum Press.

Masten, A. S. (1994). Resilience in individual development: Successful adaptation despite risk and adversity. In M. C. Wang & E. W. Gorden (Eds.), *Educational resilience in inner city America* (pp. 3–25). Hillsdale, NJ: Erlbaum.

Masten, A. S., Best, K. M., & Garmezy, N. (1990). Resilience and development: Contributions from the study of children who overcome adversity. *Development and Psychopathology, 2,* 425–444.

Rutter, M. (1982). Epidemiological-longitudinal approaches to the study of development. In W. A. Collins (Ed.), *The concept of development. The Minnesota Symposia on Child Psychology (Vol. 15)* (pp. 105–144). Hillsdale, NJ: Lawrence Erlbaum.

Rutter, M. (1987). Psychosocial resilience and protective mechanisms. *American Journal of Orthopsychiatry, 57*(3), 316–331.

Rutter, M. (1993). Resilience: Some conceptual considerations. *Journal of Adolescent Health, 14,* 626–631.

Wolin, S. J., & Wolin, S. (1993). *Bound and Determined: Growing up resilient in a troubled family.* New York: Villard Press.

11

Opening Doors to Resilience Intervention for Prevention Research

Jon E. Rolf and Jeannette L. Johnson

Introduction

Childhood and adolescence can be times of tough growing. In the 1990's, many youths are stressed-out and street-wise. Many are lacking positive connections to family, school, or community. More than any time in our country's history, youth are emersed in teen cultures in school, recreational peer groups, and part-time work. There is a general absence of parental monitoring or other adult mentoring. Today, connections to the community are defined more by individual consumerism than by citizenship distinguished by apprenticeship in adult roles. The work ethic and customs of civility characteristic of their grandparents generation seem irrelevant relics of an outdated American dream. The mass media and daily experiences in the schools and neighborhoods are providing youth with an overabundance of role models for violence and risk-taking lifestyles. It's a time for tough growing.

Research literature provides abundant evidence that many of the problem behaviors of youth are associated with conditions of social and economic environments. Some of these findings raise important questions

Jon E. Rolf • Center for Substance Abuse Prevention, Substance Abuse and Mental Health Services Administration, Rockville, Maryland 20857. **Jeannette L. Johnson** • Department of Psychiatry, Division of Alcohol and Drug Abuse, University of Maryland, Baltimore, Maryland 21201.

Resilience and Development: Positive Life Adaptations, edited by Glantz and Johnson. Kluwer Academic/Plenum Publishers, New York, 1999.

about how social learning and family training can be strengthened to reduce risks for poor outcomes during development. Unfortunately, very little is known about how environmental factors interact with attributes to make some of today's youth more resilient to trauma during development. We have a long way to go before we can declare our understanding of the emergence of risk and protective factors and their mechanisms that influence the development and maintenance of resilience across the lifespan (Luthar, 1993; Pelligrini, 1990). There is a great need for longitudinal research to discover how youth develop resilience or how they find the means to shape their own developmental trajectories towards health and competence. Even less is known from research about the ways that scientific intervention programs can increase the resiliency processes among youth. There are, however, many clues as to how resilience might be enhanced through experimental interventions. This paper discusses how some of the known intervention approaches could be adapted for a new generation of sponsored prevention research.

In this paper, it is assumed that resiliency involves an inter-play of biological, psychological and environmental processes. Emmy Werner's work (Werner, 1984; Werner, 1986; Werner, 1989; Werner & Smith, 1982) has identified a short list of processes that have apparently been protective during the development of some children growing up under considerable stress. On the biological side these processes are: (1) an "easy" temperament (or alternatively, an "emotional toughness") and (2) a tendency to explore outside the home environment. This exploration brings them into contact with alternative competence promoting environments.

The list of psychosocial processes underlying resilience is longer and it includes: (1) normal or greater intelligence (which, of course, also has a genetic/biological component); (2) ability to bond to a nurturing caretaker (e.g., a neighbor, relative, or surrogate big brother or sister, etc.); (3) social comprehension allowing one to stay connected with the mentoring adults in order to advance cognitive, communication, and self-help skills; (4) a positive self-concept; (5) an optimistic outlook on life (e.g., life has meaning and it can be shaped and improved by the youth him/herself); and (6) an ability to use spiritual beliefs, religious faith and/or humor to reduce the stressful and distressing impacts of negative life events.

For some of us, these resiliency indicators sound a lot like what used to be termed "positive personality traits". Regardless of the terminology, what's important to the prevention research field is whether or not resilience is a protective process that can be changed through intervention. There is evidence that currently accepted theories of intervention to affect behavior change are congruent with the hypothesis that resilience can be experimentally increased. Common sense also tells us that the answer might be that resilience can be learned. It seems reasonable to expect that such resilience processes as likability, humor, and attachment to mentoring adults can be trained as skills through systematic application of interventions that have been previously demonstrated to build other types of skills. There are also reasons to expect that resilience skill promoting interventions could be packaged with other types of preventive interventions. Such a promotion/prevention intervention package fits with current trends. For example, based on data from the substance abuse risk research and prevention intervention fields, a strong consensus has emerged that multi-method, multi-occasion and cross-context skills training interventions are the types of programs most likely to produce positive and enduring effects in the areas of self-concept, cognitive style and expectancies as well as in the rates of future risk-lowering behaviors (Botvin, 1982; Bukoski, 1991; Cowen, 1982; Felner, Jason, Moritsugu, & Farber, 1983). There is also reason to believe that including "resilience skills" building components into existing theory based preventive intervention programs will not be technically difficult, nor would introducing resilience promotion into the research agenda seem to be a politically unwise move. The current conservative voting trends in the United States indicate great interest in redirecting services in ways so people can help themselves through self-improvement and sustained work.

Approaching Resilience through the Science of Intervention Research

There is a sufficient body of risk research suggesting what it takes to produce bad outcomes during development (Crittenden, 1985; Garmezy, 1993; Schissel, 1993; Pellegrini, 1990; Wyman, Cowen, Work, & Parker, 1991). Similarly, there is sufficient data to predict and explain how a focused skill or knowledge building intervention produces a desired change in groups of youth (Botvin & Wills, 1985; Botvin, Baker, Dusenbury, Tortu, & Botvin, 1990). However, the developmental challenge for the prevention research community is to design sustainable and testable developmentally relevant intervention programs that are comprehensive and produce a measurable range of effects in sub-groups of youth according to the interplay of individual and contextual differences. Experienced researchers, such as Anne Masten (personal communication, 1994), assert that the prevention research field should move on to more complex, integrative prevention projects that can test the resilience promotion along with risk reduction intervention effectiveness in real world settings.

Resilience can be an attractive addition to prevention research. Public health service providers, educators, and social scientists all strive to develop,

implement, and evaluate preventive programs to reduce the future incidence and prevalence of one or more bad outcomes for youth at risk (e.g.,
drug abuse, pregnancy and STD/HIV/AIDS infections). Adding resilience
promotion to these programs could help improve the fit between a project's
research goals and the value structures of the host community and its institutions (such as the schools). The primary mission of the schools has always
been to enable their students to become increasingly competent in both
abstract intellectual abilities and in their ability to solve the practical "real
world" problems. Unfortunately, the increasing focus on developing behavioral control and discipline is beginning to predominate school culture at
the expense of the three "R's" curricula. Existing prevention programs are,
in part, accepted by the schools because they might help reduce discipline
problems in the short term. Resilience promotion should be attractive to
both educators and youth because resilience promotion offers some desirable short term benefits. For educators, more resilient youths should pose
fewer (or at least less long term) learning or disciplinary problems at school.
For their part, youths want very much to acquire skills that enable them to
master their immediate developmental challenges; to cope with the social
and academic grading systems; to accommodate their evolving self-image
to changes in their physical and psycho-sexual partners; and to attract
employers in order to get jobs to earn sufficient money to support both
basic survival needs and a chosen lifestyle. Learning to become more
resilient should sound like a good thing to most youth because it would
make them more likely to maintain valued behaviors and peer status during
stressful times.

Scope and Feasibility of Resilience Intervention
for Institutions Supporting Prevention Research
and Demonstrations

Prevention research with components that integrate resilience promotion could be both good science and affordable to research support institutions. This win-win outcome won't happen quickly or automatically
without nurturance. There needs to be some careful planning jointly guided
by program staff from the research funding institutions and by prevention
scientists. While such planning is not without cost, there is much to be
gained from such collaborative planning and technical review activities.
Also, it would not offer any impediments to an independent investigator
eager for a grant proposal during the collaborative planning interval.

Some of the benefits of collaborative planning are rather obvious. First,
it would help avoid the danger of having resilience intervention research

being labeled as soft science and unworthy of funding. Second, the national political mood and the realities of budget deficit reduction measures make it dangerous to even suggest that resilience intervention should be applied and evaluated on any type of large scale. As Emmy Werner (personal communication, 1994) and others have recently pointed out, with the possible single exception of Head Start, the will to continue the "war on poverty" has passed. Today, new programs promising greater burdens on the advocates of new social benefits must find low-cost, low-profile ways to prove real cost-benefits in advance of large scale program delivery. Consequently, it seems advisable to plan small scale demonstration research projects on resilience. Such projects should be restricted to carefully controlled experiments or quasi-experiments so that they will be viable in NIH or SAMHSA peer review and funded on their individual scientific merits. However, the rate of fundable grant proposals within the emerging resilience research field could be accelerated in affordable and politically acceptable ways.

Given agreement that the knowledge base is sufficient to begin resilience intervention studies and the political atmosphere is conducive to launching a modest program to support the studies, the key questions remain: "Do what, to whom, by whom, where, and for how long?" In an ideal world, there would be a grant to fund planning for cross-site collaborations to answer these questions and to develop a shared intervention and evaluation protocol. Certainly, sharing aspects of a research protocol could yield pooled data permitting examination of outcome data for more types of subgroups while maintaining sufficient power for longitudinal analyses. Such collaboration could produce more fundable proposals at earlier dates.

The Design of Resiliency Intervention Projects

As with all longitudinal research, great care must be given to choosing an experimental design for resilience intervention studies that minimizes most common threats to internal and external validity. This is much more easily said than done, but there are very scientifically respectable theory based designs that can be sustained for at least a one- to five-year grant cycle in the real world environments of youth. The remainder of this paper will explore some of the alternatives in the hope that it will spur debate and encourage needed collaborative planning.

We begin with three assumptions: (1) The need for precise tests of single factor low-potency interventions is past; it is better to compare state-of-the-science, multi-method intervention packages with and without a resilience promotion enhancement. The interventions should be as potent as possible in order to have a chance to obtain important and measurable intervention effects across three or four grant years; (2) Specific tests of hypotheses on the added effects of the resilience enhanced vs. nonenhanced intervention packages would not interfere with the testing of hypotheses on other popular prevention outcome variables in the alcohol and other drug use, behavior problem prevention research fields; and (3) Longitudinal measurement of stressful life events common to all adolescents can detect natural experiments on the benefits of previous "resilience skill" training for sub-groups of subjects. Therefore, it should not be necessary to restrict the initial studies to using only the highest risk youth in samples.

Choosing Comparison Sites

A scientifically sound longitudinal research project requires a high level of fidelity of protocol implementation over the years. This is possible only in sites where collaboration is sustainable with the host communities, its' institutions and subject cohorts. Thus, one would try to avoid politically unstable communities with a failed economic base, saturated with violence and disconnections of families from the community leaders and schools. Better options for the early resilience interventions studies may lie in the townships and smaller cities of rural America. These communities often have relatively small non-mobile populations, a sense of self-identity, and an interest in finding external support to develop the means to more adequately meet the prevention needs of their youth. For example, the smaller towns of Oregon and northern Arizona (to name but two areas), already have proven to be excellent research partners for NIDA and NIAAA, and NCI. Townships in the Midwest and West also offer excellent geographic separation for testing community based intervention programs.

Developmental Staging

The exciting challenge in resilience research is to demonstrate that it is a modifiable protective process during development. It would be advisable to choose a relatively brief period of development to study, for a number of reasons. The current grant environment can be expected to fund only short term longitudinal studies of no more than four or five years duration. Therefore, it is crucial to select a study cohort that will undergo a predictable and stressful developmental transition during those years. The transitions and challenges of early and middle adolescence fit this criterion, and they already have proven to be fertile grounds for NIH grantees' longitudinal studies into the interplay of biological, psychosocial, and community/environment factors. Given the near universally experienced stress of early adolescence combined with the experimentation with alcohol, tobacco, or other illicit drugs, one need not search out only highest risk early adolescents in highly stressed environments. Even typical young adolescents in any town can be expected to produce the needed range of bad outcomes without having risk factors impervious to the experimental interventions. Some researchers may prefer other developmental staging periods, but the adolescent transition will be used in this paper's discussions of intervention alternatives.

Measurement

The source of project funding will certainly shape the assessment packages. NIAAA is particularly interested in alcohol related variables, while NIMH grants have foci on cognitive, affective, and social processes involved in the etiological chains leading to behavior problems and mental disorders. CSAP may be most concerned with demonstrating how prevention can work for community based organizations. Regardless of the funding source, there should be sufficient agreement on what would constitute a desirable core of (1) independent variables (e.g., gender, age, physical development, cognitive abilities, and peer influences) and (2) dependent variables from competencies to problem behaviors. Were this agreement true, there could be some rather easily obtained cross-resilience project agreements as to how to gather some data in common (Schorr, 1988). However, it is usually more difficult to agree on the specific measures, frequency of administration, and primacy of any one domain or specific measure. Even so, it is not improbable to expect to achieve some form of cross-project collaborations. Cross-sponsored institute sponsored workgroups on desirable assessment domains and methods would facilitate such collaborations for resilience researchers as it has for other areas of research in the past (e.g., NIMH's 1980's working groups on longitudinal assessments of depressive affect in adolescence and on family research methodology).

Whatever the specifics of a common assessment core, there can be major benefits in reserving at least part of the first project year for formative research and piloting of research instruments and procedures. Preventive intervention studies integrating resilience promotion will need these opportunities to fine tune the specifics to local contexts. This fine tuning can be done without jeopardizing the essence of the standardization. Of equal importance are the positive effects that such formative research will bring in the forms of generating community acceptance and sustaining the research protocol over subsequent years.

Guidance by Theoretical Models

Ones approach to resilience promotion program development can be guided by several theoretical perspectives that are considered to be part of the mainstream of prevention research. The first of these is the human developmental perspective that describes behavioral change during development as an interaction of bio-psychological maturational processes. For example, the cognitive developmental theory of Jean Piaget describes human development as shaped by inherent urges to assimilate and accommodate experience into new cognitive schemas of reality. Bronfenbrenner and colleagues (1977, 1983) point to the wisdom of remembering that youth always develop in contexts, and that this embeddedness in school, peer, family, and community environments constantly mediates developmental changes and skill acquisition. Robert White (1959, 1979) has also theorized that becoming competent in building various schema and gaining mastery by adapting to new challenging experiences is inherently rewarding to developing individuals.

Learning theory perspectives are in agreement with developmental ones in that humans will work hard to gain mastery—especially when their physical health, their self-esteem, and their social status are enhanced. The urge to mastery (or competence) may or may not be innate, but the consequences of the efforts expended certainly shape development. Therefore, resilience promoting intervention schemes will no doubt be guided by some form of social cognitive theory and perhaps by its more public health person-in-context oriented variant known as Social Action Theory (Bandura, 1986). Combining these theoretical perspectives with the results of previous theory based intervention studies point to three useful principals for intervention protocol development: (1) Building knowledge will be insufficient for habit development without ample opportunities for socially reinforced practice (i.e., putting new knowledge into action in social contexts via work projects, role-play, etc.); (2) Building specific self-efficacy beliefs (confidence in "I can do it" expectancies) will increase the chances that an intervention subject will actually apply a new protective behavior in an appropriate health risking situation; and (3) Providing skill practicing opportunities across social contexts (in school, family, peer, and adult settings) is necessary to generalize newly acquired skills into habitual life styles and developing personality traits.

Avenues of Intervention

Should resilience intervention studies place their efforts on schools, families, youth clubs, or the media as the primary avenue of program delivery? Previous prevention research has documented successes with each one. Perhaps the initial resilience studies should attempt to research some of the best of each. This integrative approach combining the best of the above approaches seems very reasonable given the need to produce measurable and enduring intervention effects during different periods of a rapid developmental transitioning. The authors' own preference is to pursue an integrative approach as will be outlined in the following sections where we have organized discussions of intervention components according to Werner's (1989) classification of resilience indicators and Dryfoos (1990) categorizations of program elements which are characteristic of successful prevention intervention projects.

Characteristics of Successful Intervention Programs: Applications to Resilience

There are a number of predictive risk factors that have been found in several longitudinal studies of development with high risk youth. For example, there are data about characteristics that discriminate between youth who come to abuse alcohol and other drugs vs. those who abstain (Jessor & Jessor, 1977; Kandel, Simcha-Fagan, & Davis, 1986). These characteristics include: (1) Life skill deficits; (2) Low self-esteem; (3) Conduct problems; (4) Pro-drug attitudes; (5) Low academic motivation; (6) Psychological disturbance (including anxiety and depression); (7) Lack of refusal skills to counter peer pressures to use illicit substances; and (8) Rejection of prosocial values and religion as guiding principles.

One part of a comprehensive intervention program to prevent problem behaviors and to promote resilience could build skills and knowledge to address these and other types of deficits. In addition, another aspect of the program could address the protective processes linked to resilience indicators. These could also be systematically enhanced with each other as part of an integrated intervention package following Emmy Werner's suggestions. The resilience promoting interventions could be designed to increase competence in: (1) Exploring local social networks for positive role models; (2) Attracting positive adult attention by demonstrating the value of an individual ability (from humor to a potentially productive talent); (3) Developing an even-tempered/likable demeanor; (4) Experiencing guided practice in required helpfulness to younger children, to elders, and to institutions with programs valued by the youth (e.g., assisting with sports, music, etc.); (5) Encouraging connections to value and faith systems via participation in traditional culture and/or religious activities; (6) Teaching humor as a restorative and bucking-up skill through modeling and hands-on practice sessions; and (7) Opening doors to mentored apprenticeships in the worlds of work and higher education.

To be successful, any integrative resilience promotion/behavior problem prevention program will probably also have to: (a) Link itself to established, community wide interagency collaborations; (b) Broaden opportunity structures for community youth; (c) Coordinate interventions in both schools and non-school environments; (d) Provide intensive individualized interventions to build skills: (e) Use media enhanced intervention curricula; (f) Engage peers as social reinforcers; (g) Involve parents and adults; (h) Link the experimental youth programs to the adult world of work; (i) Intervene early with problem outliers; (j) Provide thorough training and monitoring of the program's interventionists to assure program fidelity; and (k) Administer the research project as a special kind of cross-cultural community based experiment. Each of these research tasks will be briefly explored in turn.

Link to Established, Community-Wide Interagency Collaborations

This is one of Dryfoos' (1990) recommended program elements. Considering our own resilience promotion research, we are proposing a new kind of research and intervention delivery collaboration built on the 130 year history of Cooperative Extension's Service's partnerships with state, county, and community based educational and recreational organizations. In one of our preliminary research designs, Cooperative Extension Specialists in the counties would help staff the resilience intervention delivery team while 4-H clubs would provide the venue for a for resilience curriculum along with 4-H mentors, after-school activity space and some materials. Resilience promotion should fit well with the 4-H tradition of learning to help oneself become more productive. The Cooperative Extension service would also provide the means to link the project's to school-based problem behavior prevention curricula and to families as many of the 4-H projects involve while at home. Other aspects of the interagency collaboration envision a public health services research team providing the expertise to obtain and manage the grant funding for the research program. These researchers and other university based Cooperative Extension service faculty would collaborate in designing the experimental interventions and their evaluations, hiring and supervising the evaluation staff, conducting staff training, providing the evaluation materials, and assisting in keeping the interagency collaboration functional.

There are a number of advantages in the two channel approach where

4-H clubs implement the resilience interventions and these schools implement the prevention curricula targeting health risking behaviors. First, it delivers a multi-method, multi-context intervention package without overburdening the staff and program/educational calendars of either institution. Second, the productivity and longevity of the research partnership is strengthened through the cross-institution collaboration. Both programs are reinforcing each other and sharing common outcome objectives. This should in turn help educate and attract community leaders and parents as advocates or project volunteers. Further discussion about school and youth club coordination is provided below. Third, the clubs and schools offer complementary recognition systems for rewarding achievement in building resilience and risk-reduction skills. For 4-H, these include county and state fair competitions, field trips, certifications, and award ribbons; for the schools, there are grades, diplomas, and varsity letters, etc. Each institution can also raise and provide supplemental funding for elements of their respective programs. Four H and school's parent booster groups do this for work-related and extracurricular projects (e.g., where youth teams plan, build/produce products, teams, bands, and other services with value to the community).

Broadening Opportunity Structures through Intensive, Individualized Attention

"Opportunity structures" is a construct describing the availability of experiences during development that can help youth make their way to a healthy, prosocially productive adulthood. Werner relates (1989) how one such opportunity structure, the "opening of doors" by mentoring adults, was a critically important transaction. Feelings of self-worth and usefulness increased among the high risk youth when the mentoring adult connected him/her to new opportunities for work, recreation, or high education. When doors were opened, the youth could show a valued skill and increase his/her worth in the eyes of the community.

Opening doors leads to opportunities to observe new role models. Mentoring relationships are believed to be one of the few key factors promoting resiliency—that is, the ability to manage stressors and to "spring back" from adversity (Rutter, 1979, 1990). Mentoring is also similar to Dryfoos (1990) "intensive individualized attention" which is one of the components of a successful prevention program. However, mentors need not be professionals (e.g., social workers, and case managers). An important component in social cognitive interventions is that observable role modeling of useful skills and the rewards that these skills bring. Resilience skill modeling would benefit from having same age peers, older youth, and adult role models both in person and media presentations helpful in promoting imitative behavior. Mentoring is a special form of modeling. Mentoring involves a transactional relationship between an experienced person who is willing and able to foster competencies and a person wanting to learn them. The mentoring relationship provides opportunities to evolve competence through ongoing communications, hands-on practice and the experience of the give and take of social and personal events. Mentors from the youth's own community can interact with cultural sensitivity and flexibility in the complex world of adolescents. Non-relative mentors may also have the ability to offer constructive boundaries and limits in a fashion that can be readily received and accepted by the youth.

Specific interventions to broaden opportunity structures could include, but are not necessarily limited to: (a) Modifying in-school and after-school curricula to include explorations into local recreation, social club and work opportunities, as well as optimal paths to vocational training and higher education; (b) Assemblies and field trips to be introduced to mentoring adults; (c) Exposure to positive older peer role models who are making it through local doors of opportunity; (d) Apprenticing in work situations; (e) Providing knowledge and skill building experiences that overcome various barriers to higher levels of autonomy or higher levels of social status; and (f) Fostering skills to clearly define realistic vocational and recreational goals to offset any sense of hopelessness.

Coordinating Interventions Both in School and Youth Clubs

We described above how youth clubs (e.g., 4-H and the schools) could provide complimentary interventions with their own space, instruction, and planning resources for working collaboratively. They can produce a very powerful multi-year integration of a multi-site, multi-method intervention package. The prevention research literature repeatedly has shown how highly structured theory-guided school-based interventions can be potent and sustainable over the years. There is less evidence about youth club based interventions, but both can provide some of the most cost-efficient means to intervene with entire age groups of youth within a community. Further, schools can be good research partners given the mounting number of county and state requirements for new types of prevention curricula targeting problem behaviors involved in illicit substance use, teen pregnancy and AIDS. In addition, new health education requirements (e.g., on nutrition, physical fitness, or hygiene) are crowding the academic calendars. Therefore, it is very possible to expect cooperation from schools in the planning and implementation of an integrated multi-year prevention curriculum. It is likely that the schools might be most interested in focusing on required ATOD, AIDS, and teen pregnancy prevention topics while the after school club based interventions could reinforce these with booster activities but mainly focus on resilience promotion.

The authors do not believe that integrative school-club prevention/promotion programs linking community schools and youth clubs are only mere fantasy. For example, in states such as Kansas, 74% of all youth under the age of 16 are enrolled in the Cooperative Extension sponsored 4-H clubs. Further, Cooperative Extension service faculty and county agents often work together to create youth programs in and for the schools. The National Cooperative Extension Service steering committee and the administrative Department of Agriculture have made the development of health promotion programs—especially for rural America—the top priority.

Provide Intensive Individualized Intervention to Build Skills

As Dryfoos (1990) points out, this widely recommended and often reviewed approach usually has the intervention team (a) teaching the youths about the consequences of their risky behavior then (b) giving them opportunity to practice decision making and communication skills about these risks among their peers. As outlined below, this typically involves opportunities to participate in role playing peer pressure situations of risky behaviors using refusal skills and suggesting safer options. Also commonly recommended are sessions to learn how to analyze peer norms and media pressures towards risk and the instilling of new local norms for socially acceptable and satisfying low-risk alternatives to high risk activities. Unlike the many extensive, individualized programs reviewed by Dryfoos (1990), this kind of intensive individualized attention would not require a professional social worker or case manager. However, actively monitored participation by adult and older peer role models is essential.

The experimental resilience skill promotion and prevention skill building curricula would be stronger were they designed to require participatory learning in groups. It seems reasonable to envision that each year in the progressive four-year curriculum sequence, youth would practice on a regular basis: (1) analogue problem solving situations in classrooms; (2) real work/productivity tasks relevant to adult vocations; and (3) other age appropriate skill enhancing tasks appropriate to the youth's own individual talents. Thus, congruent with social action theory and the resilience literature, the school and club curricula would include "hands-on" project planning and execution, role playing, cooperative group work, and regular evaluations by self and instructors at each step to insure reinforcing feedback. Each youth's progress should be carefully quantified and monitored for ongoing competency skills certification and promotion to successive stages in programs. It would be fun to think about some types of resilience skill building interventions such as increasing humor skills, enhancing likability, or skills to seek out and recruit mentors.

Use of Media Enhanced Intervention Curricula

Video media are the source of much of the information delivered to adolescents in the 1990's. Enhancing prevention curricula with video media holds great promise for integrative resilience intervention research projects involving multiple delivery sites and group based programming. Intervention components packaged in video form are very adaptable to simultaneous replications of interventions across sites and even to "distance learning" applications in rural areas. Video curricula package intervention sessions are highly interesting and motivating ways that can be used by local instructors as gateways to discussions and skill-building activities that fit well within existing local peer-group and community contexts. Videos can also integrate different educational and behavior change methods by: (1) structuring novel group learning experiences; (2) providing a variety of role models not easily brought into classrooms and youth club meetings; (3) dramatizing vicarious rewards to increase motivation to build self-efficacy beliefs and behavioral skills via follow-on projects; and (4) setting up guided, emotionally intense, but safe discussions relevant to the building of targeted knowledge, intentions, and skills.

Video based interventions are particularly useful for developing acceptable ways to handle sensitive topics. In our own work involving an NIMH SBIR funded mental health video curriculum research project, my colleagues and I have successfully used clay animation to moderate depictions of risk-taking behaviors that would be taboo if depicted by live actors. Certainly, video enhanced intervention curricula could be developed for a range of resilience and life skills for integrated applications in both youth club and school room settings. Were they to demonstrate their efficacy, such curricula would find ready national markets.

Engage Peer Norms in the Intervention Process

During adolescence, peer groups have increasing influence on shaping attitudes, behaviors, and goals. In recognition of this, a resilience promotion/

problem behavior prevention research program would be well advised to design the intervention package to affect peer group norms. The program should be mass-targeted by attempting to recruit all the community's youth into the program (i.e., including both higher and lower risk groups). This community wide approach will help shift some perceived peer norms so that it would be normal for every teen to be doing the program. Peer-peer work-team activities would explore and report on national and local epidemiologic data concerning health risking (e.g., drinking) and health protecting behaviors (e.g., seat belts, declining getting high). It's no longer expected that every 14-year-old will be getting drunk once a month.

In our current prevention project with Native American youth, we have found that it is very motivating to students to be informed of what the actual base rates are for risky behaviors. (They are lower than that believed). Further, it is negatively reinforcing of these behaviors to show the local samples' rates of accompanying problems for different subgroups (e.g., regular drinkers vs. occasional drinkers).

Involve Parents and Adults

Beyond obtaining parental permission to participate in a prevention research program, parents can be engaged in a number of ways as: (a) adult mentors; (b) community outreach workers coordinating presentations to recruit understanding and involvement in the program; and (c) providers of booster intervention activities. However, not many adults will wish to be involved on a regular basis. Further, in multi-threat neighborhoods, there may be substantial percentages of dysfunctional adults whom one wouldn't want involved in program advertisement or delivery. Still, teens from dysfunctional families need access to prosocial adult role models. Therefore, the program should have trained staff whose job is to recruit potentially mentoring well-adapted adults living and/or working in the neighborhoods. The program can then train them and structure situations to help bring them into regular contact with the youth as instructors, media role models, storytellers, teachers, and facilitators, etc.

The Family as a Potential Component

There are reports in the literature (Brennan, 1993; Resnick, Harris, & Blum, 1993; Wyman, Cowen, Work, & Parker, 1991) showing that relationships within the family play a critical role in the development of resilience in children and adolescents, even in children born to drug abusing parents (Johnson, Glassman, Fiks, & Rosen, 1990). In a study of 13,135 children born in England, Scotland, and Wales, Osborn (1990) showed that having positive, supportive, and interested parents was a decisive determinant that enabled socially vulnerable children to achieve competence. Resnick, Harris, & Blum (1993) showed in a sample of 36,000 7th through 12th graders that family and school connectedness were the most powerful protective factors against acting out behaviors among these youth. The family connectedness variable referred to a sense of belonging and closeness in the family. Central to this was the adolescent's experience of being connected to at least one caring, competent adult, similar to one of Werners' resiliency processes. School connectedness was second in importance after family connectedness as a salient protective factor for both boys and girls. The authors inferred that schools play a vital role in reducing health risking behaviors.

Preventive intervention researchers are beginning to recognize the value of including parent and family intervention components for increasing the effectiveness of prevention programs for youth. Kumpfer's research with children of substance abusing parents (DeMarsh & Kumpfer, 1986; Kumpfer & DeMarsh, 1986) supports the fact that the family is highly involved in the genesis and maintenance of chemical dependency and can be very influential in the alleviation of risk factors in children. Unfortunately, few family-focused substance abuse prevention programs have been developed for high risk children, despite the fact that the application of parent training and family skills training programs to other problems in children have been highly effective (Patterson et al., 1975; Miller, 1975; Gordon, 1970; Dinkmeyer & McKay, 1976; Forehand & McMahon, 1981; Guerney, 1964; Abate, 1977). One reason for this effectiveness is that primary caretakers (i.e., parents, grandparents, foster parents) with AOD or other associated problems are difficult to train as change agents. Recently, NIDA has been supporting several promising family-focused prevention programs, namely the Kumpfer's Strengthening Families Program (DeMarsh & Kumpfer, 1986; Kumpfer & DeMarsh, 1986a) for children of drug abusers in treatment, Alvy's Confident Parenting Program (1987) for parents of Black youth, and Szapocznik's Family Effectiveness Training (1983) for parents of high risk Hispanic adolescents.

Family involvement in a very comprehensive intervention can be problematical, but a family component involving appropriate monitoring and mentoring can be a strength if the protocol is sufficiently flexible to permit the substitution of a relative or adult friend for an unavailable and/or dysfunctional parent. Family members have a tremendous impact on the child's vulnerability or proneness to the development of problems during development. For example, parental use of alcohol and drugs as well as parental dysfunctional communications can create increased risk in the child for developmental problems (Kumpfer, 1989). Further, Dielman and associates (1989) have also found that parents who allow their children to engage in socially prohibited behavior (i.e., drinking at home under their supervision), have the most at-risk children for early alcohol use among peers. Family support for connections with the school are also important. Connell, Spencer, and Aber (1994) show that African-American youth's who show disaffected patterns of behavior and emotion in school experience have less family support than do those youth with more engaged patterns of action.

Link Youth with the World of Adult Work

As previously indicated, the proposed program curricula would increase the visibility and the viability of local options for useful work experiences. The intervention program would train youths to understand the options to access them. The program curricula would strive to strengthen connections to the world of work and the workers in it by linking knowledge-building curriculum topics to hands-on work projects based on youth-identified priorities (e.g., recreation). This might require youth-planned and led opinion surveys and focus groups to choose among proposed projects. Planning and feasibility study teams would develop estimates of the needed personnel, materials, time, approvals, and funding. Short term project work groups would prepare planning reports, resource recruitment posters, promotional videos, etc. Each of these product-oriented teams could also require the practice of peer-peer and youth-adult communications, writing up the findings, applying math skills to calculate costs and so forth. Were the chosen project to require the construction or rehabilitation of buildings, these, too, would require the planning and implementation skills (from site selection and site preparation to actual building and fitting out the interior spaces to serve their intended functions). Individual, anti-social, program-disrupting peers can be diverted to alternative programs to avoid negative contamination (e.g., it's not possible to be part of the program if you are high on drugs).

Intervene Broadly but Detect and Treat the Problem Outliers

One should expect that there will be "responders" and non-responders' to our program. They too need to be identified early. The non-responders can then be targeted for more intensive booster interventions or referrals for treatment as necessary. Experienced youth counselors trained to identify and coordinate health services interventions for outliers (the problem youth in the prevention cohorts) should be included in the overall research design. They would facilitate referrals to both professional health services (e.g., substance use, mental health, and reproductive health treatment) as well as to special services in the educational and correctional systems as needed.

Provide Thorough Training of Interventionists

It is crucial to do an excellent job of staff training and monitoring of the quality of the intervention process delivered by all participants. Professional trainers and evaluation staff will be required for a hybrid school and club intervention program that addresses a developmental transition period and crosses traditional social and administrative boundaries of middle, junior, and senior high schools.

Administer the Research Program as a Special Cross-Agency Program

Dryfoos (1990) described four types of external program management. One of these is similar to our proposed model outlined in our component pertaining to interagency collaborations. There are advantages in having the program's Principal Investigator and the project executive committee established outside but in close communication with the administrative hierarchies of the collaborating institutions. Interagency collaborations typically trigger Hawthorn-like positive expectations and willingness to try some new approaches. In a sense, this is similar to cross-cultural collaborations where the perception of shared values and commitments to work for the collective good can break down formidable bureaucratic barriers and tedious procedural routines.

References

Alvy, K. T. (1987). *Black parenting: Strategies for training*, New York, NY Irvington Publishers, Inc.

Bandura, A. (1986). *Social foundations of thought and action: A social cognitive theory*. Englewood Cliffs, NJ: Prentice-Hall.

Botvin, G. J. (1982). Broadening the focus of smoking prevention strategies. In T. Coates, A. Peterson, & C. Perry (Eds.), *Promoting adolescent health: A dialog on research and practice*. New York: Academic Press.

Botvin, G. J., & Wills, T. A. (1985). Personal and social skills training: Cognitive-behavioral approaches to substance abuse prevention. In C. S. Bell & R. Battjes (Eds.): *Prevention research: Deterring drug abuse among children and adolescents. NIDA Research Monograph 63*, 8–49.

Botvin, G. J., Baker, E., Dusenbury, L., Tortu, S., & Botvin, E. M. (1990). Preventing adolescent drug abuse through a multimodal cognitive-behavioral approach: Results of a 3 year study. *Journal of Consulting and Clinical Psychology, 58*(4), 437–446.

Brennan, J. L. (1993). Family relationships and the development of social competence in adolescence. *Journal of Pediatric Child Health, 29*, suppl 1. S37–241.

Brofenbrenner, U. (1977). Toward an experimental ecology of human development. *American Psychologist, 32*, 513–531.

Brofenbrenner, U., & Crouter, A. C. (1983). The evolution of environmental models in developmental research. In PH Mussen (Ed.), Handbook of child psychology. 4th edition. New York: Wiley.

Bukoski, W. J. (1991). A framework for drug abuse prevention research. In C. G. Leukefeld, W. J. Bukoski (Eds.), *Drug abuse prevention intervention research: Methodological issues*, NIDA Research Monograph *107*, 7–28.

Connell, J. P., Spencer, M. B., Aber, J. L. (1994). Educational Risk and resilience in African-American youth context, self, action, and outcomes in school. *Child Development, 65*(2), 493–506.

Cowen, E. L. (1982). Primary prevention research: Barriers, needs and opportunities. *Journal of Primary Prevention, 2*(3), 131–137.

Crittenden, P. M. (1985). Maltreated infants: Vulnerability and resilience. *Journal of Child Psychology and Psychiatry, 26*(1), 85–96.

DeMarsh, J. P., & Kumpfer, K. (1986). Family oriented interventions for the prevention of chemical dependency in children and adolescence. In Ezekoye, S., Kumpfer, K, & Bukoski, W. (Eds.), Childhood Chemical Abuse: Prevention and intervention (pp. 117–152). The Haworth Press, New York, NY 117–151.

Dielman, T. E., Shope, J. J., Leech, S. L., & Butchart, A. T. (1989). Differential effectiveness of an elementary school-based alcohol misuse program by type of prior drinking experience. Journal of School Health, *59*, 255–263.

Dinkmeyer, D., & McKay, G. (1976). Systematic training for effective parenting: Parent's workbook. Circle Pine Minnesota: American Guidance Service, Inc.

Dryfoos, J. (1990). *Adolescent-at-risk: Prevalence and prevention*. New York: Oxford.

Felner, R. D., Jason, L., Moritsugu, J., & Farber, S. S. (1983). (Eds.) *Preventive psychology: Theory, research and practice in community interventions.* New York: Pergamon Press.

Forehand, R. L., & McMahon, R. J. (1981). Helping the noncompliant child: A clinician's guide to parent training. New York: Guilford Press.

Garmezy, N. (1993). Children in poverty: Resilience despite risk. *Psychiatry, 56*, 127–136.

Gordon, T. (1970). Parent effectiveness training. New York; Wyden.

Johnson, H. L., Glassman, M. B., Fiks, K. B., Rosen, T. S. (1990). Resilient children: Individual differences in developmental outcome of children born to drug abusers. *Journal of Genetic Psychology, 151*(4), 523–539.

Jessor, R., & Jessor, S. L. (1977). Problem behavior and psychosocial development: A longitudinal study of youth. New York: Academic Press.

Kandel, D., Simcha-Fagan, O., Davies, M. (1986). Risk factors for delinquency and illicit drug use from adolescence to young adulthood. *Journal of Drug Issues, 15*(1), 67–90.

Kumpfer, K. L. (1989). A critical review of risk factors and prevention strategies. In D. Shaffer, I. Philips, & N Enzer (Eds.), Prevention of Mental Disorders, alcohol and other drug use in children and adolescents, A Report of Project Prevention of the American Academy of Child and Adolescent psychiatry (pp. 309–372). OSAP Prevention Monograph-2, DHHS Publication No. (ADM) 89–1646.

Kumpfer, K. L., & DeMarsh, J. (1986). Family environmental and genetic influences on children's future chemical dependency. *Journal of Children in Contemporary Society: Advances in Theory and Applied Research, 18*(1/2), 49–92.

Luthar, S. S. (1991). Vulnerability and resilience: A study of high-risk adolescents. *Child Development, 62,* 600–616.

Luthar, S. S. (1993). Annotation: Methodological and conceptual issues in research on childhood resilience. *Journal of Child Psychology and Psychiatry, 34*(4), 441–453.

Masten, A. (1994). Personal communication.

O'Grady, D., & Metz, J. R. (1987). Resilience in children at high risk for psychological disorder. *Journal of Pediatric Psychology, 12*(1), 3–23.

Osborn, A. F. (1990). Resilient children: A longitudinal study of high achieving socially disadvantaged children. *Early Child Development and Care, 62,* 23–47.

Patterson, G. (1975). Professional guide for families and living with children. Champaign, Illinois: Research Press.

Pellegrini, D. S. (1990). Psychosocial risk and protective factors in childhood. *Developmental and Behavioral Pediatrics, 11*(4), 201–209.

Parker, G. R., Cowen, E. L., Work, W. C., & Wyman, P. A. (1990). Test correlates of stress resilience among urban school children. *Journal of Primary Prevention, 11*(1), 19–34.

Resnick, M. D., Harris, L. J., Blum, R. W. (1993). The impact of caring and connectedness on adolescent health and well being. *Journal of Paediatrics and Child Health, 29,* (S1).

Rutter, M. (1979). Protective factors in children's responses to stress and disadvantage. In M. W. Kent & J. E. Rolf (Eds.), Primary Prevention of Psychopathology, Vol. III: Social Competence in Children (pp. 49–74). Hanover, N.H., University Press of New England.

Rutter, M. (1990). Psychosocial resilience and protective mechanisms. In J. E. Rolf, A. S. Masten, D. Cicchetti, K. Nuechterlein, & S. Weintraub (Eds.), Risk and Protective Factors in the Development of Psychopathology (pp. 182–210). New York: Cambridge University Press.

Schissel, B. (1993). Coping with adversity: Testing the origins of resiliency in mental health. *International Journal of Social Psychiatry, 39*(1), 34–46.

Schorr, L. B. (1988). Within our reach: Breaking the cycle of disadvantage. New York, NY: Doubleday.

Szapocznik, J., Santisteban, D., Kurtines, W., Perez-Vidal, A., & Hervis, O. (1983). Bicultural effectiveness training: A treatment intervention for enhancing intercultural adjustment in Cuban American families. Paper presented at the Ethnicity, Acculturation and Mental health Among Hispanics Conference, Albuquerque, New Mexico.

Werner, E. E. (1984). Research in Review. Resilient Children. *Young Children, 40*(1), 68–72.

Werner, E. E. (1986). Resilient offspring of alcoholics: A longitudinal study from birth to age 18. *Journal of Studies on Alcohol, 47*(1), 34–40.

Werner, E. E. (1989). High-risk children in young adulthood: A longitudinal study from birth to 32 years. *American Journal of Orthopsychiatry, 59,* 72–81.

Werner, E. E., & Smith, R. S. (1982). *Vulnerable but invincible: A study of resilient children.* New York: McGraw-Hill.

White, R. W. (1959). Motivation reconsidered: The concept of competence. *Psychological Review, 66,* 297–333.

White, R. W. (1979). Competence as an aspect of personal growth. In M. W. Kent & J. E. Rolf (Eds.), Primary prevention of psychopathology: Vol. III. Social competence in children (pp. 5–22). Hanover, NH: University Press of New England.

Wolfson, J., Fields, J. H., & Rose, S. A. (1987). Symptoms, temperament, resiliency, and control in anxiety-disordered preschool children. *Journal of the American Academy of Child and Adolescent Psychiatry*, *26*(1), 16–22.

Wyman, P. A., Cowen, E. L., Work, W. C., & Parker, G. R. (1991). Developmental and family milieu correlates of resilience in urban children who have experience major life stress. *American Journal of Community Psychology*, *19*(3), 405–426.

12

Commentary
The Promise and Perils of Resilience Research as a Guide to Preventive Interventions

Ann S. Masten

Introduction

One of the fundamental arguments for studying resilience over the past 25 years has been the premise that knowledge about how children achieve good developmental outcomes despite risk status and adversity holds great potential for guiding interventions and policies aimed at promoting better development among children at risk (Masten, 1994). Resilience investigators have argued that scientists studying psychopathology long neglected an important source of information by failing to study such children (Garmezy, 1971, 1974, 1985; Masten, 1989; Rutter, 1979).

The first generation of research by investigators attending to these phenomena has resulted in a short list of salient "protective factors" that consistently emerge as correlates of successful psychosocial development among children at risk for a variety of reasons (Masten, 1994, Masten & Coatsworth, 1998; Rutter, 1990). These correlates, such as parenting quality, intellectual functioning and self-perception, suggest protective processes that may steer development in favorable directions and thereby also suggest

Ann S. Masten • Institute of Child Development, University of Minnesota, Minneapolis, Minnesota 55455.

Resilience and Development: Positive Life Adaptations, edited by Glantz and Johnson. Kluwer Academic/Plenum Publishers, New York, 1999.

possibilities for intervention before, during, and after risk processes impinge negatively on development. In their chapter, Rolf and Johnson (1999, this volume) begin to examine how resilience research can inform preventive interventions and how prevention research can serve either to evaluate or refine a specific program and as a testing ground for hypothesized protective processes derived from studies of naturally occurring resilience.

Rolf and Johnson emphasize the need for developmental, multisystem approaches to preventive intervention. Many of the problems of grave concern to U.S. society—including behavioral and emotional problems, violence among juveniles, academic failure, substance abuse, child maltreatment—need to be viewed from a multifaceted, developmental, and dynamical systems perspective (Coie et al., 1993; Masten & Coatsworth, 1995, 1998; Masten & Wright, 1998; Yoshikawa, 1994). Evidence on etiologies of such problems does not point to single or simple causes or solutions. Instead, these problems are likely to arise from complex interplay of multiple influences over time. Many of these influences have been studied as risks, assets, vulnerabilities, and protective factors under the auspices of the new transdisciplinary science termed "developmental psychopathology" (Cicchetti & Cohen, 1995; Masten & Braswell, 1991; Masten & Garmezy, 1985). Within this framework, studies of resilience comprise part of a large effort to gain a more comprehensive and integrative understanding of why and how psychopathology does and does not occur and how a normal developmental path is recovered when psychopathology has developed.

In developmental psychopathology, similar risk and protective factors keep cropping up in studies of different problems (Masten & Coatsworth, 1995; Garmezy & Masten, 1994). Coie and his colleagues (1993) compiled a list of what they term "generic" risk factors, such as family conflict and extreme poverty. Analogous general protective factors that turn up in studies of diverse risk samples include the presence of close relationships with prosocial and caring adults (Coie et al., 1993; Masten, Best, & Garmezy, 1990). At the same time, evidence mounts for specific genetic or biological vulnerabilities that may predispose an individual child to a particular type of disorder, such as Tourette's (Cohen & Leckman, 1994).

"Cumulative risk and protection" models of etiology and intervention are rapidly emerging to encompass the complexities of developmental theory and the expanding empirical knowledge base on child and adolescent psychopathology (Conduct Problems Prevention Research Group, 1992; Catalano & Hawkins, 1996; Masten & Wright, 1998; Yoshikawa, 1994). Such models acknowledge the multiplicity of possible causal processes underlying normal and deviant behavioral patterns, the embeddedness of individual development in multiple systems of social interaction (e.g., family, school, peers, neighborhood), and the compounding of risk as disadvantages and adversities pile-up in a child's life. Concomitantly, these models suggest multiple possibilities for intervention conceptualized in terms of eliminating risk factors, reducing the pile-up of adversities, boosting compensatory assets, moderating negative consequences of risk, facilitating protective processes, etc.

Thus, contemporary models of psychopathology, which are more multifactorial, developmental, and contextual than the models of previous generations, carry profound implications for intervention. These, in brief, include the following:

- Given multicausal influences and the contextual embeddedness of behavior, "magic bullet" solutions are unlikely for most behavioral problems of great concern in present U.S. society.
- Single-factor-focused interventions are not likely to affect more than a small part of the problem or a small portion of children. Strategies targeting multiple risks and resources, processes, and contexts are likely to have more impact.
- The timing and nature of interventions should be developmentally strategic for greatest efficacy and efficiency. The salience of different contexts shift over development as do individual vulnerabilities and the significance of particular risks and assets. Interventions involving peers, for example, would not be as strategic for very young children as for older children and adolescents. Similarly, the best methods of attaining the same goal, such as improving self-efficacy, will differ across age groups.
- The embeddedness of human development in multiple interacting systems offers multiple arenas for intervention. Similarly, research on prevention and intervention programs suggest a wide variety of options for multifaceted intervention designs (e.g., Mrazek & Haggerty, 1994).
- Resilience research reinforces the importance of preventing or reducing risk exposure but also suggests the potential of boosting assets and mobilizing or enhancing protective systems (Masten, 1994).
- What "works" for one group of children in one context may not work for the same group or other groups of children in different contexts nor for all children with similar problems. Interventions need to be ecologically valid. Consequently, "one size fits all" programs are not likely to be optimal. The same basic protective processes can be achieved in different ways. The "Comer Process," for example, is a school-based intervention program in which a general set of strategies and guidelines developed in New Haven are applied in other

places to facilitate changes in school climate and student achievement (Comer, 1980; 1985). The actual process is presumed to arise
within the context in which these changes are fostered and cannot
be directly transplanted nor precisely prescribed in a "cookbook."
• The complexity of risk and resilience processes operating in multiple, embedded systems of development and diverse contexts calls for
the expertise of more than one discipline, whether the goal is to
advance empirical knowledge or to change the course of development through intervention.

The prevention characteristics generally recommended by Rolf and
Johnson and illustrated in their Cooperative Extension Prevention program
address a number of these implications. They emphasize the advantages
of programs that are multifaceted in terms of methods, processes targeted,
contexts for action, developmental systems engaged, and disciplines
involved through collaboration. They espouse short-term, lower cost
prospective studies that are strategically focused from a developmental perspective. The Extension program is "developmentally staged" during the
adolescent transition years, and program elements are informed by the
salience of social contexts during this period. Peer groups and activities,
schools, work, and media, are utilized in this program consistent with developmental tasks and influential social contexts of adolescent development.
Their program is rooted in the community, to garner the support and unique
resources of its constituents and to maximize ecological validity.

Their approach reflects the maturing of resilience research in that
intervention targets are based on hypothesized protective processes derived
from research on resilience in childhood and adolescence. These include,
for example, promoting relationships with prosocial adults, boosting self-
efficacy, and improving the social problem solving of the adolescents. These
processes have a theoretical and empirical basis in the general child development literature as well as in resilience-focused investigations.

Rolf and Johnson recognize that well-designed prevention/interven-
tion research is fundamentally basic as well as applied science. Through
theoretically based intervention studies, hypotheses about the processes
underlying risk and protective factors can be convincingly tested and
refined (Masten, 1994; Coie et al., 1993).

Intervention can be conceptualized as a deliberate effort to foster
resilience, or to redirect development in more favorable directions, toward
desired outcomes in a particular society and context (Masten, 1994). In
doing so, one is acting in the capacity of a protective factor. Interventions
become protective processes. "Prevention" describes efforts to eliminate
risks and hazards before they occur or before they have full impact, as well
as efforts to boost resources or to facilitate protective processes that

preclude or reduce progression along deviant developmental pathways. "Treatment" interventions are targeted later in the course of progress along deviant developmental pathways, when efforts are directed at facilitating recovery, preventing relapse, and reducing longer-term sequelae. A resilience perspective underscores the importance of understanding processes that avert, counterbalance, or moderate the negative influences underlying risk and vulnerability. Knowledge of these processes in addition to the processes that produce risk or increase vulnerability to psychopathology has the potential to provide a more comprehensive scientific basis for intervention.

Our knowledge of resilience and risk processes is rudimentary at this time. This fact is evident in the chapter by Rolf and Johnson, as in their intervention design; the assumptions and theory underlying this and other prevention efforts have not been rigorously tested as yet. Consequently, there are perils in overselling what we know and what we may be able to achieve for children at risk. Most fundamentally, it is unclear whether positive developmental outcomes can be successfully created or fostered through intervention.

Resilience-based concepts and research, combined with a better understanding of psychopathology and normal development, have begun to provide a framework for broadening assessment and designing better interventions. Amid growing public concern about violence, academic failure, teenage pregnancy, and a host of other social ills, resilience studies also serve as a reminder of human capacity for adaptation, recovery, self-righting, reintegration, and change in developmental pathways. The elucidation of resilience processes in human development offers hope and guidance for those who seek to improve the odds of favorable child development through preventive interventions and policy. Also, growing awareness of the complexity of the processes influencing the course of individual development serves as a cautionary note for scientists and practitioners that our current knowledge base is thin, our conceptual frameworks are rough, and much painstaking work still remains to be done.

ACKNOWLEDGMENTS. Preparation of this commentary was supported in part by grants from the William T. Grant Foundation and the National Science Foundation (NSF/SBR-9729111).

References

Catalano, R. F., & Hawkins, J. D. (1996). The social development model: A theory of antisocial behavior. In J. D. Hawkins (Ed.), *Delinquency and crime: Current theories* (pp. 149–197). New York: Cambridge University Press.

Cicchetti, D., & Cohen, D. J. (Eds.) (1995). *Developmental psychopathology.* New York: Wiley.

Cohen, D. J., & Leckman, J. F. (1994). Developmental psychopathology and neurobiology of Tourette's Syndrome. *Journal of the American Academy of Child and Adolescent Psychiatry, 33*, 2–15.

Coie, J. D., Watt, N. F., West, S. G., Hawkins, J. D., Asarnow, J. R., Markman, H. J., Ramey, S. L., Shure, M. B., & Long, B. (1993). The science of prevention: A conceptual framework and some directions for a national research program. *American Psychologist, 48*, 1013–1022.

Comer, J. P. (1980). *School power.* New York: Free Press.

Comer, J. P. (1985). The Yale-New Haven Primary Prevention Project: A follow-up study. *Journal of the American Academy of Child Psychiatry, 24*, 154–160.

Conduct Problems Prevention Research Group (1992). A developmental and clinical model for the prevention of conduct disorder: The FAST Track program. *Development and Psychopathology, 4*, 509–527.

Garmezy, N. (1971). Vulnerability research and the issue of primary prevention. *American Journal of Orthopsychiatry, 41*, 101–116.

Garmezy, N. (1974). The study of competence in children at risk for severe psychopathology. In A. Koupernik (Ed.), *The child in his family-Children at psychiatric risk* (*Vol. 3*, pp. 77–97). New York: Wiley.

Garmezy, N. (1985). Stress-resistant children: the search for protective factors. In J. E. Stevenson (Ed.), *Recent research in developmental psychopathology. Journal of Child Psychology and Psychiatry Book Supplement No. 4* (pp. 213–233). Oxford: Pergamon Press.

Garmezy, N., & Masten, A. S. (1994). Chronic adversities. In M. Rutter, E. Taylor, & L. Hersov (Eds.), *Child and adolescent psychiatry* (pp. 191–208). Oxford: Blackwell Scientific Publications.

Masten, A. S. (1989). Resilience in development: Implications of the study of successful adaptation for developmental psychopathology. In D. Cicchetti (Ed.), *The emergence of a discipline: Rochester Symposium on Developmental Psychopathology* (Vol. 1) (pp. 261–294). Hillsdale, NJ: Erlbaum.

Masten, A. S. (1994). Resilience individual development: Successful adaptation despite risk and adversity. In M. C. Wang & E. Gordon (Eds.), *Educational resilience in inner city America: Challenges and prospects* (pp. 3–25). Hillsdale, NJ: Lawrence Erlbaum.

Masten, A. S., Best, K. M., & Garmezy, N. (1990). Resilience and development: Contributions from the study of children who overcome adversity. *Development and psychopathology, 2*, 425–444.

Masten, A. S., & Brasell, L. (1991). Developmental psychopathology: An integrative framework. In P. R. Martin (Ed.), *Handbook of behavior therapy and psychological science: An integrative approach* (pp. 35–56). New York: Pergamon.

Masten, A. S., & Coatsworth, J. D. (1995). Competence, resilience, and psychopathology. In D. Cicchetti & D. Cohen (Eds.), *Developmental psychopathology Vol. 2: Risk, disorder, and adaptation* (pp. 715–752). New York: Wiley.

Masten, A. S., & Coatsworth, J. D. (1998). The development of competence in favorable and unfavorable environments: Lessons from Research on successful children. *American Psychologist, 53*, 205–220.

Masten, A. S., & Garmezy, N. (1985). Risk, vulnerability, and protective factors in developmental psychopathology. In B. B. Lahey & A. E. Kazdin (Eds.), *Advances in clinical child psychology* (Vol. 8) (pp. 1–52). New York: Plenum Press.

Masten, A. S., & Wright, M. O'D. (1998). Cumulative risk and protection models of child maltreatment. In B. B. Robbie Rossman & M. S. Rosenberg (Eds.), *Multiple victimization of children: Conceptual, developmental, research, and treatment issues* (pp. 7–30). New York: Haworth Press.

Mrazek, P. J., & Haggerty, R. J. (Eds.) (1994). *Reducing risks for mental disorders: Frontiers for preventive intervention research.* Washington, DC: National Academy Press.

Rolf, J., & Johnson, J. (1999). Opening doors to resilience intervention for prevention research. In M. Glantz & (Eds.), *Resilience and development: Positive life adaptations.* New York: Plenum Press.

Rutter, M. (1979). Protective factors in children's responses to stress and disadvantage. In M. W. Kent & J. E. Rolf (Eds.), *Primary prevention of psychopathology, Vol. III: Social competence in children* (pp. 49–74). Hanover, NH: University Press of New England.

Rutter, M. (1990). Psychosocial resilience and protective mechanisms. In J. Rolf, A. S. Masten, D. Cicchetti, K. H. Nuechterlein, & S. Weintraub (Eds.), *Risk and protective factors in the development of psychopathology* (pp. 181–214). New York: Cambridge University Press.

Yoshikawa, H. (1994). Prevention as cumulative protection; Effects of early family support and education on chronic delinquency and its risks. *Psychological Bulletin, 115*, 28–54.

13

Can We Apply Resilience?

Emmy E. Werner and Jeannette L. Johnson

Introduction

The challenges that confront us when we look for applications of the concept of resilience can be summed up by Piet Hein, a Danish physicist turned poet who wrote:

> *"The road to wisdom?—Well, it's plain and simple to express: Err and err and err again, but less and less and less."*

This captures our current dilemma: there is more promise in the concept of resilience than there are possibilities for application. In this chapter, we will examine three areas that contribute to our promise in the application of resilience: (1) resilience research as a knowledge basis for practice; (2) the application of the findings of resilience research; and (3) the building of bridges between clinicians and researchers, practitioners, and policymakers.

Resilience Research as a Knowledge Base for Practice

Our current understanding of the roots of resilience and of factors or mechanisms that protect individuals from the adverse effects of potent biological and psychosocial risk comes from a diverse body of literature gen-

Emmy E. Werner • Department of Human Development, University of California, Davis, California 95616.   **Jeannette L. Johnson** • Department of Psychiatry, Division of Alcohol and Drug Abuse, University of Maryland, Baltimore, Maryland 21201.

Resilience and Development: Positive Life Adaptations, edited by Glantz and Johnson. Kluwer Academic/Plenum Publishers, New York, 1999.

erated by investigators with different professional perspectives. Furthermore, we do not have data on resilience across the lifespan as most researchers have studied only up to the first 40 years of life, but rarely beyond. Unfortunately, there are many more possible years left for breakdown (Anthony & Cohler, 1987). The majority of existing data are on characteristics of resilient individuals in middle childhood, more so than in adolescence; or, investigations that have begun in infancy and early childhood (Anthony & Cohler, 1987; Werner & Smith, 1993). Investigations that have extended beyond the second decade of life are rare. Finally, we have more reviews of the research in resilience than we do actual studies, especially those from a developmental viewpoint. Most of the prospective studies in this field are short-term and tend to focus on middle childhood or adolescence. Other, more clinically oriented studies, use retrospective data on adults seen in therapy (Wolin & Wolin, 1993). There are only a handful of longitudinal studies that have followed individuals exposed to substance abuse and/or parental mental illness into adulthood. Among them are Anthony's studies of the resilient children of schizophrenics and manic-depressive parents in St. Louis (Anthony & Cohler, 1987); Bleuler's follow-up into adulthood of the offspring of schizophrenics in Switzerland (Bleuler, 1984); the Danish adoption studies of children of schizophrenic parents that now extend into middle age (Parnas et al., 1993); a twenty-year follow-up of Swedish children of alcoholic fathers by Rydelius (Rydelius, 1981); the Boston based studies of the natural history of alcoholism by Vaillant (Vaillant, 1983); and the longitudinal study of a cohort of Pacific-Asian children on the island of Kauai that included offspring of alcoholic and psychotic parents who were followed from birth to their mid-thirties (Werner & Smith, 1993), and now on into their forties.

In recent years, such research has demonstrated a significant shift from case studies and retrospective studies to prospective longitudinal studies. Definitions of risk in these studies vary with level of organization, namely, whether risk factors are conceived of primarily residing in the individual organism, in the immediate family, or in the broader social context that the individual inhabits. Data analyses that explore the interplay among multiple risk and protective factors at all three levels are rare, but should be on the increase in the near future as several prospective longitudinal studies with large numbers of high risk children are coming of age. Most of these longitudinal studies have focused on children who have experienced chronic economic hardships or who live in high crime neighborhoods. Other studies have focused on children raised with serious caregiving deficits or traumatic upheavals of their social conditions. While many of the studies have pointed to a common core of individual dispositions and support systems in the extended family and community that appear to foster resilience, there is accumulating evidence that resilience, however defined, exacts a price. Both Anthony and Cohler's (1987) studies of African Americans and Caucasians and Werner and Smith's (1993) research with Asian-Americans indicate that even though some individuals have grown into competent, confident, and caring adults, these same individuals usually detach themselves from family members whose domestic and emotional problems threaten to engulf them. The price that is exacted from this detachment varies from stress related health problems to a certain aloofness in their interpersonal relationships, especially with their siblings.

Indeed, one of the more challenging problems of the study of resilience is the study of differences within families who are at risk for substance abuse or mental illness; the differences within families seems to be more influential than the differences between families. Stressful experiences may not impinge the same way on all children in the family (Hoffman, 1991). Werner and Smith (1993) suggest that variables such as age, birth order, birth spacing, family size, and the gender of the child, as well as the afflicted parent, need to be taken into account when assessing the relative vulnerability or resilience of an individual growing up in a family context of substance abuse and psychopathology.

Evidence So Far

Despite the heterogeneity of risk conditions studied, and despite conceptual and methodological differences in the assessment of the quality of adaptation (mental health and competence), a common core of individual dispositions and sources of family and community support can be discerned. This common core tends to ameliorate or buffer responses to both constitutional risk factors (such as parental alcoholism or mental illness) or stressful life events (such as economic hardship or the breakdown of parenting). Three types of protective factors emerge as recurrent themes from several diverse studies: (1) dispositional attributes of the individual that elicit predominantly positive responses from the environment, such as physical robustness and vigor, an engaging "easy" temperament, good problem-solving and communication skills, and an area of competence valued by the person or society; (2) socialization practices within the family that encourage trust, autonomy, initiative, and affectional ties to a stable, caring, competent adult, whether a parent, grandparent, older sibling, or other kin; and (3) external support systems in the neighborhood, school, church, or the community that reinforce self-esteem and self-efficacy and provide the individual with a set of positive values. These "buffers" appear to make a more profound impact on the life course of children and youths who grow up under adverse conditions than do specific risk factors or stressful life events. They appear to transcend geographical, historical, and social class boundaries and have been replicated in samples of Asian, Black, Caucasian, and Hispanic youth.

Furthermore, most studies on resilience show a pattern of gender differences. These studies have shown that boys are more vulnerable than girls in childhood to the effects of biological insult, caregiving deficits, and economic hardships-including the early onset of substance abuse. This trend is reversed in the second decade, with girls becoming more vulnerable than boys in adolescence, especially with the onset of teenage childbearing. In the twenties and early thirties, the balance appears to shift back again in favor of women (Werner & Smith, 1982, 1993).

The studies, to date, imply that psychological development is highly buffered and self-righting through psychosocial resilience. Importantly, the long-lasting effects of biological and/or psychosocial risks are almost always related to organic damage or chronic and severe interference in the protective processes embedded in the caregiving system (Masten, Best, & Garmezy, 1990).

The Application of Resilience

The evidence that programs actually influence lasting positive changes in the behavior of individuals who grow up under the shadows of alcoholism, drug abuse, and mental illness is just beginning to be published. Shared catharsis among program leaders or program participants may be a good thing, but we need to ask what specific behavior is changed in the individuals who participate in programs that are called "resilience interventions". Moving from exhortation to evaluation will provide us with the necessary evidence for building better programs attempting to foster resilience. A sobering lesson from Europe is contained in a book recently published by Rutter and Smith (1995). In this book, the authors discuss the general increases in living standards and the reduction of social inequities in the European community since World War II. These improved living conditions have been associated with a falling infant mortality rate, marked improvements in physical health, and a rising life expectancy. In contrast, there have not been parallel trends for reductions in the psychopathological disorders of youth. Instead, suicide rates, rates of depressive disorders, and drug and alcohol problems have gone up. Even in a country as socially committed as Sweden, with free pre- and post-natal care for its children, paid parental leaves for both parents, subsidized daycare, and education and housing for all its children, some 28% of urban families in Stockholm are presently considered at risk because of chronic alcoholism and parental psychopathology (Nordberg, 1994).

The original longitudinal studies of resilience consisted of samples of individuals who "pulled themselves up by their own bootstraps", without benefit of formalized outside intervention. It remains to be seen how well these protective factors and processes can be actually replicated in formal education, prevention, and intervention programs. When asked who helped them succeed against the odds, the resilient children, youth, and adults in the longitudinal study of Werner and Smith (1993) overwhelmingly and exclusively gave the credit to members of their extended family (grandparents, siblings, aunts, or uncles), to neighbors and teachers who were confidants and role models, and to mentors in voluntary associations, such as 4-H, the YMCA or YWCA, and church groups. Support from such an informal network of kin and neighbors and "ordinary" members of the community was more often sought and more highly valued than the services of community organizers, mental health professionals, and social workers (Werner, 1990a,b).

Building Bridges between Clinicians and Researchers

There is a wealth of experience and knowledge that can be shared by clinicians who deal with specific individuals who have overcome the odds and with researchers and professionals who want to learn about and improve the well being of communities. We need to partner in our design and evaluation of programs that claim to foster resiliency and communicate the findings of our joint venture to policymakers. The findings from Werner and Smith (1993) suggest that programs should work toward strengthening available informal ties to kin and community rather than to introduce additional layers of bureaucracy into the delivery of social services for vulnerable children and their families.

The Shifting Balance between Vulnerability and Resilience

Just as vulnerability is relative, depending on complex interactions among constitutional factors and life circumstances, resilience appears to be governed by a similar dynamic interaction among protective factors within the individual, the family environment, and the larger social context. Longitudinal studies that have followed high risk children to adulthood find that, at each developmental stage, there is a shifting balance between the stressful life events that heighten their vulnerability and the protective factors that enhance their resilience. This balance not only changes with the stages of the life cycle, but also varies with the gender of the individual.

The Mediating Processes That Underlie Resilience

There is an urgent need for more longitudinal data that documents how a chain of protective factors is forged over time making it possible for high risk children to become competent, confident, and caring individuals and that show the different pathways that lead to positive developmental outcomes. For example, when Werner and Smith (1993) examined the links between protective factors within the individual and outside sources of support, they noted a certain continuity that appeared in the life course of the men and women who successfully overcame a variety of childhood adversities (including parental alcoholism). Their individual dispositions led them to select or construct environments that, in turn, reinforced and sustained their active, outgoing dispositions, and rewarded their competencies. In spite of occasional deviations during transitional periods, such as adolescence, their life trajectories revealed cumulative "interactional continuity" (Werner, 1991; Werner & Smith, 1993). There was, for example, a significant positive link between an "easy" infant temperament and the sources of support available to the individual in early and middle childhood. Active and sociable babies, without distressing sleeping and feeding habits, tended to elicit more positive responses from their mothers at age one and from alternate caregivers by age two. In middle childhood, such children tended to rely on a wider network of caring adults and peers both within and outside the family circle.

Positive parental interactions with the infant and toddler were, in turn, associated with greater autonomy and social maturity at age two, and with greater scholastic competence at age ten. "Difficult" temperament traits in infancy, in contrast, were moderately linked with behavior problems in the classroom and at home at age ten, which in turn, generated fewer sources of emotional support in the family and community during adolescence. Parental competence, as manifested in educational level achieved, also proved to be a significant protective factor in the lives of the men and women on Kauai who successfully overcame childhood adversity. A higher parental educational level was linked to more positive parent-child interactions in the first and second year of life, and to more emotional support provided for the offspring during early and middle childhood. Parental education was also positively linked to the infants' health and physical status by age two. There were also significant positive links between parental educational level and the child's scholastic competence at ten; one path was direct, the other was mediated through the infant's health and physical status. Better educated parents had children with better problem solving and reading skills, but they also had healthier children with fewer handicaps and absences from school, due to repeated serious illnesses.

While parental competence and the sources of support available in the childhood home were modestly linked to the quality of adult adaptation, they made less of a direct impact in adulthood than the individuals' competencies, degree of self-esteem and self-efficacy, and temperamental dispositions. Many high-risk youths left the adverse conditions of their childhood homes and/or neighborhood after high school, and sought environments they found more compatible. In short, they picked their own niches (Scarr & McCartney, 1983).

Gaps in Our Understanding of Resilience

Just as risk factors or stressful life events may co-occur within a particular group of youth or within a particular time-period of the life course, protective factors are also likely to be correlated to some degree. The functional equivalence of protective factors (and their ability to be substituted with other factors) has not yet been adequately addressed in research on risk and resilience (Gore & Eckenrode, 1992). There are several implications of the co-occurrence of protective factors in our understanding of resilience:

1. The clustering of protective factors within a population results in groups of individuals at the ends of the distribution who have either many competencies and sources of support, or virtually no such resources. Examining protective factors (and risk factors) one at a time will not uncover individuals who have multiple strengths compared to multiple deficits.

2. Explicitly recognizing the co-occurrence of protective factors within a study population protects us from overestimating the effect of a single personal or social resource. Treating all children or youth alike who score high on a protective factor (for example, a strong religious faith) may overlook the possibility that most of the stress-buffering effect is being carried by a smaller sub-group of persons having this resource paired with other resources. Alternative methods to the variable-centered approach used in much resilience research (such as cluster analysis) may be useful in detecting patterns of relationships between correlated protective factors (Magnusson, 1988).

3. The co-occurrence of multiple protective factors raises the possibility of one resource substituting for another in coping with adversity—a topic about which we know very little. For example, can lack
of social support for a child with an alcoholic parent be made up by
high levels of self-esteem? In Werner and Smith's (1993) longitudinal analyses of the life course of high-risk children on Kauai different protective factors, such as social support and positive school
experiences, may produce similar results if their impact is through
common pathways, such as an increase in self-esteem and self-
efficacy. This has practical implications for intervention.
4. A consideration of two or more protective factors lead to questions
about the ways in which they potentially combine to buffer
stressful experiences, and whether the strength of the interactions
between personal competencies and social resources vary by gender
and by developmental stage or the developmental task which has
to be accomplished.

Implications

Longitudinal studies that focus on both risk and resilience in the life
course of children and adolescents exposed to substance abuse are rare,
especially those that begin in the early childhood years, before the onset of
experimentation with tobacco, alcohol, and illicit drugs. These few studies
include a predominantly Caucasian sub-sample from Block's ego-resiliency
study in the San Francisco Bay area (Block, Block, & Keyes, 1988; Shedler
& Block, 1990), an African American sub-sample from the Woodlawn
Study, in the Chicago area (Kellam, Ensminger, & Simon, 1980), and the
Pacific-Asian children in the Kauai Longitudinal Study (Werner, 1986,
1991).

The examination of the long-term effects of childhood adversity and
of protective factors and processes in the lives of these youth has shown
that some of the most critical determinants of adult outcomes are already
present in the first decade, and that there are large individual differences
among high risk children in their responses to both negative and positive
circumstances in their caregiving environment. For example, in the
Woodlawn study, Kellam and his colleagues (1980) found that psychological characteristics assessed in the first grade (ages six to seven) foretold drug
use at ages 16 and 17. The Block study (1988) found early childhood personality and environmental precursors at age three that predicted drug use
at age 14, and differences between frequent users, experimenters, and
abstainers at age 18. The antecedents of drug use differed as a function of

gender. Data from the Kauai Longitudinal Study revealed significant differences at ages one and two in the family environment (for both boys and girls) and in temperamental dispositions (for girls) between offspring of alcoholics with coping and substance abuse problems and those without any problems by age 18.

These preliminary findings raise some important questions that need to be addressed in future research on the applications of resilience. The admittedly still fragmented research on risk and resilience suggests that individuals, from early childhood on, select, seek out, and construct environments that are compatible with their temperamental dispositions and intellectual characteristics (Scarr & McCartney, 1983). A strictly "peer" centered or "environmental" explanation of drug use (or abstinence) seems inadequate, given the present longitudinal findings (Shedler & Block, 1990). Since early initiation of substance abuse appears to be a very potent predictor of progression to heavy use and long duration of dependence, a top priority of future research should be to examine the antecedents of such use before children enter grade school and to identify protective factors in the individual, the family, and the community that act as deterrents of substance abuse in high risk individuals who live in stressful home environments—especially those that have a family history of substance abuse. Among the important questions that need to be systematically addressed are:

1. The need for attention to gender differences in both vulnerability and resilience.
2. The need for a developmental perspective that addresses the interplay between risk and protective factors at important developmental transitions.
3. The need to identify the mediating processes that underlie resilience and the differential pathways that may lead from risk status to positive adaptation.
4. The need to consider the price exacted from individuals who sustain high competence and abstain or desist from drugs despite exposure to stressful home environments.
5. The need to evaluate the effectiveness of intervention programs at every age level.

References

Anthony, E. J., & Cohler, B. J. (1987). *The invulnerable child.* New York: Guilford Press, pp. 147–184.

Bleuler, M. (1984). Different forms of childhood stress and patterns of adult psychiatric outcome. In N. S. Watt, E. J. Anthony, L. C. Wynne, & J. E. Rolf (Eds.): *Children at risk for schizophrenia: A longitudinal perspective (pp. 537–542)*. New York: Cambridge University Press.

Block, J., Block, J., & Keyes, S. (1988). Longitudinally foretelling drug usage in adolescence: Early childhood personality and environmental precursors. *Child Development, 59*, 336–355.

Gore, S., & Eckenrode, J. (1992). Context and process in research on risk and resilience. Paper presented at the Conference on Risk, Resiliency, and Development: Research and Interventions. Kiawa Island, South Carolina, May 28–31.

Hoffman, L. W. (1991). The influence of family environment on personality: Accounting for sibling differences. *Psychological Bulletin, 110*, 187–203.

Kellam, S. G., Ensminger, M. E., & Simon, M. B. (1980). Mental health in first grade and teenage drug, alcohol, and cigarette use. *Drug and Alcohol Dependence, 5*, 273–304.

Magnusson, D. (1988). *Individual development from an interactional perspective: A longitudinal study*. Hillsdale, NJ: Erlbaum.

Masten, A. S., Best, K. M., & Garmezy, N. (1990). Resilience and development: Contributions from the study of children who overcome adversity. *Developmental Psychopathology, 2*, 425–444.

Nordberg, L. (1994). Ph. D. Dissertation, Karolinska Institutet, Department of Women and Child Health, Child and Adolescent Psychiatric Unit, Stockholm.

Parnas, J., Cannon, T. D., Jacobsen, B., Schulsinger, H., Schulsinger, F., & Mednick, S. A. (1993). Lifetime DSM-III-R diagnostic outcomes in the offspring of schizophrenic mothers: results from the Copenhagen high-risk study. *Archives of General Psychiatry, 50*, 707–714.

Rutter, M., & Smith, D. (1995). *Psychosocial disorders in young people: Time trends and their causes*. Chichester: Wiley.

Rydelius, P. A. (1981). Children of alcoholic fathers: Their social adjustment and their health status over 20 years. *Acta Paediatrics Scandinavica*. Supplement 286.

Scarr, S., & McCartney, K. (1983). How people make their own environment: A theory of genotype-environment effects. *Child Development, 54*, 424–435.

Shelder, J., & Block, J. (1990). Adolescent drug use and psychological health. *American Psychologist, 45*, 612–631.

Vaillant, G. (1983). *The natural history of alcoholism*. Cambridge: Harvard University Press.

Werner, E. E. (1986). Resilient offspring of alcoholics: A longitudinal study from birth to age 18. *Journal of Studies on Alcohol, 47*, 34–40.

Werner, E. E. (1990a). Protective factors and individual resilience. In S. Meisel and J. Shonkoff (Eds.), *Handbook of Early Intervention* (pp. 97–116). Cambridge: Cambridge University Press.

Werner, E. E. (1990b). Civil Society and Human Development. *Law and Society Seminar*, Harvard Law School, Cambridge, Mass, October 10.

Werner, E. E., (1991). The role of caring adults and religious coping efforts in the lives of children of alcoholics. Final Report to Lilly Endowment, Inc.

Werner, E. E. & Smith, R. S. (1982). *Vulnerable but invincible: A longitudinal study of resilient children and youth*. New York: McGraw Hill.

Werner, E. E., & Smith, R. S. (1993). *Overcoming the Odds: High Risk Children from Birth to Adulthood*. Ithaca, New York: Cornell University Press.

Wolin, S. J., & Wolin, S. (1993). *The resilient self: How survivors of troubled families rise above adversity*. New York: Villard Books.

14

Applications of Resilience
Possibilities and Promise

Bonnie Benard

Introduction

Resilience research creates a new paradigm for both research and clinicians alike. It situates risk in the broader social context of racism, war, and poverty-not in individuals, families, and communities-and asks how it is that youth successfully develop in the face of such stressors. Resilience research provides a powerful rationale for moving our focus in the social and behavioral sciences from a concern with individual deficit and pathology to an examination of individual and community strengths. The first component of this rationale is that the pathology model, through its focus on studying problems, illnesses, disorders, deviance, and risks, has not provided information as to what interventions do work. Ultimately, the potential for prevention surely lies in increasing our knowledge and understanding of reasons why some children are not damaged by deprivation.

Secondly, even though risk is a statistical concept applicable to the study of groups, it has been applied to individuals labeled according to their perceived deficit. The application of risk factor-focused research usually leads to the identification, labeling, and stigmatizing of youth, their families, and their communities. Resilience research, on the other hand, provides the field with a compelling rationale to move beyond risks and deficits (Oakes, 1985; Rosenthal, 1992; Weinstein et al., 1991). According to Jessor

Bonnie Benard • Resiliency Associates, Berkeley, California 94703.

Resilience and Development: Positive Life Adaptations, edited by Glantz and Johnson. Kluwer Academic/Plenum Publishers, New York, 1999.

(1993), our *"univocal preoccupation with risk tends to homogenize and caricature those who are poor"* (p. 121). In contrast, resilience research focuses on the life stories of individuals and on the individual variation within particular high-risk groups.

A third component of this rationale has profound implications for practice: using resilience as the knowledge base for practice creates a sense of optimism and hope. Using resilience in this way allows health care professionals working with youth to teach them to dwell in possibility and to have confidence in their futures. Conveying this positive expectation to them offers a more optimistic outlook (Werner & Smith, 1982). Moving from a risk focus to a resilience focus grounds practice in optimism, an essential component in building internal motivation in both adults and youth. Even at the community level, a resilience paradigm provides optimism, hope, and motivation.

Focus on Human Development

Resilience research offers the field evidence for placing human development at the center of prevention, education, and treatment (Masten, 1994). Addressing our common, shared, and basic human needs, resilience research findings also may transcend ethnic, social, geographical, and historical boundaries (Werner & Smith, 1992). The development of resilience may parallel the process of healthy human development, a dynamic process in which personality and environmental influences interact in a reciprocal, transactional relationship. Some suggest that alcohol and drug abuse, as well as mental health problems, must be framed within a developmental context (Jessor & Jessor, 1977; Zucker, 1989). From a developmental perspective the following question becomes the guiding principle for practice: How does this intervention meet the developmental needs of this person?

Emphasis on Process—Not Program

Resilience research shows that fostering resilience is a process and not a program. Rutter (1987) encouraged the use of the term protective processes to capture the dynamic nature of resilience instead of the commonly used term protective factors. *"The search is not for broadly defined facts but, rather, for the development and situational mechanisms involved in protective processes"* (Rutter, 1987, p. 317). Resilience research thus promises to move the prevention and treatment fields beyond their focus on "what" to an emphasis on "how". For example, Schorr's (1988) review of successful prevention programs came to the conclusions that child-centered programs based on the establishment of mutual relationships of care, respect, and trust between clients and professionals are the critical components in program effectiveness.

The voices of those who have overcome adversity (Lefkowitz, 1987; McLaughlin, Irby, & Langman, 1994; Polakow, 1993) tell us that ultimately resilience is a process of connectedness—of linking to people, to interests, and ultimately to life itself. Rutter stated that *"Development is a question of linkages that happen within you as a person and also in the environment in which you live . . . Our hope lies in doing something to alter these linkages, to see that kids who start in a bad environment don't go on having bad environments and develop a sense of impotency"* (in Pines, p. 62). Similarly, James Coleman claimed the most fundamental task for parents, educators, and policy makers is linking children into our social fabric (in Olson, 1987, p. 16). Effective interventions must give meaning by reinforcing the natural social bonds, between young and old, between siblings, and between friends (Werner & Smith, 1982). Research on resilience challenges the field to build a connectedness or sense of belonging, by transforming our families, schools, and communities to become "psychological homes" where youth can find mutually caring and respectful relationships and opportunities for meaningful involvement.

Use in the Field

The two approaches described below build on the themes of resilience research. The approaches use resilience as a paradigm and view resilience as the process of human development innate to all human beings. These approaches are not programs but, instead, are processes focusing on relationships and opportunities. Two themes that are logical extensions of the approaches are articulated as follows: 1) fostering resilience is a community-building process; and 2) promoting resilience in youth means we have to model resilience ourselves.

Health Realization Model

A growing number of practitioners have been using an approach developed by Roger Mills called the Health Realization and Community Empowerment Model. This model began in a Dade County, Florida housing project in the late 1980's. The housing project was beset with poverty and racism, high rates of violence, drug-dealing, teen pregnancy, and school failure. The Health Realization model demonstrated its effectiveness by reducing the rates of these problems and building a sense of community pride and well-being. Some of the findings from the 142 families and 604 youth involved in the three-year Dade County project included: a) significantly improved parent-child relationships; b) a 75 per cent reduction in delinquency and school-related problem behaviors; c) a 65 per cent decrease in drug trafficking; d) an 80 per cent decrease in teen pregnancy; and e) a 60 per cent decrease in substance abuse (Mills, 1993). The underlying principle of the Health Realization model is that resilience is innate in all humans and that it is directly accessible. According to Mills (1993), the capacity for mental health, wisdom, intelligence, common sense, and positive motivation is in everyone despite his or her risk factors. The Health Realization model aims to reconnect people to themselves and each other through educational, and not therapeutic, means. It consists of teaching, accessing, and overcoming the barriers leading to innate resilience.

While several successful community change efforts are grounded in the creation of caring relationships, communicating high expectations, and creating opportunities for active participation, Health Realization makes several contributions to resilience theory. First, Health Realization demonstrates the process of inside-out change. Through realizing one's own innate health, one experiences a sense of self-efficacy, a sense of personal empowerment and motivation to work with others to build a critical mass that, in turn, creates community change. The Health Realization Model asserts that we all have an inborn capacity for social competence, autonomy, problem-solving, and optimism. In spite of powerful risk factors, participants in various Health Realization projects have been able to overcome odds when they've come to understand how thinking gets in the way of accessing their inner core of mental health and well-being. Additionally, the model demonstrates the dynamic relationship between environmental protective factors and individual resilience, also known as the relative and situational nature of resilience (Gordon & Song, 1994). Health Realization has found that a caring, nurturing environment is necessary for accessing innate resilience and mental health. All individuals have different needs and experiences, and the environmental stimulus needed to engage self-righting mechanisms and our innate resilience varies not only between individuals but within a person and over the course of a lifetime (Rutter, 1987; Werner & Smith, 1982).

A fourth contribution from the Health Realization approach demonstrates the "black box" of resilience—the internal process of health realization. Health Realization is the ability to recognize one's negative thoughts and to let go of them through "adaptive distancing." Through adaptive distancing a person resists being drawn into the negative dynamics of a dysfunctional system (be it a family, a classroom, a relationship). Adaptive distancing also involves the ability to withdraw from an unhealthy situation with reflective thought. Thought recognition is reinforced in research on "learned helplessness" and "learned optimism" (Seligman, 1990). Seligman attributes the key to either depression or psychological well-being to our explanatory styles, the way we explain both the good and bad things that happen to us. While changing the way one thinks about experience (cognitive reframing), the Health Realization approach teaches that innate wisdom and optimism will rise to the surface. Health realization also offers us a practical approach to applying resilience. Thought recognition should be taught in the context of a caring, respectful, reciprocal relationship. Health realization is not an add-on program. Rather, Health Realization involves a process of deep changes in belief systems, requiring practitioners to actively listen and connect with a person's inner core of mental health.

Western Center for Drug-Free Schools and Communities

One organization that is particularly effective at incorporating resilience research into their agenda is the Western Center for Drug-Free Schools and Communities. They have conducted extensive training in applying resilience research to the field of practice with parent educators, school personnel, community-based organizations and coalitions, professional associations, and state-level policy makers (Bernard, Burgoa, & Whealdon, 1994). The goal of the Western Center is to move practitioners from a risk model to a model of resilience and to provide a framework to guide resilience based practice. The training operates on four assumptions. First, resilience helps to build communities that support human development that is rich in caring relationships. These relationships communicate high expectations and offer ongoing opportunities for participation in families, classrooms, schools, support groups, and neighborhood organizations. Second, resilience meets youths' basic needs of belonging and having a stable psychological home. Third, resilience must be supported in the lives of the practitioner. Building community and creating belonging for youth means we must also do this for ourselves. Practitioners need caring, respectful relationships and opportunities to make decisions; without these, they cannot create them for youth. Lastly, resilience validates the wisdom of the heart or an innate intuitiveness that guides reflective practice. Giving them language and concepts from the resilience research to directly express and guide their work supports practitioners' wisdom.

These four assumptions operate on two principles. The first principle is caring. Caring is seeing the possibilities in each child and using one's wisdom. Parents, teachers, and youth workers must have a sense of compassion, looking beyond the negative words and actions of youth and seeing the underlying feelings of anger, pain, and insecurity. In Alice Miller's (1990) research on resilient survivors of childhood abuse and trauma, caring also meant being a "sympathetic witness", carefully listening to, and believing, a child's story. An ethic of caring is not a program or strategy, per se, but rather a way of being in the world, and relating to youth and their families. Caring conveys compassion, understanding, respect, and interest.

The second principle is having high expectations. Having high expectations has mitigated against alcohol and drug use (Brook, Nomura, & Cohen, 1989) and promoted academic achievement, self-efficacy, and optimism (Bandura, 1992; Rutter et al., 1979). Using school as an example, expectations can be conveyed in the curriculum (e.g., a multicultural curriculum conveys respect for other cultures) or in grouping practices (e.g., heterogeneous cooperative learning groups convey to a child that they belong). Providing youth with the opportunities for meaningful involvement and responsibility is a natural outcome of environments that convey high expectations. Infusing opportunities for participation into the life of the classroom doesn't require any special add-on programs. Adults need to see youths as a valuable resource, share power with them, and create a system based on reciprocity and collaboration rather than on control and competition. For example, strategies that help promote resilience include: 1) asking questions that encourage critical, reflective thinking; 2) encouraging hands-on and experiential learning; 3) involving youth in curriculum and program planning; 4) letting youth create the program or classroom agreements; and 5) employing approaches like cooperative learning, peer helping, or cross-age mentoring.

Challenges to Research

Interdisciplinary research across the human sciences as well as collaboration between basic and applied researchers are approaches continually advocated as steps to advancing knowledge and facilitating the application to practice (Whyte, 1991). A recent collaboration sponsored by the MacArthur Foundation's *"Successful Adolescent Development among Youth in High-Risk Settings"* offers a model for achieving both of these objectives in the study of human development. Jessor (1993) describes this initiative as holding "promise for a more comprehensive, more differentiated, and more situated understanding of adolescent behavior and development than has been achieved thus far" (p. 117). Rather than situating risks in the characteristics of youth, their families, and their communities, this initiative situates risks in the social contexts of racism and poverty. This initiative asks, "What are the personal, social, and institutional resources that promote successful adolescent development despite these risks?" Several imperatives guide the initiative in elaborating the complexity and richness of human development: 1) development over time is longitudinal; 2) transactional processes between person and environment are focused on; 3) individual variation within the risk category is emphasized; and 4) the stories, voices, and subjective experiences and personal meanings of youth are captured. These imperatives may be met through a cross-discipline approach and through a collaboration among differing research methodologies—quantitative/qualitative, etiological/evaluative, and ethnographic/empirical.

While the initiative provides a model for resilience research that can truly inform practice, the problem remains of how to move the findings into the field. For this to happen we must build projects and interventions based on the concept of creating learning communities that include researchers from a broad array of disciplines and methodologies as well as practitioners and policy makers wherein each can build on each other's strengths, knowledge, and position. The goal of these learning communities would be to produce research findings and that prove fruitful in practical application. Like any healthy functioning human system—these communities must be grounded in relationships based on mutual support, respect, and power. Practitioners must be active partners in the research process, including participation in design and application.

Certainly, a small tradition has long existed in social science research for incorporating scientific and indigenous knowledge, especially in the fields of applied anthropology and community development and in the methodology of participatory action research (Whyte, 1991). A commitment to promoting the development of people is at the core of these approaches and the approaches of resilience researchers. Changing the status quo in our society means changing paradigms, both personally and professionally from risk to resilience. Fostering resilience means changing our belief systems to see youth, their families, and their cultures as resources instead of problems. Additionally, fostering resilience requires working on the policy level for educational, social, and economic justice. As Currie (1989) concluded in his powerful examination of the drugs and the cities, *"We must take up the long postponed challenge to relieve the human misery that lies at the heart of our continuing drug crisis. We have, after all, been trying the alternatives for 40 years. We have tried moral exhortation. We have tried neglect. We have tried punishment. We have even, more grudgingly, tried treatment. We have tried everything but improving our lives"* (p. 332). Research on resilience provides the evidence we need to do this.

References

Bandura, A. (1992). Exercise of personal agency through the self-efficacy mechanism. In Schwarzer, R. (Ed.), *Self-Efficacy: Thought control of action* (pp. 3–38). Washington, DC: Hemisphere publishing.

Benard, B., Burgoa, C., & Whealdon, K. (1994). *Fostering resiliency in kids: Protective factors in the school. (Training of Trainers).* San Francisco: Far West Laboratory.

Brook, J., Nomura, C., & Cohen, P. (1989). A network of influences on adolescent drug involvement: Neighborhood, school, peer, and family. *Genetic, Social, and General Psychology Monographs, 115,* 303–321.

Currie, E. (1989). *Reckoning: drugs, the cities, and the American future.* New York: Hill and Wang.

Gordon, E., & Song, L. (1994). Variations in the experience of resilience. In Wang, M. & Gordon, E. (Eds.), *Educational resilience in inner-city America: challenges and prospects.* Hillsdale, NJ: Lawrence Erlbaum Associates.

Jessor, R. (1993). Successful adolescent development among youth in high-risk settings. *American Psychologist, 48,* 117–126.

Jessor, R. & Jessor, S. (1977). *Problem behavior and psychosocial development: A longitudinal study of youth.* New York: Academic Press.

Lefkowitz, B. (1987). *Tough change: Growing up on your own in America.* New York: Doubleday.

Masten, A. S. (1994). Resilience in individual development: Successful adaptation despite risk and adversity. In Wang, M. & Gordon, E. (Eds.), *Educational resilience in inner-city American: Challenges and prospects* (pp. 3–25). Hillsdale, NJ: Lawrence Erlbaum Associates.

McLaughlin, M., Irby, M., & Langman, J. (1994). *Urban sanctuaries: Neighborhood organizations in the lives and futures of inner-city youth.* San Francisco: Jossey-Bass.

Miller, A. (1990). *The untouched key: Tracing childhood trauma in creativity and destructiveness.* New York: Anchor/Doubleday.

Mills, R. (1993). *The Health Realization Model: A community empowerment primer.* Alhambra: California School of Professional Psychology.

Oakes, J. (1985). *Keeping track: How schools structure inequality.* New Haven: Yale University Press.

Olson, L. (1987). A prominent "boat rocker" rejoins the fray. *Education Week, January 14,* 14–17.

Pines, M. (1984). Resilient children: Interview with Michael Rutter. *Psychology Today, 18,* pp. 56–57.

Polakow, V. (1993). *Lives on the edge: Single mothers and their children in the other America.* Chicago: University of Chicago Press.

Rosenthal, R. (1992). *Pygmalion in the classroom: Teacher expectation and pupils' intellectual development.* New York: Irvington Publishers.

Rutter, M. (1987). Psychosocial resilience and protective mechanisms. *American Journal of Orthopsychiatry, 57,* 316–331.

Rutter, M., Maughan, B., Mortimore, J., Ouston, J., & Smith, A. (1979). *Fifteen thousand hours:*

Secondary schools and their effects on children. Cambridge: Harvard University Press.

Schorr, L. (1988). *Within our reach: Breaking the cycle of disadvantage.* New York: Doubleday, 1988.

Seligman, M. (1990). *Learned optimism: How to change your mind and your life.* New York: Simon and Schuster.

Weinstein, R., Soule, C., Collins, F., Cone, J., Mehlorn, M., & Stimmonacchi, K. (1991). Expectations and high school change: teacher-researcher collaboration to prevent school failure. *American Journal of Community Psychology, 19,* 333–363.

Werner, E., & Smith, R. (1982). *Vulnerable but invincible: A longitudinal study of resilient children and youth.* New York: Adams, Bannister, and Cox.

Werner, E., & Smith, R. (1992). *Overcoming the odds: High-risk children from birth to adulthood.* New York: Cornell University Press.

Whyte, W. (1991). The social sciences in the university. *American Behavioral Scientist, 34,* 618–633.

Zucker, R. (1989). Is risk for alcoholism predictable? A probabilistic approach to a developmental problem. *Drugs and Society, 3,* 69–93.

IV

EPILOGUE

15

Resilience Comes of Age
Reflections on the Past and Outlook for the Next Generation of Research

Ann S. Masten

Introduction

The first generation of resilience research has ended and the second is beginning. This volume is replete with signs of the transition from first to second generation, ranging from the intensity of the criticisms of the construct of resilience to the demands for theory and process-oriented research. The goal of this discussion is to examine where we have been and where we appear to be going by highlighting the major issues and themes across the chapters in this timely volume.

The study of resilience in psychology and psychiatry arose from efforts to understand the etiology and development of psychopathology, and most particularly from studies of children "at risk" for psychopathology due to parental mental illness, perinatal problems, interparental conflict, poverty, or a combination of such risk factors (Garmezy, 1974; Masten, 1989; Rutter, 1979). Prospective studies of high-risk children focused attention on the possibility of "false positives"—those in the risk group who did not develop disorder—and also the significance of such phenomena for theories of psychopathology. At the same time, these studies required developmental per-

Ann S. Masten • Institute of Child Development, University of Minnesota, Minneapolis, Minnesota 55455.

Resilience and Development: Positive Life Adaptations, edited by Glantz and Johnson. Kluwer Academic/Plenum Publishers, New York, 1999.

spectives in theory and methodology, and thus contributed to the rise of developmental psychopathology (Masten & Braswell, 1991).

The study of resilience was motivated in part by growing concerns about the effects on children of potentially adverse life events such as divorce and traumatic stressors such as abuse or neglect and war (Garmezy & Masten, 1994; Haggerty, Sherrod, Garmezy, & Rutter, 1994; National Research Council, 1993). Evaluating impact and investigating the possibility of recovery again brought attention to individual differences in adaptation and developmental trajectories.

The implicit or explicit rationale for focusing on "good" outcomes among high risk or high stressor-exposed children was twofold: (a) to gain a better understanding of risk factors and processes and (b) to identify protective factors and their underlying processes. Both presumably could inform prevention and intervention efforts.

The pioneers in the study of resilience argued that investigators had neglected an important perspective and set of phenomena by attending exclusively to risk factors and negative outcomes (Garmezy, 1971, 1974; Murphy & Moriarty, 1976; Rutter, 1979; Werner & Smith, 1982, 1992). They argued for the importance of examining pathways away from as well as toward deviance at different points in development. These investigators brought attention to the family of phenomena labeled variously as "resilience" or "stress-resistance" or, rather unrealistically, "invulnerability," although they never argued that this domain of inquiry was the only one of importance. Rather, they sought greater balance in the study of psychopathology in development.

Now, after two decades of research, authors in this volume raise reasonable questions about whether we still need to focus on the family of phenomena connoted by resilience, whether the pendulum has swung too far away from risk or liability processes, and whether the construct of resilience has any meaning. Those who find the concept meaningful additionally raise challenging methodological questions.

Conceptual Issues

Validity

In various ways, the chapters of this volume all address the question of validity, whether "resilience" has meaning or how it can be meaningfully defined: What does resilience refer to? Who defines it? Is it a trait or a multiply determined outcome, internal or external, narrow or broad? Is resilience a process or an outcome? Does the construct serve a useful purpose?

From a phenomenological perspective, there does appear to be agreement about the nature of the ballpark we are in when "resilience" is invoked. The construct of resilience presumes that there is a range of observable behavior or outcomes or phenotypic variation in high-risk groups. Resilience generally refers to patterns of desirable behavior in situations where adaptive functioning or development have been or currently are significantly threatened by adverse experiences or rearing conditions. Thus, resilience is a contextual and inferential construct because it depends on a combination of high risk status or exposure to experiences known to have variable but on average negative consequences for development or adaptation, plus a judgment that "good" adaptation or development has occurred despite the risks or adversity. Definitions of what constitutes good functioning or outcomes will vary in relation to historical, cultural, and developmental contexts (Masten & Coatsworth, 1995, 1998). There is considerable agreement that this general class of phenomena is real while at the same time there is a great deal of disagreement about the diagnostic criteria.

The issue of "who decides" the criteria may become more salient as cross-cultural studies of adaptation increase across and within nations (Durbrow, 1999; Ogbu, 1985). Should successful development be defined only within cultural context? What happens when subcultural norms differ from the majority culture? How can emic and etic perspectives inform each other?

The term "resiliency" appearing in this volume has a narrower connotation because of its historical roots in the personality literature, in particular the seminal work of Jack and Jeanne Block on ego-resiliency (Block & Block, 1980). The term, "resiliency," has sometimes been used to refer to a relatively global personality trait that affords better adaptation to life, and is metaphorically akin to the resiliency of rubber bands or steel in materials science, as noted by Tarter and Vanyukov (1999) in their chapter, or the buoyancy property of objects in water. However, given the present lack of evidence corroborating such a broad adaptive resiliency trait, it would seem advisable to study better delineated and measurable personality dimensions, such as ego-resiliency and ego-control (Block & Block, 1980) or positive and negative emotionality (Tellegen, 1985) in relation to good and bad developmental trajectories, life events and so forth.

Tarter and Vanyukov (1999) argue in their chapter that the concept of resilience (by which they appear to mean resiliency as a trait) is superfluous because the notion of variations in liability, within the framework of the diathesis-stressor model of psychopathology, is sufficient to account for it. Their perspective represents an interesting, although perhaps ironic, return to the origins of resilience research. The diathesis-stressor model and the reaction range concepts as applied to understanding the development of psychopathology (Gottesman & Shields, 1972, 1982) played a significant role in the history of interest in resilience. The diathesis-stressor model of mental illness, as articulated by Gottesman and Shields, incorporated genetic and environmental "assets" as well as risks in the total liability equation. The "risk consortium" of investigators turned to the study of high-risk children to learn about the etiology of schizophrenia and other major disorders (Watt, Anthony, Wynne, & Rolf, 1984). It was through the study of such children, as noted earlier in this chapter, that investigators such as Norman Garmezy and Michael Rutter and Arnold Sameroff turned their attention to the observable fact that there were good developmental trajectories among high-risk children. They recognized the potential in studying good as well as poor outcomes in search of the processes that give rise to or avert psychopathology. Resilience needed to be highlighted because it had been neglected in favor of an exclusive focus on risk and deviance— it served the purpose of bringing serious empirical attention to understudied phenomena, as noted by Windle in his chapter, thereby expanding the focus of research to a broader range of individuals and individual differences.

The study of processes that may lower liability for disorders such as schizophrenia has been hampered by the lack of knowledge about the specific biological vulnerability processes which appear to be necessary but not sufficient contributors to disorder (Gottesman & Shields, 1982). As knowledge of brain development and brain-behavior relations improves, the study of protective processes, given biological vulnerability to a particular disorder, become more feasible. Whether this area of inquiry is labeled "liability-reducing" effects or protective processes or resilience studies may be inconsequential to science, although the latter terms probably would have considerably more appeal to research participants and policy makers. Certainly, the study of liability-reducing processes does not obviate the necessity of investigating liability-augmenting processes.

Modeling Resilience

Another theme common to many of the criticisms of the resilience construct in this volume is the lack of precision in specifying models of resilience so that they can be adequately tested and replicated. Risk/ resilience studies address linkages among risk factors, behavioral outcomes, and other variables that may be correlates of outcomes or moderators and mediators or risk factors. Some of the possibilities are illustrated in Figure 1, which is a greatly simplified causal model of cumulative risk and protective effects on a single positive aspect of behavior.

Additive main effects are shown at the top of the figure, where three correlates of the outcome are illustrated. A pure asset, such as a wonderful

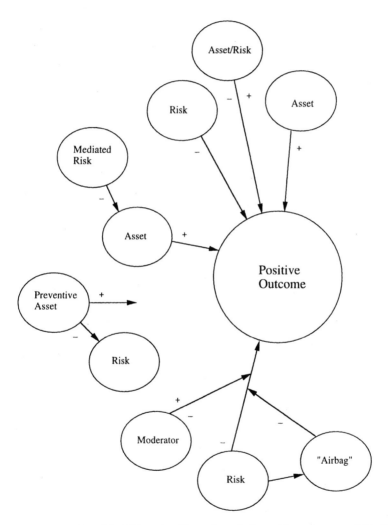

Figure 1. Multicausal model of risk and resilience for a single positive outcome variable, illustrating compensatory, moderating, and preventive types of protective processes.

friend or a talent, has a positive relation to outcome when it is present, but little effect when absent. A pure risk factor, such as a car accident or premature birth, has a negative relation to the outcome when present and little significance if not present. These are probably less common than the third type of correlate, a bipolar variable, such as intellectual ability or parenting quality, which may affect the outcome at all levels on a continuum. As shown, these risks and assets have independent effects. Given the presence of risk processes, however, assets could be conceived of as "protective factors," through counterbalancing or compensating for risk (Masten et al., 1988).

Moving to the bottom of Figure 1, interaction effects are illustrated. In these cases, the impact of the risk variable depends on another variable, a moderator, which can enhance or reduce the impact. Variables that enhance risk or increase the effects of a risk factor have been called vulnerability factors and those that reduce risk have been called protective factors (Masten et al., 1988). Two examples are provided in the figure. One shows a moderator that independently interacts with the risk variable, such as a teacher who tries to help a child feel better after a divorce or a personality trait (e.g., the tendency to experience negative emotions) or negative cognitive attributional style that increases the impact of adversity. The other shows a risk-activated protective factor, labeled "airbag" for brevity. Like an airbag in automobiles, this type of moderator is triggered by the stressor or threatening situation. Many emergency social services operate reactively in this way in efforts to protect endangered children. These services may have no functional significance in a child's life *until activated by the stressor*, much like human antibodies.

Two other types of protective effects are illustrated in this figure on the left. One shows the potential protective effect of an asset that mediates risk, although the same example also illustrates the case where risk has indirect effects by undermining key assets for the outcome criterion. For example, stressful life events in the life of an adult may affect the quality of parenting by that adult (Conger et al., 1992). Nonetheless, a highly effective parent would reduce the indirect effects on a child of a given stressor. The last example illustrated in Figure 1 is a preventive case. An alert parent may completely avert a stressor that would have harmed a child, just as good prenatal care may avert birth complications. In these cases, the outcome is better than it might have been because risk has been prevented.

Figure 1 could focus on a negative outcome, such as psychopathology, in which case the relations would be reversed for assets and risks. There are also other possible linkages among variables that are not illustrated, such as the possibility that two risk factors have a synergistic joint effect that is more than the sum of their additive influence, or curvilinear effects (Rutter,

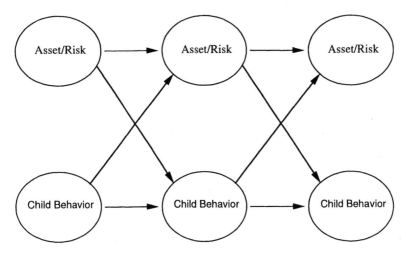

Figure 2. Transactional model of a risk/asset factor and one aspect of child behavior influencing each other over time.

1990). Most importantly, the fundamentally transactional nature of development (Sameroff & Chandler, 1975) is not illustrated in Figure 1. The behavior labeled "outcome" is likely to influence what happens next, in terms of other variables. Child behavior, for example, may influence parent behavior or the school environment (Patterson, Reid, & Dishion, 1992). Behavior problems can lead to angry parents or placements in different classrooms or school or choices of deviant peer groups that in turn influence the child's behavior or exposure to negative life events down the road. A general transactional pattern is illustrated in Figure 2.

In the resilience literature, unfortunately, it is not always clear which effects are being investigated. Moreover, every investigator seems to have a different name for the variables and relations under investigation. For example, a number of studies compare two groups of people who shared a common risk status, those with good outcome ("resilient") and those with poor outcome ("affected" or "vulnerable"). Correlates of good and poor outcome are labeled protective factors. However, in many cases the correlate is known to be a general correlate of the outcome criterion, regardless of risk status. Without the inclusion of low risk groups, it is not possible to distinguish assets and risks (main effects) from moderating variables.

Another issue in resilience studies is distinguishing lower net risk from resilience. Studies that identify a high-risk group (often by aggregating risk factors or stressful life events) and then identify groups with good versus poor outcomes often find that the two groups differed in important ways from the outset or early in development. For example, in the classic study of the children of Kauai (Werner & Smith, 1982), high risk children who turned out well were more appealing as babies, had more stable and better caregiving, and were healthier. Is it more accurate to describe these children as resilient and their parenting and disposition as protective factors, or to describe them as lower risk to begin with?

As Tarter and Vanyukov point out (1999, in this volume), risk factors are defined by population or group statistics. If we don't know precisely what the risk mechanisms are, then an individual in a high risk group may come out better simply because the significant risk effect is not present (Rutter, 1990). Similarly, stressful or traumatic life events are viewed as risk factors because of their typical effects on people. It is conceivable that there has been exposure to a stressor, but the risk process has not occurred (the child, for example, did not understand what happened).

Methodological Issues

The maturing of resilience research is also evident in the methodological issues that have been identified in this volume. Many of these issues are not unique to this are of inquiry but reflect more general issues in developmental psychopathology.

Methodological issues include the multifaceted problem of how to operationalize the predictors and moderators (risks and assets and other variables) and outcomes of interest (effective adaptation or psychopathology symptoms or diagnosis). This issue is highly complex if one is to take development and context seriously. Resilience will not arise from fixed characteristics of person or environment but from an ever-changing interplay of multiple systems. The same attribute (of person or environment) could afford an advantage at one period of development or in one situation and a disadvantage at another time or in another situation. An individual's behavior at a given time reflects countless unique interactions within the organism and with the environment. If organism and environment are comprised of multiple interacting systems (Ford & Lerner, 1992; Gunnar & Thelen, 1989), threats to development can arise from any system within or outside the organism or from bad "fits" of organism and environment. Methodology lags behind such dynamic models of behavior. Many of the measures employed in studies of risk and resilience offer only crude indicators of variance that can be measured with a reasonable degree of reliability and show some validity in their predictive power.

As discussed by Luthar and Cushing (1999, in this volume), there are several basic approaches to "risk," the variables that have shown validity as predictors of some undesirable outcome. Some studies focus on a single risk factor, such as low birth weight or poverty or divorce. However, it has become clear that risk factors rarely occur in isolation from other risks or disadvantages, which has led to more comprehensive approaches (Coie et al., 1993; Hawkins, Catalano, & Miller, 1992; Masten & Wright, 1997). Some studies tally risk variables to form a cumulative index, often by adding up the number of risk factors or stressful life events that are present. These composite variables often have more predictive power but it is not clear what is being measured. It is also unlikely that risk processes operate together as part of a single underlying dimension. It is more likely that many processes are reflected in the composite-outcome linkage, with the composite serving as a complex marker variable. Ironically, composites that "explain" more variance, may obscure causal processes, as noted in Windle's commentary in this volume. With advances in multivariate statistics and larger sample sizes, what may become more common in the future are efforts to model multiple risk variables simultaneously, while keeping them separate so that specific processes can be more readily identified.

Many methodological issues have been raised in the literature concerned with stressful life events (Cohen, 1988; Masten, Neemann, & Andenas, 1994). One of the most important is the issue of "controllability" or independence of life events. This issue arises from the acknowledgment that some life experiences are closely tied to the behavior of the individual. Some individuals behave in ways that are more likely to precipitate negative life experiences. Consequently, measures of such events tend to be confounded with the outcomes of interest and also potential moderators, such as personality variables (Masten et al., 1994). This creates problems for figuring out how life events and outcomes are related. Some investigators focus exclusively on uncontrollable events, stressors that are unlikely to result from a child's behavior. This strategy has the advantage of avoiding confounded measures, but fails to address what may be an important phenomenon in development—the ways in which people "make their own environments" (Scarr & McCartney, 1983), or fail to learn self-protective skills.

The measurement of desirable or undesirable outcome is similarly complex. Some studies focus on effective performance in salient developmental tasks as an indicator of "good" developmental status or outcome (e.g., Masten et al., 1988, 1999). Others focus on psychological well being or distress (e.g., Swearingen & Cohen, 1985) or diagnostic criteria (e.g., Conrad & Hammen, 1993). All of these criteria involve judgments about the quality of development or functioning, which have an historical, cultural, and developmental reference point (Masten & Coatsworth, 1995, 1998). Kumpfer

(1999) in this volume has discussed the challenging issue of defining adaptation. In choosing the criteria and measures by which to judge adaptation, an investigator makes many implicit or explicit conceptual decisions about cultural reference points, whether resilience will be defined in terms of external or internal functioning or both, who the most reliable informants may be, how broadly or narrowly to define it, etc. In longitudinal studies, the investigator interested in change must also figure out how to assess meaningful behavioral trajectories.

When resilience is defined by multiple criteria (e.g., doing well on several major developmental tasks), in an all or none approach, dramatic differences may emerge when maladaptive and resilient groups are compared (e.g., Werner & Smith, 1982, 1992). This approach has provided compelling evidence of where to look for protective processes. However, it may be necessary to conduct finer-grained analyses in order to identify specific effects of protective processes, because they may operate differentially in different domains of behavior. Recent studies of maltreated children (Cicchetti, Rogosch, Lynch, & Holt, 1993) and disadvantaged inner city adolescents (Luthar, 1991) illustrate what may be gained from a more differentiated approach to resilience.

Investigators must also decide which analytic strategies best address their research questions within the constraints of their sample size and measures. Person-focused strategies have used diagnostic criteria to identify groups of "resilient" and "affected" individuals who are then compared through analysis of variance. Cluster analysis is another person-focused approach to grouping individuals for comparison. Variable-focused approaches use a variety of multivariate strategies such as hierarchical regression, path analysis or structural equation modeling to identify significant linkages between risks, assets, adaptive criteria and other variables. Perhaps the most difficult to model and test are developmental changes in vulnerability and protective processes, turning points in developmental trajectories, and transactional processes, all of which have been implicated in theoretical discussions of resilience (Masten, Best, & Garmezy, 1990; Rutter, 1990).

Policy and Application Issues

As a sense of national urgency mounts in regard to child poverty, child crime, drug use, adolescent pregnancy, and so forth, the appeal of resilience as a construct and research agenda also appears to have increased, as evidenced by this volume and the conference that preceded it. Perhaps the phenomenon and even the idea of resilience provides a sense of hope for a despairing public. There is little dispute that good outcomes can be found among high-risk children. For scientists, however, the study of resilience must provide new knowledge as well as hope. In addition, researchers (and funders) have had high hopes that resilience research would inform intervention and prevention efforts to steer development in more positive directions. Kaplan (1999) argues in his chapter that the "evaluative significance" of outcomes may be *"incidental to the purpose of explaining the phenomenon in question"*. For basic science, this may be true. However, this is not the case for policy and intervention goals, when the aim is to learn how to promote desirable outcomes and/or minimize negative outcomes. Rolf and Johnson, as well as Bernard, discuss the role of resilience frameworks and research for prevention, intervention, and related policy.

The first generation of research has yielded "broad stroke" knowledge. Diverse studies implicate similar variables, such as stable relationships with caring/competent adults or good intellectual skills, as assets and protective factors for attaining competence and avoiding mental health problems among children at risk for various reasons (Masten, 1994; Masten & Coatsworth, 1998). For some criteria, such as academic achievement, more specific assets have consistently emerged, such as parent involvement (Stevenson & Baker, 1987). For the most part, however, finer-grained inquiry is just beginning. It is a central task for second-generation investigators to study in greater detail what processes may explain the broad strokes and to delineate how potential assets or protective systems work for whom under which conditions. Given the urgency of current problems, it is also incumbent upon the second-generation researchers to test their theories through intervention studies. In resilience research, intervention and prevention designs with random assignment provide the best experimental evidence of hypothesized processes. A fundamental question for the next generation of researchers is whether naturally occurring resilience can be deliberately and effectively created through intervention.

Second Generation Goals and Challenges

The first generation of resilience-focused thinking and research has resulted in a "short list" of potential protective factors that point to possible processes worth investigating, tools for analyzing resilience, a much greater awareness of the complexity of understanding the broad array of phenomena encompassed by the concept, and, most recently, incisive criticism of the construct, methods, and findings of the first generation of work. Where does this leave us at the outset of the second generation? The context for studying resilience has dramatically shifted in two major ways. As noted earlier, there is a sense of emergency rising with the tide of child casualties of violence, drug abuse, and poverty in the United States. Moral and economic imperatives are converging to provide powerful incentives to intervene in order to protect development or prevent morbidity. Second, the science of child development, both normative and pathological, has shifted toward multifactorial, multisystem, process-oriented theories and investigations.

These trends, combined with the knowledge gained from the early resilience research, suggest the following conclusions for second generation investigators to consider:

1. Longitudinal studies and normative samples with multifactorial designs and reasonably large samples, such as the Dunedin study (Silva, 1990) provide the best basic understanding of developmental pathways. Yet these studies are complex and expensive to mount and have long time horizons for pay-off.
2. It makes little sense to study single risk or protective factors or isolated problematic outcomes in children and adolescents when the evidence is overwhelming that risk factors typically co-occur, that the same risk factor can contribute to a variety of problem outcomes, that different risk factors predict the same problem, and that problem outcomes frequently co-occur (Coie et al., 1993; Jessor, 1993; Masten & Wright, 1997). Compartmentalized studies—or funding streams—do not seem sensible or cost efficient.
3. If multiple processes influence developmental pathways, it is not reasonable to expect interventions targeting a single influence to have much impact. Interventions are likely to be increasingly multifaceted and longitudinal; targeting multiple risk and protective processes involving multiple developmental systems (organism, family, peers, school, community, culture) and shifting focus strategically as the leverage for change shifts with development (Coie et al., 1993; Jessor, 1993; Weizs, Weiss, Han, Granger, & Morton, 1995; Yoshikawa, 1994; Zigler, Taussig, & Black, 1992).
4. Multisystem research, studying the human organism in context or studying two or more embedded or transactional systems simultaneously requires expertise from multiple disciplines that is unlikely to reside in single individuals (Jessor, 1993).
5. Funders have a dual challenge of fostering transdisciplinary collaboration and avoiding artificial compartmentalization of research by risk factor or problem.
6. Urgent problems may not wait for thorough and gradual accretion of a solid knowledge base on risk-reducing or asset-enhancing and

other protective processes. Urgency may justify direct testing of informed strategies of intervention, using experimental designs to test and subsequently refine protective-process hypotheses. Informed strategies will be grounded in scientific theory and knowledge as well as the practical experience of seasoned teachers, parents, clinicians, and other child educators or service providers.

7. Basic research is needed on how assets and moderators "work" and how these processes change as a function of development. Highly focused short-term longitudinal designs may be useful in identifying likely processes, which could then be experimentally tested through intervention studies.

The growth of developmental psychopathology as well as resilience research signify widespread recognition that we can not understand psychopathology without the context of normative development, nor risk and vulnerability and deviance without assets and protection and effective adaptation, nor expect to learn how to help individuals in trouble by focusing solely on either normative *or* deviant development (Masten & Coatsworth, 1995, 1998; Sroufe, 1990). For more than 20 years, the concept of resilience has played a role in bringing out the salience of neglected phenomena, strategies, and ideas. Now this construct serves to highlight the importance of intervention guided by theory and the accrued knowledge base of child development, psychiatry, psychology, and related fields. Intervention and prevention efforts can be conceptualized as deliberate protective efforts. The key to intervention could lie in triggering or facilitating natural protective systems. A crucial question for the future is whether such efforts are best modeled on naturally occurring resilience or not.

At this time, it is premature to throw out "resilience" as an organizing construct for the systematic investigation of good adaptation in risk situations. Ultimately, however, resilience concepts and studies should not be necessary. Sophisticated developmental models and studies of human behavior that accommodate the full range of organism and environmental variation and their complex interactions will absorb them. Meanwhile, we still have much to learn from the lives of children who attain normal developmental trajectories despite significant threats to their development.

ACKNOWLEDGMENTS. The author is deeply indebted to the ideas of Norman Garmezy, Michael Rutter, and many colleagues in Project Competence and the Institute of Child Development. Preparation of this chapter was supported in part by the William T. Grant Foundation, long active in support of resilience studies, and the National Science Foundation (NSF/SBR-9729111).

References

Block, J. H., & Block, J. (1980). The role of ego-control and ego-resiliency in the organization of behavior. In W. A. Collins (Ed.), *Development of cognition, affect, and social relations* (pp. 39–101). Hillsdale, NJ: Lawrence Erlbaum.

Cohen, L. H. (1988) (Ed.). *Life events and psychological functioning: Theoretical and methodological issues* (pp. 11–30). Beverly Hills, CA: Sage.

Cicchetti, D., Rogosch, F. A., Lynch, M., & Holt, K. D. (1993). Resilience in maltreated children: Processes leading to adaptive outcome. *Development and Psychopathology, 5,* 629–647.

Coie, J. D., Watt, N. F., West, S. G., Hawkins, J. D., Asarnow, J. R., Markman, H. J., Ramey, S. L., Shure, M. B., & Long, B. (1993). The science of prevention: A conceptual framework and some directions for a national research program. *American Psychologist, 48,* 1013–1022.

Conger, R. D., Conger, K. J., Elder, G. H., Lorenz, F. O., Simons, R. l., & Whitbeck, L. B. (1992). A family process model of economic hardship and adjustment of early adolescent boys. *Child Development, 63,* 526–541.

Conrad, M., & Hammen, C. (1993). Protective and resource factors in high and low-risk children: A comparison of children with unipolar, bipolar, medically ill, and normal mothers. *Development and Psychopathology, 5,* 593–607.

Durbrow, E. H. (1999). Cultural processes in child competence: how rural Caribbean parents evaluate their children. In A. S. Masten (Ed.), *Cultural processes in child development: The Minnesota Symposia on Child Psychology* (Vol. 29) (pp. 97–121). Mahwah, NJ: Erlbaum.

Ford, D. H., & Lerner, R. M. (1992). *Developmental systems theory: An integrative approach.* Newbury Park, CA: Sage.

Garmezy, N. (1971). Vulnerability research and the issue of primary prevention. *American Journal of Orthopsychiatry, 41,* 101–116.

Garmezy, N. (1974). The study of competence in children at risk for severe psychopathology. In E. J. Anthony & C. Koupernick (Eds.), *The child in his family. Vol. 3: Children at psychiatric risk* (pp. 77–97). New York: Wiley.

Garmezy, N., & Masten, A. S. (1994). Chronic adversities. In M. Rutter, L. Herzov, & E. Taylor (Eds.), *Child and adolescent psychiatry* (3rd ed; pp. 191–208). Oxford: Blackwell.

Gottesman, I. I., & Shields, J. (1972). *Schizophrenia and genetics: A twin study vantage point.* New York: Academic Press.

Gottesman, I. I., & Shields, J. (1982). *Schizophrenia: The epigenetic puzzle.* New York: Cambridge University Press.

Gunnar, J. R., & Thelen, E. (1989). *Systems and development: The Minnesota Symposia on Child Psychology, Vol. 22.* Hillsdale, NJ: Erlbaum.

Haggerty, R. J., Sherrod, L., Garmezy, N., & Rutter, M. (1994) (Eds.), *Stress, risk and resilience in children and adolescents: Processes, mechanisms, and intervention.* New York: Cambridge University Press.

Hawkins, J. D., Catalano, R. F., & Miller, J. Y. (1992). Risk and protective factors for alcohol and other drug problems in adolescence and early adulthood: Implications for substance abuse prevention. *Psychological Bulletin, 112,* 64–105.

Horowitz, F. (1989, April). The concept of risk: A re-evaluation. Invited address, biennial meeting of the Society for Research in Child Development, Kansas City, MO.

Jessor, R. (1993). Successful adolescent development among youth in high-risk settings. *American Psychologist, 48,* 117–126.

Kaplan, H. (1999). Toward an understanding of resilience: A critical review of definitions and models. In M. Glantz & J. Johnson (Eds.), *Resilience and development: Positive life adaptations.* New York: Plenum Press.

Kumpfer, K. (1999). Factors and processes contributing to resilience: The resilience framework. In M. Glantz & J. Johnson (Eds.), *Resilience and development: Positive life adaptations.* New York: Plenum Press.

Luthar, S. S. (1991). Vulnerability and resilience: A study of high-risk adolescents. *Child Development, 62,* 600–612.

Luthar, S. S., & Cushing, G. (1999). Measurement issues in the empirical study of resilience: An overview. In M. Glantz & J. Johnson (Eds.), *Resilience and development: Positive life adaptations.* New York: Plenum Press.

Masten, A. S. (1989). Resilience in development: Implications of the study of successful adaptation for developmental psychopathology. In D. Cicchetti (Ed.), *The emergence of a discipline: Rochester Symposium on Developmental Psychopathology* (Vol. 1, pp. 261–294). Hillsdale, NJ: Erlbaum.

Masten, A. S. (1994). Resilience in individual development: Successful adaptation despite risk and adversity. In M. C. Wang & E. W. Gordon (Eds.), *Educational resilience in inner-city America: Challenges and prospects.* Hillsdale, NJ: Lawrence Erlbaum.

Masten, A. S., Best, K. M., & Garmezy, N. (1990). Resilience and development: Contributions from the study of children who overcome adversity. *Development and psychopathology, 2,* 425–444.

Masten, A. S., & Braswell, L. (1991). Developmental psychopathology: An integrative framework. In P. R. Martin (Ed.), *Handbook of behavior therapy and psychological science: An integrative approach* (pp. 35–56). New York: Pergamon.

Masten, A. S., & Coatsworth, J. D. (1995). Competence, resilience, and psychopathology. In D. Cicchetti & D. Cohen (Eds.), *Developmental psychopathology Vol. 2: Risk, disorder, and adaptation* (pp. 715–752). New York: Wiley.

Masten, A. S., & Coatsworth, J. D. (1998). The development of competence in favorable and unfavorable environments. *American Psychologist, 53,* 205–220.

Masten, A. S., Garmezy, N., Tellegen, A., Pellegrini, D. S., Larkin, K., & Larsen, A. (1988). Competence and stress in school children: The moderating effects of individual and family qualities. *Journal of Child Psychology and Psychiatry, 29,* 745–764.

Masten, A. S., Hubbard, J. J., Gest, S. D., Garmezy, N., & Ramirez, M. (1999). Competence in the context of adversity: Pathways to resilience and maladaptation from childhood to late adolescence. *Development and Psychopathology, 11,* 143–169.

Masten, A. S., Neemann, J., & Andenas, S. (1994). Life events and adjustment in adolescents: The significance of event independence, desirability, and chronicity. *Journal of Research on Adolescence, 4,* 71–97.

Masten, A. S., & Wright, M. O'D. (1997). Cumulative risk and protection models of child maltreatment. In B. B. R. Rossman & M. S. Rosenberg (Eds.), *Multiple victimization of children: Conceptual, developmental, research and treatment issues* (pp. 7–30). New York: Haworth Press.

Murphy, L. B., and Moriarty, A. E. (1976). *Vulnerability, coping, and growth from infancy to adolescence.* New Haven: Yale University Press.

National Research Council, Panel on Research on Child Abuse and Neglect, Commission on Behavioral and Social Sciences and Education (1993). *Understanding child abuse and neglect.* Washington, DC: National Academy Press.

Ogbu, J. U. (1985). A cultural ecology of competence among inner-city blacks. In M. B. Spencer, G. K. Brookins, & W. R. Allen (Eds.), *Beginnings: The social and affective development of black children* (pp. 45–66). Hillsdale, NJ: Lawrence Erlbaum.

Patterson, G. R., Reid, J., & Dishion, T. (1992). *Antisocial boys.* Eugene, OR: Castaglia.

Plomin, R., & Daniels, D. (1987). Why are children in the same family so different from one another? *The Behavioral and Brain Sciences, 10,* 1–15.

Rutter, M. (1979). Protective factors in children's responses to stress and disadvantage. *Annals of the Academy of Medicine, Singapore, 8,* 324–338.

Rutter, M. (1990). Psychosocial resilience and protective mechanisms. In J. Rolf, A. S. Masten, D. Cicchetti, K. H. Nuechterlein, & S. Weintraub (Eds.), *Risk and protective factors in the development of psychopathology* (pp. 181–214). New York: Cambridge University Press.

Sameroff, A. J., & Chandler, M. J. (1975). Reproductive risk and the continuum of caretaking casualty. *Review of Child Development Research, 4,* 187–244.

Scarr, S., & McCartney, K. (1983). How people make their own environments: A theory of genotype—environment effects. *Child Development, 54,* 424–435.

Silva, P. A. (1990). The Dunedin Multidisciplinary Health and Development Study: A fifteen year longitudinal study. *Paediatric and Perinatal Epidemiology, 4,* 96–127.

Sroufe, L. A. (1990). Considering normal and abnormal together: The essence of developmental psychopathology. *Development and Psychopathology, 2,* 335–347.

Stevenson, D. L., and Baker, D. P. (1987). The family-school relation and the child's school performance. *Child Development, 58,* 1348–1357.

Swearingen, E. M., & Cohen, L. H. (1985). Life events and psychological distress: A prospective study of young adolescents. *Developmental Psychology, 21,* 1045–1054.

Tarter, R., & Vanyukov, M. (1999). Re-visiting the validity of the construct of resilience. In M. Glantz & J. Johnson (Eds.), *Resilience and development: Positive life adaptations.* New York: Plenum Press.

Tellegen, A. (1985). Structures of mood and personality and their relevance to assessing anxiety, with an emphasis on self-report. In A. H. Tuma & J. D. Maser (Eds.), *Anxiety and the anxiety disorders* (pp. 681–716). Hillsdale, NJ: Lawrence Erlbaum Associates.

Vuchinich, S., Bank, L., & Patterson, G. R. (1992). Parenting, peers, & the stability of antisocial behavior in preadolescent boys. *Developmental Psychology, 28,* 510–521.

Watt, N. F., Anthony, E. J., Wynne, L. C., & Rolf, J. E. (1984). Children at risk for schizophrenia: A longitudinal perspective. New York: Cambridge University Press.

Weisz, J. R., Weiss, B., Hann, S. S., Granger, D. A., & Morton, T. (1995). Effects of psychotherapy with children and adolescents revisited: A meta-analysis of treatment outcome studies. *Psychological Bulletin, 117,* 450–468.

Werner, E. E., & Smith, R. S. (1982). *Vulnerable but invincible: A study of resilient children.* New York: McGraw-Hill.

Werner, E. E., & Smith, R. S. (1992). *Overcoming the odds: High risk children from birth to adulthood.* Ithaca: Cornell University Press.

Yoshikawa, H. (1994). Prevention as cumulative protection: Effects of early family support and education on chronic delinquency and its risks. *Psychological Bulletin, 115,* 28–54.

Zigler, E., Taussig, C., & Black, K. (1992). Early childhood intervention: A promising preventative for juvenile delinquency. *American Psychologist, 47,* 997–1006.

Index